Two paragraphs for next
time minimum 125 words
on same subject. (med.) 125
ed (Specific details
ment (results)
(cause)

Subjects for paragraph

1. Sunday evening Church (cong's)
attendance is (declining) (same)

2. Few people use common sense
about the food they eat.

3. The war made young men restless

4. It takes more than buildings
& money to make a college

5. Unearned luxury is bad for
young people.

6. Friendship involves sacrifice.

7. The College community seems
to ignore the student who
does the hard quiet work for
college enterprise

8. Too much study leaves a man no time to think.

9 A sense of humor is the best domestic lubricant.

10 We are happiest when busiest.

11.

SPECIMENS OF
PROSE COMPOSITION

EDITED BY

FRANK WILSON CHENEY HERSEY, A.M.
INSTRUCTOR IN ENGLISH AT HARVARD COLLEGE

AND

CHESTER NOYES GREENOUGH, Ph.D.
PROFESSOR OF ENGLISH AT HARVARD COLLEGE

REVISED EDITION

GINN AND COMPANY
BOSTON · NEW YORK · CHICAGO · LONDON
ATLANTA · DALLAS · COLUMBUS · SAN FRANCISCO

𝕿𝖍𝖊 𝕬𝖙𝖍𝖊𝖓𝖆𝖚𝖒 𝕻𝖗𝖊𝖘𝖘

GINN AND COMPANY · PRO-
PRIETORS · BOSTON · U.S.A.

CONTENTS

CONTENTS

NARRATION

MODELS OF NARRATION

INCIDENTS AND ADVENTURES

SHORT STORIES

STUDENTS' THEMES: NARRATION

SIGNALS BEFORE ACTION

In view of the success of case-books in teaching the principles of law, economics, and business, it is hoped that this revision of an early attempt to apply the same method to the study of English Composition may prove useful. For, after all, such models as are here given rather than any treatise on rhetoric are the sources from which authority is derived.

The principles of composition which have thus been founded on the practice of the best writers are discussed in the Notes and Comments (p. 451). There introductory chapters explain how these principles, usually studied as if they applied to all kinds of writing inflexibly, vary in application according as the writer's purpose is expository, argumentative, descriptive, or narrative.

Manifold differences in the tone and procedure of these specimens remind us that there is no one orthodox, hard-and-fast way of writing. Monotonous correctness is better than incorrectness, but the college student should not be satisfied with that: he is reaching the point where he can see that there are many kinds of correctness, and that "every single one of them is right."

By means of the Index of Practical Devices (p. 507) those who use this book can cut paths through it in any direction they like, quite without regard to the "kinds of writing" under which the selections are arranged.

The subject-matter, especially in Exposition and Argument, should stimulate thinking and writing. The selections, dealing as they do with many topics of public interest today, such as government, banking, science, labor unions, railroads, literature, and American life, will suggest a variety of subjects for original themes and discussions in class. The specimens may serve equally well for deliberate study and for rapid reading. It is well to vary the pace occasionally.

The short biographies of authors in the Notes and Comments have been added in order to make quickly accessible some information about their careers and works. Try to read the sketch of an author before reading a selection by him. Knowledge of the man will bring keener appreciation of his work, and both together might happily lead to reading the rest of the book from which the extract comes and other books of his. Thus there is an opportunity to become acquainted with many of the best writers of our time. In the case of the more important authors longer lives should be read.

One of the great benefits to be derived from a study of these models is the critical comparison of them with unsuccessful themes in college courses and with some of the many examples of inferior work which are unfortunately so abundant. To know exactly why bad writing is bad one must know why great literature is great.

Everyone understands the advantages of memorizing poetry: it is only a little less valuable to commit to memory certain passages of really excellent prose (for example, the conclusion of Stevenson's *Æs Triplex*, p. 95) in order that the rhythm of fine prose may echo in one's mind.

SPECIMENS OF
PROSE COMPOSITION

MODELS OF EXPOSITION

TAXATION AND GOVERNMENT[1]

John Fiske

What, then, are taxes? The question is one which is apt to come up, sooner or later, to puzzle children. They find no difficulty in understanding the butcher's bill for so many pounds of meat, or the tailor's bill for so many suits of clothes, where the value received is something that can be 5 seen and handled. But the tax bill, though it comes as inevitably as the autumnal frosts, bears no such obvious relation to the incidents of domestic life; it is not quite so clear what the money goes for; and hence it is apt to be paid by the head of the household with more or less grumbling, while 10 for the younger members of the family it requires some explanation.

It only needs to be pointed out, however, that in every town some things are done for the benefit of all the inhabitants of the town, things which concern one person just as 15 much as another. Thus roads are made and kept in repair, school-houses are built and salaries paid to school-teachers, there are constables who take criminals to jail, there are engines for putting out fires, there are public libraries, town cemeteries, and poor-houses. Money raised for these pur- 20 poses, which are supposed to concern all the inhabitants, is supposed to be paid by all the inhabitants, each one furnishing his share; and the share which each one pays is his town tax.

[1] From *Civil Government in the United States*, pp. 3–8. Houghton Mifflin Company, Boston, 1896.

From this illustration it would appear that taxes are private property taken for public purposes; and in making this statement we come very near the truth. Taxes are portions of private property which a government takes for its public
5 purposes. Before going farther, let us pause to observe that there is one other way, besides taxation, in which government sometimes takes private property for public purposes. Roads and streets are of great importance to the general public; and the government of the town or city in which you live
10 may see fit, in opening a new street, to run it across your garden, or to make you move your house or shop out of the way for it. In so doing, the government either takes away or damages some of your property. It exercises rights over your property without asking your permission. This power
15 of government over private property is called "the right of eminent domain." It means that a man's private interests must not be allowed to obstruct the interests of the whole community in which he lives. But in two ways the exercise of eminent domain is unlike taxation. In the first place, it
20 is only occasional, and affects only certain persons here or there, whereas taxation goes on perpetually and affects all persons who own property. In the second place, when the government takes away a piece of your land to make a road, it pays you money in return for it; perhaps not quite so
25 much as you believe the piece of land was worth in the market; the average human nature is doubtless such that men seldom give fair measure for measure unless they feel compelled to, and it is not easy to put a government under compulsion. Still it gives you something; it does not ask you to
30 part with your property for nothing. Now in the case of taxation, the government takes your money and seems to make no return to you individually; but it is supposed to return to you the value of it in the shape of well-paved streets, good schools, efficient protection against criminals, and so forth.
35 In giving this brief preliminary definition of taxes and taxation, we have already begun to speak of "the govern-

ment" of the town or city in which you live. We shall
presently have to speak of other "governments,"—as the
government of your state and the government of the United
States; and we shall now and then have occasion to allude
to the governments of other countries in which the people are 5
free, as, for example, England; and of some countries in
which the people are not free, as, for example, Russia. It is
desirable, therefore, that we should here at the start make
sure what we mean by "government," in order that we may
have a clear idea of what we are talking about.   10

Our verb "to govern" is an old French word, one of the
great host of French words which became a part of the English language between the eleventh and fourteenth centuries,
when so much French was spoken in England. The French
word was *gouverner*, and its oldest form was the Latin *guber-* 15
nare, a word which the Romans borrowed from the Greek,
and meant originally "to steer the ship." Hence it very
naturally came to mean "to guide," "to direct," "to command." The comparison between governing and steering was
a happy one. To govern is not to command as a master 20
commands a slave, but it is to issue orders and give directions
for the common good; for the interests of the man at the
helm are the same as those of the people in the ship. All
must float or sink together. Hence we sometimes speak of
the "ship of state," and we often call the state a "common- 25
wealth," or something in the weal or welfare of which all the
people are alike interested.

Government, then, is the directing or managing of such
affairs as concern all the people alike,—as, for example, the
punishment of criminals, the enforcement of contracts, the 30
defence against foreign enemies, the maintenance of roads
and bridges, and so on. To the directing or managing of
such affairs all the people are expected to contribute, each
according to his ability, in the shape of taxes. Government
is something which is supported by the people and kept alive 35
by taxation. There is no other way of keeping it alive.

The business of carrying on government—of steering the ship of state—either requires some special training, or absorbs all the time and attention of those who carry it on; and accordingly, in all countries, certain persons or groups of
5 persons are selected or in some way set apart, for longer or shorter periods of time, to perform the work of government. Such persons may be a king with his council, as in the England of the twelfth century; or a parliament led by a responsible ministry, as in the England of to-day; or a president
10 and two houses of congress, as in the United States; or a board of selectmen, as in a New England town. When we speak of "a government" or "the government," we often mean the group of persons thus set apart for carrying on the work of government. Thus, by "the Gladstone government"
15 we mean Mr. Gladstone, with his colleagues in the cabinet and his Liberal majority in the House of Commons; and by "the Lincoln government," properly speaking, was meant President Lincoln, with the Republican majorities in the Senate and House of Representatives.

20 "The government" has always many things to do, and there are many different lights in which we might regard it. But for the present there is one thing which we need especially to keep in mind. "The government" is the power which can rightfully take away a part of your property, in
25 the shape of taxes, to be used for public purposes. A government is not worthy of the name, and cannot long be kept in existence, unless it can raise money by taxation, and use force, if necessary, in collecting its taxes. The only general government of the United States during the Revolutionary
30 War, and for six years after its close, was the Continental Congress, which had no authority to raise money by taxation. In order to feed and clothe the army and pay its officers and soldiers, it was obliged to *ask* for money from the several states, and hardly ever got as much as was needed. It was
35 obliged to borrow millions of dollars from France and Holland, and to issue promissory notes which soon became worth-

less. After the war was over it became clear that this so-called government could neither preserve order nor pay its debts, and accordingly it ceased to be respected either at home or abroad, and it became necessary for the American people to adopt a new form of government. Between the old Conti- 5 nental Congress and the government under which we have lived since 1789, the differences were many; but by far the most essential difference was that the new government could raise money by taxation, and was thus enabled properly to carry on the work of governing. 10

If we are in any doubt as to what is really the government of some particular country, we cannot do better than observe what person or persons in that country are clothed with authority to tax the people. Mere names, as customarily applied to governments, are apt to be deceptive. Thus in 15 the middle of the eighteenth century France and England were both called "kingdoms"; but so far as kingly power was concerned, Louis XV. was a very different sort of king from George II. The French king could impose taxes on his people, and it might therefore be truly said that the govern- 20 ment of France was in the king. Indeed, it was Louis XV.'s immediate predecessor[1] who made the famous remark, "The state is myself." But the English king could not impose taxes; the only power in England that could do that was the House of Commons, and accordingly it is correct to say that 25 in England, at the time of which we are speaking, the government was (as it still is) in the House of Commons.

I say, then, the most essential feature of a government— or at any rate the feature with which it is most important for us to become familiar at the start—is its power of taxa- 30 tion. The government is that which taxes. If individuals

---

[1] Louis XIV., the Grand Monarch, who personally ruled France from 1661 until his death in 1715. That he addressed the words "L'État c'est moi" to the President of the Parliament of Paris is a fairly well established tradition; that the famous dictum represents his belief and practice is a matter of history.

take away some of your property for purposes of their own, it is robbery; you lose your money and get nothing in return. But if the government takes away some of your property in the shape of taxes, it is supposed to render to you an equiva-
5 lent in the shape of good government, something without which our lives and property would not be safe. Herein seems to lie the difference between taxation and robbery. When the highwayman points his pistol at me and I hand him my purse and watch, I am robbed. But when I pay the
10 tax-collector, who can seize my watch or sell my house over my head if I refuse, I am simply paying what is fairly due from me toward supporting the government.

THE STORY OF FINANCE AND BANKING[1]

William Cameron Forbes

It is the object of this chapter[2] to set forth the nature and growth of that kind of service rendered to us all by those whose business is connected with finance—the banks, the bankers, and the brokers.

We return to our elemental community and find ourselves 5 watching a development that comes after the people have begun to specialize, save, and lay something by for the future. Perhaps they have already learned to use crude metal coins, or perhaps their wealth is represented in important measure by the jewels and ornaments of their women- 10 folk. Each wants to safeguard his property. He might build a strong box and watch it, but that would leave him no time to make a living. He might hide his treasure away. That can be done, but who will find it if he dies? And if he tells any one else where it is hidden, some fine day he may wake 15 up to find his savings are gone. So presently our ingenious man speaks up and says:

"Let us all put our interests together and build a strong box that can be watched by three people whom we select especially for their trustworthiness and who will serve to 20 watch our property and watch one another."

And so they agree, and all their savings, or most of them, are put in the keeping of one agency that safeguards them

---

[1] From *The Romance of Business*, chap. vii. By permission of, and by special arrangement with, Houghton Mifflin Company, Boston, 1921.

[2] It is a pleasure to acknowledge with gratitude my indebtedness to Ray Morris, Esq., of Brown Brothers & Co., New York, and to the officers of the First National Bank, of Boston, for valuable assistance in the preparation of this chapter.—W. C. F.

for all. By combined effort they can build a much safer
place than each one could afford separately; and by each
contributing something, they can afford to hire people to
watch it. Each member of the community now feels free to
5 go farther afield in his work. His mind is at ease.

The first requirement of a bank is thus obtained, namely,
security. If a man dies, his heirs know where to find his
possessions, and the guardians of these things have their instructions as to how to dispose of them. The business of
10 these men is faithfully to guard the property of the rest; and
the others, by increased devotion to their specialties, can
earn enough more to pay them handsomely for it.

Now let us look at a second service performed by a bank.
To make a striking if somewhat grotesque illustration, let us
15 imagine our community as more civilized than when we first
saw it, but still using measures of corn as its currency. Let
us imagine that A, who is the butcher, wants to pay B, who
is the baker, for the supplies received from him during the
month. B is a vegetarian and does not eat meat. A loads
20 up his cart with corn, swings the two oxen into the yoke, and
laboriously goes four miles out into the country and delivers
to B his payment in sacks of corn. B, the baker, has owed
C, who lives in town and who may be the clothier, the confectioner, or perhaps the candlestick-maker, for things which
25 have been due him, and he has been waiting for A to pay
him before he pays C. So B hitches up his yoke of oxen,
loads the corn into his cart and puts in a day hauling the
corn four miles back to town, delivering it to C, who has
been visited several times by D, the doctor, who, liking the
30 air of the country, lives four miles out the other side of
the town. So once again another yoke of patient oxen are
called out and C puts in a day hauling his corn into the
country to hand it over to his friend the doctor, who has
been waiting for this auspicious moment to pay for the
35 meat he has received from A and for which the bill is some
time overdue. So the doctor, instead of making his rounds

on horseback as usual, hitches his horse to a cart, puts in the corn, and hauls it back to A, where it started. All four men have paid their bills and the corn is just where it was, a little the worse for wear, having been wet down perhaps one day when it was raining. There is a decrease in the quantity too, for some of the corn has dropped out through a hole in one of the bags. And four days' work of man and beast has been wasted.

One of the services rendered by a bank is the elimination of all this kind of waste. Even if corn were the currency, it could have stayed in the granary and been represented by receipts. Each of these persons could have given an order on the bank for the money necessary to pay his bill, and the value behind the currency, whether it were corn or gold or silver, would have remained stationary while the slips of paper indicating ownership were passed about.

When our village has grown to a city and the number of persons concerned has increased from a hundred families to a million families, a place or series of places of common meeting to provide a method by which the bills can be paid is not only a convenience, but an imperative necessity. It is perfectly easy to see that people would have to go without most of the things that they now enjoy, as they would spend a very important proportion of their time hunting up and paying the people who made the things that they use if they had to carry the money, particularly if it were in bulky form, to arrange the payment. It is not too much to say that business as we do it to-day is made possible only by the facilities rendered us by banking institutions. They are an essential part of our civilization, just as a link is an essential part of a chain; and if that link were taken out, the whole chain would fall apart, and our civilization in its present form would collapse.

Now let us take another service rendered by banks and see how that develops. This is to make beneficial use of their deposits. They put this money at work and it thus

serves the purposes of the community a thousand times better than it would were it to lie idle. If invested or loaned, money can earn, let us say, six per cent, which, as we know, means that for every hundred dollars the owner gets a reve-
5 nue of six dollars each year. And if that same money were to be buried under the house, the owner not only fails to receive that six dollars, but the community loses something besides, because the person who borrows one hundred dollars from the bank for his business and pays six dollars a year
10 for it knows that he can make more than just that six dollars or there would be nothing in it for him.

What do we mean by putting money to work, and how does it come to pass that a bank can do it?

Let us take a simple case. Suppose our village has one
15 hundred families and that each family keeps its spare money in the bank. Some are farmers and sell their produce—fruit, vegetables, barley, corn, and wheat—as it is harvested, in the spring, summer, or autumn. Much of the money thus received will not be needed till the winter, when there are no
20 more harvests and the expenses roll right on. Some deal in cordwood and coal and get their largest receipts in the winter. Others raise sheep or cattle and have wool to sell in the spring, and meat and hides at other times. Some work for wages and get their pay weekly and try to save a little
25 against a rainy day. Suppose, just for example, there is an average deposit in the bank of one hundred dollars per family, or for one hundred families ten thousand dollars. The banks are unlikely to carry on their operations on so small a scale as this, but this will serve for the illustration. Experi-
30 ence tells the bank manager how much of the money it is safe to lend and how much must be kept in cash. The laws under which our banks operate fix a minimum reserve of cash in hand below which the bank manager cannot go if he wants to keep out of jail.

35 Now let us see how the bank puts this money to work. We will say a ship comes in with a load of sugar and there

will not be another for three months. The grocer wants to lay in a sufficient stock of sugar to meet what he knows will be the requirements of the villagers for that length of time, but he has money enough to pay for only half what he wants. He goes to the bank and asks for a loan and gets it. He has to pay interest to the bank on his loan and pledge some of his property to secure payment, but he can easily afford, from the profit he makes on the sale of sugar, the amount necessary to pay for the interest. The bank knows that it can safely loan the grocer the amount he needs. The grocer repays the loan when he has sold the first half of the sugar and so closes the transaction. This money thus loaned has rendered service to the community. It has assured them a supply of sugar which otherwise they would have been without.

Let us take another illustration. One of our villagers cuts and stores ice for sale in the summer. But the cold spells are of short duration and to fill his ice-house he has to employ many helpers. He cannot do it alone in the time nature has allowed him before the next thaw. He has not money to pay these men and they unfortunately cannot wait for their pay till the summer comes and the ice is sold, for they need food and coal and clothing and other things that take money from day to day. He goes to the bank. He offers his house or his ice-house and its contents, and perhaps his horse and wagon used to deliver the ice, as security; insures the life of his horse with an insurance company, as the bank is very careful to see that its loans are properly protected; and borrows the amount necessary to pay for the labor that cuts his ice. In the summer he sells the ice for enough to repay the bank all it loaned with interest and also to provide himself with a nice profit, so that perhaps next year he will have enough money to pay his laborers without having to borrow.

Carrying on the same principle, people's money while on deposit is made to build railroads and public buildings, provide funds to tradespeople, to farmers and manufacturers,

and to help out all sorts of enterprises. Besides its deposits the bank has its own capital to start with. It puts part of the earnings that it gets from use of the money of its depositors into the business and calls it surplus, and the amount
5 of the capital and surplus is enough to secure the depositors from loss if from an unforeseen reason some of the loans the bank has made turn out to be ill-advised.

In the first example of a bank's usefulness, we have the depositors paying something for the service they receive.
10 But as the usefulness of a bank grows, we find it receiving and handling people's money and making no charge for it, as it makes a profit from the use of the money enough to pay all the costs of running the bank, and it even goes so far as to pay depositors something for the use of their money if the
15 deposit be large and continuous.

The funds available for loaning purposes by banks are not, however, only the funds first deposited with the banks in the form of cash. The great foundation of deposits is loans, direct or indirect. When the merchant who wants to buy
20 sugar gets his loan at the bank, what does the bank, in fact, do? It probably merely writes down the amount which has been loaned as a deposit in the merchant's favor. There would be, say, three entries in the case of an ordinary discounted note; on one side of the books the "avails" of the
25 note would be credited to the merchant as a deposit; and a record showing that the face amount of the note was owed the bank by the merchant at maturity would offset it. To make these sums balance, it is necessary to add as "earned discount" a sum equal to the difference between the par
30 amount of the note and the "avails" of the note, this representing the bank's profit. But the salient point is that, so far, no money has passed.

The merchant, if he pays for his sugar by check, is transferring to another individual, and very probably to another
35 bank, the claim for such part of that bank deposit of his as represents the amount which the sugar costs. The seller

of the sugar then deposits in his own bank the check thus received, and still no money has passed. Now, if we assume that we are dealing with two active commercial banks, it is probable that many transactions pass between them every day, and that only the balance of debits and credits is received by one from the other in settlement.

The net result of all this (and it is the essence of this part of the banking function) is that the amount of available bank deposits, which work just like currency in payment of obligations, is many times the amount of the currency in the country. The banks, in other words, enable us to do business on what we are going to earn, instead of on what we have earned already, and thus permit commercial growth on the basis of ascertained future needs, instead of on the slow basis of the exchange of currency based on past performance. But the process carries the dangers of its conveniences, and the difference between good banking and bad banking is mostly measured by the control and regulation of credit machinery, which is where our important new development, the Federal Reserve Bank, comes in.

If a bank can be serviceable to people who live near one another and are within easy reach, how greatly multiplied is its service when its payments are to be made to people at a distance! And this service is still more accentuated if the money is to be paid in a country that has a different unit of value for its currency and does business in a different language. The bank has enough of these transactions to be able to afford to keep men familiar with the languages used by foreign people with whom their customers deal.

The old method by which trading was done is filled with the glamour that attached to the days of the clipper ships, the China and East-Indian trade, when interchange of commodities was slow and difficult and letters took half a year to go halfway round the world. In these days, when a cable can reach the same distances in half an hour, it is hard to realize the difficulties of business in the old days.

A century ago the ships set forth from Boston or New York loaded with such of the products and manufactures of our Atlantic seaboard as could find sale in the ports to be visited. The goods were bought and paid for here and the ships set sail. There was no need of international banking operations, as each ship did her own banking. An officer known as the supercargo accompanied her and had charge of the goods with which she was freighted. The captain was also a merchant and business man. Arrived at China, he made his way to Hong Kong, or Canton, or Tientsin, or Shanghai, and unloaded. Chinese merchants crowded around and purchased his wares, or perhaps the owners of the vessel maintained a house there and his vessel's supplies were placed in the warehouse and thence sold to the local merchants in small quantities or in bulk, according as seemed best at the time. All this involved a good deal of judgment. Perhaps the owners had miscalculated the market and shipped too much of some one commodity. Perhaps they knew that another ship was on the ocean headed that way with a still larger supply of the same goods. Often the whole success of a voyage depended on the speed of the ship and her ability to get to port ahead of other vessels trading in competition, thus giving her a chance to take advantage of some favorable condition of the market. Sometimes these cargoes had ready sale at good prices, and sometimes the sale was retarded; or perhaps the ship was sent on to some other port where there might be a better demand.

But suppose that the cargo has been well selected and is all absorbed by the market. What then? The money received is immediately paid out in the purchase of other wares, silks, teas, and perhaps porcelain ware. The ship is loaded and starts. No large amount of money for sale of merchandise is needed to be carried by the ship—only goods. The ship carries only enough money to pay for expenses of the voyage, such as the wages of the crew and the food and supplies. Even in the Chinese port, let us call it Shanghai, there may be little passing of money. The same merchant who takes the American-made cargo will pay for it in bales of silk or cases of tea, and the only money that passes is the difference in value between his purchases and his sales.

My grandfather went to work at the age of fifteen years 5 in the counting-house of his uncles, Messrs. Perkins, of Boston, who had a China business. One of the practices of those days was to let the officers of the ship, and sometimes ship's clerks, have the "privilege" of a little space, free of freight, in the ship and to allow them to undertake what they called 10 "adventures." They could buy on their own account and at their own risk a supply of goods, silk scarfs or shawls, jewels, lace, or perhaps some of the rare vases from Satsuma, a little tea, or raw silk, and this they sold for their own account either at the home port or at some of the ports that 15 the ship visited on the way home. My grandfather as a small boy had several of these "adventures" and made a thousand dollars as a result of these operations by the time he was seventeen years old.

Sometimes, of course, these voyages were more complex, 20 and instead of loading for one port a ship carried cargoes for three ports in as many different countries. If at each of these places the value of the sales equaled the value of the purchases, no money was needed; the transactions "washed" each other, as it is now expressed. But when there was a 25 balance owed or owing, the shipmaster had to make arrangements with some bank or banking-house, or make up the difference with silver or gold.

Let us take a very simple case. Thompson, living in Boston, wants to buy some coffee raised in Brazil for his grocery 30 stores, and Brown, of Lynn, wants to sell some shoes in Rio de Janeiro. To reduce the transaction to its simplest terms we will suppose that the values concerned are equal, say one thousand dollars of each commodity. Thompson and Brown do not know each other and have no way of getting into 35 touch. But both know the bank and ask its assistance, and

the bank makes a transaction very advantageous to all parties. It takes Thompson's money paid for the coffee and
gives it to Brown in payment for his shoes, and notifies its
agent in Brazil of this transaction, and the agent in Brazil
5 collects the same amount from the shoe-dealer in Rio and
pays it over to the coffee-planter in São Paulo. The transaction is not quite so direct as all this, as in between there
are a number of other transactions involving insurance,
freight charges, bills of lading, warehouse receipts, etc., all
10 of which care for the value of the goods during the period
they are on the water and for the cost of handling and
moving them.

When the values are not the same, the transactions are
similar, but compound instead of simple. That is, there may
15 be on one day fifty concerns interested in trying to get
money to Brazil, and perhaps as many more trying to get
money from Brazil. Their operators patronize different
banks, but usually only a few of the larger ones specialize
in this sort of business and so it is a simple matter for one
20 bank to telephone around to some central source of information for quotations: "I want money in Rio. Can you let me
have it?"

The rate of exchange, as it is called, responds very readily to the law of supply and demand. If much more money
25 is needed in Brazil than in North America, an effort is made
to find some other way of getting the balance restored. For
example, Brazil may be marketing her coffee crop, of which
she sells annually about 12,000,000 bags at 132 pounds per
bag, valued in 1919 at more than $36,000,000, and yet at the
30 same time Brazil may be purchasing railroad equipment in
England and rails in Belgium. Instead of having money sent
from the United States to Rio to pay for coffee and then
shipping this same money to Europe to pay for purchases
there, Brazil arranges by cable with the banks to send the
35 American money to Europe to pay Brazil's debts there. Perhaps, however, it will be found that no money may be needed

for the transaction, as it may be that England wants to pay the United States for wheat shipped from Minnesota, and Belgium may be desirous of paying interest on a loan its Government made from ours; and so the banks manage to bring it to pass that each party gets his proper payment and that the actual transfer of cash is reduced to a minimum, just as in an earlier example we see the operations of the bank preventing the necessity for the laborious delivery of loads of corn from house to house.

Think what a tremendous service these triumphs of commercial and financial art have rendered mankind! In the first place, the transfers of cash are avoided and the exchange is made in an hour by sending and receiving a cable. All chance of loss is eliminated, for if the cable goes astray another is easily sent. Besides saving the cost and risk of sending money, there is saved the interest on it during its period of transit when it is, comparatively speaking, useless.

In the chapter on textiles we showed how the services rendered by the bank helped out the cotton-grower. In fact, it was explained how it made it possible for him to carry on his business, even though it is done indirectly and without lending the farmer a dollar. That is, the bank lends money to the grocer and the dry-goods man, who in turn let the farmer supply his needs on credit, as it is called; that is, they allow him to delay paying for the things he uses until his crop is sold. So in every step of finance the bank helps out. It helps the farmer, the tradesman, the broker, the railroad that transports the raw or unmanufactured and later the finished product, the manufacturer and the ultimate consumer. It takes money that otherwise would be held idle waiting for future use and makes it work.

We have supposed the case of a small bank in a village merely to illustrate the nature of a bank's service. Let us now take the case of a large bank in a large city and get some measure of the extent of the service it renders. One of the largest banks in Boston has 15,000 depositors, with total

deposits of $150,000,000, or an average of $10,000 per depositor. It has a capital of $12,000,000 and a surplus of $20,000,000, which means that $32,000,000 has been paid into the treasury with which it can conduct its business and add
5 to the security of its depositors. It has 9000 stockholders.

Let us carry our observations a step farther and see what this service means when extended to the whole United States. In 1920 the clearings of the national banks of the United States, which represent the transfers of funds between banks,
10 largely for the accounts of customers, amounted to over $451,000,000,000. This means that on every business day of the year about $1,500,000,000 was transferred. The deposits in the national banks at the close of 1920 amounted to about $13,867,000,000, from which it is apparent that the money on
15 deposit was turned over about thirty-three times in the course of the year, which does not indicate any idleness. The loans outstanding at the close of 1920 aggregated $12,311,500,000. The nearly 7800 national banks last year had $1,118,600,000 capital and nearly $1,000,000,000 surplus; and these figures
20 do not include the State banking institutions, which reported deposits of about $6,500,000,000.

Yet mere figures only suggest the magnitude of our system of banking, for there is no way to show adequately the tremendous range of the services that it renders, and it is im-
25 possible for us fully to realize the desperate straits in which we should find ourselves if it were to collapse.

SELF–CULTIVATION IN ENGLISH[1]

George Herbert Palmer

First, then, "Look well to your speech." It is commonly
supposed that when a man seeks literary power he goes to his
room and plans an article for the press. But this is to begin
literary culture at the wrong end. We speak a hundred times
for every once we write. The busiest writer produces little ₅
more than a volume a year, not so much as his talk would
amount to in a week. Consequently through speech it is
usually decided whether a man is to have command of his
language or not. If he is slovenly in his ninety-nine cases of
talking, he can seldom pull himself up to strength and exacti- ₁₀
tude in the hundredth case of writing. A person is made in
one piece, and the same being runs through a multitude of
performances. Whether words are uttered on paper or to the
air, the effect on the utterer is the same. Vigor or feebleness
results according as energy or slackness has been in com- ₁₅
mand. I know that certain adaptations to a new field are
often necessary. A good speaker may find awkwardnesses
in himself when he comes to write, a good writer when he
speaks. And certainly cases occur where a man exhibits distinct strength in one of the two, speaking or writing, and not ₂₀
in the other. But such cases are rare. As a rule, language
once within our control can be employed for oral or for written purposes. And since the opportunities for oral practice
enormously outbalance those for written, it is the oral which
are chiefly significant in the development of literary power. ₂₅
We rightly say of the accomplished writer that he shows a
mastery of his own tongue.

[1] From *Self-Cultivation in English*, pp. 9 ff. Thomas Y. Crowell Company, New York, 1897.

Fortunate it is, then, that self-cultivation in the use of English must chiefly come through speech; because we are always speaking, whatever else we do. In opportunities for acquiring a mastery of language, the poorest and busiest are
5 at no large disadvantage as compared with the leisured rich. It is true the strong impulse which comes from the suggestion and approval of society may in some cases be absent, but this can be compensated by the sturdy purpose of the learner. A recognition of the beauty of well-ordered words, a strong
10 desire, patience under discouragements, and promptness in counting every occasion as of consequence,—these are the simple agencies which sweep one on to power. Watch your speech, then. That is all which is needed. Only it is desirable to know what qualities of speech to watch for. I find
15 three,—accuracy, audacity, and range,—and I will say a few words about each.

Obviously, good English is exact English. Our words should fit our thoughts like a glove, and be neither too wide nor too tight. If too wide, they will include much vacuity
20 beside the intended matter. If too tight, they will check the strong grasp. Of the two dangers, looseness is by far the greater. There are people who say what they mean with such a naked precision that nobody not familiar with the subject can quickly catch the sense. George Herbert and
25 Emerson strain the attention of many. But niggardly and angular speakers are rare. Too frequently words signify nothing in particular. They are merely thrown out in a certain direction, to report a vague and undetermined meaning or even a general emotion. The first business of every one
30 who would train himself in language is to articulate his thought, to know definitely what he wishes to say, and then to pick those words which compel the hearer to think of this and only this. For such a purpose two words are often better than three. The fewer the words, the more pungent the im-
35 pression. Brevity is the soul not simply of a jest, but of wit in its finest sense where it is identical with wisdom. He who

can put a great deal into a little is the master. Since firm texture is what is wanted, not embroidery or superposed ornament, beauty has been well defined as the purgation of superfluities. And certainly many a paragraph might have its beauty brightened by letting quiet words take the place 5 of its loud words, omitting its "verys," and striking out its purple patches of "fine writing." Here is Ben Jonson's description of Bacon's language: "There happened in my time one noble speaker who was full of gravity in his speech. No man ever spoke more neatly, more pressly, more weightily, 10 or suffered less emptiness, less idleness, in what he uttered. No member of his speech but consisted of his own graces. His hearers could not cough or look aside without loss. He commanded when he spoke, and had his judges angry or pleased at his discretion." Such are the men who command, 15 men who speak "neatly and pressly." But to gain such precision is toilsome business. While we are in training for it, no word must unpermittedly pass the portal of the teeth. Something like what we mean must never be counted equivalent to what we mean. And if we are not sure of our meaning 20 or of our word, we must pause until we are sure. Accuracy does not come of itself. For persons who can use several languages, capital practice in acquiring it can be had by translating from one language to another and seeing that the entire sense is carried over. Those who have only their 25 native speech will find it profitable often to attempt definitions of the common words they use. Inaccuracy will not stand up against the habit of definition. Dante boasted that no rhythmic exigency had ever made him say what he did not mean. We heedless and unintending speakers, under no 30 exigency of rhyme or reason, say what we mean but seldom and still more seldom mean what we say. To hold our thoughts and words in significant adjustment requires unceasing consciousness, a perpetual determination not to tell lies; for of course every inaccuracy is a bit of untruthfulness. 35 We have something in mind, yet convey something else to our

hearer. And no moral purpose will save us from this untruthfulness unless that purpose is sufficient to inspire the
daily drill which brings the power to be true. Again and
again we are shut up to evil because we have not acquired
5 the ability of goodness.

But after all, I hope that nobody who hears me will quite
agree. There is something enervating in conscious care.
Necessary as it is in shaping our purposes, if allowed too
direct and exclusive control consciousness breeds hesitation
10 and feebleness. Action is not excellent, at least, until spontaneous. In piano playing we begin by picking out each
separate note; but we do not call the result music until we
play our notes by the handful, heedless how each is formed.
And so it is everywhere. Consciously selective conduct is
15 elementary and inferior. People distrust it, or rather they
distrust him who exhibits it. If anybody talking to us visibly
studies his words, we turn away. What he says may be well
enough as school exercise, but it is not conversation. Accordingly, if we would have our speech forcible, we shall need to
20 put into it quite as much of audacity as we do of precision,
terseness, or simplicity. Accuracy alone is not a thing to be
sought, but accuracy and dash. Of Patrick Henry, the orator
who more than any other could craze our Revolutionary
fathers, it was said that he was accustomed to throw himself
25 headlong into the middle of a sentence, trusting to God
Almighty to get him out. So must we speak. We must not,
before beginning a sentence, decide what the end shall be;
for if we do, nobody will care to hear that end. At the beginning, it is the beginning which claims the attention of
30 both speaker and listener, and trepidation about going on
will mar all. We must give our thought its head, and not
drive it with too tight a rein, nor grow timid when it begins
to prance a bit. Of course we must retain coolness in courage, applying the results of our previous discipline in accu-
35 racy; but we need not move so slowly as to become formal.
Pedantry is worse than blundering. If we care for grace and

flexible beauty of language, we must learn to let our thought run. Would it, then, be too much of an Irish bull to say that in acquiring English we need to cultivate spontaneity? The uncultivated kind is not worth much; it is wild and hap-hazard stuff, unadjusted to its uses. On the other hand, no speech is of much account, however just, which lacks the element of courage. Accuracy and dash, then, the combination of the two, must be our difficult aim; and we must not rest satisfied so long as either dwells with us alone.

But are the two so hostile as they at first appear? Or can, indeed, the first be obtained without the aid of the second? Supposing we are convinced that words possess no value in themselves, and are correct or incorrect only as they truly report experience, we shall feel ourselves impelled in the mere interest of accuracy to choose them freshly, and to put them together in ways in which they never co-operated before, so as to set forth with distinctness that which just we, not other people, have seen or felt. The reason why we do not naturally have this daring exactitude is probably twofold. We let our experiences be blurred, not observing sharply, nor knowing with any minuteness what we are thinking about; and so there is no individuality in our language. And then, besides, we are terrorized by custom, and inclined to adjust what we would say to what others have said before. The cure for the first of these troubles is to keep our eye on our object, instead of on our listener or ourselves; and for the second, to learn to rate the expressiveness of language more highly than its correctness. The opposite of this, the disposition to set correctness above expressiveness, produces that peculiarly vulgar diction known as "school-ma'am English," in which for the sake of a dull accord with usage all the picturesque, imaginative, and forceful employment of words is sacrificed. Of course we must use words so that people can understand them, and understand them, too, with ease; but this once granted, let our language be our own, obedient to our special needs. "Whenever," says Thomas

Jefferson, "by small grammatical negligences the energy of an idea can be condensed, or a word be made to stand for a sentence, I hold grammatical rigor in contempt." "Young man," said Henry Ward Beecher to one who was pointing
5 out grammatical errors in a sermon of his, "when the English language gets in my way, it does n't stand a chance." No man can be convincing, writer or speaker, who is afraid to send his words wherever they may best follow his meaning, and this with but little regard to whether any other person's words have
10 ever been there before. In assessing merit, let us not stupefy ourselves with using negative standards. What stamps a man as great is not freedom from faults, but abundance of powers.

   Such audacious accuracy, however, distinguishing as it does noble speech from commonplace speech, can be prac-
15 tised only by him who has a wide range of words. Our ordinary range is absurdly narrow. It is important, therefore, for anybody who would cultivate himself in English to make strenuous and systematic efforts to enlarge his vocabulary. Our dictionaries contain more than a hundred thousand
20 words. The average speaker employs about three thousand. Is this because ordinary people have only three or four thousand things to say? Not at all. It is simply due to dulness. Listen to the average school-boy. He has a dozen or two nouns, half a dozen verbs, three or four adjectives, and
25 enough conjunctions and prepositions to stick the conglomerate together. This ordinary speech deserves the description which Hobbes gave to his *State of Nature*, that "it is solitary, poor, nasty, brutish, and short." The fact is, we fall into the way of thinking that the wealthy words are for others and that
30 they do not belong to us. We are like those who have received a vast inheritance, but who persist in the inconveniences of hard beds, scanty food, rude clothing, who never travel, and who limit their purchases to the bleak necessities of life. Ask such people why they endure niggardly living while wealth in
35 plenty is lying in the bank, and they can only answer that they have never learned how to spend. But this is worth

learning. Milton used eight thousand words, Shakespeare fifteen thousand. We have all the subjects to talk about that these early speakers had; and in addition, we have bicycles and sciences and strikes and political combinations and all the complicated living of the modern world. 5

Why, then, do we hesitate to swell our words to meet our needs? It is a nonsense question. There is no reason. We are simply lazy; too lazy to make ourselves comfortable. We let our vocabularies be limited, and get along rawly without the refinements of human intercourse, without refinements in 10 our own thoughts; for thoughts are almost as dependent on words as words on thoughts. For example, all exasperations we lump together as "aggravating," not considering whether they may not rather be displeasing, annoying, offensive, disgusting, irritating, or even maddening; and without observ- 15 ing, too, that in our reckless usage we have burned up a word which might be convenient when we should need to mark some shading of the word "increase." Like the bad cook, we seize the frying-pan whenever we need to fry, broil, roast, or stew, and then we wonder why all our dishes taste alike while 20 in the next house the food is appetizing. It is all unnecessary. Enlarge the vocabulary. Let any one who wants to see himself grow, resolve to adopt two new words each week. It will not be long before the endless and enchanting variety of the world will begin to reflect itself in his speech, and in 25 his mind as well. I know that when we use a word for the first time we are startled, as if a firecracker went off in our neighborhood. We look about hastily to see if any one has noticed. But finding that no one has, we may be emboldened. A word used three times slips off the tongue with 30 entire naturalness. Then it is ours forever, and with it some phase of life which had been lacking hitherto. For each word presents its own point of view, discloses a special aspect of things, reports some little importance not otherwise conveyed, and so contributes its small emancipation to our 35 tied-up minds and tongues.

But a brief warning may be necessary to make my meaning clear. In urging the addition of new words to our present poverty-stricken stock, I am far from suggesting that we should seek out strange, technical, or inflated expressions, which do not appear in ordinary conversation. The very opposite is my aim. I would put every man who is now employing a diction merely local and personal in command of the approved resources of the English language. Our poverty usually comes through provinciality, through accepting without criticism the habits of our special set. My family, my immediate friends, have a diction of their own. Plenty of other words, recognized as sound, are known to be current in books, and to be employed by modest and intelligent speakers, only we do not use them. Our set has never said "diction," or "current," or "scope," or "scanty," or "hitherto," or "convey," or "lack." Far from unusual as these words are, to adopt them might seem to set me apart from those whose intellectual habits I share. From this I shrink. I do not like to wear clothes suitable enough for others, but not in the style of my own plain circle. Yet if each one of that circle does the same, the general shabbiness is increased. The talk of all is made narrow enough to fit the thinnest there. What we should seek is to contribute to each of the little companies with which our life is bound up a gently enlarging influence, such impulses as will not startle or create detachment, but which may save from humdrum, routine, and dreary usualness. We cannot be really kind without being a little venturesome. The small shocks of our increasing vocabulary will in all probability be as helpful to our friends as to ourselves.

Such, then, are the excellences of speech. If we would cultivate ourselves in the use of English, we must make our daily talk accurate, daring, and full. I have insisted on these points the more because in my judgment all literary power, especially that of busy men, is rooted in sound speech.

ON THE STUDY OF ZOÖLOGY[1]

THOMAS HENRY HUXLEY

Certain broad laws have a general application throughout both the animal and the vegetable worlds, but the ground common to these kingdoms of nature is not of very wide extent, and the multiplicity of details is so great, that the student of living beings finds himself obliged to devote his attention exclusively either to the one or the other. If he elects to study plants, under any aspect, we know at once what to call him. He is a botanist, and his science is botany. But if the investigation of animal life be his choice, the name generally applied to him will vary according to the kind of animals he studies, or the particular phenomena of the animal life to which he confines his attention. If the study of man is his object, he is called an anatomist, or a physiologist, or an ethnologist; but if he dissects animals, or examines into the mode in which their functions are performed, he is a comparative anatomist or comparative physiologist. If he turns his attention to fossil animals, he is a palæontologist. If his mind is more particularly directed to the description specific, discrimination, classification, and distribution of animals, he is termed a zoölogist.

For the purposes of the present discourse, however, I shall recognize none of these titles save the last, which I shall employ as the equivalent of botanist, and I shall use the term zoölogy as denoting the whole doctrine of animal life, in contradistinction to botany, which signifies the whole doctrine of vegetable life.

[1] From "On the Study of Zoölogy," in *Lay Sermons, Addresses, and Reviews*, pp. 95–109. D. Appleton and Company, New York, 1874. Originally published in 1861.

Employed in this sense, zoölogy, like botany, is divisible into three great but subordinate sciences, morphology, physiology, and distribution, each of which may, to a very great extent, be studied independently of the other.

5 Zoölogical morphology is the doctrine of animal form or structure. Anatomy is one of its branches; development is another; while classification is the expression of the relations which different animals bear to one another, in respect of their anatomy and their development.

10 Zoölogical distribution is the study of animals in relation to the terrestrial conditions which obtain now, or have obtained at any previous epoch of the earth's history.

Zoölogical physiology, lastly, is the doctrine of the functions or actions of animals. It regards animal bodies as
15 machines impelled by certain forces, and performing an amount of work which can be expressed in terms of the ordinary forces of nature. The final object of physiology is to deduce the facts of morphology, on the one hand, and those of distribution on the other, from the laws of the molecular
20 forces of matter.

Such is the scope of zoölogy. But if I were to content myself with the enunciation of these dry definitions, I should ill exemplify that method of teaching this branch of physical science, which it is my chief business to-night to recommend.
25 Let us turn away then from abstract definitions. Let us take some concrete living thing, some animal, the commoner the better, and let us see how the application of common sense and common logic to the obvious facts it presents, inevitably leads us into all these branches of zoölogical science.

30 I have before me a lobster. When I examine it, what appears to be the most striking character it presents? Why, I observe that this part which we call the tail of the lobster, is made up of six distinct hard rings and a seventh terminal piece. If I separate one of the middle rings, say the third, I
35 find it carries upon its under surface a pair of limbs or appendages, each of which consists of a stalk and two terminal

pieces. So that I can represent a transverse section of the ring and its appendages upon the diagram board in this way.

If I now take the fourth ring I find it has the same structure, and so have the fifth and the second; so that, in each of these divisions of the tail, I find parts which correspond with one another, a ring and two appendages; and in each appendage a stalk and two end pieces. These corresponding parts are called, in the technical language of anatomy, "homologous parts." The ring of the third division is the "homologue" of the ring of the fifth; the appendage of the former is the homologue of the appendage of the latter. And, as each division exhibits corresponding parts in corresponding places, we say that all the divisions are constructed upon the same plan. But now let us consider the sixth division. It is similar to, and yet different from, the others. The ring is essentially the same as in the other divisions; but the appendages look at first as if they were very different; and yet when we regard them closely, what do we find? A stalk and two terminal divisions, exactly as in the others, but the stalk is very short and very thick, the terminal divisions are very broad and flat, and one of them is divided into two pieces.

I may say, therefore, that the sixth segment is like the others in plan, but that it is modified in its details.

The first segment is like the others, so far as its ring is concerned, and though its appendages differ from any of those yet examined in the simplicity of their structure, parts corresponding with the stem and one of the divisions of the appendages of the other segments can be readily discerned in them.

Thus it appears that the lobster's tail is composed of a series of segments which are fundamentally similar, though each presents peculiar modifications of the plan common to all. But when I turn to the fore part of the body I see, at first, nothing but a great shield-like shell, called technically the "carapace," ending in front in a sharp spine, on either side of which are the curious compound eyes, set upon the

ends of stout moveable stalks. Behind these, on the under
side of the body, are two pairs of long feelers, or antennæ,
followed by six pairs of jaws, folded against one another
over the mouth, and five pairs of legs, the foremost of these
5 being the great pinchers, or claws, of the lobster.

It looks, at first, a little hopeless to attempt to find in this
complex mass a series of rings, each with its pair of appendages, such as I have shown you in the abdomen, and yet it is
not difficult to demonstrate their existence. Strip off the legs,
10 and you will find that each pair is attached to a very definite
segment of the under wall of the body; but these segments,
instead of being the lower parts of free rings, as in the tail,
are such parts of rings which are all solidly united and bound
together; and the like is true of the jaws, the feelers, and the
15 eye-stalks, every pair of which is borne upon its own special
segment. Thus the conclusion is gradually forced upon us,
that the body of the lobster is composed of as many rings as
there are pairs of appendages, namely, twenty in all, but that
the six hindmost rings remain free and moveable, while the
20 fourteen front rings become firmly soldered together, their
backs forming one continuous shield—the carapace.

Unity of plan, diversity in execution, is the lesson taught
by the study of the rings of the body, and the same instruction is given still more emphatically by the appendages. If
25 I examine the outermost jaw I find it consists of three distinct portions, an inner, a middle, and an outer, mounted
upon a common stem; and if I compare this jaw with the legs
behind it, or the jaws in front of it, I find it quite easy to see,
that, in the legs, it is the part of the appendage which corre-
30 sponds with the inner division, which becomes modified into
what we know familiarly as the "leg," while the middle division disappears, and the outer division is hidden under the
carapace. Nor is it more difficult to discern that, in the appendages of the tail, the middle division appears again and
35 the outer vanishes; while, on the other hand, in the foremost
jaw, the so-called mandible, the inner division only is left;

and, in the same way, the parts of the feelers and of the eye-stalks can be identified with those of the legs and jaws.

But whither does all this tend? To the very remarkable conclusion that a unity of plan, of the same kind as that discoverable in the tail or abdomen of the lobster, pervades the whole organization of its skeleton, so that I can return to the diagram representing any one of the rings of the tail, which I drew upon the board, and by adding a third division to each appendage, I can use it as a sort of scheme or plan of any ring of the body. I can give names to all the parts of that figure, and then if I take any segment of the body of the lobster, I can point out to you exactly, what modification the general plan has undergone in that particular segment; what part has remained moveable, and what has become fixed to another; what has been excessively developed and metamorphosed, and what has been suppressed.

But I imagine I hear the question, How is all this to be tested? No doubt it is a pretty and ingenious way of looking at the structure of any animal, but is it anything more? Does Nature acknowledge, in any deeper way, this unity of plan we seem to trace?

The objection suggested by these questions is a very valid and important one, and morphology was in an unsound state, so long as it rested upon the mere perception of the analogies which obtain between fully formed parts. The unchecked ingenuity of speculative anatomists proved itself fully competent to spin any number of contradictory hypotheses out of the same facts, and endless morphological dreams threatened to supplant scientific theory.

Happily, however, there is a criterion of morphological truth, and a sure test of all homologies. Our lobster has not always been what we see it; it was once an egg, a semifluid mass of yolk, not so big as a pin's head, contained in a transparent membrane, and exhibiting not the least trace of any one of those organs, whose multiplicity and complexity, in the adult, are so surprising. After a time a delicate patch of

cellular membrane appeared upon one face of this yolk, and that patch was the foundation of the whole creature, the clay out of which it would be moulded. Gradually investing the yolk, it became subdivided by transverse constrictions into
5 segments, the forerunners of the rings of the body. Upon the ventral surface of each of the rings thus sketched out, a pair of bud-like prominences made their appearance—the rudiments of the appendages of the ring. At first, all the appendages were alike, but, as they grew, most of them became
10 distinguished into a stem and two terminal divisions, to which, in the middle part of the body, was added a third outer division; and it was only at a later period, that by the modification, or absorption, of certain of these primitive constituents, the limbs acquired their perfect form.

15 Thus the study of development proves that the doctrine of unity of plan is not merely a fancy, that it is not merely one way of looking at the matter, but that it is the expression of deep-seated natural facts. The legs and jaws of the lobster may not merely be regarded as modifications
20 of a common type,—in fact and in nature they are so, —the leg and the jaw of the young animal being, at first, indistinguishable.

These are wonderful truths, the more so because the zoölogist finds them to be of universal application. The
25 investigation of a polype, of a snail, of a fish, of a horse, or of a man, would have led us, though by a less easy path, perhaps, to exactly the same point. Unity of plan everywhere lies hidden under the mask of diversity of structure—the complex is everywhere evolved out of the simple. Every animal
30 has at first the form of an egg, and every animal and every organic part, in reaching its adult state, passes through conditions common to other animals and other adult parts; and this leads me to another point. I have hitherto spoken as if the lobster were alone in the world, but, as I need hardly re-
35 mind you, there are myriads of other animal organisms. Of these, some, such as men, horses, birds, fishes, snails, slugs,

oysters, corals, and sponges, are not in the least like the
lobster. But other animals, though they may differ a good
deal from the lobster, are yet either very like it, or are like
something that is like it. The cray fish, the rock lobster, and
the prawn, and the shrimp, for example, however different, 5
are yet so like lobsters, that a child would group them as of
the lobster kind, in contradistinction to snails and slugs; and
these last again would form a kind by themselves, in contradistinction to cows, horses, and sheep, the cattle kind.

But this spontaneous grouping into "kinds" is the first 10
essay of the human mind at classification, or the calling by a
common name of those things that are alike, and the arranging them in such a manner as best to suggest the sum of their
likenesses and unlikenesses to other things.

Those kinds which include no other subdivisions than the 15
sexes, or various breeds, are called, in technical language,
species. The English lobster is a species, our cray fish is
another, our prawn is another. In other countries, however,
there are lobsters, cray fish, and prawns, very like ours, and
yet presenting sufficient differences to deserve distinction. 20
Naturalists, therefore, express this resemblance and this
diversity by grouping them as distinct species of the same
"genus." But the lobster and the cray fish, though belonging
to distinct genera, have many features in common, and hence
are grouped together in an assemblage which is called a 25
family. More distant resemblances connect the lobster with
the prawn and the crab, which are expressed by putting all
these into the same order. Again, more remote, but still very
definite, resemblances unite the lobster with the wood-louse,
the king crab, the water-flea, and the barnacle, and separate 30
them from all other animals; whence they collectively constitute the larger group, or class, *Crustacea*. But the *Crustacea* exhibit many peculiar features in common with insects,
spiders, and centipedes, so that these are grouped into the
still larger assemblage or "province" *Articulata*; and, finally, 35
the relations which these have to worms and other lower

animals, are expressed by combining the whole vast aggregate into the sub-kingdom of *Annulosa*.

If I had worked my way from a sponge instead of a lobster,
I should have found it associated, by like ties, with a great
number of other animals into the sub-kingdom *Protozoa*;
if I had selected a fresh-water polype or a coral, the members
of what naturalists term the sub-kingdom *Coelenterata*
would have grouped themselves around my type; had a snail
been chosen, the inhabitants of all univalve and bivalve, land
and water, shells, the lamp shells, the squids, and the sea-mat
would have gradually linked themselves on to it as members
of the same sub-kingdom of *Mollusca*; and finally, starting
from man, I should have been compelled to admit first, the
ape, the rat, the horse, the dog, into the same class; and then
the bird, the crocodile, the turtle, the frog, and the fish, into
the same sub-kingdom of *Vertebrata*.

And if I had followed out all these various lines of classification fully, I should discover in the end that there was no
animal, either recent or fossil, which did not at once fall into
one or other of these sub-kingdoms. In other words, every
animal is organized upon one or other of the five, or more,
plans, whose existence renders our classification possible.
And so definitely and precisely marked is the structure of
each animal, that, in the present state of our knowledge,
there is not the least evidence to prove that a form, in the
slightest degree transitional between any two of the groups
Vertebrata, *Annulosa*, *Mollusca*, and *Coelenterata*, either
exists, or has existed, during that period of the earth's history
which is recorded by the geologist. Nevertheless, you must
not for a moment suppose, because no such transitional forms
are known, that the members of the sub-kingdoms are dis-
connected from, or independent of, one another. On the contrary, in their earliest condition they are all alike, and the
primordial germs of a man, a dog, a bird, a fish, a beetle, a
snail, and a polype are, in no essential structural respects,
distinguishable.

In this broad sense, it may with truth be said, that all living animals, and all those dead creations which geology reveals, are bound together by an all-pervading unity of organization, of the same character, though not equal in degree, to that which enables us to discern one and the same plan amidst the twenty different segments of a lobster's body. Truly it has been said, that to a clear eye the smallest fact is a window through which the Infinite may be seen.

Turning from these purely morphological considerations, let us now examine into the manner in which the attentive study of the lobster impels us into other lines of research.

Lobsters are found in all the European seas; but on the opposite shores of the Atlantic and in the seas of the southern hemisphere they do not exist. They are, however, represented in these regions by very closely allied, but distinct forms— the *Homarus Americanus* and the *Homarus Capensis*: so that we may say that the European has one species of *Homarus*; the American, another; the African, another; and thus the remarkable facts of geographical distribution begin to dawn upon us.

Again, if we examine the contents of the earth's crust, we shall find in the latter of those deposits, which have served as the great burying grounds of past ages, numberless lobster-like animals, but none so similar to our living lobster as to make zoölogists sure that they belonged even to the same genus. If we go still further back in time, we discover, in the oldest rocks of all, the remains of animals, constructed on the same general plan as the lobster, and belonging to the same great group of *Crustacea*; but for the most part totally different from the lobster, and indeed from any other living form of crustacean; and thus we gain a notion of that successive change of the animal population of the globe, in past ages, which is the most striking fact revealed by geology.

Consider, now, where our inquiries have led us. We studied our type morphologically, when we determined its anatomy and its development, and when comparing it, in these re-

spects, with other animals, we made out its place in a system
of classification. If we were to examine every animal in a
similar manner, we should establish a complete body of
zoölogical morphology.

5 Again, we investigated the distribution of our type in
space and in time, and, if the like had been done with every
animal, the sciences of geographical and geological distribution would have attained their limit.

But you will observe one remarkable circumstance, that,
10 up to this point, the question of the life of these organisms
has not come under consideration. Morphology and distribution might be studied almost as well, if animals and plants
were a peculiar kind of crystals, and possessed none of those
functions which distinguish living beings so remarkably.
15 But the facts of morphology and distribution have to be
accounted for, and the science, whose aim it is to account for
them, is Physiology.

Let us return to our lobster once more. If we watched the
creature in its native element, we should see it climbing
20 actively the submerged rocks, among which it delights to
live, by means of its strong legs; or swimming by powerful
strokes of its great tail, the appendages of whose sixth joint
are spread out into a broad fan-like propeller: seize it, and
it will show you that its great claws are no mean weapons of
25 offence; suspend a piece of carrion among its haunts, and it
will greedily devour it, tearing and crushing the flesh by
means of its multitudinous jaws.

Suppose that we had known nothing of the lobster but as
an inert mass, an organic crystal, if I may use the phrase,
30 and that we could suddenly see it exerting all these powers,
what wonderful new ideas and new questions would arise in
our minds! The great new question would be, "How does
all this take place?" the chief new idea would be, the idea
of adaptation to purpose,—the notion, that the constituents
35 of animal bodies are not mere unconnected parts, but organs
working together to an end. Let us consider the tail of the

lobster again from this point of view. Morphology has
taught us that it is a series of segments composed of homologous parts, which undergo various modifications—beneath
and through which a common plan of formation is discernible.
But if I look at the same part physiologically, I see that it is 5
a most beautifully constructed organ of locomotion, by means
of which the animal can swiftly propel itself either backwards or forwards.

But how is this remarkable propulsive machine made to
perform its functions? If I were suddenly to kill one of these 10
animals and to take out all the soft parts, I should find the
shell to be perfectly inert, to have no more power of moving
itself than is possessed by the machinery of a mill, when dis-
connected from its steam-engine or water-wheel. But if I
were to open it, and take out the viscera only, leaving the 15
white flesh, I should perceive that the lobster could bend and
extend its tail as well as before. If I were to cut off the tail,
I should cease to find any spontaneous motion in it; but on
pinching any portion of the flesh, I should observe that it
underwent a very curious change—each fibre becoming 20
shorter and thicker. By this act of contraction, as it is
termed, the parts to which the ends of the fibre are attached
are, of course, approximated; and according to the relations
of their points of attachment to the centres of motion of the
different rings, the bending or the extension of the tail re- 25
sults. Close observation of the newly-opened lobster would
soon show that all its movements are due to the same cause
—the shortening and thickening of these fleshy fibres, which
are technically called muscles.

Here, then, is a capital fact. The movements of the lobster 30
are due to muscular contractility. But why does a muscle
contract at one time and not at another? Why does one
whole group of muscles contract when the lobster wishes
to extend his tail, and another group when he desires to
bend it? What is it originates, directs, and controls the 35
motive power?

Experiment, the great instrument for the ascertainment of truth in physical science, answers this question for us. In the head of the lobster there lies a small mass of that peculiar tissue which is known as nervous substance. Cords of simi-
5 lar matter connect this brain of the lobster, directly or indirectly, with the muscles. Now, if these communicating cords are cut, the brain remaining entire, the power of exerting what we call voluntary motion in the parts below the section is destroyed; and on the other hand, if, the cords
10 remaining entire, the brain mass be destroyed, the same voluntary mobility is equally lost. Whence the inevitable conclusion is, that the power of originating these motions resides in the brain, and is propagated along the nervous cords.

15 In the higher animals the phenomena which attend this transmission have been investigated, and the exertion of the peculiar energy which resides in the nerves has been found to be accompanied by a disturbance of the electrical state of their molecules.

20 If we could exactly estimate the signification of this disturbance; if we could obtain the value of a given exertion of nerve force by determining the quantity of electricity, or of heat, of which it is the equivalent; if we could ascertain upon what arrangement, or other condition of the molecules of
25 matter, the manifestation of the nervous and muscular energies depends, (and doubtless science will some day or other ascertain these points,) physiologists would have attained their ultimate goal in this direction; they would have determined the relation of the motive force of animals to the other
30 forms of force found in nature; and if the same process had been successfully performed for all the operations which are carried on in, and by, the animal frame, physiology would be perfect, and the facts of morphology and distribution would be deducible from the laws which physiologists had estab-
35 lished, combined with those determining the condition of the surrounding universe.

There is not a fragment of the organism of this humble animal, whose study would not lead us into regions of thought as large as those which I have briefly opened up to you; but what I have been saying, I trust, has not only enabled you to form a conception of the scope and purport of zoölogy, but has given you an imperfect example of the manner in which, in my opinion, that science, or indeed any physical science, may be best taught. The great matter is, to make teaching real and practical, by fixing the attention of the student on particular facts; but at the same time it should be rendered broad and comprehensive, by constant reference to the generalizations of which all particular facts are illustrations. The lobster has served as a type of the whole animal kingdom, and its anatomy and physiology have illustrated for us some of the greatest truths of biology. The student who has once seen for himself the facts which I have described, has had their relations explained to him, and has clearly comprehended them, has, so far, a knowledge of zoölogy, which is real and genuine, however limited it may be, and which is worth more than all the mere reading knowledge of the science he could ever acquire. His zoölogical information is, so far, knowledge and not mere hearsay.

THE WONDER–WORLD OF ATOMS[1]

Professor John Arthur Thomson

The exploration of this wonder-world of atoms and mole-cules by the physicists and chemists of to-day is one of the most impressive triumphs of modern science. Quite apart from radium and electrons and other sensational discoveries of recent years, the study of ordinary matter is hardly in-ferior, either in interest or audacity, to the work of the astronomer. And there is the same foundation in both cases —marvellous apparatus, and trains of mathematical reason-ing that would have astonished Euclid or Archimedes. Ex-traordinary, therefore, as are some of the facts and figures we are now going to give in connection with the minuteness of atoms and molecules, let us bear in mind that we owe them to the most solid and severe processes of human thought.

Yet the principle can in most cases be made so clear that the reader will not be asked to take much on trust. It is, for instance, a matter of common knowledge that gold is soft enough to be beaten into gold leaf. It is a matter of common sense, one hopes, that if you beat a measured cube of gold into a leaf six inches square, the mathematician can tell the thickness of that leaf without measuring it. As a matter of fact, a single grain of gold has been beaten into a leaf seventy-five inches square. Now the mathematician can easily find that when a single grain of gold is beaten out to that size, the leaf must be $\frac{1}{367.000}$ of an inch thick, or about a thousand times thinner than the paper on which these words are printed; yet the leaf must be several molecules thick.

[1] From *The Outline of Science*, Vol. I, pp. 249–253. Copyrighted in the United States, 1922, by G. P. Putnam's Sons, New York.

The finest gold leaf is, in fact, too thick for our purpose, and we turn with a new interest to that toy of our boyhood, the soap-bubble. If you carefully examine one of these delicate films of soapy water, you notice certain dark spots or patches on them. These are their thinnest parts, and by two quite independent methods—one using electricity and the other light—we have found that at these spots the bubble is less than the three-millionth of an inch thick! But the molecules in the film cling together so firmly that they must be at least twenty or thirty deep in the thinnest part. A molecule, therefore, must be far less than the three-millionth of an inch thick.

We found next that a film of oil on the surface of water may be even thinner than a soap-bubble. Professor Perrin, the great French authority on atoms, got films of oil down to the fifty-millionth of an inch in thickness! He poured a measured drop of oil upon water. Then he found the exact limits of the area of the oil-sheet by blowing upon the water a fine powder which spread to the edge of the film and clearly outlined it. The rest is safe and simple calculation, as in the case of the beaten grain of gold. Now this film of oil must have been at least two molecules deep, so a single molecule of oil is considerably less than a hundred-millionth of an inch in diameter.

Innumerable methods have been tried, and the result is always the same. A single grain of indigo, for instance, will colour a ton of water. This obviously means that the grain contains billions of molecules which spread through the water. A grain of musk will scent a room—pour molecules into every part of it—for several years, yet not lose one-millionth of its mass in a year. There are a hundred ways of showing the minuteness of the ultimate particles of matter, and some of these enable us to give definite figures. On a careful comparison of the best methods we can say that the average molecule of matter is less than the $\frac{1}{125,000,000}$ of an inch in diameter. In a single cubic centimetre of air—a

globule about the size of a small marble—there are thirty
million billion molecules. And since the molecule is, as we
saw, a group or cluster of atoms, the atom itself is smaller.
Atoms, for reasons which we shall see later, differ very greatly
from each other in size and weight. It is enough to say that
some of them are so small that it would take 400,000,000 of
them, in a line, to cover an inch of space; and that it takes
at least a trillion atoms of gold to weigh a single gramme.
Five million atoms of helium could be placed in a line across
the diameter of a full stop.

And this is only the beginning of the wonders that were
done with "ordinary matter," quite apart from radium and
its revelations, to which we will come presently. Most people
have heard of "atomic energy," and the extraordinary things
that might be accomplished if we could harness this energy
and turn it to human use. A deeper and more wonderful
source of this energy has been discovered in the last twenty
years, but it is well to realise that the atoms themselves have
stupendous energy. The atoms of matter are vibrating or
gyrating with extraordinary vigour. The piece of cold iron
you hold in your hand, the bit of brick you pick up, or the
penny you take from your pocket is a colossal reservoir of
energy, since it consists of billions of moving atoms. To
realise the total energy, of course, we should have to witness
a transformation such as we do in atoms of radio-active elements, about which we shall have something to say presently.

If we put a grain of indigo in a glass of water, or a grain
of musk in a perfectly still room, we soon realise that molecules travel. Similarly, the fact that gases spread until they
fill every "empty" available space shows definitely that they
consist of small particles travelling at great speed. The physicist brings his refined methods to bear on these things, and
he measures the energy and velocity of these infinitely minute
molecules. He tells us that molecules of oxygen, at the temperature of melting ice, travel at the rate of about 500 yards
a second—more than a quarter of a mile a second. Molecules

of hydrogen travel at four times that speed, or three times
the speed with which a bullet leaves a rifle. Each molecule
of the air, which seems so still in the house on a summer's
day, is really travelling faster than a rifle bullet does at the
beginning of its journey. It collides with another molecule
every twenty-thousandth of an inch of its journey. It is
turned from its course 5,000,000,000 times in every second by
collisions. If we could stop the molecules of hydrogen gas,
and utilise their energy, as we utilise the energy of steam or
the energy of the water at Niagara, we should find enough in
every gramme of gas (about two-thousandths of a pound) to
raise a third of a ton to a height of forty inches.

I have used for comparison the speed of a rifle bullet, and
in an earlier generation people would have thought it impossible even to estimate this. It is, of course, easy. We put
two screens in the path of the bullet, one near the rifle and
the other some distance away. We connect them electrically
and use a fine time-recording machine, and the bullet itself
registers the time it takes to travel from the first to the
second screen.

Now this is very simple and superficial work in comparison with the system of exact and minute measurements which
the physicist and chemist use. In one of his interesting
works Mr. Charles R. Gibson gives a photograph of two
exactly equal pieces of paper in the opposite pans of a fine
balance. A single word has been written in pencil on one of
these papers, and that little scraping of lead has been enough
to bring down the scale! The spectroscope will detect a
quantity of matter four million times smaller even than this;
and the electroscope is a million times still more sensitive than
the spectroscope. We have a heat-measuring instrument, the
bolometer, which makes the best thermometer seem Early
Victorian. It records the millionth of a degree of temperature. It is such instruments, multiplied by the score, which
enable us to do the fine work recorded in these pages.

THE DISCOVERY OF X–RAYS AND RADIUM[1]

PROFESSOR JOHN ARTHUR THOMSON

But these wonders of the atom are only a prelude to the more romantic and far-reaching discoveries of the new physics—the wonders of the electron. Another and the most important phase of our exploration of the material universe opened with the discovery of radium in 1898.

In the discovery of radio-active elements, a new property of matter was discovered. What followed on the discovery of radium and of the X-rays we shall see.

As Sir Ernest Rutherford, one of our greatest authorities, recently said, the new physics has dissipated the last doubt about the reality of atoms and molecules. The closer examination of matter which we have been able to make shows positively that it is composed of atoms. But we must not take the word now in its original Greek meaning (an "indivisible" thing). The atoms are not indivisible. They can be broken up. They are composed of still smaller particles.

The discovery that the atom was composed of smaller particles was the welcome realisation of a dream that had haunted the imagination of the nineteenth century. Chemists said that there were about eighty different kinds of atoms —different kinds of matter—but no one was satisfied with the multiplicity. Science is always aiming at simplicity and unity. It may be that science has now taken a long step in the direction of explaining the fundamental unity of all matter. The chemist was unable to break up these "elements" into something simpler, so he called their atoms "indivisible" in that sense. But one man of science after another

[1] From *The Outline of Science*, Vol. I, pp. 253–258. Copyrighted in the United States, 1922, by G. P. Putnam's Sons, New York.

expressed the hope that we would yet discover some fundamental matter of which the various atoms were composed—
*one primordial substance from which all the varying forms
of matter have been evolved or built up.* Prout suggested
this at the very beginning of the century, when atoms were
rediscovered by Dalton. Father Secchi, the famous Jesuit
astronomer, said that all the atoms were probably evolved
from ether; and this was a very favoured speculation.
Sir William Crookes talked of "prothyl" as the fundamental
substance. Others thought hydrogen was the stuff out of
which all the other atoms were composed.

The work which finally resulted in the discovery of radium
began with some beautiful experiments of Professor (later
Sir William) Crookes in the eighties.

It had been noticed in 1869 that a strange colouring was
caused when an electric charge was sent through a vacuum
tube—the walls of the glass tube began to glow with a greenish phosphorescence. A vacuum tube is one from which
nearly all the air has been pumped, although we can never
completely empty the tube. Crookes used such ingenious
methods that he reduced the gas in his tubes until it was
twenty million times thinner than the atmosphere. He then
sent an electric discharge through, and got very remarkable
results. The negative pole of the electric current (the
"cathode") *gave off rays which faintly lit the molecules of
the thin gas in the tube,* and caused a pretty fluorescence on
the glass walls of the tube. What were these rays? Crookes
at first thought they corresponded to a "new or fourth state
of matter." Hitherto we had only been familiar with matter
in the three conditions of solid, liquid, and gaseous.

Now Crookes really had the great secret under his eyes.
But about twenty years elapsed before the true nature of
these rays was finally and independently established by various experiments. The experiments proved "that the rays
consisted of a stream of negatively charged particles travelling with enormous velocities from 10,000 to 100,000 miles a

second. In addition, it was found that the mass of each particle was exceedingly small, about $\frac{1}{1800}$ of the mass of a hydrogen atom, the lightest atom known to science." *These particles or electrons, as they are now called, were being liberated from the atom.* The atoms of matter were breaking down in Crookes tubes. At that time, however, it was premature to think of such a thing, and Crookes preferred to say that the particles of the gas were electrified and hurled against the walls of the tube. He said that it was ordinary matter in a new state—"radiant matter." Another distinguished man of science, Lenard, found that, when he fitted a little plate of aluminium in the glass wall of the tube, the mysterious rays passed through this as if it were a window. They must be waves in the ether, he said.

So the story went on from year to year. We shall see in a moment to what it led. Meanwhile the next great step was when, in 1895, Röntgen discovered the X-rays, which are now known to everybody. He was following up the work of Lenard, and he one day covered a "Crookes tube" with some black stuff. To his astonishment a prepared chemical screen which was near the tube began to glow. *The rays had gone through the black stuff; and on further experiment he found that they would go through stone, living flesh, and all sorts* of *"opaque" substances.* In a short time the world was astonished to learn that we could photograph the skeleton in a living man's body, locate a penny in the interior of a child that had swallowed one, or take an impression of a coin through a slab of stone.

And what are these X-rays? They are not a form of matter; they are not material particles. X-rays were found to be a new variety of *light* with a remarkable power of penetration. We have seen what the spectroscope reveals about the varying nature of light wave-lengths. Light-waves are set up by vibrations in ether,[1] and, as we shall see, these ether

---

[1] We refer throughout to the "ether" because, although modern theories dispense largely with this conception, the theories of physics are so inex-

disturbances are all of the same kind; they only differ as
regards wave-lengths. The X-rays which Röntgen discovered, then, are light, but a variety of light previously unknown to us; they are ether waves of very short length.
X-rays have proved of great value in many directions, as all 5
the world knows, but that we need not discuss at this point.
Let us see what followed Röntgen's discovery.

While the world wondered at these marvels, the men of
science were eagerly following up the new clue to the mystery
of matter which was exercising the mind of Crookes and 10
other investigators. In 1896 Becquerel brought us to the
threshold of the great discovery.

Certain substances are phosphorescent—they become luminous after they have been exposed to sunlight for some time,
and Becquerel was trying to find if any of these substances 15
give rise to X-rays. One day he chose a salt of the metal
uranium. He was going to see if, after exposing it to sunlight, he could photograph a cross with it through an opaque
substance. He wrapped it up and laid it aside, to wait for
the sun, but he found the uranium salt did not wait for the 20
sun. Some strong radiation from it went through the opaque
covering and made an impression of the cross upon the plate
underneath. Light or darkness was immaterial. The mysterious rays streamed night and day from the salt. This was
something new. Here was a substance which appeared to be 25
producing X-rays; the rays emitted by uranium would penetrate the same opaque substances as the X-rays discovered
by Röntgen.

Now, at the same time as many other investigators, Professor Curie and his Polish wife took up the search. They 30
decided to find out whether the emission came from the
uranium itself or *from something associated with it*, and for
this purpose they made a chemical analysis of great quantities of minerals. They found a certain kind of pitchblende

tricably interwoven with it that it is necessary, in an elementary exposition,
to assume its existence.

which was very active, and they analysed tons of it, concentrating always on the radiant element in it. After a time, as they successively worked out the non-radiant matter, the stuff began to glow. In the end they extracted from eight
5 tons of pitchblende about half a teaspoonful of something *that was a million times more radiant than uranium.* There was only one name for it—Radium.

That was the starting-point of the new development of physics and chemistry. From every laboratory in the world
10 came a cry for radium salts (as pure radium was too precious), and hundreds of brilliant workers fastened on the new element. The inquiry was broadened, and, as year followed year, one substance after another was found to possess the power of emitting rays, that is, to be radio-active. We know
15 to-day that nearly every form of matter can be stimulated to radio-activity; which, as we shall see, means that *its atoms break up into smaller and wonderfully energetic particles which we call "electrons."* This discovery of electrons has brought about a complete change in our ideas in many
20 directions.

So, instead of atoms being indivisible, they are actually dividing themselves, spontaneously, and giving off throughout the universe tiny fragments of their substance. We shall explain presently what was later discovered about the elec-
25 tron; meanwhile we can say that every glowing metal is pouring out a stream of these electrons. Every arc-lamp is discharging them. Every clap of thunder means a shower of them. Every star is flooding space with them. We are witnessing the spontaneous breaking up of atoms, atoms
30 which had been thought to be indivisible. The sun not only pours out streams of electrons from its own atoms, but the ultra-violet light which it sends to the earth is one of the most powerful agencies for releasing electrons from the surface-atoms of matter on the earth. It is fortunate for
35 us that our atmosphere absorbs most of this ultra-violet or

invisible light of the sun—a kind of light which will be explained presently. It has been suggested that, if we received the full flood of it from the sun, our metals would disintegrate under its influence and this "steel civilisation" of ours would be impossible !   5

But we are here anticipating, we are going beyond radium to the wonderful discoveries which were made by the chemists and physicists of the world who concentrated upon it. The work of Professor and Mme. Curie was merely the final clue to guide the great search. How it was followed up, how 10 we penetrated into the very heart of the minute atom and discovered new and portentous mines of energy, and how we were able to understand, not only matter, but electricity and light, will be told in the next chapter.

LIFE IN THE WILDERNESS[1]

THEODORE ROOSEVELT

Long before the first Continental Congress assembled, the backwoodsmen, whatever their blood, had become Americans, one in speech, thought, and character, clutching firmly the land in which their fathers and grandfathers had lived
5 before them. They had lost all remembrance of Europe and all sympathy with things European; they had become as emphatically products native to the soil as were the tough and supple hickories out of which they fashioned the handles of their long, light axes. Their grim, harsh, narrow lives were
10 yet strangely fascinating and full of adventurous toil and danger; none but natures as strong, as freedom-loving, and as full of bold defiance as theirs could have endured existence on the terms which these men found pleasurable. Their iron surroundings made a mould which turned out all alike in the
15 same shape. They resembled one another, and they differed from the rest of the world—even the world of America, and infinitely more the world of Europe—in dress, in customs, and in mode of life.

Where their lands abutted on the more settled districts to
20 the eastward, the population was of course thickest, and their peculiarities least. Here and there at such points they built small backwoods burgs or towns, rude, straggling, unkempt villages, with a store or two, a tavern,—sometimes good, often a "scandalous hog-sty," where travellers were devoured by
25 fleas, and every one slept and ate in one room,[18]—a small log

[1] From *The Winning of the West*, Vol. I, chap. v, pp. 108–113. G. P. Putnam's Sons, New York, 1889.

[18] MS. Journal of Matthew Clarkson, 1766. See also La Rochefoucauld-Liancourt, *Voyage dans les États-Unis*, tome i, p. 104. Paris, L'an VII.

school-house, and a little church, presided over by a hard-featured Presbyterian preacher, gloomy, earnest, and zealous, probably bigoted and narrow-minded, but nevertheless a great power for good in the community.[19]

However, the backwoodsmen as a class neither built towns nor loved to dwell therein. They were to be seen at their best in the vast, interminable forests that formed their chosen home. They won and kept their lands by force, and ever lived either at war or in dread of war. Hence they settled always in groups of several families each, all banded together for mutual protection. Their red foes were strong and terrible, cunning in council, dreadful in battle, merciless beyond belief in victory. The men of the border did not overcome and dispossess cowards and weaklings; they marched forth to spoil the stout-hearted and to take for a prey the possessions of the men of might. Every acre, every rood of ground which they claimed had to be cleared by the axe and held with the rifle. Not only was the chopping down of the forests the first preliminary to cultivation, but it was also the surest means of subduing the Indians, to whom the unending stretches of choked woodland were an impenetrable cover behind which to move unseen, a shield in making assaults, and a strong tower of defence in repelling counter-attacks. In the conquest of the west the backwoods axe, shapely, well-poised, with long haft and light head, was a servant hardly standing second even to the rifle; the two were the national weapons of the American backwoodsman, and in their use he has never been excelled.

When a group of families moved out into the wilderness they built themselves a station or stockadé fort; a square palisade of upright logs, loop-holed, with strong block-houses as bastions at the corners. One side at least was generally formed by the backs of the cabins themselves, all standing

[19] The borderers had the true Calvinistic taste in preaching. Clarkson, in his journal of his western trip, mentions with approval a sermon he heard as being "a very judicious and alarming discourse."

in a row; and there was a great door or gate, that could be strongly barred in case of need. Often no iron whatever was employed in any of the buildings. The square inside contained the provision sheds and frequently a strong central block-house as well. These forts, of course, could not stand against cannon, and they were always in danger when attacked with fire; but save for this risk of burning they were very effectual defences against men without artillery, and were rarely taken, whether by whites or Indians, except by surprise. Few other buildings have played so important a part in our history as the rough stockade fort of the backwoods.

The families only lived in the fort when there was war with the Indians, and even then not in the winter. At other times they all separated out to their own farms, universally called clearings, as they were always made by first cutting off the timber. The stumps were left to dot the fields of grain and Indian corn. The corn in especial was the stand-by and invariable resource of the western settler; it was the crop on which he relied to feed his family, and when hunting or on a war trail the parched grains were carried in his leather wallet to serve often as his only food. But he planted orchards and raised melons, potatoes, and many other fruits and vegetables as well; and he had usually a horse or two, cows, and perhaps hogs and sheep, if the wolves and bears did not interfere. If he was poor his cabin was made of unhewn logs, and held but a single room; if well-to-do, the logs were neatly hewed, and besides the large living- and eating-room with its huge stone fireplace, there was also a small bedroom and a kitchen, while a ladder led to the loft above, in which the boys slept. The floor was made of puncheons, great slabs of wood hewed carefully out, and the roof of clapboards. Pegs of wood were thrust into the sides of the house, to serve instead of a wardrobe; and buck antlers, thrust into joists, held the ever ready rifles. The table was a great clapboard set on four wooden legs; there were three-legged stools, and in the better sort of houses old-fashioned rocking chairs.[20] The couch or bed was warmly covered with blankets, bear-skins, and deer-hides.[21]

These clearings lay far apart from one another in the wilderness. Up to the door-sills of the log-huts stretched the solemn and mysterious forest. There were no openings to break its continuity; nothing but endless leagues on leagues of shadowy, wolf-haunted woodland. The great trees towered aloft till their separate heads were lost in the mass of foliage above, and the rank underbrush choked the spaces between the trunks. On the higher peaks and ridge-crests of the mountains there were straggling birches and pines, hemlocks and balsam firs;[22] elsewhere, oaks, chestnuts, hickories, maples, beeches, walnuts, and great tulip trees grew side by side with many other kinds. The sunlight could not penetrate the roofed archway of murmuring leaves; through the gray aisles of the forest men walked always in a kind of midday gloaming. Those who had lived in the open plains felt when they came to the backwoods as if their heads were hooded. Save on the border of a lake, from a cliff top, or on a bald knob,—that is, a bare hill-shoulder,—they could not anywhere look out for any distance.

[20] McAfee MSS.

[21] In the McAfee MSS. there is an amusing mention of the skin of a huge bull elk, killed by the father, which the youngsters christened "old ellick"; they used to quarrel for the possession of it on cold nights, as it was very warm, though if the hairside was turned in it became slippery and apt to slide off the bed.

[22] On the mountains the climate, flora, and fauna were all those of the north, not of the adjacent southern lowlands. The ruffed grouse, red squirrel, snow bird, various Canadian warblers, and a peculiar species of boreal field-mouse, the evotomys, are all found as far south as the Great Smokies.

THE PLEASANTNESS OF AMERICAN LIFE[1]

James Bryce

I have never met a European of the upper or middle classes who did not express astonishment when told that America was a more agreeable place than Europe to live in. "For working men," he would answer, "yes; but for men of
5 education or property, how can a new rough country, where nothing but business is talked and the refinements of life are only just beginning to appear, how can such a country be compared with England, or France, or Italy?"

It is nevertheless true that there are elements in the life
10 of the United States which may well make a European of any class prefer to dwell there rather than in the land of his birth. Let us see what they are.

In the first place there is the general prosperity and material well-being of the mass of the inhabitants. In Europe, if
15 an observer takes his eye off his own class and considers the whole population of any one of the greater countries (for I except Switzerland and parts of Scandinavia and Portugal), he will perceive that by far the greater number lead very laborious lives, and are, if not actually in want of the neces-
20 saries of existence, yet liable to fall into want, the agriculturists when nature is harsh, the wage-earners when work is scarce. In England the lot of the labourer has been hitherto a hard one, incessant field toil, with rheumatism at fifty and the workhouse at the end of the vista; while the misery
25 massed in such cities as London, Liverpool, and Glasgow is only too well known. In France there is less pauperism, but

[1] From *The American Commonwealth*, Vol. III, chap. cxii. Macmillan & Co., London, 1888.

nothing can be more pinched and sordid than the life of the
bulk of the peasantry. In the great towns of Germany there
is constant distress and increasing discontent. The riots of
1886 in Belgium told an even more painful tale of the
wretchedness of the miners and artisans there. In Italy the 5
condition of the rural population of Lombardy and Venetia
as well as of the southern provinces seems to grow worse, and
fills her statesmen with alarm. Of Russia, with her eighty
millions of ignorant peasants living in half-barbarism, there
is no need to speak. Contrast any one of these countries with 10
the United States, where the working classes are as well fed,
clothed, and lodged as the lower middle-class in Europe, and
the farmers who till their own land (as nearly all do) much
better, where a good education is within the reach of the
poorest, where the opportunities for getting on in one way 15
or another are so abundant that no one need fear any physical ill but disease or the results of his own intemperance.
Pauperism already exists and increases in some of the larger
cities, where drink breeds misery, and where recent immi-
grants, with the shiftlessness of Europe still clinging round 20
them, are huddled together in squalor. But outside these
few cities one sees nothing but comfort. In Connecticut and
Massachusetts the operatives in many a manufacturing town
lead a life far easier, far more brightened by intellectual
culture and by amusements, than that of the clerks and shop- 25
keepers of England or France. In cities like Cleveland or
Chicago one finds miles on miles of suburb filled with neat
wooden houses, each with its tiny garden plot, owned by the
shop assistants and handicraftsmen who return on the horse
cars in the evening from their work. All over the wide West, 30
from Lake Ontario to the Upper Missouri, one travels past
farms of two to three hundred acres, in every one of which
there is a spacious farmhouse among orchards and meadows,
where the farmer's children grow up strong and hearty on
abundant food, the boys full of intelligence and enterprise, 35
ready to push their way on farms of their own or enter busi-

ness in the nearest town, the girls familiar with the current literature of England as well as of America. The life of the new emigrant in the further West has its privations in the first years, but it is brightened by hope, and has a singular
5 charm of freedom and simplicity. The impression which this comfort and plenty makes is heightened by the brilliance and keenness of the air, by the look of freshness and cleanness which even the cities wear, all of them except the poorest parts of those few I have referred to above. The fog and
10 soot-flakes of an English town, as well as its squalor, are wanting; you are in a new world, and a world which knows the sun. It is impossible not to feel warmed, cheered, invigorated by the sense of such material well-being all around one, impossible not to be infected by the buoyancy and hope-
15 fulness of the people. The wretchedness of Europe lies far behind; the weight of its problems seems lifted from the mind. As a man suffering from depression feels the clouds roll away from his spirit when he meets a friend whose good humour and energy present the better side of things and
20 point the way through difficulties, so the sanguine temper of the Americans, and the sight of the ardour with which they pursue their aims, stimulates a European, and makes him think the world a better place than it had seemed amid the entanglements and sufferings of his own hemisphere.

25   To some Europeans this may seem fanciful. I doubt if any European can realize till he has been in America how much difference it makes to the happiness of any one not wholly devoid of sympathy with his fellow-beings, to feel that all round him, in all classes of society and all parts of
30 the country, there exist in such ample measure so many of the external conditions of happiness: abundance of the necessaries of life, easy command of education and books, amusements and leisure to enjoy them, comparatively few temptations to intemperance and vice.

35   The second charm of American life is one which some Europeans will smile at. It is social equality. To many

THE PLEASANTNESS OF AMERICAN LIFE 59

Europeans—to Germans, let us say, or Englishmen—the word has an odious sound. It suggests a dirty fellow in a blouse elbowing his betters in a crowd, or an ill-conditioned villager shaking his fist at the parson and the squire; or, at any rate, it suggests obtrusiveness and bad manners. The exact contrary is the truth. Equality improves manners, for it strengthens the basis of all good manners, respect for other men and women simply as men and women, irrespective of their station in life. Probably the assertion of social equality was one of the causes which injured American manners forty years ago, for that they were then bad among townsfolks can hardly be doubted in face of the testimony, not merely of sharp tongues like Mrs. Trollope's, but of calm observers like Sir Charles Lyell and sympathetic observers like Richard Cobden. In those days there was an obtrusive self-assertiveness among the less refined classes, especially towards those who, coming from the Old World, were assumed to come in a patronizing spirit. Now, however, social equality has grown so naturally out of the circumstances of the country, has been so long established, and is so ungrudgingly admitted, that all excuse for obtrusiveness has disappeared. People meet on a simple and natural footing, with more frankness and ease than is possible in countries where every one is either looking up or looking down.[1] There is no servility on the part of the humbler, and if now and then a

[1] A trifling anecdote may illustrate what I mean. In a small Far Western town the stationmaster lent me a locomotive to run a few miles out along the railway to see a remarkable piece of scenery. The engine took me and dropped me there, as I wished to walk back, much to the surprise of the driver and the stoker, for in America no one walks if he can help it. The same evening, as I was sitting in the hall of the hotel, I was touched on the arm, and turning round found myself accosted by a well-mannered man, who turned out to be the engine-driver. He expressed his regret that the locomotive had not been cleaner and better "fixed up," as he would have liked to make my trip as agreeable as possible, but the notice given him had been short. He talked with intelligence, and we had some pleasant chat together. It was fortunate that I had resisted in the forenoon the British impulse to bestow a gratuity.

little of the "I am as good as you" rudeness be perceptible, it is almost sure to proceed from a recent immigrant, to whom the attitude of simple equality has not yet become familiar as the evidently proper attitude of one man to another. There is no condescension on the part of the more highly placed, nor is there even that sort of scrupulously polite coldness which one might think they would adopt in order to protect their dignity. They have no cause to fear for their dignity, so long as they do not themselves forget it. And the fact that your shoemaker or your factory hand addresses you as an equal does not prevent him from respecting, and showing his respect for, all such superiority as your birth or education or eminence in any line of life may entitle you to receive.

This naturalness of intercourse is a distinct addition to the pleasure of social life. It enlarges the circle of possible friendship, by removing the *gêne* which in most parts of Europe persons of different ranks feel in exchanging their thoughts on any matters save those of business. It raises the humbler classes without lowering the upper; indeed, it improves the upper no less than the lower by expunging that latent insolence which deforms the manners of so many of the European rich or great. It relieves women in particular, who in Europe are specially apt to think of class distinctions, from that sense of constraint and uneasiness which is produced by the knowledge that other women with whom they come in contact are either looking down on them, or at any rate trying to gauge and determine their social position. It expands the range of a man's sympathies, and makes it easier for him to enter into the sentiments of other classes than his own. It gives a sense of solidarity to the whole nation, cutting away the ground for all sorts of jealousies and grudges which distract people, so long as the social pretensions of past centuries linger on to be resisted and resented by the levelling spirit of a revolutionary age. And I have never heard native Americans speak of any drawbacks corresponding to and qualifying these benefits.

There are, moreover, other rancours besides those of social inequality whose absence from America brightens it to a European eye. There are no quarrels of churches and sects. Judah does not vex Ephraim, nor Ephraim envy Judah. No Established Church looks down scornfully upon Dissenters from the height of its titles and endowments, and talks of them as hindrances in the way of its work. No Dissenters pursue an Established Church in a spirit of watchful jealousy, nor agitate for its overthrow. One is not offended by the contrast between the theory and the practice of a religion of peace, between professions of universal affection in pulpit addresses and forms of prayer, and the acrimony of clerical controversialists. Still less, of course, is there that sharp opposition and antagonism of Christians and anti-Christians which lacerates the private as well as public life of France. Rivalry between sects appears only in the innocent form of the planting of new churches and raising of funds for missionary objects, while most of the Protestant denominations, including the four most numerous, constantly fraternize in charitable work. Between Roman Catholics and Protestants there is little hostility, and sometimes co-operation for a philanthropic purpose. The sceptic is no longer under a social ban, and discussions on the essentials of Christianity and of theism are conducted with good temper. There is not a country in the world where Frederick the Great's principle, that every one should be allowed to go to heaven his own way, is so fully applied. This sense of religious peace as well as religious freedom all around one is soothing to the weary European, and contributes not a little to sweeten the lives of ordinary people.

I come last to the character and ways of the Americans themselves, in which there is a certain charm, hard to convey by description, but felt almost as soon as one sets foot on their shore, and felt constantly thereafter. They are a kindly people. Good nature, heartiness, a readiness to render small services to one another, an assumption that neighbours in

the country, or persons thrown together in travel, or even in
a crowd, were meant to be friendly rather than hostile to one
another, seem to be everywhere in the air, and in those who
breathe it. Sociability is the rule, isolation and moroseness
5 the rare exception. It is not merely that people are more
vivacious or talkative than an Englishman expects to find
them, for the Western man is often taciturn and seldom
wreathes his long face into a smile. It is rather that you feel
that the man next you, whether silent or talkative, does not
10 mean to repel intercourse or convey by his manner his low
opinion of his fellow-creatures. Everybody seems disposed
to think well of the world and its inhabitants, well enough
at least to wish to be on easy terms with them and serve them
in those little things whose trouble to the doer is small in
15 proportion to the pleasure they give to the receiver. To help
others is better recognized as a duty than in Europe. Nowhere is money so readily given for any public purpose;
nowhere, I suspect, are there so many acts of private kindness done, such, for instance, as paying the college expenses
20 of a promising boy, or aiding a widow to carry on her husband's farm; and these are not done with ostentation. People
seem to take their own troubles more lightly than they do in
Europe, and to be more indulgent to the faults by which
troubles are caused. It is a land of hope, and a land of hope
25 is a land of good humour. And they have also, though this
is a quality more perceptible in women than in men, a remarkable faculty for enjoyment, a power of drawing more
happiness from obvious pleasures, simple and innocent
pleasures, than one often finds in overburdened Europe.

30   As generalizations like this are necessarily comparative,
I may be asked with whom I am comparing the Americans.
With the English, or with some attempted average of European nations? Primarily I am comparing them with the
English, because they are the nearest relatives of the English.
35 But there are other European countries, such as France, Belgium, Spain, in which the sort of cheerful friendliness I have

sought to describe is less common than it is in America. Even in Germany and German Austria, simple and kindly as are the masses of the people, the upper classes have that *roideur* which belongs to countries dominated by an old aristocracy, or by a plutocracy trying to imitate aristocratic ways. The upper class in America (if one may use such an expression) has not in this respect differentiated itself from the character of the nation at large.

If the view here presented be a true one, to what causes are we to ascribe this agreeable development of the original English type, a development in whose course the sadness of Puritanism seems to have been shed off?

Perhaps one of them is the humorous turn of the American character. Humour is a sweetener of temper, a copious spring of charity, for it makes the good side of bad things even more visible than the weak side of good things: but humour in Americans may be as much a result of an easy and kindly turn as their kindliness is of their humour. Another is the perpetuation of a habit of mutual help formed in colonial days. Colonists need one another's aid more constantly than the dwellers in an old country, are thrown more upon one another, even when they live scattered in woods or prairies, are more interested in one another's welfare. When you have only three neighbours within five miles, each of them covers a large part of your horizon. You want to borrow a plough from one; you get another to help you to roll your logs; your children's delight is to go over for an evening's merrymaking to the lads and lasses of the third. It is much pleasanter to be on good terms with these few neighbours, and when others come one by one, they fall into the same habits of intimacy. Any one who has read those stories of rustic New England or New York life which delighted the English children of thirty years ago—I do not know whether they delight children still, or have been thrown aside for more highly spiced food—will remember the warm-hearted simplicity and atmosphere of genial goodwill which softened

the roughness of peasant manners and tempered the stern-
ness of a Calvinistic creed. It is natural that the freedom
of intercourse and sense of interdependence which existed
among the early settlers, and which have always existed since
5 among the pioneers of colonization in the West as they moved
from the Connecticut to the Mohawk, from the Mohawk to
the Ohio, from the Ohio to the Mississippi, should have left
on the national character traces not effaced even in the more
artificial civilization of our own time. Something may be set
10 down to the feeling of social equality, creating that respect
for a man as a man, whether he be rich or poor, which was
described a few pages back; and something to a regard for
the sentiment of the multitude, a sentiment which forbids
any man to stand aloof in the conceit of self-importance, and
15 holds up geniality and good fellowship as almost the first of
social virtues. I do not mean that a man consciously sup-
presses his impulses to selfishness or gruffness because he
knows that his faults will be ill regarded; but that, having
grown up in a society which is infinitely powerful as com-
20 pared with the most powerful person in it, he has learnt to
realize his individual insignificance, as members of the upper
class in Europe never do, and has become permeated by the
feeling which this society entertains—that each one's duty
is not only to accept equality, but also to relish equality, and
25 to make himself pleasant to his equals. Thus the habit is
formed even in natures of no special sweetness, and men become kindly by doing kindly acts.

Whether, however, these suggestions be right or wrong,
there is, I think, no doubt as to the fact which they attempt
30 to explain. I do not, of course, give it merely as the casual
impression of European visitors, whom a singularly frank
and ready hospitality welcomes and makes much of. I base
it on the reports of European friends who have lived for years
in the United States, and whose criticism of the ways and
35 notions of the people is keen enough to show that they are
no partial witnesses.

THE BOW OF A BOAT[1]

John Ruskin

Of all things, living or lifeless, upon this strange earth, there is but one which, having reached the mid-term of appointed human endurance on it, I still regard with unmitigated amazement. I know, indeed, that all around me is wonderful—but I cannot answer it with wonder: a dark veil, with the foolish words, NATURE OF THINGS, upon it, casts its deadening folds between me and their dazzling strangeness. Flowers open, and stars rise, and it seems to me they could have done no less. The mystery of distant mountain-blue only makes me reflect that the earth is of necessity mountainous; the sea-wave breaks at my feet, and I do not see how it should have remained unbroken. But one object there is still, which I never pass without the renewed wonder of childhood, and that is the bow of a Boat. Not of a racing-wherry, or revenue cutter, or clipper yacht; but the blunt head of a common, bluff, undecked sea-boat, lying aside in its furrow of beach sand. The sum of Navigation is in that. You may magnify it or decorate as you will: you do not add to the wonder of it. Lengthen it into hatchet-like edge of iron—strengthen it with complex tracery of ribs of oak— carve it and gild it till a column of light moves beneath it on the sea—you have made no more of it than it was at first. That rude simplicity of bent plank, that can breast its way through the death that is in the deep sea, has in it the soul of shipping. Beyond this, we may have more work, more men, more money; we cannot have more miracle.

For there is, first, an infinite strangeness in the perfection

[1] From *The Harbours of England*, pp. 1 ff. London, 1856.

of the thing, as work of human hands. I know nothing else
that man does, which is perfect, but that. All his other do-
ings have some sign of weakness, affectation, or ignorance in
them. They are overfinished or underfinished; they do not
5 quite answer their end, or they show a mean vanity in answering it too well.

But the boat's bow is naïvely perfect: complete without
an effort. The man who made it knew not he was making
anything beautiful, as he bent its planks into those mysteri-
10 ous, ever-changing curves. It grows under his hand into the
image of a sea-shell; the seal, as it were, of the flowing of the
great tides and streams of ocean stamped on its delicate
rounding. He leaves it when all is done, without a boast. It
is simple work, but it will keep out water. And every plank
15 thenceforward is a Fate, and has men's lives wreathed in the
knots of it, as the cloth-yard shaft had their deaths in its
plumes.

Then, also, it is wonderful on account of the greatness of
the thing accomplished. No other work of human hands
20 ever gained so much. Steam engines and telegraphs indeed
help us to fetch, and carry, and talk; they lift weights for
us, and bring messages, with less trouble than would have
been needed otherwise; this saving of trouble, however, does
not constitute a new faculty, it only enhances the powers we
25 already possess. But in that bow of the boat is the gift of another world. Without it, what prison wall would be so strong
as that 'white and wailing fringe' of sea? What maimed
creatures were we all, chained to our rocks, Andromeda-like,
or wandering by the endless shores, wasting our incommuni-
30 cable strength, and pining in hopeless watch of unconquer-
able waves? The nails that fasten together the planks of the
boat's bow are the rivets of the fellowship of the world.
Their iron does more than draw lightning out of heaven; it
leads love round the earth.

35 Then, also, it is wonderful on account of the greatness of
the enemy that it does battle with. To lift dead weight; to

overcome length of languid space; to multiply or systematize a given force; this we may see done by the bar, or beam, or wheel, without wonder. But to war with that living fury of waters, to bare its breast, moment after moment, against the unwearied enmity of ocean—the subtle, fitful, implacable 5 smiting of the black waves, provoking each other on, endlessly, all the infinite march of the Atlantic rolling on behind them to their help—and still to strike them back into a wreath of smoke and futile foam, and win its way against them, and keep its charge of life from them—does any other 10 soulless thing do as much as this?

I should not have talked of this feeling of mine about a boat, if I had thought it was mine only; but I believe it to be common to all of us who are not seamen. With the seaman, wonder changes into fellowship and close affection; but to 15 all landsmen, from youth upwards, the boat remains a piece of enchantment.

STUDENTS' THEMES: EXPOSITION

THE SEA SLED

A few years ago, there arose a demand for a small but sea-worthy speed boat. Many people believed that the construction of such a craft was impossible, and indeed the experience of engineers seemed to show that high speed and seaworthi-ness could not be combined in a small boat. Then, while arguments and experiments were still going on, it was announced that someone had solved the whole problem by inventing the "Sea Sled." The name is ingenious, and drew people's attention. For a long while, interest centered on this strange craft, and, after many exhaustive tests, it was finally accepted as a boat, and not as an experiment. The result of the tests was the general admission that there could be such a thing as a seaworthy speed boat, although it seemed incredible that one could hit a six-foot wave at fifty miles an hour without even getting wet.

Perhaps a brief explanation of the construction of a boat which can perform such a feat would be of interest. Imagine a high-sided, flat-bottomed scow with a square stern and a bow hollowed out so that it looks like the front of a sled, and you have a rough picture of a Sea Sled. Its sides descend perpendicularly into the water, and at the stern a slight "overhang" projects above the propellers. The bow, from which this remarkable craft derives its name, is usually very high, and there is a decided slope of the deck from bow to stern. At the stern, the bottom of the boat is perfectly flat. About six feet forward from the stern a V-shaped crease, or "valley," begins, which deepens and widens as it curves upward, until, at the very tip of the bow, the bottom of this valley nearly touches the under side of the deck above. Hence, there is not as much room inside a Sea Sled as one would expect in such a square, wide craft. Because of this lack of space, the full weight of the engines lies at the stern, where there is most displacement, and the propellers extend 5 not only outwards, but downwards. Thus the forward motion of the boat is the component of both an upward and a forward force, with the result that, when a certain speed is reached, she "planes" over the water's surface after the manner of the stepped hydroplane racing boats. But there is one 10 difference. The hydroplane rides on a cushion of air; the Sea Sled on a cushion of water.

This type of boat was exactly what many people were looking for, and soon the Sea Sled was a familiar sight everywhere. Well do I remember my first sight of one. It was 15 early one calm evening, and the "Thoroughfare" was as still as a mill pond. I was furling the sail of a small knockabout, when I realized that both shores were echoing a strange sound, at first dull and low, then louder and more vibrant. Three minutes later, the little fishing wharves were reëcho- 20 ing a furious roar, and a bright searchlight was carefully "picking up" the channel buoys as it sped past. I had a brief impression of a high, reaching bow, and a streak of white foam. Three minutes later, the gulls settled on the rocks again, and all was silent. I asked a fisherman if he 25 knew who owned the boat. He replied: "Boston man. He leaves his office at three every Friday afternoon, and gets to Bar Harbor in time for dinner." But that was in the early days, when the Sea Sled had not been perfected. Even the Boston man could not stand the steady roar for five hours at 30 a stretch, and he soon gave up this unique way of commuting —possibly through inability to pay the gasoline bills, which must have been tremendous. But anyone who has sailed New England waters will not doubt the seaworthiness of the boat which can cut across the open sea from Boston to the 35 Maine coast, and make the trip in five hours.

Another early type of Sea Sled was the model designed for the U. S. Navy. Four were built, and I believe all four were discarded because of expense of upkeep. Two of these boats I have seen out of water in the Lawley Shipyard at Neponset.
5 They are forty feet long, and are equipped with *four* large heavy oil engines. When built, they were guaranteed to go fifty miles an hour, and during subsequent Navy tests they made fifty-five. But how the super-heated engineer managed to live, I cannot imagine. He had about four cubic feet of
10 head room in which to tend as many roaring engines. The steersman, too, must have been a versatile man. For he sat behind a small steel cowl above the cockpit, managing four clutch levers, eight spark and gas controls, and a double rudder. These boats were built to be lifted onto the deck of
15 a battleship, and their construction is very strong. Since they were rarely slowed down to less than thirty miles an hour, even in the roughest kinds of weather, their seaworthiness has been well tested.

As far as utility is concerned, these two examples may
20 seem to show the Sea Sled in a rather unfavorable light. But let me hasten to say that they show only the first step in the development of what has now become a well-recognized type of fast boat. That development has been in progress ever since, and the speedy, quiet, economical craft which skim
25 over Long Island Sound and Southern waters, for business and for pleasure, have most certainly demonstrated both their utility, and their ability to stand a heavy sea.

FLOATING LABOR

There are many kinds of work in this country that last for only a short time, but during that time they are conducted on a vast scale. Harvesting is the biggest and most important work of this kind. To harvest the wheat crops of the West, many thousand workers are needed. Men cannot have a trade of harvesting, as it occupies only a month or two each year. Consequently, a large body of men must come into a certain section for a short time, and then move on. This condition has created the moving body of workers known as "floating labor."

The men who form this body have many jobs in many places. They flock to Kansas, Nebraska, and the Dakotas in July and August to harvest the wheat. When all the wheat is harvested, they move to another place. What place? Any place where labor is needed. If there is a great labor shortage in the East, these men will drift there, and soon the shortage has ceased. Of course, this drifting is true only of unskilled labor. The trained mechanic can almost always get work, and he does not have to go far to get it. But the common laborer, the man who shovels hot steel into wheelbarrows in a steel mill, who acts as a carpenter's helper when a new roof is built on a roundhouse, who digs ditches and lays railroad tracks, is the man who makes up the body known as floating labor. He is the unskilled, underpaid man who, when the country is threatened with a labor shortage, arrives on the scene and prevents a shutdown. But he does this for no patriotic or friendly motive. He wants work and he will go where the work is. He thrives when labor is scarce. When it is plentiful, he stands freezing in the bread lines on the Bowery or Madison Street.

The floating laborer has no home; generally he wants no
home. He has been "on the bum" (his own expression for
being a floating laborer) for many years; and he will stay on
the bum for many more. He has been all over the country.
5 He knows all the big cities and is at home in all of them. I
do not say he is at home everywhere. He is not. His home,
even though I have said he has none, is in the city. *What*
city doesn't matter. He never works all the time. He makes
three or four hundred dollars, goes back to town, hires a room
10 for a few months, and has a good time. When all his money
is gone, he gets a job and is off for another six months. The
money that he earns is never saved. The future does not
concern him, the past does not haunt him, the present is all
that interests him. But he does save while he is working.
15 He knows he can get more fun out of a lot of money for a
short time than out of a little money for a long time. I met
men who were working thirteen hours a day five days in a
week and nine hours on Saturday for fifty dollars. They
saved most of this, and at the end of a few months spent it
20 all in Chicago.

These men have no cares or worries: no relatives, but
many friends. Most of their fellow laborers are their friends.
They are always ready to accept you as a friend if you treat
them decently. They never ask your name or past history,
25 but they are always ready to listen to all your experiences
and to tell you theirs.

The best way to get acquainted with them is to travel
with them. Most people think that this class of men travel
on a freight train. This is not so. A freight is slow and
30 uncomfortable. Their favorite mode of travel is the free
shipment.

In every large city in this country there is a street corresponding to the Bowery in New York. If you walk down
one of these streets, you will see many posters in what seem
35 to be empty shop windows. Stop for a moment and read one.
You will see something like this.

LABORERS WANTED
JANESVILLE, WIS.
50¢ an hour.   *Good Board.*
SHIP TODAY.   FREE FARE.

Before you can finish reading, a seedy-looking man will approach you and ask, "Want to ship West today, boys?"

This is your introduction to the labor agency and to the labor agent. When a factory needs laborers, it notifies a labor agency. The agency puts out posters telling about the work, pay, etc. The tramp who is out of money, or pretty nearly out of it, sees the poster, goes into the agency, and signs up for the job. Generally he has to pay the agent two dollars, which goes straight to the agent and is pure graft. The agent finds out if the man has baggage and signs him up if he has. The reason for this is simple. When a company ships men from a city, it has to pay their railroad fare. This seems a very good way for a man to obtain a free ride: it would be very easy to get off before reaching the proper destination. If many men did this, and practically all would, the companies would lose a lot of money. To avoid this, they make a simple but effective rule. No man will be shipped unless he has baggage. When he gets to the station, his baggage is checked. When he arrives at the end of the journey, he finds his bag in a building. He can go in, open his bag, take out his working clothes, and go out again. But until he has worked out his fare, he cannot take his bag from that building. As the floating laborer generally travels with all he owns, he cannot afford to leave his baggage to be sold by the company.

This kind of shipment is known as the company shipment. It is all right for the man who is in no hurry. He gets a shipment in the direction he wants to go, works for a week, and then moves on. But when a man is in a hurry, he uses another kind of shipment.

To meet the demands of the tramp anxious to reach California before winter, the railroad shipment was invented. Railroads need laborers just as much as factories. They, too, get men through the labor agents. But they do not take
5 the fare out of the men's pay, as it costs them nothing to hitch an extra car on a passenger train and fill it with men. Therefore, on a railroad shipment a man does not have to check his baggage. As in the company shipment, he is put on the right train by the labor agent, who also arranges about
10 the number of men with the conductor. The men are free to get off at any time. In this way many men obtain a free ride, and yet do not have to stop and work out their fare. As a result, men seldom turn up on the job; in fact, they never do unless they have no money.

15 This method of helping labor to float seems like a great loss of time and money to the railroad. But the men have to get work somewhere. The more men in a section of the country, the more work is done, and hence the more freight, and thus more money for the railroad. So even though the
20 men never show up on the railroad's job, the railroad gains by shipping men into a state and thus developing the industries of that state.

AN EAST AFRICAN CARAVAN

The caravans traveling between the coast and the inland
markets of East Africa differ from the caravans of Arabia or
North Africa mainly in this, that they are totally made up
of men. The stately "ship of the desert," which we are
accustomed to associate with the word "caravan," is entirely 5
absent. Indeed, it would hardly be needed, because the German and British Colonies, to which the name of East Africa
applies, have no extensive deserts, for the regular tropical
rains keep the country fertile and green all the year round.
In this paper I shall speak of the African Caravan that plies 10
between the coast and the inland centers of German East
Africa, and tell how it is formed in the interior by the traders,
and slowly marched to the coast.

Let us, then, imagine a white trader after six months of
successful business in Tabora, the great Unyanyembi market 15
between Lake Nyanza and Lake Tanganyika. During these
months our trader has carried on an active barter with the
natives, gathering in his store large quantities of ivory, rubber, gums, skins, and such products of the country. But now
August approaches with the great tropical rains which draw 20
the natives to their fields, turn the land into a swamp, and
stop all business and travel. The trader must get ahead of
the rains and take his goods to the coast, eight hundred
miles away, before the porters become scarce and the paths
impracticable. 25

Porters are needed because, although East Africa has
beasts of burden, wild and domestic, the presence of the
tse-tse fly makes it impossible for the cattle to live in most
districts, and prevents the introduction of the camel. If to
this difficulty we add the absolute absence of roads, as we 30

understand them, only one method of transportation is left to the trader: the native porter. And so it is that the natives do all the carrying in East Africa, where everything, from the sugar of the trader to the steamboat of the government, must
5 be made up in loads to be carried on the shoulders of men. For fast traveling a porter is given a load of sixty pounds, to which must be added the weight of his baggage, consisting of a pot, a gourd, a mat, some clothes, and provisions for a day or two. But where there is little hurry, or little humane
10 feeling, the load of a man is sometimes increased to one hundred pounds, although the government is trying to standardize the sixty pounds weight through legislation. Our trader, a white man, will distribute his goods in loads of sixty pounds, calculate the number of porters he needs, and
15 make known that he intends to leave for the coast.

For this he needs no advertising, because in a market place like Tabora, the news that a white trader wishes to organize a caravan spreads very quickly, and soon some chief, with a crowd of retainers anxious to earn something and travel to
20 the coast, applies for the job. This is what our trader has been waiting for, because a chief, being a well-known person with authority over his tribe, will be a good headman for the caravan and somewhat responsible for his men. He is received in solemn audience by the trader; he is told the
25 number of men required and the salary offered; and after some haggling a date is fixed for the gathering of the porters in Tabora. The chief is then dismissed with a small present, and warned not to lose sight of the moon.

The moon is the infallible calendar by which time is
30 reckoned in East Africa, and since every native has got one, the date is kept with fair accuracy. On the day appointed the men are mustered, the loads are weighed and distributed, each man shaping his bundle to suit himself. A score of porters is selected to carry the trader's personal baggage, his
35 tent, camp furniture, cooking battery, curiosities, and what not. Ten more men, called *askari*, are armed with guns and

kept as guards and reserves. When the evening comes, everything is packed, every man enrolled by name, and the caravan ready for departure at dawn.

The chief, who has been appointed headman with half a dozen *wanyapara*, or leaders, under his orders, has been very busy during this time. Yet the white man is the real headman, the one who keeps the discipline, which can be summed up in a word,—*kiboko*, the name of a strong whip made of hippopotamus hide.

After emptying his house and store, the trader has lived for the last few days in his tent from which, long before sunrise on the morning of departure, he gives the order to break up. Instantly everything is in a bustle; the tent is quickly pulled down and made into loads by the men appointed, and after a few minutes, at the firing of a gun, every porter lifts his load, and amid singing, shouting, and rapping of boxes, the caravan files out of the dark and silent village.

Thus the caravan starts singing, and the singing must be kept up through all the journey in order to increase the endurance of the porters. Indeed, it is an important duty of the headman to get at least one good singer with a drum in the caravan. This singer, walking up and down the column, begins a monotonous tune which the whole caravan takes up with sometimes impressive, sometimes weird, effect. But life is not a continuous song anywhere, and a great deal of trouble comes up all the time among the porters. Here a man gets tired, another suddenly sick; there some one sprains his foot, another steps on a thorn, still another is bitten by a snake. These men need a good deal of exhorting and "disciplining." It may also happen that a straggler is carried off by a lion in the early morning, and a leader or one of the *askari* is thereby forced to take the load of the deceased, and carry it on until another porter can be procured at a village.

In spite of these and many other annoyances, the trader does not lack diversions. The beautiful country teems with all kinds of game, and though the shooting is often very dangerous, even the largest animals stand a poor chance against a modern rifle. The caravan is kept well supplied with fresh meat, a sufficient compensation for the freely administered *kiboko*.

5 The first day's march is usually short. A mile or two is added every day until an average of fifteen miles is reached. Thus the journey lasts about sixty days. Yet two months are too much for the trader, who is usually in a hurry. If he makes the loads very light and provides plenty of meat, he 10 can increase the daily march to twenty miles and shorten the journey considerably.

The twenty miles average, however, cannot be kept with much accuracy, because the camp must be pitched every night where water can be obtained. Yet the trader knows 15 the way sufficiently well, having gone over it before, and can divide the journey in fairly equal marches, each to end at some village or place where water and food can be procured. A village, of course, is much preferred, because the native chiefs are usually expected or compelled to provide the white 20 traveler with food, water, and fuel.

When the village is reached and the halt made, the loads are put down in a heap and covered with tarpaulins, while the porters, after helping in the pitching of the tent, scatter to get what they need for their meal. For this purpose they 25 receive a small daily allowance in cloth or money. The trader, too, against heavy odds, manages to cook a fair meal with the help of his native chef, and though he may not always be able to fill his bathtub, he gets enough dirty water for his tea. After eating he may lie down and read, or stroll 30 about the village watching his men, or, if there is time, he may make a little hunting expedition with a couple of *askari*, and return with a trophy before sunset.

At sunset a big fire is built before the tent—a ring of fires in lion infested districts—and the caravan, with pots and 35 mats, collects around the blaze. There is a good deal of talking and eating, some quarreling and fighting, but by and by every one stretches down on his mat, and by eight o'clock the whole camp is asleep. The *askari* on duty watch by the fire and keep it burning, a hyena whines near the camp and a couple of lions roar in the distance, as the trader, after inspecting everything, lies down to sleep in his camp bed.   5

So ends the day. Yet sometimes the camp must be defended against wild animals or men; sometimes there is a rebellion to quell or a runaway to catch; but day by day the march goes on, until the air becomes warmer and moister, the sky cloudier and whiter, until the line of the ocean glit- 10 ters before the eyes of the tired caravan, and the goal is reached.

The little coast town is entered in triumph amid loud rejoicing, the loads are stored at the trader's headquarters, and the caravan musters on the road to be paid and dismissed. 15 The pay is very small. Five or six dollars actual worth, half in cloth, half in money, for carrying a sixty-pound load over eight hundred miles of wilderness. Yet everyone is satisfied and happy, for the Coast is reached, the Mecca of every native of the Interior.   20

After being paid, the men disband. The wise ones collect around their chief, spend a few days sightseeing, invest their money in trifles for the ladies at home, and look about for loads to carry back inland. The foolish ones, and they are the majority, hasten to get rid of all they have, are speedily 25 reduced to want and compelled to hire themselves out on plantations. Very often they never see their homes again.

MODELS OF ESSAYS

COURAGE[1]

RALPH WALDO EMERSON

I observe that there are three qualities which conspicuously
attract the wonder and reverence of mankind:—

1. Disinterestedness, as shown in indifference to the ordinary bribes and influences of conduct,—a purpose so sincere
5 and generous that it cannot be tempted aside by any prospects of wealth or other private advantage. Self-love is, in
almost all men, such an over-weight, that they are incredulous of a man's habitual preference of the general good to his
own; but when they see it proved by sacrifices of ease, wealth,
10 rank, and of life itself, there is no limit to their admiration.
This has made the power of the saints of the East and West,
who have led the religion of great nations. Self-sacrifice is
the real miracle out of which all the reported miracles grew.
This makes the renown of the heroes of Greece and Rome,—
15 of Socrates, Aristides, and Phocion; of Quintus Curtius,
Cato, and Regulus; of Hatem Tai's hospitality; of Chatham,
whose scornful magnanimity gave him immense popularity;
of Washington, giving his service to the public without salary
or reward.

20 2. Practical power. Men admire the man who can organize their wishes and thoughts in stone and wood, and steel and
brass,—the man who can build the boat, who has the impiety
to make the rivers run the way he wants them, who can lead

[1] From *Society and Solitude*, 1870. By permission of, and by special
arrangement with, Houghton Mifflin Company, Boston. Portions of the
essay have been omitted.

his telegraph through the ocean from shore to shore; who, sitting in his closet, can lay out the plans of a campaign,— sea-war and land-war; such that the best generals and admirals, when all is done, see that they must thank him for success; the power of better combination and foresight, however exhibited, which, whether it only plays a game of chess, or whether, more loftily, a cunning mathematician, penetrating the cubic weights of stars, predicts the planet which eyes had never seen; or whether, exploring the chemical elements whereof we and the world are made, and seeing their secret, Franklin draws off the lightning in his hand, suggesting that one day a wiser geology shall make the earthquake harmless and the volcano an agricultural resource. Or here is one who, seeing the wishes of men, knows how to come at their end; whispers to this friend, argues down that adversary, moulds society to his purpose, and looks at all men as wax for his hands,—takes command of them as the wind does of clouds, as the mother does of the child, or the man that knows more does of the man that knows less; and leads them in glad surprise to the very point where they would be: this man is followed with acclamation.

3. The third excellence is courage, the perfect will, which no terrors can shake, which is attracted by frowns, or threats, or hostile armies, nay, needs these to awake and fan its reserved energies into a pure flame, and is never quite itself until the hazard is extreme; then it is serene and fertile, and all its powers play well. There is a Hercules, an Achilles, a Rustam, an Arthur, or a Cid in the mythology of every nation; and in authentic history, a Leonidas, a Scipio, a Cæsar, a Richard Cœur de Lion, a Cromwell, a Nelson, a Great Condé, a Bertrand de Guesclin, a Doge Dandolo, a Napoleon, a Massena, and Ney. 'Tis said courage is common, but the immense esteem in which it is held proves it to be rare. Animal resistance, the instinct of the male animal when cornered, is no doubt common; but the pure article, courage with eyes, courage with conduct, self-possession at the cannon's

mouth, cheerfulness in lonely adherence to the right, is the endowment of elevated characters. I need not show how much it is esteemed, for the people give it the first rank. They forgive everything to it. What an ado we make through two thousand years about Thermopylæ and Salamis! What a memory of Poitiers and Crécy, and Bunker Hill, and Washington's endurance! And any man who puts his life in peril in a cause which is esteemed, becomes the darling of all men. The very nursery-books, the ballads which delight boys, the romances which delight men, the favourite topics of eloquence, the thunderous emphasis which orators give to every martial defiance and passage of arms, and which the people greet, may testify. How short a time since this whole nation rose every morning to read or to hear the traits of courage of its sons and brothers in the field, and was never weary of the theme! We have had examples of men who, for showing effective courage on a single occasion, have become a favourite spectacle to nations, and must be brought in chariots to every mass meeting.

But man begins life helpless. The babe is in paroxysms of fear the moment its nurse leaves it alone, and it comes so slowly to any power of self-protection, that mothers say the salvation of the life and health of a young child is a perpetual miracle. The terrors of the child are quite reasonable, and add to his loveliness; for his utter ignorance and weakness, and his enchanting indignation on such a small basis of capital, compel every bystander to take his part. Every moment, as long as he is awake, he studies the use of his eyes, ears, hands, and feet, learning how to meet and avoid his dangers, and thus every hour loses one terror more. But this education stops too soon. A large majority of men being bred in families, and beginning early to be occupied day by day with some routine of safe industry, never come to the rough experiences that make the Indian, the soldier, or the frontiersman self-subsistent and fearless. Hence the high price of courage indicates the general timidity.

Cowardice shuts the eyes till the sky is not larger than a calf-skin; shuts the eyes so that we cannot see the horse that is running away with us; worse, shuts the eyes of the mind and chills the heart. Fear is cruel and mean. The political reigns of terror have been reigns of madness and malignity— a total perversion of opinion; society is upside down, and its best men are thought too bad to live. Then the protection which a house, a family, neighbourhood, and property, even the first accumulation of savings, give, goes in all times to generate this taint of the respectable classes. Voltaire said, "One of the chief misfortunes of honest people is that they are cowardly." Those political parties which gather in the well-disposed portion of the community—how infirm and ignoble! what white lips they have! always on the defensive, as if the lead were intrusted to the journals, often written in great part by women and boys, who, without strength, wish to keep up the appearance of strength. They can do the hurras, the placarding, the flags—and the voting, if it is a fair day; but the aggressive attitude of men who will have right done, will no longer be bothered with burglars and ruffians in the streets, counterfeiters in public offices, and thieves on the bench; that part, the part of the leader and soul of the vigilance committee, must be taken by stout and sincere men who are really angry and determined. In ordinary, we have a snappish criticism which watches and contradicts the opposite party. We want the will which advances and dictates. When we get an advantage, as in Congress the other day, it is because our adversary has committed a fault, not that we have taken the initiative and given the law. Nature has made up her mind that what cannot defend itself shall not be defended. Complaining never so loud, and with never so much reason, is of no use. One heard much cant of peace-parties long ago in Kansas and elsewhere, that their strength lay in the greatness of their wrongs, and dissuading all resistance, as if to make this strength greater.

But with this pacific education, we have no readiness for bad times. I am much mistaken if every man who went to the army in the late war had not a lively curiosity to know how he should behave in action. Tender, amiable boys, who had never encountered any rougher play than a base-ball match or a fishing excursion, were suddenly drawn up to face a bayonet charge or capture a battery. Of course, they must each go into that action with a certain despair. Each whispers to himself: "My exertions must be of small account to the result; only will the benignant Heaven save me from disgracing myself and my friends and my State. Die! Oh, yes; I can well die; but I cannot afford to misbehave; and I do not know how I shall feel." So great a soldier as the old French Marshal Montluc acknowledges that he has often trembled with fear, and recovered courage when he said a prayer for the occasion. I knew a young soldier who died in the early campaign, who confided to his sister that he had made up his mind to volunteer for the war. "I have not," he said, "any proper courage, but I shall never let any one find it out." And he had accustomed himself always to go into whatever place of danger, and do whatever he was afraid to do, setting a dogged resolution to resist this natural infirmity. Coleridge has preserved an anecdote of an officer in the British Navy, who told him that when he, in his first boat expedition, a midshipman in his fourteenth year, accompanied Sir Alexander Ball, "as we were rowing up to the vessel we were to attack, amid a discharge of musketry, I was overpowered with fear, my knees shook, and I was ready to faint away. Lieutenant Ball seeing me, placed himself close beside me, took hold of my hand and whispered, 'Courage, my dear boy! you will recover in a minute or so; I was just the same when I first went out in this way.' It was as if an angel spoke to me. From that moment I was as fearless and as forward as the oldest of the boat's crew. But I dare not think what would have become of me, if, at that moment, he had scoffed and exposed me."

Knowledge is the antidote to fear,—Knowledge, Use, and Reason, with its higher aids. The child is as much in danger from a staircase, or the fire-grate, or a bath-tub, or a cat, as the soldier from a cannon or an ambush. Each surmounts the fear as fast as he precisely understands the peril, and learns the means of resistance. Each is liable to panic, which is, exactly, the terror of ignorance surrendered to the imagination. Knowledge is the encourager, knowledge that takes fear out of the heart, knowledge and use, which is knowledge in practice. They can conquer who believe they can. It is he who has done the deed once who does not shrink from attempting it again. It is the groom who knows the jumping horse well who can safely ride him. It is the veteran soldier, who, seeing the flash of the cannon, can step aside from the path of the ball. Use makes a better soldier than the most urgent considerations of duty,—familiarity with danger enabling him to estimate the danger. He sees how much is the risk, and is not afflicted with imagination; knows practically Marshal Saxe's rule, that every soldier killed costs the enemy his weight in lead.

The sailor loses fear as fast as he acquires command of sails and spars and steam; the frontiersman, when he has a perfect rifle and has acquired a sure aim. To the sailor's experience every new circumstance suggests what he must do. The terrific chances which make the hours and the minutes long to the passenger, he whiles away by incessant application of expedients and repairs. To him a leak, a hurricane, or a water-spout is so much work,—no more. The hunter is not alarmed by bears, catamounts, or wolves, nor the grazier by his bull, nor the dog-breeder by his bloodhound, nor an Arab by the simoom, nor a farmer by a fire in the woods. The forest on fire looks discouraging enough to a citizen: the farmer is skilful to fight it. The neighbours run together; with pine boughs they can mop out the flame, and, by raking with the hoe a long but little trench, confine to a patch the fire which would easily spread over a hundred acres.

In short, courage consists in equality to the problem before us. The school-boy is daunted before his tutor by a question of arithmetic, because he does not yet command the simple steps of the solution which the boy beside him has mastered. These once seen, he is as cool as Archimedes, and cheerily proceeds a step farther. Courage is equality to the problem, in affairs, in science, in trade, in council, or in action; consists in the conviction that the agents with whom you contend are not superior in strength or resources or spirit to you. The general must stimulate the mind of his soldiers to the perception that they are men, and the enemy is no more. Knowledge, yes; for the danger of dangers is illusion. The eye is easily daunted; and the drums, flags, shining helmets, beard, and mustache of the soldier have conquered you long before his sword or bayonet reaches you.

But we do not exhaust the subject in the slight analysis; we must not forget the variety of temperaments, each of which qualifies this power of resistance. It is observed that men with little imagination are less fearful; they wait till they feel pain, whilst others of more sensibility anticipate it, and suffer in the fear of the pang more acutely than in the pang. 'Tis certain that the threat is sometimes more formidable than the stroke, and 'tis possible that the beholders suffer more keenly than the victims. Bodily pain is superficial, seated usually in the skin and the extremities, for the sake of giving us warning to put us on our guard; not in the vitals, where the rupture that produces death is perhaps not felt, and the victim never knew what hurt him. Pain is superficial, and therefore fear is. The torments of martyrdoms are probably most keenly felt by the bystanders. The torments are illusory. The first suffering is the last suffering, the later hurts being lost on insensibility. Our affections and wishes for the external welfare of the hero tumultuously rush to expression in tears and outcries; but we, like him, subside into indifferency and defiance, when we perceive how short is the longest arm of malice, how serene is the sufferer.

It is plain that there is no separate essence called courage, no cup or cell in the brain, no vessel in the heart containing drops or atoms that make or give this virtue; but it is the right or healthy state of every man, when he is free to do that which is constitutional to him to do. It is directness,—the instant performing of that which he ought. The thoughtful man says, You differ from me in opinion and methods; but do you not see that I cannot think or act otherwise than I do? that my way of living is organic? And to be really strong we must adhere to our own means. On organic action all strength depends.

There is a courage in the treatment of every art by a master in architecture, in sculpture, in painting, or in poetry, each cheering the mind of the spectator or receiver as by true strokes of genius, which yet nowise implies the presence of physical valour in the artist. This is the courage of genius, in every kind.

It gives the cutting edge to every profession. The judge puts his mind to the tangle of contradictions in the case, squarely accosts the question, and, by not being afraid of it, by dealing with it as business which must be disposed of, he sees presently that common arithmetic and common methods apply to this affair. Perseverance strips it of all peculiarity, and ranges it on the same ground as other business. You may see the same dealing in criticism; a new book astonishes for a few days, takes itself out of common jurisdiction, and nobody knows what to say of it: but the scholar is not deceived. The old principles which books exist to express are more beautiful than any book; and out of love of the reality he is an expert judge how far the book has approached it and where it has come short. In all applications 'tis the same power,—the habit of reference to one's own mind, as the home of all truth and counsel, and which can easily dispose of any book because it can very well do without all books. When a confident man comes into a company magnifying this or that author he has freshly read, the company grow silent

and ashamed of their ignorance. But I remember the old
professor, whose searching mind engraved every word he
spoke on the memory of the class, when we asked if he had
read this or that shining novelty, "No, I have never read that
5 book"; instantly the book lost credit, and was not to be
heard of again.

Every creature has a courage of his constitution fit for
his duties:—Archimedes, the courage of a geometer to stick
to his diagram, heedless of the siege and sack of the city;
10 and the Roman soldier his faculty to strike at Archimedes.
Each is strong, relying on his own, and each is betrayed when
he seeks in himself the courage of others.

> "'Tis still observed those men most valiant are,
> Who are most modest ere they came to war."

15 True courage is not ostentatious; men who wish to inspire
terror seem thereby to confess themselves cowards. Why
do they rely on it, but because they know how potent it is
with themselves?

There is a persuasion in the soul of man that he is here for
20 cause, that he was put down in this place by the Creator to
do the work for which He inspires him, that thus he is an
overmatch for all antagonists that could combine against
him. The pious Mrs. Hutchinson says of some passages in
the defence of Nottingham against the Cavaliers, "It was a
25 great instruction that the best and highest courages are
beams of the Almighty." And whenever the religious sentiment is adequately affirmed, it must be with dazzling courage.
Sacred courage indicates that a man loves an idea better than
all things in the world; that he is aiming neither at pelf nor
30 comfort, but will venture all to put in act the invisible
thought in his mind. He is everywhere a liberator, but of a
freedom that is ideal; not seeking to have land or money or
conveniences, but to have no other limitation than that which
his own constitution imposes. He is free to speak truth; he
35 is not free to lie. He wishes to break every yoke all over

the world which hinders his brother from acting after his thought.

There are degrees of courage, and each step upward makes us acquainted with a higher virtue. Let us say then frankly that the education of the will is the object of our existence. Poverty, the prison, the rack, the fire, the hatred and execrations of our fellow-men, appear trials beyond the endurance of common humanity; but to the hero whose intellect is aggrandised by the soul, and so measures these penalities against the good which his thought surveys, these terrors vanish as darkness at sunrise.

He has not learned the lesson of life who does not every day surmount a fear. I do not wish to put myself or any man into a theatrical position, or urge him to ape the courage of his comrade. Have the courage not to adopt another's courage. There is scope and cause and resistance enough for us in our proper work and circumstance. And there is no creed of an honest man, be he Christian, Turk, or Gentoo, which does not equally preach it. If you have no faith in beneficent power above you, but see only an adamantine fate coiling its folds about nature and man, then reflect that the best use of fate is to teach us courage, if only because baseness cannot change the appointed event. If you accept your thoughts as inspirations from the Supreme Intelligence, obey them when they prescribe difficult duties, because they come only so long as they are used; or, if your scepticism reaches to the last verge, and you have no confidence in any foreign mind, then be brave, because there is one good opinion which must always be of consequence to you, namely, your own.

ÆS TRIPLEX[1]

ROBERT LOUIS STEVENSON

The changes wrought by death are in themselves so sharp
and final, and so terrible and melancholy in their consequences, that the thing stands alone in man's experience, and
has no parallel upon earth. It outdoes all other accidents
5 because it is the last of them. Sometimes it leaps suddenly
upon its victims, like a Thug; sometimes it lays a regular
siege and creeps upon their citadel during a score of years.
And when the business is done, there is sore havoc made in
other people's lives, and a pin knocked out by which many
10 subsidiary friendships hung together. There are empty chairs,
solitary walks, and single beds at night. Again, in taking
away our friends, death does not take them away utterly, but
leaves behind a mocking, tragical, and soon intolerable resi-
due, which must be hurriedly concealed. Hence a whole
15 chapter of sights and customs striking to the mind, from the
pyramids of Egypt to the gibbets and dule trees of mediæval
Europe. The poorest persons have a bit of pageant going
towards the tomb; memorial stones are set up over the least
memorable; and, in order to preserve some show of respect
20 for what remains of our old loves and friendships, we must
accompany it with much grimly ludicrous ceremonial, and
the hired undertaker parades before the door. All this, and
much more of the same sort, accompanied by the eloquence
of poets, has gone a great way to put humanity in error;
25 nay, in many philosophies the error has been embodied and
laid down with every circumstance of logic; although in
real life the bustle and swiftness, in leaving people little

[1]From *Virginibus Puerisque*. Charles Scribner's Sons, New York.

time to think, have not left them time enough to go danger-
ously wrong in practice.

As a matter of fact, although few things are spoken of
with more fearful whisperings than this prospect of death,
few have less influence on conduct under healthy circum- 5
stances. We have all heard of cities in South America built
upon the side of fiery mountains, and how, even in this tremendous neighbourhood, the inhabitants are not a jot more
impressed by the solemnity of mortal conditions than if they
were delving gardens in the greenest corner of England. 10
There are serenades and suppers and much gallantry among
the myrtles overhead; and meanwhile the foundation shud-
ders underfoot, the bowels of the mountain growl, and at any
moment living ruin may leap sky-high into the moonlight,
and tumble man and his merry-making in the dust. In the 15
eyes of very young people, and very dull old ones, there is
something indescribably reckless and desperate in such a picture. It seems not credible that respectable married people,
with umbrellas, should find appetite for a bit of supper within
quite a long distance of a fiery mountain; ordinary life begins 20
to smell of high-handed debauch when it is carried on so close
to a catastrophe; and even cheese and salad, it seems, could
hardly be relished in such circumstances without something
like a defiance of the Creator. It should be a place for nobody but hermits dwelling in prayer and maceration or mere 25
born-devils drowning care in a perpetual carouse.

And yet, when one comes to think upon it calmly, the
situation of these South American citizens forms only a very
pale figure for the state of ordinary mankind. This world
itself, travelling blindly and swiftly in overcrowded space, 30
among a million other worlds travelling blindly and swiftly
in contrary directions, may very well come by a knock that
would set it into explosion like a penny squib. And what,
pathologically looked at, is the human body with all its organs, but a mere bagful of petards? The least of these is 35
as dangerous to the whole economy as the ship's powder-

magazine to the ship; and with every breath we breathe, and
every meal we eat, we are putting one or more of them in
peril. If we clung as devotedly as some philosophers pretend
we do to the abstract idea of life, or were half as frightened as
they make out we are, for the subversive accident that ends
it all, the trumpets might sound by the hour and no one
would follow them into battle—the blue-peter might fly at
the truck, but who would climb into a sea-going ship? Think
(if these philosophers were right) with what a preparation
of spirit we should affront the daily peril of the dinner-table:
a deadlier spot than any battle-field in history, where the far
greater proportion of our ancestors have miserably left their
bones! What woman would ever be lured into marriage,
so much more dangerous than the wildest sea? And what
would it be to grow old? For, after a certain distance, every
step we take in life we find the ice growing thinner below our
feet, and all around us and behind us we see our contempora-
ries going through. By the time a man gets well into the
seventies, his continued existence is a mere miracle; and
when he lays his old bones in bed for the night, there is an
overwhelming probability that he will never see the day.
Do the old men mind it, as a matter of fact? Why, no. They
were never merrier; they have their grog at night, and tell
the raciest stories; they hear of the death of people about
their own age, or even younger, not as if it was a grisly warning, but with a simple childlike pleasure at having outlived
some one else; and when a draught might puff them out like
a guttering candle, or a bit of a stumble shatter them like so
much glass, their old hearts keep sound and unaffrighted, and
they go on, bubbling with laughter, through years of man's
age compared to which the valley at Balaclava was as safe
and peaceful as a village cricket-green on Sunday. It may
fairly be questioned (if we look to the peril only) whether
it was a much more daring feat for Curtius to plunge into
the gulf, than for any old gentleman of ninety to doff his
clothes and clamber into bed.

We live the time that a match flickers; we pop the cork of a ginger-beer bottle, and the earthquake swallows us on the instant. Is it not odd, is it not incongruous, is it not, in the highest sense of human speech, incredible, that we should think so highly of the ginger-beer, and regard so little the devouring earthquake? The love of Life and the fear of Death are two famous phrases that grow harder to understand the more we think about them. It is a well-known fact that an immense proportion of boat accidents would never happen if people held the sheet in their hands instead of making it fast; and yet, unless it be some martinet of a professional mariner or some landsman with shattered nerves, every one of God's creatures makes it fast. A strange instance of man's unconcern and brazen boldness in the face of death!

We confound ourselves with metaphysical phrases, which we import into daily talk with noble inappropriateness. We have no idea of what death is, apart from its circumstances and some of its consequences to others; and although we have some experience of living, there is not a man on earth who has flown so high into abstraction as to have any practical guess at the meaning of the word *life*. All literature, from Job and Omar Khayyam to Thomas Carlyle or Walt Whitman, is but an attempt to look upon the human state with such largeness of view as shall enable us to rise from the consideration of living to the Definition of Life. And our sages give us about the best satisfaction in their power when they say that it is a vapour, or a show, or made out of the same stuff with dreams. Philosophy, in its more rigid sense, has been at the same work for ages; and after a myriad bald heads have wagged over the problem, and piles of words have been heaped one upon another into dry and cloudy volumes without end, philosophy has the honour of laying before us, with modest pride, her contribution towards the subject: that life is a Permanent Possibility of Sensation. Truly a fine result! A man may very well love beef, or hunting, or a

woman; but surely, surely, not a Permanent Possibility of
Sensation! He may be afraid of a precipice, or a dentist, or
a large enemy with a club, or even an undertaker's man; but
not certainly of abstract death. We may trick with the word
5 life in its dozen senses until we are weary of tricking; we
may argue in terms of all the philosophies on earth, but one
fact remains true throughout—that we do not love life, in the
sense that we are greatly preoccupied about its conservation;
that we do not, properly speaking, love life at all, but living.
10 Into the views of the least careful there will enter some degree of providence; no man's eyes are fixed entirely on the
passing hour; but although we have some anticipation of
good health, good weather, wine, active employment, love,
and self-approval, the sum of these anticipations does not
15 amount to anything like a general view of life's possibilities
and issues; nor are those who cherish them most vividly, at
all the most scrupulous of their personal safety. To be deeply
interested in the accidents of our existence, to enjoy keenly
the mixed texture of human experience, rather leads a man
20 to disregard precautions, and risk his neck against a straw.
For surely the love of living is stronger in an Alpine climber
roping over a peril, or a hunter riding merrily at a stiff fence,
than in a creature who lives upon a diet and walks a measured distance in the interest of his constitution.

.   .   .   .

25 And, after all, what sorry and pitiful quibbling all this is!
To forego all the issues of living in a parlour with a regulated
temperature—as if that were not to die a hundred times over,
and for ten years at a stretch! As if it were not to die in
one's own lifetime, and without even the sad immunities of
30 death! As if it were not to die, and yet be the patient
spectators of our own pitiable change! The Permanent Possibility is preserved, but the sensations carefully held at
arm's length, as if one kept a photographic plate in a dark
chamber. It is better to lose health like a spendthrift than
35 to waste it like a miser. It is better to live and be done with

it, than to die daily in the sickroom. By all means begin your folio; even if the doctor does not give you a year, even if he hesitates about a month, make one brave push and see what can be accomplished in a week. It is not only in finished undertakings that we ought to honour useful labour. A spirit goes out of the man who means execution, which outlives the most untimely ending. All who have meant good work with their whole hearts, have done good work, although they may die before they have the time to sign it. Every heart that has beat strong and cheerfully has left a hopeful impulse behind it in the world, and bettered the tradition of mankind. And even if death catch people, like an open pitfall, and in mid-career, laying out vast projects, and planning monstrous foundations, flushed with hope, and their mouths full of boastful language, they should be at once tripped up and silenced: is there not something brave and spirited in such a termination? and does not life go down with a better grace, foaming in full body over a precipice, than miserably straggling to an end in sandy deltas? When the Greeks made their fine saying that those whom the gods love die young, I cannot help believing they had this sort of death also in their eye. For surely, at whatever age it overtake the man, this is to die young. Death has not been suffered to take so much as an illusion from his heart. In the hot-fit of life, a-tiptoe on the highest point of being, he passes at a bound on to the other side. The noise of the mallet and chisel is scarcely quenched, the trumpets are hardly done blowing, when, trailing with him clouds of glory, this happy-starred, full-blooded spirit shoots into the spiritual land.

OF SILVER PAPER[1]

Edward Verrall Lucas

Opening a new box of cigarettes this morning, I came upon
the usual piece of silver paper. But I did not as usual disregard it, but held it in my hand, examining it in a kind of
wonder for some minutes, and asking myself why such beau-
5 tiful stuff should be at the disposal of tobacconists in such
profusion, how it was made, how it could be so cheap, and so
forth. And I then shed some dozens of years from my shoulders by wrapping a penny in it and, by infinite smoothings
with the back of a finger-nail, transmuting that coin into a
10 lustrous half-crown—as I used to do when the world was
young and silver paper a treasured rarity. And, having finished playing with it, I came back to the question, How is
silver paper made? and from that to the question, How are
most things made? and so to a state of stupor occasioned by
15 the realisation of my abysmal ignorance. For I have no notion how silver paper is made, and I am sufficiently bold and
sceptical to doubt too if the Swiss Family Robinson could
have made it, to save their lives.

What would one first look for if one were told, out of a
20 clear sky, to make some silver paper? Obviously not paper,
for there is no paper about it; and obviously not silver, for
if silver came into its preparation tobacconists and chocolate
manufacturers could not throw it about as they do. Thus
it is borne in upon me, and I recognise the verity with pro-
25 found sadness, that, heir of the ages as I am, I am as ignorant
of the making of silver paper as though I were a South Sea

[1] From *Cloud and Silver*, pp. 66–69. Copyright, 1916, by George H.
Doran Company, New York, Publisher.

savage. Not only am I at a loss as to its preparation, but also as to what kind of people make it; where their factories are; what they call themselves. It may be a by-product of something else; it may be a business alone. Boys at Eton may be the sons of silver-paper makers or they may not. I don't know, nor do I know whether they would mention the source of their fathers' wealth or conceal it.

And I am equally ignorant as to the origin of thousands of other things which I fancy one ought to know. Looking round the room, my eyes alight on one thing after another. Colour printing, for example—how would one, *ab initio*, set about that? An ordinary printing press I could see myself laboriously building up, with some rude success; but how do they take a Royal Academy picture, such as that on the wall above me, and translate it into mechanical reproduction? I have no notion beyond the vaguest. I know that photography comes in, and that three colours provide all the necessary tints and gradations; but how, I know not. And glass? What is the first step in the making of glass—that most mysterious of all substances: a great sheet of hard nothingness through which at this moment I watch a regiment of soldiers marching by? Could Robinson Crusoe have had glass? I feel convinced that he could not. Pens and ink, yes; and some substitute for paper (so long as it was not silver paper), yes; but never glass. Even such an ordinary matter as soap baffles me. I know that fat goes to its making, but I know also that, normally, fat rubbed on the hands makes them not clean but peculiarly beastly. How, then, does soap get its cleansing properties? I have no notion. And I am considered by those who meet me as not wholly an uninstructed man.

I look through my pockets. Money—yes, one could make some kind of an attempt at money, if one could get metal. A pencil?—yes, that is just black lead cut into a strip and enclosed in wood: easy. A knife?—not so simple, but obviously possible, because all castaways make things to cut with.

Even, however, if I could not make these things, I know
where they are made, and more or less how they are made.
There are books to tell me this. What no book knows anything about is silver paper. Not even those friends of the
5 ignorant, the Encyclopædists, help me. Their books lie before me, but all their million pages are silent as to silver
paper; or if they do mention it, they carefully abstain from
associating the information either with "paper" or "silver."

Did I, I ask myself, merely go to the wrong school, or are
10 all schools equally taciturn about this kind of thing? There
should be special classes for potential castaways. In fact,
all education that does not fit scholars to be, one day,
marooned, is defective: I would go as far as to say that. The
height of mountains, the intricacies of algebra, the length of
15 rivers, the dates of kings, matter nothing. But it does matter
that one should know something about the ordinary daily
things of life, their constituents and manufacture. Suppose
the Government appointed me—as—after all the books I
have written, with their show of information, it might easily
20 do, at, of course, an insufficient wage—to be the companion
of some gentle inquisitive barbarian visiting these shores—
some new Prince Lee Boo—a nice kind of idiot I should look
when he began to fire his questions at me! And silver paper
is precisely the kind of glittering attractive stuff with which
he would begin.

STUDENTS' THEMES: ESSAYS

IN DEFENCE OF THE APPLE

The Apple is the gift of the gods. What other fruit offers the wide range of variety in itself that apples do?—big, hard, juicy Northern Spies that crackle when you bite into them; beautiful red-cheeked Baldwins and delicately tinted Snow Apples; sharp, tangy, green "cookers" and tiny biting crabs; 5 thorn apples; Michigan apples; the shiny thick-skinned beauties of the fruit vender; pear-apples; homely burnished russets—the sweetest of all,—in short, a kind for every man. There breathes not a man with palate so dead who hasn't a weakness for hot "cinnamonny" apple pie, or steaming baked 10 apples with their browned, sugary skins bursting to disclose a delectable, snowy softness, or apple turnovers, or rich apple sauce with heavy cream. What is turkey without apple dressing, or roast suckling without the inevitable apple in its mouth? What is Hallowe'en without tart apple cider? 15 There is no other single food so relished by man and beast and bird, alike, as is the Apple.

And here is the injustice,—that this noble fruit, this delight of children and old folks, this delicious gift of Nature should be so maligned. Maligned? Yes, doesn't this plain, 20 unassuming fruit,—not snobbish like grapefruit or sour like lemon,—bear the brunt of the blame for the downfall of mankind? Where in Holy Scripture does it state that the grandmother of human beings, Lady Eve, ate of, and gave her husband to eat of, a forbidden *Apple*, thereby causing 25 irreparable stain on the former purity of our ancestors? Nowhere! And yet, this is the slanderous story in common

belief. God wouldn't have banned a blessing; it is only the *fruit* of a certain tree that was *verboten*. It must have been some low scoundrel who, having a grudge against some green apples that his own piggishness caused him to overindulge
5 in, linked the Apple with the Eden Episode, and gave it its unsavory reputation.

Let us have justice done. Let us praise the Apple for the benefits it has rendered society on Hallowe'ens innumerable, when it has cheerfully floated in tubs of water for hours; or
10 let us remember its value as an asset to young lovers who count its seeds,—"She loves; she loves me not"; but greatest, far greatest, of all, recall that we should never have learned one of the great secrets of science had not an Apple taken it upon itself to fall on the head of Isaac Newton.
15 This is the real Apple—a benefactor of man, not the cause of his ruin. This falsehood about Adam and the "Apple" must be tracked and nailed to the ground. *Fiat Justitia.*

OUR LODGERS

In those days I seem always to have been dusting. There must have been interludes for school, of course, but the dusting sticks in my memory—and another thing. This was my mother's glowing face when the front door bell was pulled suddenly.

"Lodgers, Fan!" she would gasp. "Is this apron clean enough? Would you charge fifty cents extra for the front room—on account of the new lamp? Is my hair all right?" All this on her way to the door. And if it were only the postman or naughty children, how woeful her face would grow.

Our whole existence hinged on those lodgers. While they stayed with us, we lived royally, and when they went, we faced an existence bleak as the rooms they quitted. There were times when we even referred to them in terms of food. I can remember coming home from school and meeting my mother at our door. She clapped her hands and said gayly, "Lamb chops and maybe custard pie!" By this I knew that the front room was let and the rent paid in advance. Beneath my jubilation at our bettered fortunes was the rankling prospect of long stretches of dusting ahead. We must all pay for our lamb chops and custard pie in life, but there were times when I felt that dusting was too high a fee. It is only nowadays that I sometimes wonder if my mother did not weary at her eternal round of mussed rooms.

Curiously enough, though my memory of lodgers in the abstract is so clear, I can recall few of them as individuals. Except Elmira. I remember her because of the piano. Other lodgers had brought bags and suitcases and even trunks, but Elmira brought the first and only piano. It was old like herself and almost as battered, but it isn't every lodger that

sports a piano. She played on it sometimes for me (when I
came in to dust!) when she was in good humor. The very
hopeless keys had faded postage stamps stuck on to distinguish them from their more tuneful brethren. I cannot remember the tunes Elmira played, but I do remember thinking
what a scandalous waste of stamps. Then there was the
Fishman—the loathsome Fishman!—who persisted in hanging his fish baskets out of our garret window through a
stifling midsummer week. He met my mother's gentle remonstrance with a sneer, "I paid fur a week, I stays fur a
week," and stay he did. The rest of the neighborhood was
singularly free from flies that week; we had them all!

There was one other vivid lodger. He was the Man-in-
front. He had books—not three or four meagre ones—but
whole satisfying sets of O. Henry, Kipling, Stevenson. The
front room was the room I dusted most assiduously. I lingered until I heard a footfall on the stairs and then fled. The
incoming lodger saw only a pig-tailed scrawny child with a
duster. How could he know she was a High Adventurer who
had lately been creeping through the heather with Alan
Breck and David Balfour, or riding out with the Brushwood
Boy, or listening to the shrewd wit of the Caliph of Bagdad-
on-the-Subway!

My mother had a sliding scale of prices for her lodgers.
Their condition frequently decided their room rent. If a
prospective lodger had a cough or a thin overcoat, a quarter
or fifty cents was deducted from his week's rent. This
method is not one to be recommended to those who would
amass wealth. My mother never grew rich through keeping
lodgers.

Though they gave me a livelihood through my leanest years,
those lodgers never seemed real persons to me, only shabby
shadows that flitted from our furnished rooms into blackness. I pitied them their skimped lives. For at the most
they were, to me, "lamb chops and custard pie," and at the
least only a little dust.

"BUT WHEN *WE* WERE YOUNG . . ."

The Present Generation of any age in history has always been an unfailing source of conversation—acidly satirical, bitterly reproachful, and disgustedly superior conversation and comment for all the fortunate and extremely sage members of the adult, or Parental generation. Without a doubt the fond mothers of the good old antediluvian days held many a despondent conclave over their camp-fires while the men were busily engaged tracking prehistoric beasts with prehistoric weapons, or shooting prehistoric dice in prehistoric corners, and the subject of this pessimistic discussion was not the unfavorable weather, or the distressing lack of humanity on the part of the grasping profiteer in shark's-teeth, or the exasperatingly inferior quality of herbage used in the manufacture of the popular and simple, but none the less necessary, garment of the day. No, these dutiful parents discussed the Youth of the Day in tones of extreme cynicism and disgust, not unmixed with awe. They were righteously scandalized by the carryings-on of their blasé offspring, and "When *we* were young," they would chant in numbers mournful, "*we* never thought of doing such things. We were steady, serious, and responsible. Of course, we had our pleasure, our recreation; but we took it in a quiet way, and in a way that would make it beneficial to ourselves mentally and physically. But the youth of today! My dear! Absolutely no restraint, no responsibility, no respect for age and wisdom, no religion, . . . no anything! . . . But in *our* day . . ." And they would take up again the old, dolorous refrain of *O tempora, o mores*, and the prehistoric and prodigiously hungry gentlemen of the period would grumble because their good wives spent so much of their time in

mournful reminiscence that they became quite oblivious of
the necessity of preparing the present dinner.

And so it is found throughout the centuries. How the
scandalized mother of Eva rebuked that popular maiden for
her lack of decorum and propriety in bowing to poor, love-
sick Walther in the old Nuremberg Cathedral! And how
that same good mother tore her maternal bosom with painful
soliloquy on the decadence of Youth and the level-headedness
and seriousness of purpose of her own days of florescence,
long since passed!

But let us leave this research into the prehistoric and
mediæval periods and examine the conditions existing in our
own native land today. Of course, in America, the home of
new customs and new ideas, one would scarcely expect to find
the same old theme of discussion in existence. But it is
nevertheless flourishing, and as a topic of conversation it is
much more popular than the tariff, the Volstead act, or the
latest divorce case. The modern maiden, especially, has
come in for more than her share of acrid comment and criticism from the worthies of the preceding generation. Let corrupt politicians wreck the peace of the world in sixty-three
different ways, let profiteers boost the rent and the price of
chocolate ice-cream sodas *ad astra per aspera*, let divorce
cases and murder cases and Heaven knows what-not fill the
chaste front page of the yellow journals with red letters
a half-foot high,—all this is bad enough, to be sure, but it
pales into the merest inconsequence when your neighbor's
eighteen-year-old daughter lights a Fatima and dons open-
work hosiery! Then does the reformer seize his typewriter
and the poet his Waterman; then does the editor invest in a
new dictionary and startle his readers with bizarre and vivid
adjectives; then does the evangelist wax eloquent and the
sentimental novelist, maudlin. And off they go into rhetori-
cal and oratorical fireworks in condemning the Present Generation. Everyone is perfectly sure that the world has never
seen such a degenerate generation. What's going to become

of us, anyway? In *our* day we never did such things; our
girls never smoked cigarettes, nor did they dream of going
to dinner-parties and the theatre without the salutary, if
somnolent, chaperone! Much less dances! Why, when we
were young, our dances always stopped at eleven o'clock, and
each girl was carefully escorted to her home by her brother
or her father. And we never heard of the toddle, or the
shimmy, or of petting-parties, or of morality tests in the
colleges. O the decadence of the race! O the degeneracy of
Youth! . . . And so on, *ad nauseam* if not *finem*!

Now, it may be that my ideas are abnormal, are warped,
in reference to the condition of things that I am discussing;
I am informed by my adult relatives that they are. Nevertheless, I object most heartily to this wholesale condemnation
of my generation as vicious and irresponsible. And I furthermore object no less heartily to the glorification of my
father's generation, with all due respect to my father. I do
not believe that I am morally depraved because I do not consider the girl who occasionally smokes a cigarette degenerate.
It is true, I, personally, do not enjoy the sight of one of my
girl-friends indulging in the practice, but that is all a matter
of taste, and has no place in this discussion. I do not see
why the freedom allowed us has harmed us, or has lowered
our ideals. I believe that our ideals are as high as, if not
higher than, the ideals of twenty years ago. Certainly it
was the ideals of the past few generations that brought the
calamity of the Great War upon the world, just as surely
as it was the older part of the presumably vicious generation that delivered the world from the scourge of that great
conflict.

And I might close this little protest with a sort of creed:
I believe in youth, in the freedom of youth, in the pleasures
of youth, and in the ideas of youth. I believe that in the
youth of today lies the future of the world; and therefore
how ridiculous it is to attempt to confine it by narrow, outlived, and unsuccessful conventionalities! I most heartily

condemn the sentiment of Bernard of Cluny: "*Hora novissima, TEMPORA PESSIMA SUNT, vigilemus!*" which has been translated and amplified into a church hymn by some exceedingly pessimistic person, of which joyous canticle the
5 first line is: "The world is very evil." I consider this statement both unchristianlike and false. The world is not very evil; it is surprisingly good, considering the wretched botch of things that the ideas of the foregoing ages of self-confessed perfection have made; and, what is more, it is going to be a
10 great deal better, and this change is coming not through the old man's dreams of *what has been*, but through the young man's knowledge of and striving toward *what is to be!*

AMERICAN PLACE-NAMES

The atlas, together with the dictionary and the encyclopedia, constitutes for most of us our intellectual reserve to be called out, like the militia, only in emergencies. Yet when variety and veracity combine in the proportions demanded by an atlas, the result cannot be dull; and indeed, few books contain so much potential entertainment. The trouble is that we do not credit the book with possessing social possibilities. We insist on maintaining with it purely commercial relations, accounting it only a storehouse of necessary information; whereas it is, in point of fact, also a tinderbox for the imagination, with every square inch crowded with names which either arrest us by their familiarity or pique us by their strangeness.

Only the other day I had occasion to study in some detail the map of the United States and that of England, and no printed page could have been more engrossing than the particolored maps clouded with place-names. To be sure, the kind of weathered beauty which distinguishes English place-names—especially those of very small villages—is lacking in the newer country; we have no Wems and Reeths and Cluns and Clitheroes, mere pebbles of words worn smooth by centuries of attrition. But if we do not compass so lovely an average, we achieve greater extremes, both of commonplaceness and of picturesqueness. Besides, our nomenclature has the merit of expressiveness, reflecting pretty accurately, for better or for worse, our national growth and some of our popular tendencies.

I have always liked our Indian names, which are as distinctively American as they are widespread and beautiful. No other country has its Winona and Minnehaha, its Cara-

tunk and Kenduskeag and Katahdin. I own I like the tang
of the last three better than the somewhat insipid flavor of
the first two, and that I liked them all better before they
became fashionable appellatives for all the steam yachts on
the coast and all the bungalows in the interior. Yet divested
of the taint of indiscriminate popularity, they hold by right
a unique place in our gazetteer. For they are survivals, re-
minders still of a picturesque past. Mattawamkeag, Winne-
pesaukee, Ogunquit, Tallahassee,—could they be spared from
the map?

Standing in relation to these as immigrant to native-born
is the great body of imported names, brought, for the most
part, from the other side of the water,—a suggestive but by
no means an infallible index of foreign population. A cursory glance over one Eastern state alone reveals Mexico,
Peru, China, Egypt, Norway, Sweden, and Denmark, all set
down within its borders. In the same state Etna, Corinth,
Hermon, and Damascus fall within a twenty-mile radius; in
another, Syracuse and Ithaca, Rome and Troy, hob-nob with
each other. Thus little by little the New World has perpetuated the names of the Old. It is rare in England to come on
a recognizable name borrowed from the Continent; but here,
through the working of the filial impulse, it is still possible
to trace the French, Dutch, and Spanish colonial holdings of
the seventeenth and eighteenth centuries; and ever since
Plymouth and Boston set the fashion, we have drawn heavily
on the mother country.

A characteristic of our map which must early strike an
observant foreigner is the predominance of surnames, in-
corporated as place-names. "Has a man done anything
noteworthy? Let us name a town for him!" seems to be the
American attitude. Nearly every state has its Washington
and its Lincoln; Columbus, Jefferson, Sherman, Roosevelt,
do not escape the hero-worshipper; Houston, Jackson, Lee,
and many a lesser patriot have pitched permanent camp
along our rivers and railroads. In this respect again we seem

to differ from England; but it is hard to institute a comparison with a country whose names were all bestowed some centuries before we began our task, with the result that their original outlines are more or less obliterated.

The great mass of undeniably commonplace American town-names derive, without doubt, from this ingenuous, and to some extent commendable, habit of nomenclature. A little town begins to grow up; either by accident or intention, the name of a well-known local family, ten to one with the inevitable -*ville* appended, becomes attached to it, and it is launched on its career. We owe the French a grudge on the score of this particular suffix. Is there a weaker one to be found, or one of wider acceptance? It is the bane of American rural districts. Indeed, when a place-name is to be manufactured out of hand, our poverty in the matter of vigorous name-endings stands out in sharp contrast to the English wealth: -shire, -hurst, -hall, -ford, -ton, -ham, -bury, -combe, -stead, terminate a host of beautiful English names, all based on particular features of the land, or instinct with the suggestion of long possession. These do not bear transplanting well; taken from their natural setting they somehow come to look as artificial as did the Pre-Raphaelite adaptations in another province of æsthetics. What an absurd lot of hybrid-English names has grown up in this country from our habit of abstracting a pleasing English tail-piece and joining it to a stem of our own choosing! If we must have the English ending, let us not filch it from its stem, but let us borrow the word boldly as a whole. But, although they are not as yet compacted by long usage into one word, we are not entirely without names with significant endings. Island Falls, Weston Mills, Cherry Valley, seem to hold in trust the seed-corn of a definitely American class of suffixes.

On the whole, we have been rather servile, as well as rather stupid, in naming our towns and cities. With a whole new country to experiment upon, it would seem that we might have done better. Yet in some parts of the country there is

a startling vigor and originality of nomenclature,—notably on the edges of uninhabited regions, wherever settled land fringes off into forest or desert. Even in Maine, up on the edge of the woods, lie Grindstone and Dead River; and in
5 Arizona and Nevada one receives a series of galvanic shocks, not unwelcome after the monotony of Whitneyville and Dodge City. Conventionality is left to the East; the West names places offhand, and, be sure, not listlessly. The name may be grotesque but it is seldom flabby. Oldglory, Tombstone,
10 Chloride, Oxbow, Skull Valley, Chin Lee, have about them a splendid and unfamiliar spontaneity. Here is vigor, color, individuality, piquing the curiosity, or telling a tale in one word. Yet even in the neighborhood of Borax and Johnnie, Searchlight and Ruby Valley, the East, in the guise of
15 Sodaville, has thrust in a jealous finger, which one finds it hard to overlook. Crude these outpost names undoubtedly are; crude and positive, good material for time to work on. Who in secret does not envy the magnificent independence of the men who christened those two towns in Arizona, not
20 impeccable "Readville" or "Harrison," but, with revolutionary disregard for tradition, Strawberry and Bumble Bee? Here, whether or not one likes to admit it, is at present the chief source of the distinctively American section of our gazetteer.

MODELS OF CRITICISM

SIR WALTER SCOTT[1]

Gilbert Keith Chesterton

Walter Scott is a writer who should just now be re-emerging into his own high place in letters, for unquestionably the recent, though now dwindling, schools of severely technical and æsthetic criticism have been unfavourable to him. He was a chaotic and unequal writer, and if there is one thing in which artists have improved since his time, it is in consistency and equality. It would perhaps be unkind to inquire whether the level of the modern man of letters, as compared with Scott, is due to the absence of valleys or the absence of mountains. But in any case we have learnt in our day to arrange our literary effects carefully, and the only point in which we fall short of Scott is in the incidental misfortune that we have nothing particular to arrange.

It is said that Scott is neglected by modern readers; if so, the matter could be more appropriately described by saying that modern readers are neglected by Providence. The ground of this neglect, in so far as it exists, must be found, I suppose, in the general sentiment that, like the beard of Polonius, he is too long. Yet it is surely a peculiar thing that in literature alone a house should be despised because it is too large, or a host impugned because he is too generous. If romance be really a pleasure, it is difficult to understand the modern reader's consuming desire to get it over, and if it be not a pleasure, it is difficult to understand his desire to have

[1] From *Varied Types*. Dodd, Mead & Company, New York, 1903.

it at all. Mere size, it seems to me, cannot be a fault. The fault must lie in some disproportion. If some of Scott's stories are dull and dilatory, it is not because they are giants, but because they are hunchbacks or cripples. Scott was very far indeed from being a perfect writer, but I do not think that it can be shown that the large and elaborate plan on which his stories are built was by any means an imperfection. He arranged his endless prefaces and his colossal introductions just as an architect plans great gates and long approaches to a really large house. He did not share the latter-day desire to get quickly through a story. He enjoyed narrative as a sensation; he did not wish to swallow a story like a pill, that it should do him good afterwards. He desired to taste it like a glass of port, that it might do him good at the time. The reader sits late at his banquets. His characters have that air of immortality which belongs to those of Dumas and Dickens. We should not be surprised to meet them in any number of sequels. Scott, in his heart of hearts, probably would have liked to write an endless story without either beginning or close.

Walter Scott is a great, and, therefore, mysterious man. He will never be understood until Romance is understood, and that will only be when Time, Man, and Eternity are understood. To say that Scott had more than any other man that ever lived a sense of the romantic seems, in these days, a slight and superficial tribute. The whole modern theory arises from one fundamental mistake—the idea that romance is in some way a plaything with life, a figment, a conventionality, a thing upon the outside. No genuine criticism of romance will ever arise until we have grasped the fact that romance lies not upon the outside of life, but absolutely in the centre of it. The centre of every man's existence is a dream. Death, disease, insanity, are merely material accidents, like toothache or a twisted ankle. That these brutal forces always besiege and often capture the citadel does not prove that they are the citadel. The boast of the realist (applying what the reviewers call his scalpel) is that he cuts into the heart of life; but he makes a very shallow incision, if he only reaches as deep as habits and calamities and sins. Deeper than all these lies a man's vision of himself, as swaggering and sentimental as a penny novelette. The literature of candour unearths innumerable weaknesses and elements of lawlessness which is called romance. It perceives superficial habits like murder and dipsomania, but it does not perceive the deepest of sins—the sin of vanity—vanity which is the mother of all day-dreams and adventures, the one sin that is not shared with any boon companion, or whispered to any priest.

In estimating, therefore, the ground of Scott's preëminence in romance we must absolutely rid ourselves of the notion that romance or adventure are merely materialistic things involved in the tangle of a plot or the multiplicity of drawn swords. We must remember that it is, like tragedy or farce, a state of the soul, and that, for some dark and elemental reason which we can never understand, this state of the soul is evoked in us by the sight of certain places or the contemplation of certain human crises, by a stream rushing under a heavy and covered wooden bridge, or by a man plunging a knife or a sword into tough timber. In the selection of these situations which catch the spirit of romance as in a net, Scott has never been equalled or even approached. His finest scenes affect us like fragments of a hilarious dream. They have the same quality which is often possessed by those nocturnal comedies—that of seeming more human than our waking life—even while they are less possible. Sir Arthur Wardour, with his daughter and the old beggar crouching in a cranny of the cliff as night falls and the tide closes around them, are actually in the coldest and bitterest of practical situations. Yet the whole incident has a quality that can only be called boyish. It is warmed with all the colours of an incredible sunset. Rob Roy trapped in the Tolbooth, and confronted with Bailie Nicol Jarvie, draws no sword, leaps

from no window, affects none of the dazzling external acts
upon which contemporary romance depends, yet that plain
and humorous dialogue is full of the essential philosophy of
romance which is almost equal betting upon man and destiny.
5 Perhaps the most profoundly thrilling of all Scott's situations is that in which the family of Colonel Mannering are
waiting for the carriage which may or may not arrive by
night to bring an unknown man into a princely possession.
Yet almost the whole of that thrilling scene consists of a
10 ridiculous conversation about food, and flirtation between
a frivolous old lawyer and a fashionable girl. We can say
nothing about what makes these scenes, except that the wind
bloweth where it listeth, and that here the wind blows strong.

It is in this quality of what may be called spiritual ad-
15 venturousness that Scott stands at so different an elevation
to the whole of the contemporary crop of romancers who
have followed the leadership of Dumas. There has, indeed,
been a great and inspiriting revival of romance in our time,
but it is partly frustrated in almost every case by this rooted
20 conception that romance consists in the vast multiplication
of incidents and the violent acceleration of narrative. The
heroes of Mr. Stanley Weyman scarcely ever have their
swords out of their hands; the deeper presence of romance
is far better felt when the sword is at the hip ready for
25 innumerable adventures too terrible to be pictured. The
Stanley Weyman hero has scarcely time to eat his supper
except in the act of leaping from a window or whilst his other
hand is employed in lunging with a rapier. In Scott's heroes,
on the other hand, there is no characteristic so typical or so
30 worthy of humour as their disposition to linger over their
meals. The conviviality of the Clerk of Copmanhurst or of
Mr. Pleydell, and the thoroughly solid things they are described as eating, is one of the most perfect of Scott's poetic
touches. In short, Mr. Stanley Weyman is filled with the
35 conviction that the sole essence of romance is to move with
insatiable rapidity from incident to incident. In the truer

romance of Scott, there is more of the sentiment of "Oh! still delay, thou art so fair!" more of a certain patriarchal enjoyment of things as they are—of the sword by the side and the wine-cup in the hand. Romance, indeed, does not consist by any means so much in experiencing adventures, as in being ready for them. How little the actual boy cares for incidents in comparison to tools and weapons may be tested by the fact that the most popular story of adventure is concerned with a man who lived for years on a desert island with two guns and a sword, which he never had to use on an enemy.

ROBERT LOUIS STEVENSON[1]

CHARLES TOWNSEND COPELAND

I

The term *fin de siècle* has come to be one of unmitigated reproach. Whatsoever things are weary, whatsoever things are corrupt, whatsoever things are (or used to be) unmentionable in polite society, are all opprobriously grouped under these three hard-working words. With but four more New Year's Days in the nineteenth century for robust resolutions, four happy new years for a decadent keeping of the same, the anxious question rises whether the hour that begins a hundred new years will mark a stage of progress or only an imaginary line. Will the decadents stop decaying, and the symbolists devise a healthier code of signals demanded by a healthier art? Will there be all sorts of dewy beginnings in literature, and will Paris, ever equal to the occasion, produce some matutinal phrase that shall drive out this hateful vesper term of ennui and disease?

Whatever the event, men may be sure that when the glass has been turned, the scythe whetted, and the joy-bells rung, they will still find time for many backward glances at the hundred years behind them. And they will note the fact that although prose romance in English died with Scott long before the sand was half run out, it was born again, but in less vigor, with Stevenson, another man of his race, while the century-glass yet lacked twenty years of turning. It will be recorded that while the historian of Wessex celebrated the three Fates until people shuddered to see the thread both spun and cut, and a strong young Occidental in the East took

[1] From "Robert Louis Stevenson," in the *Atlantic Monthly*, April, 1895.

pains to show that men's motives are not always better than those which stir the jungle, this northern teller of tales, who shared his empire with them, took upon himself the different and truly romantic task of giving the world pleasure un- mixed with pain. And it will likewise be observed, I think, 5 with the wisdom which, I seem to hear the reader say, sits so easily upon critics, whether for prophecy or for retrospect, that Stevenson not only quickened an admirable art, but also founded a school of more and less unsuccessful imitators of himself. 10

Judgment of Mr. Stevenson in his varied activity must be left to *aube de siècle* judges. He will take the place proper to him without our help; it may be, without theirs. Of obituary lament there has been already enough and to spare; but the moment admits, perhaps, now that the multitude 15 who mourn him have recovered somewhat from the sorrow and confusion brought by his death to all who care for letters, a brief lingering over a few of those qualities which one reader, at least, has found most salient. That Stevenson was gay and resolute enough to found a school of romance in the 20 midst of opposing tendencies is, of course, the chief quality of all. He loves the past for the courageous picture of it which survives. He blows his wild war-note, unfurls his banner to the breeze of long ago, and goes forth always to the motto, "*Espérance* and set on." This watchword, 25 indeed, might be set above essay as well as story, travels and verse as well as essay, for in almost all the extraor- dinary variety of his writing Robert Louis Stevenson is the consistent preacher of courage and cheer. The writer's own brave and most pathetic life was, as the world knows, 30 a consistent practicing of what he preached. In most of his published words, optimism is at the height of the Selkirk grace, or of Happy Thought in *A Child's Garden of Verses*:—

> "The world is so full of a number of things, 35
> I'm sure we should all be as happy as kings."

And never, even in A Christmas Sermon or Pulvis et Umbra,
does he decline farther into the vale of pessimism than the
stage once dubbed meliorism by a great novelist whom he
did not love. It is indubitably a help to this philosophy that
5 arrival and success are not among its dreams. The beckon-
ing road and the roadside inn are ever better with Stevenson
than the end of the passage. Pleasure lies in running, not
in reaching the goal; and hunger is an infinitely sweeter thing
than satiety. "A man's reach"—I have wondered that he
10 nowhere quotes a line with which he everywhere agrees—"a
man's reach should exceed his grasp, or what's a heaven for?"

II

Next in importance, perhaps, to the cardinal trait of
Mr. Stevenson's career, that he was a romantic in an age of
realism, come the facts that he was a Scotchman, born within
15 the frown of Edinburgh Castle, and that his father and
grandfather were engineers to the Board of Northern Lights.
This sounds like a business connection with the Aurora
Borealis, but it means merely that the lives of the Stevensons
had the relish both of salvation and of adventure, because
20 they were the builders of Skerryvore, the Bell Rock, and
other great sea-lights along the northern coast of Britain.
Much of the best writing of the author of David Balfour—
can any one forget the dedication of that book?—thrills and
tingles with the feeling of race and native land. I have in
25 mind at this moment The Foreigner at Home, a page or two
of The Silverado Squatters, and portions of the paper entitled
The Manse, ending with the triumphant picture of ascent
from the writer, through engineers, Picts, and what-not clans
and tribes, to Probably Arboreal chattering in the top of the
30 family tree. Less often, yet again and again, both in verse
and in prose, does Stevenson dwell proudly upon the exploits
and the hardy lives of his forbears, and mourn the degeneracy in bodily frame and strength of their hearth-keeping

descendant. His whole feeling about all this is in some enchanting lines written at Bournemouth, in a house named
after the chief memorial of his family:—

> "Say not of me that weakly I declined
> The labours of my sires, and fled the sea,   5
> The towers we founded and the lamps we lit,
> To play at home with paper like a child.
> But rather say: *In the afternoon of time*
> *A strenuous family dusted from its hands*
> *The sand of granite, and beholding far*   10
> *Along the sounding coast its pyramids*
> *And tall memorials catch the dying sun,*
> *Smiled well content, and to this childish task*
> *Around the fire addressed its evening hours.*"

It never occurred to him that he was the brightest of all the 15
lamps they lit, but many men, even of the not inhuman,
would be content to see Skerryvore itself quenched in the
ocean, if by that extinction the light might shine again on
Vaea Mountain.

III

That Mr. Stevenson is a sworn romantic, and that he is 20
so much a Scot as to keep a strong flavor of the wilding, in
spite of each exotic graft, are truths no less conspicuous than
that he is an exquisite and a secure artist in prose narrative,
in verse, the essay, and the sketch. So perfectly, indeed,
does he write that the Philistines—and not the mere *bour-* 25
geois citizens of the country, but the first families of Philistia
—are often heard to accuse him of having naught to say.
To them, it is more than probable, he has nothing at all to
say, unless they first master certain remarks once made by
Mr. Joseph Addison on the subject of Literary Taste. But 30
to the minds of men who have a humble and hearty admiration for good writing, Stevenson's tales of adventure gain
much from his care about form; and his kind and sagacious
thoughts gain very much indeed from the "continual slight

novelty" of his style. This loved and lost story-teller of ours
could no more content himself with the construction used by
Dumas in his gay and ragged volumes than with the disposition and English of the scene in *Guy Mannering* which jars
on him like a false note in music or color. Yet he had read
Le Vicomte de Bragelonne five times, and hoped—let us trust
the hope was realized—to read it once again before he died.
And the jarring scene—which happens, by the way, to have
been that of Harry Bertram's landing at Ellangowan—he
respects as being in general "a model instance of the romantic method." The Meredith jargon Mr. Stevenson would no
more think of putting into the mouths of his own people than
he would that uttered by the purely symbolic young men and
maidens whom Scott fobs off upon us as heroes and heroines.
Mr. Meredith is nevertheless the breath of life to him, and
Sir Walter "out and away the king of the romantics."

In these references to Stevenson's art and the frequent
artlessness of Scott and Dumas, there is no slightest intention of matching him with them. He would not, if he could,
have written like them; he could not, if he would, have imagined and invented and swung the whole thing along as
they did. They, with all their faults, are great romantics:
he, with all his gifts and graces, is a little romantic; and the
many well-meaning persons who range him persistently with
Scott do him nothing but disservice. The appearance of
Meg Merrilies to Godfrey Bertram, the abdication of Queen
Mary at Lochleven, the installation of the abbot of Kenna-
quhair, the appeal of Jeanie Deans for Effie, a certain scene
in *Old Mortality*,—the play and stretch and headlong vigor
of sheer improvisation that made all these possible, and easily
possible, to Scott, are "out of the star" of the author of
Kidnapped and *David Balfour*. Nor, in writing, do I forget
Alan and Davie beside the stream, or the bewitching scenes
of the windmills in Holland, or the duel of the two brothers
outside the distracted house of Durrisdeer, when all was so
still that the flame of the candles went up straight and steady

into the night. But Sir Walter's books seem to me like a large symphony which has many discords; Mr. Stevenson's, like a discreet yet moving theme, perfectly played on fewer instruments.

To leave the unseemly task of comparison, I am well aware that there are those who find Mr. Stevenson's art at fault by times within his chosen province. But *The Master of Ballantrae*, the chief object of their criticisms, has been dispraised too harshly. The details, to be sure, are ill blended, but each in itself is admirably worked out; and the failure (or half failure) at last seems to have come through a sheer lack of power to fuse the well-selected elements of the tale. Of details and bits and episodes there is a vast and engaging variety in the writings of this author. That quaint episode, Providence and the Guitar, which must be taken as one of the Stevensonian *cruces*, reflects within its narrow term all the sweetness and light of Bohemia. That fierce episode, A Story of Francis Villon, shows forth all the bitterness and blackness which may sometimes darken and make sinister the same cheerful land. Pictures are often evoked with a few words, as when the redcoats are seen down the valley from the high-placed rock among the heather; or as when Jekyll discovers the unconscious transformation into Hyde by seeing his hand upon the bedclothes. There has not been such a shudder as that in our literature since Crusoe found the footprint in the sand. *Prince Otto*, an *opéra bouffe* in Dresden china, is another Stevensonian *crux*, acceptable only to the esoteric and the inner circle; but the going of night and the coming of dawn in the forest of Gerolstein charm the eyes like the sunrise on the Bass Rock.

And so on, indefinitely, these thick-coming memories might be set down; but it is full time for a word about Stevenson's style, which is, in the opinion of many, his chief distinction. Several London critics, in the attempt, perhaps, to avenge certain "Bards" upon their "Reviewers," have spoken grudgingly of his wonderful skill, because, forsooth, he learned

to write before he wrote for publication. The offense was
deeper dyed because the young Scot sought aid from France,
the ancient ally of Scotland, and scrupled not to avow that
his sojourn in Paris and the study of French writers had
5 taught him secrets of technique. Even British critics allow
a painter to study pigments before he exhibits a picture, a
sculptor to model in clay before he carves the nation's heroes
in marble; but, in the face of repeated blows, the fine old
superstition dies hard, that ill-regulated impulse is an im-
10 portant element in the "inspiration" of an art more subtle
than either painting or sculpture. Stevenson chose to reduce
this element to a minimum, and to make himself the most
faithful of apprentices. He became at last the most impeccable of artists; and although the ardent study of an
15 extraordinary variety of masters did not dull his keen, original gift,—as if, indeed, the right use of even the one talent
ever failed to multiply it,—he yet keeps in his most ornate
pages the good tradition of the language, the classic note of
the best English prose. Stevenson loves and practices the
20 *belle phrase*, the harmonious sentence; but scarce ever does
he descend to the indolent *cheville*. Never, to the best of my
memory, does he make the Wegg-like change,—so often
made by Wegg's creator, that great, imperfect genius,—the
change from rhythm to metre. In few, he nicely observes the
25 adjective in Dryden's saying, "the *other* harmony of prose."

ON THE THANKSGIVING AND CHRISTMAS STORY[1]

WILLIAM DEAN HOWELLS

While the Americans have greatly excelled in the short story generally, they have almost created a species of it in the Thanksgiving story. We have transplanted the Christmas story from England, while the Thanksgiving story is native to our air; but both are of Anglo-Saxon growth. Their 5 difference is from a difference of environment; and the Christmas story when naturalized among us becomes almost identical in motive, incident, and treatment with the Thanksgiving story. If I were to generalize a distinction between them, I should say that the one dealt more with marvels and 10 the other more with morals; and yet the critic should beware of speaking too confidently on this point. It is certain, however, that the Christmas season is meteorologically more favorable to the effective return of persons long supposed lost at sea, or from a prodigal life, or from a darkened mind. 15 The longer, denser, and colder nights are better adapted to the apparition of ghosts, and to all manner of signs and portents; while they seem to present a wider field for the active intervention of angels in behalf of orphans and outcasts. The dreams of elderly sleepers at this time are apt to 20 be such as will effect a lasting change in them when they awake, turning them from the hard, cruel, and grasping habits of a lifetime, and reconciling them to their sons, daughters, and nephews, who have thwarted them in marriage; or softening them to their meek, uncomplaining wives, 25

[1] From *Criticism and Fiction*, chap. xxvi. Harper & Brothers, New York, 1891.

whose hearts they have trampled upon in their reckless pursuit of wealth; and generally disposing them to a distribution of hampers among the sick and poor, and to a friendly reception of chubby gentlemen with charity subscription papers.
5 Ships readily drive upon rocks in the early twilight, and offer exciting difficulties of salvage; and the heavy snows gather thickly round the steps of wanderers who lie down to die in them, preparatory to their discovery and rescue by immediate relatives. The midnight weather is also very suitable to
10 encounter with murderers and burglars; and the contrast of its freezing gloom with the light and cheer in-doors promotes the gayeties which merge, at all well-regulated country-houses, in love and marriage. In the region of pure character no moment could be so available for flinging off the mask
15 of frivolity, or imbecility, or savagery, which one has worn for ten or twenty long years, say, for the purpose of foiling some villain, and surprising the reader, and helping the author out with his plot. Persons abroad in the Alps, or Apennines, or Pyrenees, or anywhere seeking shelter in the
20 huts of shepherds or the dens of smugglers, find no time like it for lying in a feigned slumber, and listening to the whispered machinations of their suspicious-looking entertainers, and then suddenly starting up and fighting their way out; or else springing from the real sleep into which they have sunk
25 exhausted, and finding it broad day and the good peasants whom they had so unjustly doubted, waiting breakfast for them. We need not point out the superior advantages of the Christmas season for anything one has a mind to do with the French Revolution, or the Arctic explorations, or the
30 Indian Mutiny, or the horrors of Siberian exile; there is no time so good for the use of this material; and ghosts on shipboard are notoriously fond of Christmas Eve. In our own logging camps the man who has gone into the woods for the winter, after quarrelling with his wife, then hears her sad
35 appealing voice, and is moved to good resolutions as at no other period of the year; and in the mining regions, first in

California and later in Colorado, the hardened reprobate, dying in his boots, smells his mother's doughnuts, and breathes his last in a soliloquized vision of the old home, and the little brother, or sister, or the old father coming to meet him from heaven; while his rude companions listen round him, and dry their eyes on the butts of their revolvers.

It has to be very grim, all that, to be truly effective; and here, already, we have a touch in the Americanized Christmas story of the moralistic quality of the American Thanksgiving story. This was seldom written, at first, for the mere entertainment of the reader; it was meant to entertain him, of course; but it was meant to edify him, too, and to improve him; and some such intention is still present in it. I rather think that it deals more probably with character to this end than its English cousin, the Christmas story, does. It is not so improbable that a man should leave off being a drunkard on Thanksgiving, as that he should leave off being a curmudgeon on Christmas; that he should conquer his appetite as that he should instantly change his nature, by good resolutions. He would be very likely, indeed, to break his resolutions in either case, but not so likely in the one as in the other.

Generically, the Thanksgiving story is cheerfuler in its drama and simpler in its persons than the Christmas story. Rarely has it dealt with the supernatural, either the apparition of ghosts or the intervention of angels. The weather being so much milder at the close of November than it is a month later, very little can be done with the elements; though on the coast a north-easterly storm has been, and can be, very usefully employed. The Thanksgiving story is more restricted in its range; the scene is still mostly in New England, and the characters are of New England extraction, who come home from the West usually, or New York, for the event of the little drama, whatever it may be. It may be the reconciliation of kinsfolk who have quarrelled; or the union of lovers long estranged; or husbands and wives who have

had hard words and parted; or mothers who had thought their sons dead in California and find themselves agreeably disappointed in their return; or fathers who for old time's sake receive back their erring and conveniently dying daugh-
5 ters. The notes are not many which this simple music sounds, but they have a Sabbath tone, mostly, and win the listener to kindlier thoughts and better moods. The art is at its highest in some strong sketch of Mrs. Rose Terry Cooke's, or some perfectly satisfying study of Miss Jewett's, or some graphic
10 situation of Miss Wilkins's; and then it is a very fine art. But mostly it is poor and rude enough, and makes openly, shamelessly, sickeningly, for the reader's emotions, as well as his morals. It is inclined to be rather descriptive. The turkey, the pumpkin, the cornfield, figure throughout; and
15 the leafless woods are blue and cold against the evening sky behind the low hip-roofed, old-fashioned homestead. The parlance is usually the Yankee dialect and its western modifications.

The Thanksgiving story is mostly confined in scene to the
20 country; it does not seem possible to do much with it in town; and it is a serious question whether with its geographical and topical limitations it can hold its own against the Christmas story; and whether it would not be well for authors to consider a combination with its elder rival.

25 The two feasts are so near together in point of time that they could be easily covered by the sentiment of even a brief narrative. Under the agglutinated style of A Thanksgiving-Christmas Story, fiction appropriate to both could be produced, and both could be employed naturally and probably
30 in the transaction of its affairs and the development of its characters. The plot for such a story could easily be made to include a total-abstinence pledge and family reunion at Thanksgiving, and an apparition and spiritual regeneration over a bowl of punch at Christmas.

35 Not all Thanksgiving-Christmas stories need be of this pattern precisely; I wish to suggest merely one way of doing

them. Perhaps when our writers really come to the work they will find sufficient inspiration in its novelty to turn to human life and observe how it is really affected on these holidays, and be tempted to present some of its actualities. This would be a great thing to do, and would come home to readers 5 with surprise.

STUDENTS' THEMES: CRITICISM

I

The story of Jael and Sisera illustrates the immense gulf between what was considered righteous then and what is now. People may behave as badly nowadays, but in their songs of triumph they omit to state the mean expedients by which they conquered. Traitors, though useful, are kept out of sight in summing up the results. Then, to Deborah and Barak, confident, in true Hebrew style, that the "stars in their courses fought against Sisera," Jael was "blessed above women" for her cruelty and treachery; and savage was their rejoicing at the grief of Sisera's mother as they pictured her looking through the window crying, "Why is his chariot so long in coming?"

At the present day woman has assumed many of man's prerogatives, while retaining, it is said, her inborn guile; but there are only isolated instances of her borrowing his more savage grandeur, such as patriotic homicide or diplomatic treachery. Antiquity seems to have revelled in women like Jael, Judith, Herodias, who sharpened frank brutality with the edge of feminine deception.

II

Why do women dislike the character of Falstaff? Well, for one reason because he is fat. Thomas B. Reed once said that no gentleman ever weighs over two hundred pounds. If we change the word gentleman to hero, any woman might say the same. Nevertheless, stout men are sometimes very popular with the opposite sex, and of this Mr. Pickwick is an

example. Falstaff, however, is also a rascal. Now a gentle-
manly rascal, such as Robin Hood or Raffles, is also occasionally admired on account of some good trait in his
character, such as generosity, courteousness, or daring. But
to crown all, Falstaff is a coward. That defect can be counter- 5
balanced only by other extremely prominent virtues, or ex-
cused by physical weakness. A man who is not only fat but
a rascal, and not only a fat rascal, but a cowardly fat rascal,
is a person who is deservedly despised by any decent, self-
respecting woman. 10

III

Thackeray conducts the characters in *Pendennis* in a very
easy, almost lazy manner. He realizes that the interests of
the whole troupe must be looked after equally, and that it is
not fair to give any of the excursionists too big a lead. So
every now and then he says to Pendennis, "You lie down and 15
rest awhile. I'll go back and bring up the Major, Foker, and
Captain Costigan, so that you can all start even again in the
morning." Then, when the party get tired, they go and sit
under a tree and the manager gives them a sermon on "How
to be happy with nothing to do," or "High life among the 20
British aristocracy." Thus they stroll happily on for about
six hundred and fifty miles, having a few quarrels on the
way but nothing serious. Suddenly the starter yells "sprint,"
and they rush on the next fifty miles at full speed till the
announcer calls out, "Pendennis, first! Laura, second! 25
Blanche Amory, distanced!"

IV

Roughly speaking, Ruskin uses color for two purposes,—
for mere physical description, and for the further description
of character. "Blue islands of Paduan hills, poised in the
golden west" suggests chiefly gorgeous sunset hues; the color 30
in this description appeals to the eye. So does the "pride of
purple rocks and river pools of blue" of the Yorkshire hills.

Yet in Ruskin's descriptive passages, words denoting color may suggest more; they may reveal character. "The low bronzed gleaming of sea-rusted armor shot angrily under *blood-red* mantle-folds." In the "blood-red" of the mantle-
5 folds is summed up and presented all the fearlessness, the authority, and the grimness of the "majestic" warriors of the sea. Here color suggests not merely physical aspect, but character.

As Ruskin uses color for two purposes, so he handles it in
10 two ways,—through direct statement, and through the suggestion of a color by the naming of an object that possesses that color. The "white clouds of heaven" floating over English hills are directly pictured; so, too, are the "black barges" of the Thames. In the phrase, however, "the mothers and
15 maidens, pure as her pillars of alabaster," the whiteness of purity is suggested through "pillars of alabaster." A more striking example of color-suggestion is the description of Venice,—"the city of marble, the golden city paved with emerald, a glowing jewel set in an unsullied sea." The first
20 method of using color is more concrete; the second allows more play to the imagination. Ruskin employs both, with the skill of a master, in his descriptions of physical aspect and character.

RANDOM THOUGHTS ON *DAVID COPPERFIELD*

Even as some children are born blondes or brunettes, I am persuaded that I was born a Dickens child. One of the earliest remembrances of my childhood is that of lying out under the trees in my cradle and hearing my mother, who is also a passionate lover of Dickens, read *Pickwick* aloud to my older brothers. Of course, I was too young to appreciate the humor of *Pickwick*, but this early association with Dickens was surely an auspicious beginning. I had a delightfully rosy old nurse, too, that in later years I constantly associated with Peggotty. Thus born a lover of Dickens, I shall live and die his lover. All of his books I have devoured, admired, and loved, and they have opened a new world to me. Much traveling in the realms of gold since I first followed Mr. Pickwick and David and little Nell through absorbing adventures, has never dimmed the pleasure given by a page of Dickens.

David Copperfield was Charles Dickens's "favorite child." He was certainly wise in his choice, wiser than many great masters have been in the choice of their favorites. *Copperfield* came to him early. Forster, in his celebrated biography, says: "The story bore him irresistibly along, . . . and he probably was never less harassed by interruptions." Public opinion, strangely enough, did not like *Copperfield* as well as *Dombey and Son* at first, but after 1850 it became the most popular, with the *Pickwick Papers*, of Dickens's books. I cannot say that *Copperfield* is my favorite any more than I can say that *Pickwick* is my favorite. It is like trying to choose between a father and a mother, a thing wholly heretical, barbaric, and impossible. *Copperfield* is an inimitable work, full of delights. Thackeray thought it charmingly

fresh and considered its tender humor admirable. Even Matthew Arnold, who did not seem able to understand why anyone read modern authors, judged it a sound, rich work, full
of treasures of gaiety, invention, life, and resource. I wonder
5 if he found that *Copperfield* agreed with his theory that the
ancients paid attention only to the excellences and full sweep
of the plot, whereas modern writers fall into the lamentable
way of considering only the embellishments of a piece of
writing, only the characters, only the brilliant lines? It cer-
10 tainly lives up to his idea of the modern point of view; it
has lines, pages, chapters, even, of sparkling brilliancy, and
its characters are superb creations. It does not, however,
have the broad full sweep of ancient writing; its characters
and lines are too brilliant. No modern writing does have
15 that classical continuity, but *Copperfield* has a comprehen-
siveness that requites this loss. The picture is a complete
one. No details are omitted; character on character is introduced merely to add to the general effect, to round out
the story. Most of the plot is simplicity itself. Nothing
20 could be simpler, for instance, than the Steerforth-Emily affair. It is all obvious—the aristocratic seducer, the confiding
rural maid, the poor but honest parents. Critics have dwelt
on this fault of obviousness, but who cares? "*Copperfield*
is so excellent that criticism is swallowed up in pleasure,"
25 says Andrew Lang.

The book is fascinating from beginning to end! It seems
to me as much the total deliverance of a great man as *Tom
Jones* or *Vanity Fair*. The first chapters are almost the best.
As with Pip, Dickens has made of David a delightful boy, a
30 more real child than Paul or Florence. There is a tender
grace about those opening chapters that draws the heart out in
unfeigned delight and amusement. The pretty mother twist-
ing her bright curls; ruddy Peggotty with her needle-marked
thumb, her work-box with St. Paul's on the cover, the croco-
35 dile book, and the buttons popping off her broad back; nervous little Dr. Chillip, whom Miss Trotwood so terrified—

who can forbear smiling at them? Mr. Chesterton has said
in one of his charming essays: "The real achievement of the
earlier part of *David Copperfield* lies in a certain impression
of the little Copperfield living in a land of giants. It is at
once Gargantuan in its fancy and grossly vivid in its facts." 5
Nothing could be truer. David struggling with the easy
good-nature of O and S and the difficulties of the other letters, or David trembling before Mr. Murdstone, invariably
seems a Lilliputian.

Then come the Murdstones, terrible, awesome, rolling up 10
like a black thunder-cloud. I always felt sure that Mr. Murdstone dyed his whiskers and I always hated him, and was
glad when David bit his hand. The gloominess inspired by
him and his steel-adorned sister is indescribable. M. Taine,
who considers *Copperfield* Dickens's best novel, found little 15
David's griefs as acute, as heartfelt as the sorrows of a grown
man. We are all glad for the comic relief furnished by the
immortal waiter, with his fable about Mr. Topsawyer. And
so we might follow David through all his adventures, meeting with him the strangest and most astonishing galaxy of 20
characters that an author has ever put into one book.

Dickens as ever is admirable in his minor characters, to
whom he gives life by one or two deft touches. A phrase
here, a repetition there, a few clauses for shading, and you
have good-natured, good-hearted Mr. Dick, who couldn't 25
keep Charles I out of his Memorial; kindly Dr. Strong;
Traddles, who grew up from a fat, skeleton-drawing school-
boy into a lovable barrister, with his hair sticking up very
straight; Julia Mills, who knew the world because she had
early suffered from a misplaced affection; those little birds, 30
the Misses Spenlow; Littimer, the grave hypocrite, who
always made David feel so young—surely these are all real?
Who would not like to know more about the poor old pawnbroker, with the stubbly gray beard, who rushed out of his
dirty den, and seizing the terrified David by the hair, whined 35
fiercely, as if he were screwing each word out, "Oh, what do

you want? Oh, my eyes and limbs, what do you want?
Oh, my lungs and liver, what do you want? Goroo, goroo!"
Who would not like to find out what became of that husky-
voiced fellow-traveler of David's, that "actually brought a
rash out upon himself with boiled beef"? There are hundreds
of such characters in every book of Charles Dickens, characters vivified into a blinding light by a single sentence, created,
and more pity for it, only to die.

Carlyle, in his *Heroes and Hero-Worship*, declares that
a history of the world lies in the history of the heroes that
have aided its development. In the same way a comprehensive criticism of *David Copperfield* would be an essay on
its characters. What a host of great ones greet such an essayist! Dickens himself preferred the Peggotty group, but
with the exception of "love lorn" Mrs. Gummidge, who "felt
it more" than the others, and of Clara Peggotty, whose greatness is undeniable, they do not seem so real or stay so long
with us as, say, Mrs. Crupp, with her hand pressed to her
nankeen bosom and with her alarming attacks of faintness,
followed by requests for a mite of brandy. She is delightful,
this Mrs. Crupp, who thanked Heaven, when David took her
chambers ("and a sweet set they is for sich") that now "she
had found summun she could care for." I cannot believe
that Mrs. Crupp is an exaggeration. In fact, the more I read
Dickens, the more I am persuaded that he is not the Great
Caricaturist! More and more I believe that he is a realist.
Surely people will not deny that nankeen bosoms exist?
Surely they will not deny that Mrs. Crupp's objections to
any of the work in connection with David's first party are
natural? For they certainly are natural—any housewife will
corroborate me. It is the height of realism. Before the
reader hastily condemns Dickens as a gross caricaturist, let
him think carefully, and if I am not greatly mistaken he will
find Nature, not Dickens, the exaggerator.

Then there are the more important and famous characters—Uriah Heep, Miss Betsey Trotwood, Agnes Wickfield,

Dora Spenlow, and, greatest of all, Mr. Wilkins Micawber.
Uriah is an excellent conception. For all his early "'umbleness" he is consumed internally by villainy. It always has
appeared to me that the effect of Uriah's personality is far
more impressive on the reader and on the plot, than are the 5
forgeries and underhand work which he perpetrates. His
writhings and leerings, his red eyes and his "'umbleness" are
capitally portrayed. No wonder Miss Trotwood exclaimed
passionately: "If you're an eel, sir, conduct yourself like one.
If you're a man, control your limbs, sir. . . . Good God! I 10
am not going to be serpentined and corkscrewed out of my
senses!" He is splendid at the end in jail, 'umble again,
cured of his "follies," as he calls them, the pious favorite of
the visiting committee.

Miss Trotwood is firm like Miss Jane Murdstone but in 15
quite another and lovable way. Her eccentricities are delightful—especially her war with the donkeys. She is so
sure that Mr. Dick is a great man that she almost persuades
us that he is. Anyway, we agree with him that she is a most
wonderful woman and we love her all the more for always 20
referring to Miss Murdstone as "that murdering woman."

For years there has been a controversy among critics about
Agnes Wickfield and Dora Spenlow. Most have, with Lang,
taken the stand that whereas Agnes is very lovely and has a
beautiful soul, she is a bit too spiritual for our world. One 25
never feels that she is quite real—she is too good, too up-
lifting. I infinitely prefer Dora to her, but it does seem to
me that there is a great tendency among modern critics to
lay too much stress on Agnes's saintliness, to overdo her perfection—surpassing the author's intentions. This is surely 30
wrong. I do not see how the modern critical conception of
Agnes could have charmed Uriah very much. Mr. Chesterton becomes really violent about Dora and Agnes. He
roundly criticizes Dickens for allowing David and Agnes
to sit comfortably at their fireside. "They will never be 35
really happy—their marriage is not human. David Copper-

field and Dora quarreled over cold mutton; and if they had
gone on quarreling to the end of their lives they would have
gone on loving each other to the end of their lives; and it
would have been a human marriage. But David Copperfield
and Agnes would agree about the mutton. And that mutton
would be very cold indeed." Having created a splendid character like Dora, he continues, Dickens became alarmed and
had to do away with her, because he did not know what
else to do with her. In the same way Mr. Chesterton com-
plains that the Micawbers and Peggotty should never have
been bundled off to Australia (represented as a patent cure-
all for all troubles) but should have remained in England to
be comforted and helped by David and their other friends.
He finds David and Agnes smug and selfish at the end, and
in his own characteristic way frankly admits he does not like
the end. I am not so sweeping as Mr. Chesterton. With him
I find Dora a more lovable and human character than Agnes.
No one wonders that her "Doady" adored her. We dote
on her with him. She confuses the housekeeping, but, as
Mr. Chesterton says, we are not angry with her, but rather
with the housekeeping. She is impractical, young and delightful; sweet when playing with Jip. How innocent, how
fresh! But I greatly doubt, to use Mr. Chesterton's own
metaphor, whether Dora's mutton would be any less cold
than that of Agnes, or if David's digestion and temper could
have withstood a life-time of Dora. After twenty years her
nonsensical eccentricities might have become a trifle tiresome,—don't you think so, Mr. Chesterton? David is going
to be happy with Agnes; the Peggottys are pleased and
Mr. Micawber delighted with Australia. Why not let them
go? Why hold them back to England? Mr. Chesterton
makes a point that Dora is thoroughly avenged by "this
spiritualised and sublimated marriage of convenience." This
may be true, but I am glad, for one, to remember Dora as an
inconsequential, heart-capturing young trifle. Dora at forty
would have been odious.

The last of the characters I intend to speak of is the greatest—so great that, as Mr. Chesterton observes, "the world has never been able to do anything but walk round and round him wondering what it shall say." Beside the great comic figures of the world's literature, Figaro, Falstaff, Uncle Toby, Tartarin, beside these, Wilkins Micawber has taken a high place. His proportions are gigantic. His character compels as much wonder as amusement. Whether beaming and expanding in joy and happiness or plunged into the deepest gloom, he is a source of inexhaustible merriment. No wonder Mrs. Micawber swore that she would never, never leave him. No one ever wants to leave him. He is like a great magnet that attracts laughter instead of steel. Whether he is brewing one of his delightful punches, or writing one of his letters (surely the most extraordinary epistles that the world has ever known, with their inimitable endings and their flowing style)— no matter what he is doing, Mr. Micawber is ever a delight. Once one had heard his florid speech and beheld the enjoyment he took in the luscious roll of an unctuous phrase, the heart would have been captured. Mr. Micawber seems scarcely born for the part he has to act in regard to Uriah, "but," as Lang sagely remarks, "some one has to act it!" And Mr. Micawber does it with extraordinary grace, falling naturally into an epistolary denouncement of the villain. He is perhaps the greatest work of a great and exceptionally gifted artist. Micawber without Copperfield would be Micawber, but Copperfield without Micawber would be very little.

MARK TWAIN AND THE MISSISSIPPI VALLEY

The valley of the Mississippi, stretching over half the habitable portion of the continent, is second in extent only to that of the Amazon, and as a dwelling-place for civilized man is by far the first upon our globe. That it must eventu-
5 ally become the center of the nation, both in population and in wealth, cannot be doubted. Indeed, it is fast assuming this position. During the period of economic development following the Civil War the Mississippi valley grew amaz-ingly. From a purely agricultural section, backward and
10 undeveloped, it became a vast region of modern farmlands, dotted with great industrial centers. Today, the Middle West is typically American, enthusiastic, aggressive, hard-headed, practical.

There is another Mississippi valley, however—the valley
15 whose story is scarcely surpassed, for sheer romantic interest, in the annals of the continent. These fertile prairies have been trodden by the Indian, the Spaniard, the Frenchman, the American. This broad river still conceals beneath its relentless flood the mortal remains of its discoverer. Here
20 La Salle made that daring voyage which brought a vast em-pire beneath the crown of France. Here Père Marquette and his brave followers fared forth upon their mission of mercy. Here, for centuries, was fought that fascinating struggle be-tween civilization and savagery, a struggle whose fate hung
25 long in the balance. And then, in a trice, all was changed. In Paris, an emperor scrawled illegibly upon a piece of paper, and the valley of the Mississippi had witnessed its final change of sovereign. At once the Atlantic seaboard poured forth its great wave of pioneers. The struggle was ended;
30 civilization had come to stay.

This new civilization is no less interesting and no less diverse than the period of conquest which preceded it. The river is now alive with a strange new life; shrieking steamboats race up its muddy current; long strings of flatboats float placidly down past bustling river ports and sleepy plantations. A thousand different types throng its banks. North and South meet in a single restless people. Cavalier and tradesman, adventurer and teacher, Yankee and Virginian, mingle and stamp their characteristics upon society.

Such was the valley of old when, in 1835, was born the man who was to make deathless its marvelous life. Born in a quiet little Missouri slave town, nurtured in its traditions, Mark Twain was peculiarly fitted to tell the story of the valley. His early training as pilot of a Mississippi steamboat added tremendously to his knowledge of the river and its peoples. Finally, his native genius, and the varied experiences of his career as journalist and lecturer gave him the literary skill necessary to make his work successful.

With the bulk of Mark Twain's works we are not here concerned; nor need we consider, in general, his place in literature. But since no work, however accurately it may reproduce the spirit and aspect of an age, can survive unless it be truly literature, we must pay some attention not only to the content of the stories, but to the way in which they are written.

Mark Twain has written three great books upon the Mississippi valley. The first of these is "Life on the Mississippi," an account of his youthful experience as a pilot. The book concludes with a description of the author's return to the river, now almost deserted and wholly colorless. This conclusion, to a certain extent, mars the unity of the book, and, through its somewhat pessimistic tone, destroys something of the glamour and illusion of the first part. But it cannot be denied that the Mississippi book deserves high rank among Mark Twain's writings. It is amazingly complete; it touches upon the great river in a thousand different moods; it de-

scribes with rare feeling the many types which flocked to this
gigantic highway. It is personal, arising from the fund of
the author's own experience. Throughout it all there runs a
thread of humor, rarely coarse, rarely burlesque, as in his
"Connecticut Yankee." Humor, indeed, as someone has
sagely observed, is useful, like salt, as a preservative; like
salt, also, it is hardly in itself a suitable article of diet. In
all of those works of Mark Twain which will endure, there
is something behind the humor, a something which the humor
serves but to heighten and display. In "Life on the Mississippi" this quality is the fidelity of the description, the skill
with which the life of the past is brought before us—in a
word, it is the spirit of the Mississippi.

In his other stories of the valley, those two epics of boyhood, "Tom Sawyer" and "Huckleberry Finn," Mark Twain
is no less faithful to the land of his boyhood. "Tom Sawyer"
is a boys' book, with a singularly thrilling plot. "Huckleberry Finn," its sequel, is artistically greater. Huck's long
struggle between his heart and his conscience as to whether
he should hand over his friend, Nigger Jim, a runaway
slave, his final decision to "go to hell rather than give up
his friend," the flight to safety down the Mississippi—this
is the basis of an intensely interesting tale, a tale in which
the quiet humor and kindly philosophy of Mark Twain are
seen at their best. Throughout it all flows the great river,
now calm and smiling, now turbulent and remorseless, but
alluring ever.

One of the chief functions of literature has always been to
perpetualize the spirit of an epoch. Homer has given us the
fire and ardor of ancient Greece; Dante has breathed into a
single poem the whole meaning of the Middle Ages; Shakespeare has made the youth and freshness of Elizabethan
England eternal. In modern times, the sphere of creative
literature seems to have become more limited, less epic. The
literature of locality has arisen. Dickens and his London,

Hardy and his Wessex, Kipling and his India—all are examples of this tendency. They are more restricted in their
field than the older masters, but their appeal is none the less
universal. To their rank belongs Mark Twain. Much of his
work is rough, journalistic, filled with forced humor. But he 5
has caught the spirit, the romance of the Mississippi valley
of the past, and has made it deathless; he, too, is deathless.

KIM

For me, a lover and almost a worshiper of Rudyard Kipling, *Kim* has always held a peculiarly seductive charm. I have read reviews which criticized *Kim* viciously and pointed out its immeasurable inferiority to Kipling's shorter stories.
5 Be that as it may, I only intend to express my very humble admiration for the book. That it has faults I should never dare to deny, for every book has faults. To me, however, it has always seemed that its faults are few and that its admirable qualities are many.

10 The chief of these faults, to leave out matters of detail, is the lack of a sustained plot. Exciting at times and always lively, the plot is not steadily interesting. Kim's first journey with the lama, his life in barracks and afterwards at St. Xavier's, his later adventures with the lama and Hurree
15 Gus Chunder, the Babu, seem definitely separated from one another. The interest in the plot almost ceases at the end of each division. *Kim*, unlike some novels which are far inferior to it in other respects, has no suspended interest, gradually increasing until the climax. As far as plot is concerned,
20 then, the interest in *Kim* is not sustained.

This, however, may well be forgiven. For instead of this sort of interest, there is the much more charming interest of description and portrayal of character. For one who has read the book with the slightest appreciation of its beauties, the
25 descriptive passages have great fascination. The description of the Great Road of India, for instance, can hardly be surpassed. The color, glare, and glitter of Indian life leap forth into startling distinctness. It is no mere catalogue of details that is presented there: one sees the bright sun, and feels the
30 warm dust of the road between his toes. As the glamour of

the scene overcomes him he wishes to wander with these crowded thousands and to share forever their brilliant, improvident existence.

This, however, is mere external description. So too is the description of the Himalayas, magnificent as it is. One feels that a great deal of its beauty lies in the subject. It is in another scene, almost the last in the book, that the description reaches its climax. Kim, after weeks in bed, is at last allowed to come out. The whole outdoor scene, in its sleepy quietude, is warmed and brightened by a hot, glowing sun. The almost indescribable feeling of the convalescent, which most persons have known at one time or another, infuses the whole scene. I defy anyone who has experienced it to read this passage without again feeling that delicious languor, that sense of remoteness from the surroundings, and that serene, untroubled joy in being alive. Here Kipling has done more than describe externals; he has placed the reader within the character and made him hear, see, feel, smell, and even think as a convalescent. This is more than mere literary skill; it is genius.

This description naturally leads to the consideration of character portrayal, for it is more than half a character sketch in itself. Such touches abound in *Kim*. Even the characterization of the minor actors in the book is fascinating. A sentence, a phrase, or sometimes even a word, is enough to give us a swift view of the character. The English chaplain, unimportant as he is, belongs to us forever. We know by heart this wrong-headed, bigoted, honest old gentleman. The Babu, fat, fearful of pain, yet courageous in the face of death, is a real person. Every little quirk and turn of his nature is represented. We love profane, wicked, lying, treacherous, and faithful Malibub Ali, faults and all. The Maharanee, the Jat, that mysterious gentleman known as "E 23," and a score of others are not mere marionettes, but real flesh and blood people who live and breathe, and love and hate as naturally as our nearest and dearest friends.

Even more intensely human are the major characters of
the book. If not the greatest, Kimball O'Hara is the most
skilfully drawn. His situation is beyond a doubt original.
An Irish lad brought up among the lowest type of Orientals,
he is acted upon by opposite influences. His Irish ancestry
impels him to a life of adventure for its own sake, of violence for the joy of conflict; his Indian environment drags
him to a life of narrow quiet, of deceit as a means to an end.
His Occidental birth enforces late maturity; his Oriental
training tends toward an early manhood. One cannot give
even an outline of his character in a sentence. Suffice it to
say that he is the triumph of reconciling an Irish birth with
an Indian training, an hereditary tendency toward the open
fight with an environment tending toward deceit.

However, if Kim is the best drawn character of the book,
the greatest creation of character is Tathoo Lama, benevo-
lent, simple, kind, and good. He is a man who sees the mote
in his own eye, but disregards the beam in his brother's eye.
The dogmas of creed are nothing to him; the prejudices of
caste trouble him but little. He spends the declining years
of his life hunting for the "River of Healing which sprang
from the Arrow of our Lord Buddha." Tenderly he loves his
"Little Friend of all the World." Mightily he struggles to
free him from his fate. Truly one may say that here was a
man who reached the fitting consummation of a blameless
life when, at last, freed from the "Wheel," "he crossed his
hands upon his lap and smiled, as a man may who has won
salvation for himself and his beloved."

MODELS OF BIOGRAPHY

JOHN GILLEY[1]

Charles William Eliot

John Gilley's first venture was the purchase of a part of a
small coasting schooner called the *Preference*, which could
carry about one hundred tons, and cost between eight and
nine hundred dollars. He became responsible for one-third
of her value, paying down one or two hundred dollars, which 5
his father probably lent him. For the rest of the third he
obtained credit for a short time from the seller of the vessel.
The other two owners were men who belonged on Great Cran-
berry Island. The owners proceeded to use their purchase
during all the mild weather—perhaps six months of each 10
year—in carrying paving-stones to Boston. These stones,
unlike the present rectangular granite blocks, were smooth
cobblestones picked up on the outside beaches of the neigh-
boring islands. They of course were not found on any inland
or smooth-water beaches, but only where heavy waves rolled 15
the beach-stones up and down. The crew of the *Preference*
must therefore anchor her off an exposed beach, and then,
with a large dory, boat off to her the stones which they
picked up by hand. This work was possible only during
moderate weather. The stones must be of tolerably uniform 20
size, neither too large nor too small; and each one had to be
selected by the eye and picked up by the hand. When the
dory was loaded, it had to be lifted off the beach by the men
standing in the water, and rowed out to the vessel; and there

[1] From *John Gilley, Maine Farmer and Fisherman*, pp. 31–35, 62–72.
The American Unitarian Association, Boston, 1904. Copyright owned by
The Century Co., New York.

every single stone had to be picked up by hand and thrown on to the vessel. A hundred tons having been thus got aboard by sheer hard work of human muscle, the old craft, which was not too seaworthy, was sailed to Boston, to be discharged at what was then called the "Stone Wharf" in Charlestown. There the crew threw the stones out of her hold on to the wharf by hand. They therefore lifted and threw these hundred tons of stone three times at least before they were deposited on the city's wharf. The cobblestones were the main freight of the vessel; but she also carried dried fish to Boston, and fetched back goods to the island stores of the vicinity. Some of the island people bought their flour, sugar, dry-goods, and other family stores in Boston through the captain of the schooner. John Gilley soon began to go as captain, being sometimes accompanied by the other owners and sometimes by men on wages. He was noted among his neighbors for the care and good judgment with which he executed their various commissions, and he knew himself to be trusted by them. This business he followed for several years, paid off his debt to the seller of the schooner, and began to lay up money. It was an immense satisfaction to him to feel himself thus established in an honest business which he understood, and in which he was making his way. There are few solider satisfactions to be won in this world by anybody, in any condition of life. The scale of the business—large or small —makes little difference in the measure of content.

In 1884 the extreme western point of Sutton's Island was sold to a "Westerner," a professor in Harvard College, and shortly after a second sale in the same neighborhood was effected; but it was not until 1886 that John Gilley made his first sale of land for summering purposes. In the next year he made another sale, and in 1894 a third. The prices he obtained, though moderate compared with the prices charged at Bar Harbor or North-East Harbor, were forty or fifty times any price which had ever been put on his farm by the

acre. Being thus provided with what was for him a considerable amount of ready money, he did what all his like do
when they come into possession of ready money—he first
gave himself and his family the pleasure of enlarging and
improving his house and other buildings, and then lent the 5
balance on small mortgages on village real estate. Suddenly
he became a prosperous man, at ease, and a leader in his
world. Up to this time, since his second marriage, he had
merely earned a comfortable livelihood by diversified industry; but now he possessed a secured capital in addition to his 10
farm and his buildings. At last, he was highly content, but
nevertheless ready as ever for new undertakings. His mind
was active, and his eye and hand were steady.

When three cottages had stood for several years on the
eastern foreside of North-East Harbor,—the nearest point 15
of the shore of Mount Desert to Sutton's Island,—John
Gilley, at the age of seventy-one, undertook to deliver at
these houses milk, eggs, and fresh vegetables every day, and
chickens and fowls when they were wanted. This undertaking involved his rowing in all weathers nearly two miles from 20
his cove to the landings of these houses, and back again,
across bay waters which are protected indeed from the heavy
ocean swells, but are still able to produce what the natives
call "a big chop." Every morning he arrived with the utmost
punctuality, in rain or shine, calm or blow, and alone, unless 25
it blew heavily from the northwest (a head wind from Sutton's), or his little grandson—his mate, as he called the boy
—wanted to accompany him on a fine, still morning. Soon
he extended his trips to the western side of North-East Harbor, where he found a much larger market for his goods than 30
he had found thirty-five years before, when he first delivered
milk at Squire Kimball's tavern. This business involved
what was new work for John Gilley, namely, the raising of
fresh vegetables in much larger variety and quantity than he
was accustomed to. He entered on this new work with in- 35
terest and intelligence, but was of course sometimes defeated

in his plans by wet weather in spring, a drought in summer,
or by the worms and insects which unexpectedly attacked his
crops. On the whole he was decidedly successful in this enterprise undertaken at seventy-one. Those who bought of
him liked to deal with him, and he found in the business
fresh interest and pleasure. Not many men take up a new
out-of-door business at seventy, and carry it on successfully
by their own brains and muscles. It was one of the sources
of his satisfaction that he thus supplied the two daughters
who still lived at his house with a profitable outlet for their
energies. One of these—the school-teacher—was an excellent laundress, and the other was devoted to the work of the
house and the farm, and was helpful in her father's new
business. John Gilley transported the washes from North-
East Harbor and back again in his rowboat, and under the
new conditions of the place washing and ironing proved to be
more profitable than school-keeping.

In the fall of 1896 the family which had occupied that
summer one of the houses John Gilley was in the habit of
supplying with milk, eggs, and vegetables, and which had a
young child dependent on the milk, lingered after the other
summer households had departed. He consented to continue
his daily trips a few days into October that the child's milk
might not be changed, although it was perfectly clear that
his labor could not be adequately recompensed. On the last
morning but one that he was to come across from the island
to the harbor a strong northeast wind was blowing, and some
sea was running through the deep passage between Sutton's
Island and Bear Island, which he had to cross on his way to
and fro. He took with him in his boat the young man who
had been working for him on the farm the few weeks past.
They delivered the milk, crossed to the western side of
North-East Harbor, did some errands there, and started
cheerfully for home, as John Gilley had done from that shore
hundreds of times before. The boy rowed from a seat near
the bow, and the old man sat on the thwart near the stern,

facing the bow, and pushing his oars from him. They had
no thought of danger; but to ease the rowing they kept to
windward under Bear Island, and then pushed across the
deep channel, south by west, for the western point of Sutton's
Island. They were more than half-way across when, through 5
some inattention or lack of skill on the part of the young
man in the bow, a sea higher or swifter than the rest threw a
good deal of water into the boat. John Gilley immediately
began to bail, and told the rower to keep her head to the
waves. The overweighted boat was less manageable than 10
before, and in a moment another roller turned her completely
over. Both men clung to the boat and climbed on to her
bottom. She drifted away before the wind and sea toward
South-West Harbor. The oversetting of the boat had been
seen from both Bear Island and Sutton's Island; but it was 15
nearly three quarters of an hour before the rescuers could
reach the floating boat, and then the young man, though unconscious, was still clinging to the boat's keel, but the old
man, chilled by the cold water and stunned by the waves
which beat about his head, had lost his hold and sunk into 20
the sea. In half an hour John Gilley had passed from a
hearty and successful old age in this world, full of its legitimate interests and satisfactions, into the voiceless mystery of
death. No trace of his body was ever found. It disappeared
into the waters on which he had played and worked as boy 25
and man all his long and fortunate life. He left his family
well provided for, and full of gratitude and praise for his
honorable career and his sterling character.

This is the life of one of the forgotten millions. It contains no material for distinction, fame, or long remembrance; 30
but it does contain the material and present the scene for a
normal human development through mingled joy and sorrow,
labor and rest, adversity and success, and through the tender
loves of childhood, maturity, and age. We cannot but believe that it is just for countless quiet, simple lives like this 35
that God made and upholds this earth.

QUEEN VICTORIA[1]

Lytton Strachey

When all was over,[2] the Archbishop and the Lord Chamberlain ordered a carriage, and drove post-haste from Windsor to Kensington. They arrived at the Palace at five o'clock, and it was only with considerable difficulty that they gained
5 admittance. At six the Duchess woke up her daughter, and told her that the Archbishop of Canterbury and Lord Conyngham were there, and wished to see her. She got out of bed, put on her dressing-gown, and went, alone, into the room where the messengers were standing. Lord Conyngham fell
10 on his knees, and officially announced the death of the King; the Archbishop added some personal details. Looking at the bending, murmuring dignitaries before her, she knew that she was Queen of England. "Since it has pleased Providence," she wrote that day in her journal, "to place me in
15 this station, I shall do my utmost to fulfil my duty towards my country; I am very young, and perhaps in many, though not in all things, inexperienced, but I am sure, that very few have more real good will and more real desire to do what is fit and right than I have." But there was scant time for
20 resolutions and reflections. At once, affairs were thick upon her. Stockmar came to breakfast, and gave some good advice. She wrote a letter to her uncle Leopold, and a hurried note to her sister Feodora. A letter came from the Prime Minister, Lord Melbourne, announcing his approaching ar-
25 rival. He came at nine, in full court dress, and kissed her

[1] From *Queen Victoria*, pp. 68-70. Copyright, 1921, by Harcourt, Brace and Company, New York.

[2] The death of William IV, Victoria's predecessor.

hand. She saw him alone, and repeated to him the lesson
which, no doubt, the faithful Stockmar had taught her at
breakfast. "It has long been my intention to retain your
Lordship and the rest of the present Ministry at the head
of affairs"; whereupon Lord Melbourne again kissed her   5
hand and shortly after left her. She then wrote a letter of
condolence to Queen Adelaide. At eleven, Lord Melbourne
came again; and at half-past eleven she went downstairs into
the red saloon to hold her first Council. The great assembly
of lords and notables, bishops, generals, and Ministers of   10
State, saw the doors thrown open and a very short, very slim
girl in deep plain mourning come into the room alone and
move forward to her seat with extraordinary dignity and
grace; they saw a countenance, not beautiful, but prepossessing—fair hair, blue prominent eyes, a small curved nose, an   15
open mouth revealing the upper teeth, a tiny chin, a clear
complexion, and, over all, the strangely mingled signs of
innocence, of gravity, of youth, and of composure; they heard
a high unwavering voice reading aloud with perfect clarity;
and then, the ceremony over, they saw the small figure   20
rise and, with the same consummate grace, the same amazing
dignity, pass out from among them, as she had come in, alone.

SIR WILLIAM TEMPLE[1]

Thomas Babington Macaulay

To say of a man that he occupied a high position in times
of misgovernment, of corruption, of civil and religious fac-
tion, and that, nevertheless, he contracted no great stain, and
bore no part in any crime;—that he won the esteem of a
profligate court and of a turbulent people, without being
guilty of any great subserviency to either,—seems to be very
high praise; and all this may with truth be said of Temple.

Yet Temple is not a man to our taste. A temper not naturally good, but under strict command,—a constant regard to
decorum,—a rare caution in playing that mixed game of skill
and hazard, human life,—a disposition to be content with
small and certain winnings rather than go on doubling the
stake,—these seem to us to be the most remarkable features
of his character. This sort of moderation, when united, as
in him it was, with very considerable abilities, is, under ordinary circumstances, scarcely to be distinguished from the
highest and purest integrity; and yet may be perfectly
compatible with laxity of principle, with coldness of heart,
and with the most intense selfishness. Temple, we fear, had
not sufficient warmth and elevation of sentiment to deserve
the name of a virtuous man. He did not betray or oppress
his country: nay, he rendered considerable service to her;
but he risked nothing for her. No temptation which either
the King or the Opposition could hold out ever induced him
to come forward as the supporter either of arbitrary or of
factious measures. But he was most careful not to give offence by strenuously opposing such measures. He never put
himself prominently before the public eye, except at conjunc-

[1] From *Critical and Miscellaneous Essays*. Written in 1838.

tures when he was almost certain to gain, and could not possibly lose;—at conjunctures when the interest of the state, the views of the court, and the passions of the multitude all appeared for an instant to coincide. By judiciously availing himself of several of these rare moments, he succeeded in establishing a high character for wisdom and patriotism. When the favourable crisis was passed, he never risked the reputation which he had won. He avoided the great offices of state with a caution almost pusillanimous, and confined himself to quiet and secluded departments of public business, in which he could enjoy moderate but certain advantage without incurring envy. If the circumstances of the country became such that it was impossible to take any part in politics without some danger, he retired to his Library and his Orchard; and, while the nation groaned under oppression, or resounded with tumult and with the din of civil arms, amused himself by writing Memoirs and tying up Apricots. His political career bore some resemblance to the military career of Louis XIV. Louis, lest his royal dignity should be compromised by failure, never repaired to a siege, till it had been reported to him by the most skilful officers in his service that nothing could prevent the fall of the place. When this was ascertained, the monarch, in his helmet and cuirass, appeared among the tents, held councils of war, dictated the capitulation, received the keys, and then returned to Versailles to hear his flatterers repeat that Turenne had been beaten at Mariendal, that Condé had been forced to raise the siege of Arras, and that the only warrior whose glory had never been obscured by a single check was Louis the Great! Yet Condé and Turenne will always be considered captains of a very different order from the invincible Louis; and we must own that many statesmen who have committed very great faults, appear to us to be deserving of more esteem than the faultless Temple. For in truth his faultlessness is chiefly to be ascribed to his extreme dread of all responsibility;—to his determination rather to leave his country in a scrape than to run any chance of being in a scrape himself. He seems to have been averse from danger; and it must be admitted that the dangers to which a public man was exposed, in those days of conflicting tyranny and sedition, were of the most serious kind. He could not bear discomfort, bodily or mental. His lamentations when, in the course of his diplomatic journeys, he was put a little out of his way, and forced, in the vulgar phrase, to *rough* it, are quite amusing. He talks of riding a day or two on a bad Westphalian road, of sleeping on straw for one night, of travelling in winter when the snow lay on the ground, as if he had gone on an expedition to the North Pole or to the source of the Nile. This kind of valetudinarian effeminacy, this habit of coddling himself, appears in all parts of his conduct. He loved fame, but not with the love of an exalted and generous mind. He loved it as an end, not at all as a means;—as a personal luxury, not at all as an instrument of advantage to others. No wonder if such a person did little or nothing which deserves positive blame. But much more than this may justly be demanded of a man possessed of such abilities and placed in such a situation.

Of course a man is not bound to be a politician any more than he is bound to be a soldier; and there are perfectly honourable ways of quitting both politics and the military profession. But neither in the one way of life, nor in the other, is any man entitled to take all the sweet and leave all the sour. A man who belongs to the army only in time of peace,—who appears at reviews in Hyde Park, escorts the sovereign with the utmost valour and fidelity to and from the House of Lords, and retires as soon as he thinks it likely that he may be ordered on an expedition,—is justly thought to have disgraced himself. Some portion of the censure due to such a holiday-soldier may justly fall on the mere holiday-politician, who flinches from his duties as soon as those duties become difficult and disagreeable;—that is to say, as soon as it becomes peculiarly important that he should resolutely perform them.

THEODORE ROOSEVELT[1]

HENRY CABOT LODGE

Theodore Roosevelt always believed that character was of
greater worth and moment than anything else. He possessed
abilities of the first order, which he was disposed to under-
rate, because he set so much greater store upon the moral
qualities which we bring together under the single word 5
"character."

Let me speak first of his abilities. He had a powerful, well-
trained, ever-active mind. He thought clearly, independently, and with originality and imagination. These priceless
gifts were sustained by an extraordinary power of acquisi- 10
tion, joined to a greater quickness of apprehension, a greater
swiftness in seizing upon the essence of a question, than I
have ever happened to see in any other man. His reading
began with natural history, then went to general history, and
thence to the whole field of literature. He had a capacity 15
for concentration which enabled him to read with remarkable
rapidity anything which he took up, if only for a moment,
and which separated him for the time being from everything
going on about him. The subjects upon which he was well
and widely informed would, if enumerated, fill a large space, 20
and to this power of acquisition was united not only a tenacious but an extraordinary accurate memory. It was never
safe to contest with him on any question of fact or figures,
whether they related to the ancient Assyrians or to the
present-day conditions of the tribes of central Africa, to the 25

[1] From *Address in Honor of Theodore Roosevelt before the Congress
of the United States, Sunday, February 9, 1919*, pp. 40–56. Senate Docu-
ment No. 384, Washington, 1919.

Syracusan Expedition, as told by Thucydides, or to protective coloring in birds and animals. He knew and held details always at command, but he was not mastered by them.
He never failed to see the forest on account of the trees or
5 the city on account of the houses.

He made himself a writer, not only of occasional addresses
and essays, but of books. He had the trained thoroughness
of the historian, as he showed in his history of the War of 1812
and of the "Winning of the West," and nature had endowed
10 him with that most enviable of gifts, the faculty of narrative
and the art of the teller of tales. He knew how to weigh evidence in the historical scales and how to depict character.
He learned to write with great ease and fluency. He was
always vigorous, always energetic, always clear and forcible
15 in everything he wrote—nobody could ever misunderstand
him—and when he allowed himself time and his feelings were
deeply engaged he gave to the world many pages of beauty
as well as power, not only in thought but in form and style.
At the same time he made himself a public speaker, and here
20 again, through a practice probably unequaled in amount, he
became one of the most effective in all our history. In speaking, as in writing, he was always full of force and energy; he
drove home his arguments and never was misunderstood. In
many of his more carefully prepared addresses are to be
25 found passages of impressive eloquence, touched with imagination and instinct with grace and feeling.

He had a large capacity for administration, clearness of
vision, promptness in decision, and a thorough apprehension
of what constituted efficient organization. All the vast and
30 varied work which he accomplished could not have been done
unless he had had most exceptional natural abilities, but behind them, most important of all, was the driving force of an
intense energy and the ever-present belief that a man could
do what he willed to do. As he made himself an athlete, a
35 horseman, a good shot, a bold explorer, so he made himself
an exceptionally successful writer and speaker. Only a most

abnormal energy would have enabled him to enter and conquer in so many fields of intellectual achievement. But
something more than energy and determination is needed for
the largest success, especially in the world's high places. The
first requisite of leadership is ability to lead, and that ability 5
Theodore Roosevelt possessed in full measure. Whether in
a game or in the hunting field, in a fight or in politics, he
sought the front, where, as Webster once remarked, there is
always plenty of room for those who can get there. His
instinct was always to say "come" rather than "go," and he 10
had the talent of command.

His also was the rare gift of arresting attention sharply and
suddenly, a very precious attribute, and one easier to illustrate than to describe. This arresting power is like a common
experience, which we have all had on entering a picture gal- 15
lery, of seeing at once and before all others a single picture
among the many on the walls. For a moment you see nothing
else, although you may be surrounded with masterpieces. In
that particular picture lurks a strange, capturing, gripping
fascination as impalpable as it is unmistakable. Roosevelt 20
had this same arresting, fascinating quality. Whether in the
legislature at Albany, the Civil Service Commission at Washington, or the police commission in New York, whether in
the Spanish War or on the plains among the cowboys, he was
always vivid, at times startling, never to be overlooked. Nor 25
did this power stop here. He not only without effort or intention drew the eager attention of the people to himself, he
could also engage and fix their thoughts upon anything which
happened to interest him. It might be a man or a book,
reformed spelling or some large historical question, his travel- 30
ing library or the military preparation of the United States,
he had but to say, "See how interesting, how important, is
this man or this event," and thousands, even millions, of
people would reply, "We never thought of this before, but
it certainly is one of the most interesting, most absorbing 35
things in the world." He touched a subject and it sud-

denly began to glow as when the high-power electric current touches the metal and the white light starts forth and dazzles the onlooking eyes. We know the air played by the Pied Piper of Hamelin no better than we know why Theodore
5 Roosevelt thus drew the interest of men after him. We only know they followed wherever his insatiable activity of mind invited them..

Men follow also most readily a leader who is always there before them, clearly visible and just where they expect him.
10 They are especially eager to go forward with a man who never sounds a retreat. Roosevelt was always advancing, always struggling to make things better, to carry some much-needed reform, and help humanity to a larger chance, to a fairer condition, to a happier life. Moreover, he looked al-
15 ways for an ethical question. He was at his best when he was fighting the battle of right against wrong. He thought soundly and wisely upon questions of expediency or of polit-ical economy, but they did not rouse him or bring him the absorbed interest of the eternal conflict between good and
20 evil. Yet he was never impractical, never blinded by coun-sels of perfection, never seeking to make the better the enemy of the good. He wished to get the best, but he would strive for all that was possible even if it fell short of the highest at which he aimed. He studied the lessons of history, and did
25 not think the past bad simply because it was the past, or the new good solely because it was new. He sought to try all questions on their intrinsic merits, and that was why he suc-ceeded in advancing, in making government and society bet-ter, where others, who would be content with nothing less than
30 an abstract perfection, failed. He would never compromise a principle, but he was eminently tolerant of honest differences of opinion. He never hesitated to give generous credit where credit seemed due, whether to friend or opponent, and in this way he gathered recruits and yet never lost adherents.
35   The criticism most commonly made upon Theodore Roose-velt was that he was impulsive and impetuous; that he acted

without thinking. He would have been the last to claim infallibility. His head did not turn when fame came to him and choruses of admiration sounded in his ears, for he was neither vain nor credulous. He knew that he made mistakes, and never hesitated to admit them to be mistakes, and to correct them or put them behind him when satisfied that they were such. But he wasted no time in mourning, explaining, or vainly regretting them. It is also true that the middle way did not attract him. He was apt to go far, both in praise and censure, although nobody could analyze qualities and balance them justly in judging men better than he. He felt strongly, and as he had no concealments of any kind, he expressed himself in like manner. But vehemence is not violence, nor is earnestness anger, which a very wise man defined as a brief madness. It was all according to his nature, just as his eager cordiality in meeting men and women, his keen interest in other people's care or joys, was not assumed, as some persons thought who did not know him. It was all profoundly natural, it was all real, and in that way and in no other was he able to meet and greet his fellow men. He spoke out with the most unrestrained frankness at all times and in all companies. Not a day passed in the Presidency when he was not guilty of what the trained diplomatist would call indiscretions. But the frankness had its own reward. There never was a President whose confidence was so respected or with whom the barriers of honor which surround private conversation were more scrupulously observed. At the same time, when the public interest required, no man could be more wisely reticent. He was apt, it is true, to act suddenly and decisively, but it was a complete mistake to suppose that he therefore acted without thought or merely on a momentary impulse. When he had made up his mind he was resolute and unchanging, but he made up his mind only after much reflection, and there never was a President in the White House who consulted not only friends but political opponents and men of all kinds and conditions more than Theodore Roosevelt. When he had reached his conclusion he acted quickly and drove hard at his object, and this it was, probably, which gave an impression that he acted sometimes hastily and thoughtlessly, which was a complete misapprehension of the man. His action was emphatic, but emphasis implies reflection, not thoughtlessness. One can not even emphasize a word without a process, however slight, of mental differentiation.

Very many people, powerful elements in the community, regarded him at one time as a dangerous radical, bent upon overthrowing all the safeguards of society and planning to tear out the foundations of an ordered liberty. As a matter of fact, what Theodore Roosevelt was trying to do was to strengthen American society and American Government by demonstrating to the American people that he was aiming at a larger economic equality and a more generous industrial opportunity for all men, and that any combination of capital or of business, which threatened the control of the Government by the people who made it, was to be curbed and resisted, just as he would have resisted an enemy who tried to take possession of the city of Washington. He had no hostility to a man because he had been successful in business or because he had accumulated a fortune. If the man had been honestly successful and used his fortune wisely and beneficently, he was regarded by Theodore Roosevelt as a good citizen. The vulgar hatred of wealth found no place in his heart. He had but one standard, one test, and that was whether a man, rich or poor, was an honest man, a good citizen, and a good American. He tried men, whether they were men of "big business" or members of a labor union, by their deeds, and in no other way. The tyranny of anarchy and disorder, such as is now desolating Russia, was as hateful to him as any other tyranny, whether it came from an autocratic system like that of Germany or from the misuse of organized capital. Personally he believed in every man earning his own living, and he earned money and was glad to do so; but he had no desire or taste for making money, and he was entirely indifferent to it. The simplest of men in his own habits, the only thing he really would have liked to have done with ample wealth would have been to give freely to the many good objects which continually interested him.

Theodore Roosevelt's power, however, and the main source of all his achievement, was not in the offices which he held, for those offices were to him only opportunities, but in the extraordinary hold which he established and retained over great bodies of men. He had the largest personal following ever attained by any man in our history. I do not mean by this the following which comes from great political office or from party candidacy. There have been many men who have held the highest offices in our history by the votes of their fellow countrymen who have never had anything more than a very small personal following. By personal following is meant here that which supports and sustains and goes with a man simply because he is himself; a following which does not care whether their leader and chief is in office or out of office, which is with him and behind him because they, one and all, believe in him and love him and are ready to stand by him for the sole and simple reason that they have perfect faith that he will lead them where they wish and where they ought to go. This following Theodore Roosevelt had, as I have said, in a larger degree than anyone in our history, and the fact that he had it and what he did with it for the welfare of his fellow men have given him his great place and his lasting fame.

All men admire courage, and that he possessed in the highest degree. But he had also something larger and rarer than courage, in the ordinary acceptation of the word. When an assassin shot him at Milwaukee he was severely wounded; how severely he could not tell, but it might well have been mortal. He went on to the great meeting awaiting him and

there, bleeding, suffering, ignorant of his fate, but still un-
conquered, made his speech and went from the stage to the
hospital. What bore him up was the dauntless spirit which
could rise victorious over pain and darkness and the unknown
5 and meet the duty of the hour as if all were well. A spirit
like this awakens in all men more than admiration, it kindles
affection and appeals to every generous impulse.

Very different, but equally compelling, was another quality. There is nothing in human beings at once so sane and
10 so sympathetic as a sense of humor. This great gift the good
fairies conferred upon Theodore Roosevelt at his birth in
unstinted measure. No man ever had a more abundant sense
of humor—joyous, irrepressible humor—and it never deserted him. Even at the most serious and even perilous
15 moments if there was a gleam of humor anywhere he saw it
and rejoiced and helped himself with it over the rough places
and in the dark hour. He loved fun, loved to joke and
chaff, and, what is more uncommon, greatly enjoyed being
chaffed himself. His ready smile and contagious laugh made
20 countless friends and saved him from many an enmity.

He was very human and intensely American, and this knit
a bond between him and the American people which nothing
could ever break. And then he had yet one more attraction,
not so impressive, perhaps, as the others, but none the less
25 very important and very captivating. He never by any
chance bored the American people. They might laugh at him
or laugh with him, they might like what he said or dislike
it, they might agree with him or disagree with him, but they
were never wearied of him, and he never failed to interest
30 them. He was never heavy, laborious, or dull. If he had
made any effort to be always interesting and entertaining
he would have failed and been tiresome. He was unfailingly
attractive, because he was always perfectly natural and his
own unconscious self. And so all these things combined to
35 give him his hold upon the American people, not only upon

their minds, but upon their hearts and their instincts, which
nothing could ever weaken, and which made him one of the
most remarkable, as he was one of the strongest, characters
that the history of popular government can show. He was
also—and this is very revealing and explanatory, too, of his 5
vast popularity—a man of ideals. He did not expose them
daily on the roadside with language fluttering about them
like the Thibetan who ties his slip of paper to the prayer
wheel whirling in the wind. He kept his ideals to himself
until the hour of fulfillment arrived. Some of them were the 10
dreams of boyhood, from which he never departed, and
which I have seen him carry out shyly and yet thoroughly
and with intense personal satisfaction. He had a touch of
the knight errant in his daily life, although he would never
have admitted it; but it was there. It was not visible in the 15
medieval form of shining armor and dazzling tournaments,
but in the never-ceasing effort to help the poor and the oppressed, to defend and protect women and children, to right
the wronged and succor the downtrodden. Passing by on
the other side was not a mode of travel through life ever 20
possible to him; and yet he was as far distant from the professional philanthropist as could well be imagined, for all he
tried to do to help his fellow men he regarded as part of the
day's work to be done and not talked about. No man ever
prized sentiment or hated sentimentality more than he. He 25
preached unceasingly the familiar morals which lie at the
bottom of both family and public life. The blood of some
ancestral Scotch covenanter or of some Dutch reformed
preacher facing the tyranny of Philip of Spain was in his
veins, and with his large opportunities and his vast audiences 30
he was always ready to appeal for justice and righteousness.
But his own personal ideals he never attempted to thrust
upon the world until the day came when they were to be
translated into realities of action.

When the future historian traces Theodore Roosevelt's ex- 35
traordinary career he will find these embodied ideals planted

like milestones along the road over which he marched. They never left him. His ideal of public service was to be found in his life, and as his life drew to its close he had to meet his ideal of sacrifice face to face. All his sons went from him to
5 the war, and one was killed upon the field of honor. Of all the ideals that lift men up, the hardest to fulfill is the ideal of sacrifice. Theodore Roosevelt met it as he had all others and fulfilled it to the last jot of its terrible demands. His country asked the sacrifice and he gave it with solemn pride
10 and uncomplaining lips.

This is not the place to speak of his private life, but within that sacred circle no man was ever more blessed in the utter devotion of a noble wife and the passionate love of his children. The absolute purity and beauty of his family life tell
15 us why the pride and interest which his fellow countrymen felt in him were always touched with the warm light of love. In the home so dear to him, in his sleep, death came, and—

So Valiant-for-Truth passed over and all the trumpets sounded for him on the other side.

ABRAHAM LINCOLN[1]

Theodore Roosevelt

We have met here to celebrate the hundredth anniversary
of the birth of one of the two greatest Americans; of one of
the two or three greatest men of the nineteenth century; of
one of the greatest men in the world's history. This rail-
splitter, this boy who passed his ungainly youth in the dire ₅
poverty of the poorest of the frontier folk, whose rise was by
weary and painful labor, lived to lead his people through the
burning flames of a struggle from which the nation emerged,
purified as by fire, born anew to a loftier life.

After long years of iron effort, and of failure that came ₁₀
more often than victory, he at last rose to the leadership of
the Republic, at the moment when that leadership had
become the stupendous world-task of the time. He grew to
know greatness, but never ease. Success came to him, but
never happiness, save that which springs from doing well a ₁₅
painful and a vital task. Power was his, but not pleasure.
The furrows deepened on his brow, but his eyes were un-
dimmed by either hate or fear. His gaunt shoulders were
bowed, but his steel thews never faltered as he bore for a
burden the destinies of his people. His great and tender ₂₀
heart shrank from giving pain; and the task allotted him was
to pour out like water the life-blood of the young men, and
to feel in his every fibre the sorrow of the women. Disaster
saddened but never dismayed him.

As the red years of war went by they found him ever doing ₂₅
his duty in the present, ever facing the future with fearless

[1] Address delivered at Lincoln's birthplace, Hodgenville, Kentucky,
February 12, 1909. Reprinted from *Collier's Weekly*, February 13, 1909.

front, high of heart, and dauntless of soul. Unbroken by
hatred, unshaken by scorn, he worked and suffered for the
people. Triumph was his at the last; and barely had he
tasted it before murder found him, and the kindly, patient,
fearless eyes were closed forever.

As a people we are indeed beyond measure fortunate in the
characters of the two greatest of our public men, Washington
and Lincoln. Widely though they differed in externals, the
Virginia landed gentleman and the Kentucky backwoodsman, they were alike in essentials, they were alike in the
great qualities which made each able to do service to his nation and to all mankind such as no other man of his generation could or did render. Each had lofty ideals, but each
in striving to attain these lofty ideals was guided by the
soundest common sense. Each possessed inflexible courage
in adversity, and a soul wholly unspoiled by prosperity. Each
possessed all the gentler virtues commonly exhibited by good
men who lack rugged strength of character. Each possessed
also all the strong qualities commonly exhibited by those
towering masters of mankind who have too often shown
themselves devoid of so much as the understanding of the
words by which we signify the qualities of duty, of mercy,
of devotion to the right, of lofty disinterestedness in battling
for the good of others.

There have been other men as great and other men as
good; but in all the history of mankind there are no other
two great men as good as these, no other two good men as
great. Widely though the problems of to-day differ from the
problems set for solution to Washington when he founded
this nation, to Lincoln when he saved it and freed the slave,
yet the qualities they showed in meeting these problems are
exactly the same as those we should show in doing our
work to-day.

Lincoln saw into the future with the prophetic imagination usually vouchsafed only to the poet and the seer. He
had in him all the lift toward greatness of the visionary, with-

out any of the visionary's fanaticism or egotism, without any
of the visionary's narrow jealousy of the practical man and
inability to strive in practical fashion for the realization of
an ideal. He had the practical man's hard common sense
and willingness to adapt means to ends; but there was in 5
him none of that morbid growth of mind and soul which
blinds so many practical men to the higher aims of life. No
more practical man ever lived than this homely backwoods
idealist; but he had nothing in common with those practical
men whose consciences are warped until they fail to distin- 10
guish between good and evil, fail to understand that strength,
ability, shrewdness, whether in the world of business or of
politics, only serve to make their possessor a more noxious,
a more evil, member of the community if they are not guided
and controlled by a fine and high moral sense.   15

   We of this day must try to solve many social and industrial problems, requiring to an especial degree the combination of indomitable resolution with cool-headed sanity. We
can profit by the way in which Lincoln used both these traits
as he strove for reform. We can learn much of value from 20
the very attacks which following that course brought upon
his head, attacks alike by the extremists of revolution and
by the extremists of reaction. He never wavered in devotion
to his principles, in his love for the Union, and in his abhor-
rence of slavery. Timid and lukewarm people were always 25
denouncing him because he was too extreme; but as a matter
of fact he never went to extremes, he worked step by step;
and because of this the extremists hated and denounced him
with a fervor which now seems to us fantastic in its deifica-
tion of the unreal and the impossible. At the very time when 30
one side was holding him up as the apostle of social revolution because he was against slavery, the leading abolitionist
denounced him as the "slave hound of Illinois." When he
was the second time candidate for President, the majority of
his opponents attacked him because of what they termed his 35
extreme radicalism, while a minority threatened to bolt his

nomination because he was not radical enough. He had continually to check those who wished to go forward too fast, at the very time that he overrode the opposition of those who wished not to go forward at all. The goal was never dim before his vision; but he picked his way cautiously, without either halt or hurry, as he strode toward it, through such a morass of difficulty that no man of less courage would have attempted it, while it would surely have overwhelmed any man of judgment less serene.

Yet perhaps the most wonderful thing of all, and, from the standpoint of the America of to-day and of the future, the most vitally important, was the extraordinary way in which Lincoln could fight valiantly against what he deemed wrong and yet preserve undiminished his love and respect for the brother from whom he differed. In the hour of a triumph that would have turned any weaker man's head, in the heat of a struggle which spurred many a good man to dreadful vindictiveness, he said truthfully that so long as he had been in his office he had never willingly planted a thorn in any man's bosom, and besought his supporters to study the incidents of the trial through which they were passing as philosophy from which to learn wisdom and not as wrongs to be avenged; ending with the solemn exhortation that, as the strife was over, all should reunite in a common effort to save their common country.

He lived in days that were great and terrible, when brother fought against brother for what each sincerely deemed to be the right. In a contest so grim the strong men who alone can carry it through are rarely able to do justice to the deep convictions of those with whom they grapple in mortal strife. At such times men see through a glass darkly; to only the rarest and loftiest spirits is vouchsafed that clear vision which gradually comes to all, even the lesser, as the struggle fades into distance, and wounds are forgotten, and peace creeps back to the hearts that were hurt.

But to Lincoln was given this supreme vision. He did not
hate the man from whom he differed. Weakness was as foreign as wickedness to his strong, gentle nature; but his courage was of a quality so high that it needed no bolstering of
dark passion. He saw clearly that the same high qualities, 5
the same courage, and willingness for self-sacrifice, and devotion to the right as it was given them to see the right,
belonged both to the men of the North and to the men of the
South. As the years roll by, and as all of us, wherever we
dwell, grow to feel an equal pride in the valor and self- 10
devotion, alike of the men who wore the blue and the
men who wore the gray, so this whole nation will grow to
feel a peculiar sense of pride in the man whose blood was
shed for the union of his people and for the freedom of a
race; the lover of his country and of all mankind; the 15
mightiest of the mighty men who mastered the mighty days,
Abraham Lincoln.

STUDENTS' THEMES: BIOGRAPHY

SILAS BRITTINGHAM

"Yaas, suh, w'en the Wah closed, Ah was so good-fur-nothin' lazy that if Ah'd been in six foot o' water Ah'd a hollered fur a niggah to come fotch me a drink. All Ah wanted to do was to lie 'roun' on the grass an' listen to the
5 bullfrogs; yaas, suh, Ah was jest that lazy."

With such a prelude, musically drawled from a true South-ern heart, Silas Brittingham, argumentative philosopher, philologist, and theologian, customarily began the story of his life. It is true that he spoke somewhat hyperbolically
10 concerning the depth of the water, for Silas, barely five feet tall and a poor swimmer, would have been desiring the colored gentleman for other purposes: but concerning the degree of his laziness either then or later—who could doubt him after even a cursory inspection? His ragged felt hat of
15 the "Colonel" variety overshadowed his gleaming, rat-like eyes, whose brightness pierced a pair of dusty spectacles. The rest of his face was merely an aquiline nose and a scraggy, grey beard, here and there tinted by an excessive use of "'Lasses Plug" and "Ole Virginia." Below his beard,
20 a sordid flannel shirt lay open at the neck, and to the shirt were slovenly "gallused" a pair of baggy homespun trousers. Before his grass-toed, cowhide boots lay a con-fused pile of basket-slats, waiting his pleasure to be woven into bushel measures; but inasmuch as he was always ready
25 to lay aside work for conversation, the slats often waited until they were no longer pliant. As in the case of Socrates of old, not even the voice of Xantippe from within the house was sufficient to stir him, if someone was at hand to discuss

the sphericity of the earth, or to listen to his entertaining biography. Silas was surely what the world calls *lazy*.

There was no excellent reason, however, why he should have begun the story of his life with so candid an admission of this laziness. He might easily have gone back some few years to a more promising occasion than the close of the war; he might even have boasted that the only child of "Marse Tom" and "Missus Lottie" was not ushered into this world "unwept, unhonored, and unsung." But he chose rather to set aside those ante-bellum days as a short, sweet dream of his youth, too sacred for public exposure. He remembered seeing his father ride gayly away, as so many Southern fathers did; and after all the "niggahs" had left, he remembered having a decided inclination to do "nothin'," simply "nothin'."

But even "nothing'" becomes tiresome if pursued at too great length, and besides, Silas was neither a fowl of the air nor a beast of the field. So, packing together what few necessaries he could take with him, he left the deserted plantation in South Carolina and started northward towards Virginia. Everywhere he was received with such genuine cordiality as his father's friends, already "po' white trash," could afford. No one, however, with slaves gone, fields ravaged, and houses burned, knew how to aid or advise him. At last he came to the James River; and upon its muddy banks, near a little town, Port Norfolk, he found a farmer who was willing to "work him for his board and keep." "To work or not to work," soliloquized Silas with all the earnestness of Hamlet. He had never seen anyone but slaves work, and then only when they were forced to. Nevertheless, these were uncommon times; every arm was needed; laziness could not be tolerated—so Silas worked.

Long hours of weary labor caused Silas to slip away into almost total forgetfulness of an outside world. Yet in the midst of his afflictions he had two things which might have made him a famous statesman: the one, his Bible, which he

tried to read every Sunday; the other, on rainy days, a Lin-
colnian chance to go to school provided he would trudge
three miles of pathless fields each way. Notwithstanding
such a reasonable deterrent, he went as often as possible even
though he stood at the end of a long line because he could
not spell Mississippi in the following approved fashion:—

M-i-s, Mis, s-i-s, sis, Mis-sis, s-i-p, sip, Mis-sis-sip, p-i, pi,
Mis-sis-sip-pi ! ! !

Perseverance is the mother of success, and Silas was soon
able to spell not only Mississippi but "Chicaincrominico" as
well. Indeed, he became an authority on "sticklers," a president at spelling-bees, a philologist whom Roosevelt would
have shocked beyond recovery. Furthermore, he began to
commit long passages of the Bible to memory, so that he
might recite them to the farmer in the evening, when no
lamp was convenient. Some of them he did not understand,
but others thoroughly convinced him that many people,
Columbus and Drake especially, had been gravely mistaken.
For instance, does not God, himself, say that "the winds
blew from the four corners of the earth"?

"Now, does 'four courners' mean roun'?" Thus Silas
Brittingham, increasing in manhood, began to think deeply
if not always correctly.

Philosophical researches, however, are not known to assist one materially in guiding a plough. The farmer noticed
that there was a diminution of work in proportion as there
was an increase of knowledge; and inasmuch as he preferred
the ploughing to the researches, he and Silas agreed to dis-
solve their partnership. It was a fortunate move for them
both. The farmer, who was getting old and needed much
assistance, secured a laborer who was not troubled with
ponderous theories; while Silas, more and more philosophic,
now found time to fall in love. The future Xantippe, really
Mary Georges, was the daughter of one of those lucky but
not over-conscientious men who were "rebels" when "rebels"
were in the neighborhood, and "unions" when the "rebels"

were gone. Consequently, he still retained the greater part
of his property.

The happy day came at last, and Silas, strangely clad in
borrowed "togs," awaited Mary at the parson's. His hat, one
of those pearl-grey "high-silks," sank so low over his ears 5
that he must have looked like the Hatter of "Alice in Won-
derland." His coat and vest had declared hostile relations as
soon as he had put them on. His trousers were long enough
to make a quintuple fold. One thing and only one was
distinctly Silas—his brass-toed, cowhide boots. 10

"Ah sure was a joyful man that hour," said Silas afterwards. "The Bible says that the bridegroom rejoiceth over
the bride, and Ah know Ah did. Mah heart was pumpin' up
and down with gladness; yaas, suh, it was. Ah felt as if Ah
didn't want to do nothin' except set and look at Mary." 15

As one of the most important steps toward the fulfillment
of this desire, Silas withdrew his belongings to Mary's home,
where he immediately became installed as a member of the
family. The old folks, whose cup was now filled to the brim,
died conveniently, if such a thing may be said; for the lazi- 20
ness which Silas felt "w'en the Wah closed" had begun to
trouble him almost chronically. He needed leisure to read
his Bible, to consider the questions of nature, and occasionally to teach the passing children "a little som'thin' about
correct spellin'." 25

"Look here, chile," was his usual salutation from the
shady side of the house, where he sat surrounded by his weaving. "Come over heah an' tell me som'thin' 'bout your
schoolin'. Can you spell 'auroraborealis'? Naw, Ah don't
mean to jest say the letters,—anybody could do that—Ah 30
mean to *spell* it. Heah! Dan! Heah!—Ah wouldn't send
this purp to these heah modern schools.—If they tell you
that the earth's roun', you ask 'em to try holdin' a bucket o'
water upside down. If they tell you that the earth goes
'roun' the sun, you ask 'em 'bout Joshua w'en he tole the 35
sun to stan' still."

Now and then for a special favorite, who had managed to answer his questions satisfactorily, Silas would venture a cracked strain from some of the delightful pickaninny songs, which he had heard in the cabin quarters. The stories which
5 he interspersed among them were perhaps not so charmingly conceived as those of "Br'er Rabbit" and "Br'er Fox," but at any rate they teemed with vague superstitions which pleased the child's fanciful mind.

Thus it was that in spite of the persistent reproaches of
10 his "old wummon" and also her thrifty example, Silas gradually, unintentionally, but inevitably, degenerated into a rasping town-pump. Sometimes, indeed, he struggled to overthrow his established reputation. The world—his world— did not understand that he was born tired; and consequently,
15 just as ancient generations had considered Alcibiades a strange mixture of talents and evil, so modern generations considered Silas a fruitless product of wit and indolence. Still he fought against it, and during occasional periods, he succeeded in weaving an extra "bushel" once each week.
20 The forthcoming profits, together with such earnings as Mary was always contributing to the family credit, were bundled up in the indispensable shot-bags. At last, this rainy-day special reached those proportions when it began to give Silas some concern. To keep it under the old feather
25 bed seemed somewhat risky; on the other hand, to deposit it in a bank was too much like "laying up treasures on earth where moth and rust doth corrupt, and where thieves break through and steal." Furthermore, the complicated intricacies of a bank, the locking safe-door, the great books, the silent
30 men—all these worried Silas as much as his Biblical precept. Finally, however, he decided upon the bank. After convincing himself by two or three sudden appearances at the teller's window, that his money was always there when he wanted it, he began to view the exertions by which the sum had been
35 accumulated with over-appropriate satisfaction, and—accordingly—to diminish them. Once more he was truly lazy.

By this time Silas was becoming an old man. The children, always objects of his uncouth affection, offered him the reverence due a sage. Young men and women were entertained by his beliefs and stories. And even the older heads respected him for his sincerity. Meanwhile, the Fates were 5 spinning darker threads around his life. Mary, his hope, his inspiration, his solace, died suddenly. For a time, all was gloom; but the clouds lifted and Silas once more told the story of his life. He left off saying "w'en the Wah closed"; he changed it to "w'en me an' Mary were together." 10

LE PÈRE PUPPEY-GIRARD

Nature is a funny old dame, after all. She chooses a stagnant pool to house the soul of a lily; she gives to a crawling worm the after-glow of God's inspiration; and she shelters the greatest of hearts behind her most curious bodies. Just such a heart, and just such a funny old body did she choose for le Père Puppey-Girard.

If it hadn't been for his beard, you would have easily mistaken him for an overgrown brownie; for his round, little head was carefully placed on a round little body, which, in turn, was supported by a pair of round little legs. But you couldn't possibly have been so deceived; for who has ever heard of a brownie with a large, snow-white beard sticking straight out from his chin, like a challenge? And Puppey-Girard's beard certainly did stick straight out. I often used to wonder if it would bear the weight of a tea-kettle, filled—say—half full of tea. I am sure it was stiff enough to support an empty one. However, I never tried this experiment, for the old priest was very proud of his "white crop," as he called it. Besides, one look into his small wrinkled eyes would have quickly stayed my hand. Small eyes they were,—a quizzical blue in color; but a blue that could on occasion change to an illusive gray. And when they did change, a valorous man who knew his Shakespeare would make a hasty exit. For then his gentle mouth would compress itself into a thin line, and his white beard would stick out straighter than ever. Personally, I am glad that such occasions were not of frequent occurrence, because I loved him best when he was in truth a disciple of God—one who guided others into the paths he knew so well—paths of harmony, of justice, of truth.

I well remember the first time I benefited from his kindly interference. I had failed to pay my respects to one of the "adjudants" of our division, and when I finally went to apologize for my negligence the latter was very indignant. Although I did not realize it at the time, the crime that I had committed was very great, according to the dictates of French society, and "mon adjudant" was entirely French. He greeted me very coolly, asking me if all Americans were of my calibre. I naturally resented his manner of speaking, and told him so in what might be termed military English (or rather French). Thereupon we both became rigidly civil, and "mon adjudant" was just about to show me the way out —when in walked Puppey-Girard. He had been washing in the adjoining room, and his cheeks were rosy from the effects of cold water. His lips were framed in a gentle smile, and his eyes were quizzically blue.

"Well, my frien'," he exclaimed jovially, "at las' we 'ave Amérique come to la France, eh? For shame," pointing his finger playfully at my ribs, "for shame, zat you did not come more queekly, yong man—is it not, mon adjudant? But now, zat you air with us, we will not so easily let you go again. For—how is it you say?—for cha'tisemen', we will ponish you in making you drink some of our horrible French wine."

"Mon adjudant" looked somewhat shamefacedly over at the "yong man," and the "yong man" equally abashed looked over at "mon adjudant." We both smiled simultaneously, and then became profuse in our apologies and charitable pardons,—while Puppey-Girard laughed happily, so delighted at the success of his little ruse that he forgot for a moment his English, exclaiming "Voilà! les beaux anges ont bien travaillé!" (The good angels have done their work well.)

Later, when I came to know him better, I was often reminded of this little expression of his. Whenever he accomplished any especially difficult manœuvre he would always end with, "Les beaux anges ont bien travaillé!"—saying

it with such naïveté that it really seemed as if he did give all
the credit for the happy result he had brought about to the
good angels, who worked well in spite of mortal interference.
He also had another expression which he used invariably
5 when we were speaking of people whom we knew or had
heard of. "Tiens, je le connais!" (Why, I know him!) And
in fact he did know pretty nearly everyone that was worth
knowing.

One of the "ambulanciers" in our section learned, quite by
10 accident, that his brother was in Paris, and we were discussing his chances of getting into the city to see him, one night,
when Puppey-Girard happened in. He was immediately very
much excited.

"Monsieur Guillaume Crowley? Non! C'est impossible!
15 Your brother? Tiens, je le connais! Yes, he was at Sor-
bonne to study, before ze war, is it not? Oui, c'est ça! Well,
well! And you would go to Paris to see him? H-m-m. Ze
général, he and I, we air ver' good frien'. Qui sait? It might
be that it could be possibul."

20 A few days later the brother of "Monsieur Guillaume
Crowley" left for Paris, acting as special messenger from the
general of our division to general headquarters. But when
we went around to see the old priest, he only laughed joyfully,
saying in his naïve manner, "Oui, les beaux anges ont bien
25 travaillé!"

He had a much more serious work, however, when the
division was in the lines, and Death was constantly cutting
more notches in the handle of his swinging scythe. Then the
priest was constantly in the Red Cross stations, or out on the
30 field of battle, braving death himself so that he could help
other men to die. On such occasions I entirely forgot his
white beard. I saw only his eternal blue eyes, and his gentle
lips which muttered a constant prayer for everlasting salvation. I saw not his brownie-like figure, but the simple soul
35 of a being truly great. Strange as it may seem, however, my
most vivid memory-picture of him is not on the battle-field,

but afterwards, in one of those field-hospitals which the French had scattered every so often, about twelve miles behind the lines.

The incident was at the death-bed of one of the fellows in our section,—a wonderful chap who had made a heroic struggle for life, only to lose it.

"Am I really to die, then, Father?" he had asked finally.

"Well," said Puppey-Girard, "I do not know. If it be that God is ready to receive you, yes. But none of us can die until He is willing. We all have to wait our turn to be admitted to the Kingdom. The most important thing is for us to be ready to go to Him."

"I am ready. But it will seem long for Mother to wait."

"Oh, not so long; and think what a consolation it will be for her—to know that you are there, waiting to receive her when her turn comes." And they both united in "Notre Père qui est aux ciels," and Puppey-Girard performed the last consecrations that are observed before the dying enter upon the Higher Life.

Afterward, in speaking of our lost friend, the old priest was sadly reminiscent.

"Pauvre garçon, he died one of the most beautifully I did ever see. He—how do you say it—he resigned himself to his Mastaire with much courage and faith. You must write zat to his Muzzaire, pauvre femme! zat he died 'bon Chrétien'." He mused a while in silence, and then continued, "But he is locky. He has found his God—which is also my God, malgré que je suis Catholique."

Good old Puppey-Girard! Many's the time that I have thought of all your whimsical little sayings, your thoughtful little ruses to help others into the right path, and your queer little figure with your white beard that sticks straight out. Les beaux anges ont bien travaillé! Surely the good angels worked well, when they conceived your soul, even though they did choose such a funny little body in which to hide your great heart.

MODELS OF ARGUMENT

THE EXPENDITURE OF RICH MEN[1]

EDWIN LAWRENCE GODKIN

From the earliest times of which we have any historical knowledge rich men have had to exercise a good deal of ingenuity in expending their income. The old notion that wealth is desired for the sake of power was never completely
5 true. It has always been desired also, as a rule, for the sake of display. The cases have been rare in which rich men have been content to be secretly or unobtrusively rich. They have always wished people to know they were rich. It has, also, from the earliest times, been considered appropriate that
10 display should accompany power. A powerful man who was not wealthy and made no display, has, in all ages, been considered a strange, exceptional person. As soon as a man became powerful, the world has always thought it becoming that he should also be rich, and should furnish evidences of
15 his riches that would impress the popular imagination. As a rule, he has sought to make this impression. He has liked people at least to see what he could do if he would. Of course, except in the case of rulers, he could not put his money into armies or fleets. Consequently, as a private man,
20 he has put it into tangible, visible property, things which people could see and envy, or wonder over. A rich man who did not do this was always set down as a miser, or something very like it, in some way queer or eccentric. He, too, has been held bound to spend his money in ways in which

[1] From *Problems of Modern Democracy.* Copyright, 1896, by Charles Scribner's Sons, New York. By permission of the publishers.

the public in general expected him to spend it, and in which it had become usual for men of his kind to expend it. His expenditure was, therefore, in a certain sense, the product of the popular manners. If a man in England, for instance, expends money like a rich Turkish pacha, or Indian prince, he is frowned on or laughed at. But if he keeps a great racing-stable, or turns large tracts of land into a grouse moor or a deer forest, in which to amuse himself by killing wild animals, it is thought natural and simple.

But one of the odd things about wealth is the small impression the preachers and moralists have ever made about it. From the very earliest times its deceitfulness, its inability to produce happiness, its fertility in temptation, its want of connection with virtue and purity, have been among the commonplaces of religion and morality. Hesiod declaims against it, and exposes its bad effects on the character of its possessors, and Christ makes it exceedingly hard for the rich man to get to heaven. The folly of winning wealth or caring for it has a prominent place in mediæval theology. Since the Reformation there has not been so much declamation against it, but the rich man's position has always been held, even among Protestants, to be exceedingly perilous. His temptations might not be so great as they used to be, but his responsibilities were quadrupled. The modern philanthropic movement, in particular, has laid heavy burdens on him. He is now allowed to have wealth, but the ethical writers and the clergy supervise his expenditure closely. If he does not give freely for charitable objects, or for the support of institutions of beneficence, he is severely criticised. His stewardship is insisted on. In the Middle Ages this was his own lookout. If he endowed monasteries, or bequeathed foundations for widows, or old men, or orphans, it was with the view of making provision for his own soul in the future world, and did not stand much higher in morals or religion than that old English legacy for the expenses of burning heretics. But in our times he is expected to endow for love of his kind or country, and gifts for his soul's sake would be considered an expression of selfishness.

In Europe, as I have said, the association of displays of wealth with political power has lasted since states were founded. It was largely made possible in the ancient world through slavery. From what we know through architectural remains, or historic record, there was no length, in that world, to which a great man could not go in the display of his possessions. What we hear or see of Hadrian's villa, or Diocletian's palace at Spalatro, makes Versailles seem a mere bauble. The stories told of the villas of Lucullus, or Mæcenas, even if half true, show that our modern rich men know but little of the possibilities of luxury. Pliny's description of his own villa in his Letters shows that they were far more than half true, that not one of our modern rich men has done one-quarter of what he might have done for material enjoyment. Undoubtedly the non-existence of slavery has been the greatest check on his extravagance. Could he have the same absolute control over domestic servants, he would probably treat himself to more extraordinary varieties of luxury in the matter of habitation and clothing and equipages. The traditions of the Roman Empire in this matter perished with the Empire. When the modern rich man came into possession of the means and appliances of civilization, he found himself in a new world, in which it was vastly more difficult to secure steady, uncomplaining personal service, and in which money was harder to get hold of. But what was within his reach, he readily used. The mediæval noble all over Europe after the Renaissance, transferred himself to magnificent abodes, and surrounded himself with a small army of servants. But he did this in obedience, I will not say to public opinion, for there was no such thing, but to popular notions of the fitting. It was held, as I have said, but becoming that a man who occupied his political place, who counted for so much in the state, whose descent was considered so illustrious, who owned such vast tracts of land, should live in a very great house, and be followed by a great retinue, should have his gentlemen and pages, and his numerous servants to wait upon him. When Madame de Sévigné travelled in the seventeenth century to Paris from her château in the country, she went with two carriages, seven horses, and four men on horseback, and each carriage had four horses; yet she was only a person of moderate fortune. Madame de Montespan, when she went to Vichy, had six horses in her coach; another behind with six maids. Then she had two *fourgons*, or baggage-wagons, six mules, and a dozen men on horseback, forty-five persons in all. Once when Madame de Sévigné's son came home from the army, her man of business had fifteen hundred men under arms to receive him in the court of the château. When the Marquis de Lavardin came to see her, he had officers and guards and trumpets and twenty gentlemen. The Montmorencis and Rohans and Soubises and Colignys made still greater display. The same thing went on in England. The rich men lived and travelled surrounded by splendor, because they were really great men. They had power over hundreds and thousands of fortunes, if not of lives. They had a share in the government. They were largely above the law. "God Almighty," as a pious but well-born French woman said, "thought twice before damning one of them." Down to the end of the last century the enmity of a peer, as was recently remarked, was enough to ruin a man in England.

All this is now changed in Europe. As power has left the upper classes, display has ceased. To be quiet and unobserved is the mark of distinction. Women of Madame de Sévigné's rank travel in dark-colored little broughams. Peers in England are indistinguishable when they move about in public, from any one else. Distinction is sought in manners, in speech, in general simplicity of demeanor, rather than in show of any kind. An attempt to produce on anybody, high or low, any impression but one of envy, by sumptuousness of

living or equipage, would prove a total failure. It may be
said, without exaggeration, that the quietness of every description is now the "note" of the higher class in all countries
in Europe—quietness of manner, of voice, of dress, of equi-
5 pages, of, in short, nearly everything which brings them in
contact with their fellow-men. Comfort is the quest of the
"old nobility" generally. Ostentation is left to the newly
enriched, but there can hardly be a doubt that this is largely
due to loss of power. Wealth now means nothing but wealth.
10 The European noble was, in fact, everywhere but in Venice,
a great territorial lord. It was incumbent on him as a mark
of his position, as soon as he came out of his mediæval
"keep," to live in a great house, if only for purposes of
entertainment. His retinue required large accommodation;
15 his guests required more, and more still was added for the
needs of the popular imagination. But the system of which
he was the product, which made his château or mansion grow
out of the soil like his crops, was never transferred to this
country. The few large grants which marked our early his-
20 tory never brought forth large mansions or great retinues.
The great houses of that period, such as those of the Van
Rensselaers or Livingstons on the Hudson, or of the planters
on the James River, are simply moderate-sized mansions
which, on most estates in England or France, would be con-
25 sidered small. Hospitality was in none of them exercised
on anything like the European scale. None of them was
ever occupied by anybody who exercised anything more than
influence over his fellow-citizens. In fact most of them are
to-day mainly interesting as showing the pains taken to put
30 up comfortable abodes in what were then very out-of-the-
way places.

All this amounts to saying that the building of great
houses was, down to our own time, a really utilitarian mode
of spending wealth. It was intended to maintain and support
35 the influence of the ruling class by means which was sure to
impress the popular mind, and which the popular mind called

for. The great territorial owners had a recognized place in government and society, which demanded, at first a strong, and later, an extensive, dwelling-place. It was, in short, the product and indication of contemporary manners as dwelling-places generally are. If we travel through a country in which castles and fortified houses are numerous, as they used to be prior to the fourteenth century all over Europe, we conclude infallibly that the law is weak, and that neighbors make armed attacks on each other in the style described in the Paston Letters. If we find, coming down later, as in the Elizabethan period, strongholds abandoned for extensive and ornamental residences with plenty of unprotected windows, we conclude that the government is omnipotent and the great men live in peace. If we go through a democratic country like Switzerland, and find moderation in the size of houses and in the manner of living, the custom of the country, we conclude that the majority is in power, and that every man has his say in the management of the state. In short it may be truly said that dwelling-places, from the Indian's tepee up to the palace of the great noble, indicate, far more clearly than books or constitutions, the political and social condition of the country.

It is only of late years that we have had among us a class capable of equalling or outdoing the European aristocracy in wealth. American fortunes are now said to be greater than any of those of Europe, and nearly, if not quite, as numerous. But the rich American is face to face with a problem by which the European was not, and is not, troubled. He has to decide for himself, what is decided for the European by tradition, by custom, by descent, if not by responsibilities, how to spend his money. The old rich class in Europe may be said to inherit their obligations of every kind. When a man comes of age, if he inherits wealth, and is of what is called "good family," he finds settled for him the kind of house he shall live in, the number of horses and servants he shall keep, the extent to which he shall entertain. His in-

come is, in truth, already disposed of by will, or settlement, or custom. There are certain people he is expected to maintain in a certain way, a certain style in which he is to live. This has led to, what appears to the American, the curious
5 reluctance of the Englishman "to lay down his carriage." To certain families, houses, and properties, to certain social positions, in short, is attached the obligation of "keeping a carriage." It is one of the outward and visible signs of the owner's place in the state. To the American it is generally
10 a mere convenience, which some years he possesses and other years he does not, and the absence of which excites no remark among his neighbors. If an Englishman of a certain rank gives it up, it indicates the occurrence of a pecuniary catastrophe. It advertises misfortune to the world. It says that
15 he has been vanquished in a struggle, that his position is in danger, and his friends sympathize with him accordingly, partly because the women of his family do not, as with us, use public conveyances in the cities.

From all these responsibilities and suggestions the Ameri-
20 can, when he "makes his pile," is free. He can say for himself how the owner of millions in a country like this ought to live. He may have one servant, eat in the basement, sup on Sunday evenings on scalloped oysters, and sit in his shirtsleeves on his own stoop in a one-hundred-thousand-dollar
25 house, and nobody will make any remark. Or he may surround himself with lackeys, whom he treats as equals, and who teach him how the master of lackeys should behave, give gorgeous entertainments to other rich men like himself, at which his wife will eclipse in finery all other wives, and
30 nobody will express interest or surprise except people who long for invitations from him. Or he may, after a period of such luxury, "burst up," sell everything out, and go live in Orange or Flushing. Or his wife may "tire of housekeeping," and they may retire to an expensive apartment in the
35 Waldorf, or Savoy, after storing their furniture, or selling it at auction. What this indicates is simply that great wealth

has not yet entered into our manners. No rules have yet been drawn to guide wealthy Americans in their manner of life. Englishmen, Frenchmen, Prussians, Austrians, Swiss, of rank and of fortune, have ways of spending their money, notions of their own of what their position and personal dignity require. But nothing of the kind is yet national in America. The result is that we constantly see wealthy Americans travelling in Europe, without the slightest idea of what they will or ought to do next, except get rid of their money as fast as possible, by the payment of monstrous prices and monstrous fees, or the committal of other acts which to Europeans are simply vulgar eccentricities, but which our countrymen try to cover up by calling them "American" when "irrational" would be a more fitting appellation. Some of this confusion of mind is due, as Matthew Arnold has suggested in one of his letters, to the absence among us of an aristocracy to set an example of behavior to our rich men. In European countries the newly enriched drop easily into the ranks of the aristocracy by a mere process of imitation. They try to dress and behave in the same way, and though a little fun may be made of them at first, they and their sons soon disappear in the crowd.

Ours do not enjoy such an advantage. They have to be, therefore, their own models, and there are finesses of manners and points of view in an aristocracy which are rarely got hold of except by long contact. By aristocracy I do not mean simply rich or well-born people, but people who have studied and long practised the social art, which is simply another name for the art of being agreeable. The notion that it consists simply in being kindly, and doing pleasant things for people, and having plenty of money, is one of the American delusions. The social art, like all other arts, is only carried to perfection, or to high excellence, by people who carefully practise it, or pay great attention to it. It consists largely in what are called "minor morals," that is, in doing things in society which long custom has settled on as suitable

for the set of people with whom one associates. But it is full
of what seem trifles, and which often become absurd if practised as a branch of learning acquired out of books. Like a
large number of other things in civilized life, to be well prac-
5 tised it needs to be practised without thought, as something
one is bred to. It is better obtained from books, or by study,
than not at all, but it is most easily learned by observation.
Ease of manner, taste in dress, tone of voice, insight into the
ways of looking at small things of well-mannered people, are
10 most easily acquired by seeing them in others. The benefit
of watching adepts in this art have been enjoyed by but few
rich men in America, and the result is that the rich world
with us can hardly be called a social world at all. There can
hardly be said to be among us what is called in Europe a
15 "world" or "monde," in which there is a stock of common
traditional manners and topics and interests, which men and
women have derived from their parents, and a common mode
of behavior which has assumed an air of sanctity. Our very
rich people are generally simply rich people with everything
20 in the way of social life to learn, but with a desire to learn
which is kept in check by the general belief in the community
that they have nothing at all to learn, and that it is enough
to be rich.

That, under these circumstances, they should, in somewhat
25 slavish imitation of Europe, choose the most conspicuous
European mode of asserting social supremacy, the building
of great houses, is not surprising. But in this imitation they
make two radical mistakes. They want the two principal
reasons for European great houses. One is that great houses
30 are in Europe signs either of great territorial possessions, or
of the practice of hospitality on a scale unknown among us.
A very large house in the country in Europe indicates either
that the owner is the possessor of great estates, or that he
means to draw on some great capital for a large body of
35 guests whom he will amuse by field sports out-of-doors, or
who will amuse each other in-doors. These are the excuses

for great houses in England, France, or Austria. The owner is a great landholder, and has in this way from time immemorial given notice of the fact. Or he is the centre of a large circle of men and women who have practised the social art, who know how to idle and have the means to idle, can talk to each other so as to entertain each other, about sport, or art, or literature, or politics, are, in short, glad to meet each other in luxurious surroundings.

No such conditions exist in America. In the first place, we have no great landholders, and there is no popular recognition of the fact that a great landowner, or great man of any sort, needs a great house. In the second place, we have no capital to draw on for a large company of men and women who will amuse each other in a social way, even from Friday to Monday. The absence of anything we can call society, that is, the union of wealth and culture in the same persons, in all the large American cities, except possibly Boston, is one of the marked and remarkable features of our time. It is, therefore, naturally what one might expect, that we rarely hear of Americans figuring in cultivated circles in England. Those who go there with social aspirations desire most to get into what is called "the Prince of Wales's set," in which their national peculiarities furnish great amusement among a class of people to whom amusement is the main thing. It would be easy enough to fill forty or fifty rooms from "Friday to Monday" in a house near New York or Boston. But what kind of company would it be? How many of the guests would have anything to say to each other? Suppose "stocks" to be ruled out, where would the topics of conversation be found? Would there be much to talk about except the size of the host's fortune, and that of some other persons present? How many of the men would wish to sit with the ladies in the evening and participate with them in conversation? Would the host attempt two such gatherings, without abandoning his efforts in disgust, selling out the whole concern, and going to Europe?

One fatal difficulty in the way of such modes of hospitality with us is the difference of social culture between our men and women. As a rule, in the European circle called "society" the men and women are interested in the same topics,
5 and these topics are entirely outside what is called "business"; they are literary or artistic, or in some degree intellectual, or else sporting. With us such topics are left almost entirely to women. Whatever is done among us for real society is done by women. It is they, as a general rule, who
10 have opinions about music, or the drama, or literature, or philosophy, or dress, or art. It is they who have reflected on these things, who know something and have something to say about them. It is a rare thing for husbands or sons to share in these interests. For the most part they care little
15 about them; they go into no society but dinners, and at dinners they talk stocks and money. A meeting of women for discussion on such subjects would be a dreadful bore to them. The husband feels better employed in making money for his wife and daughters to spend seeing the sights abroad.
20 This difference in the culture of the sexes, and in the practice of the social art, is in fact so great in some parts of the country as to make happy marriages rare or brief. It makes immense houses, with many chambers, in town or country, almost an absurdity in our present stage of progress.

25   Another, and the most serious reason against spending money in America in building great dwelling-houses, is, as I have already indicated, that the dwellings of leading men in every country should be in some sort of accord with the national manners. If there be what is called a "note" in
30 American polity, it is equality of conditions, that there should neither be an immoderate display of wealth, nor of poverty, that no man should be raised so far above the generality in outward seeming as to excite either envy, hatred, or malice; that, above all things, wealth should not become
35 an object of apprehension. We undoubtedly owe to suspicion and dislike of great wealth and displays of it, the Bryan

platform, with its absurdities and its atrocities. The accumulation of great fortunes since the war, honestly it may
be, but in ways mysterious or unknown to the plain man, has
introduced among us the greatest of European curses—class
hatred, the feeling among one large body of the community 5
that they are being cheated or oppressed by another body.
To erect "palatial abodes" is to flaunt in the faces of the
poor and the unsuccessful and greedy the most conspicuous
possible evidence that the owner not only has enormous
amounts of money, but does not know what to do with it. 10
We know that from the earliest times there has not been,
and we know that there is not now, the smallest popular
dislike to the successful man's "living like a gentleman," as
the saying is, that is, with quiet comfort, and with a reasonable amount of personal attendance. But the popular gall 15
rises when an American citizen appears, in the character of a
Montmorenci, or a Noailles, or a Westminster, in a gorgeous
palace, at the head of a large army of foreign lackeys. They
ask themselves what does this mean? Whither are we tending? Is it possible we are about to renew on this soil, at the 20
end of the nineteenth century, the extravagances and follies
of the later Roman Empire and of the age of Louis XIV?
What it does mean, in most cases, is simply that the citizen
has more money than he finds it easy to dispose of. Consequently the only thing he can think of is building a residence 25
for himself, which, like Versailles, shall astonish the world,
if in no other way, by its cost.

All this may be said without denying in the least the great
liberality of American millionaires. What colleges, schools,
museums, and charities owe to them is something new in the 30
history of the world. They have set Europe an example in
this matter which is one of the glories of America. It is a
pity to have them lessen its effect or turn attention away
from it, by extravagance or frivolity, the more so because
there is a mode still open to them of getting rid of cumber- 35
some money, which is untried, and is full of honest fame and

endless memory. We mean the beautifying of our cities with
monuments and buildings. This should really be, and, I
believe, will eventually become, the American way of *dis-*
playing wealth. Considering what our wealth is and what
the burden of our taxation is, and, as shown by the Chicago
Exhibition, what the capabilities of our native architecture
are, the condition of our leading cities as regards monuments
of sculpture or architecture, is one of the sorrowful wonders
of our condition. We are enormously rich, but except one or
two things, like the Boston Library and the Washington
public buildings, what have we to show? Almost nothing.
Ugliness from the artistic point of view is the mark of all our
cities. The stranger looks through them in vain for anything
but population and hotels. No arches, no great churches, no
courthouses, no city halls, no statues, no tombs, no municipal splendors of any description, nothing but huge inns.

I fear, too, of this poverty we are not likely soon to be rid,
owing to the character of the government. It will always,
under the régime of universal suffrage, be difficult in any city
to get the average tax-payer to do much for art, or to allow
art, as we see in the case of the Sherman Monument, to be
made anything but the expression of his own admiration for
somebody. It is almost impossible to prevent monuments or
buildings being jobs or caricatures, through the play of popular politics on a subject which was no more meant for its
treatment by majorities than the standard of value. Governments in all European countries do much for art. They erect
fine public buildings under the best artistic conditions. They
endow and maintain picture-galleries and museums. In fact
the cultivation of art is one of their accepted functions.
Nothing of the kind is known among us. It would infuriate
Populists and Bryanites to know that our Treasury was putting tens of thousands of dollars into books and paintings, or
bric-à-brac, or even into art-education. An École des Beaux
Arts, or National Gallery, seems to be an impossibility for
us. Whatever is done for beauty in America, must, it seems,

at least for a long time to come, be done by private munifi-
cence. If we are to have noble arches, or gateways, or buildings, or monuments of any description, if our cities are to
have other attractions than large hotels, it is evident our rich
men must be induced to use for this purpose the wealth which 5
it seems often to puzzle them to spend. Such works would
be a far more striking evidence of the owner's opulence than
any private palace, would give his name a perpetuity which
can never be got from a private house, and would rid him
completely from the imputation of selfishness. For our ex- 10
perience with regard to great houses, hitherto, is that the
children of the men who cause them to be built rarely wish
to live in them, and often have not the means to do so. Such
buildings become after their death either hotels or some kind
of charitable institutions. They are in no sense memorials 15
in men's minds of anything but somebody's folly or extravagance. All they say to coming generations, if they are not
pulled down, is that So-and-so made a fortune.

In erecting public monuments a rich man would have the
great advantage of doing what he pleased. If the thing were 20
more than a building, were, for instance, an arch or a fountain, all he would have to get from the public would be permission to build, which would be seldom difficult. To obtain
from a popular government large expenditure of money in a
way which artists would approve, especially a government 25
resting on a public as little instructed in art matters as ours,
is likely to be for a long time to come at least almost an impossibility. Men in office are rarely experts in such matters,
and if thoroughly honest, are apt to plume themselves on
their economy and rigid devotion to utility, rather than on 30
any regard for beauty. The banker in New York who refused, some time ago, to give in aid of an Academy of Design,
money which might be used, he said, in setting "a young man
up in the grocery business," fairly represented the state of
mind of any official class which we are likely to have for a 35
good while. Our reliance for the ornamentation of the new

world must therefore be mainly on our rich men. They can choose their subject and their architect, without let or hindrance, and they have thus far shown themselves fully alive to the value of professional advice and criticism. They have, in fact, before them a wonderful opportunity, of which we trust the next generation at least will avail itself, without servile imitation of a society which is passing away in the places in which history produced it.

TOO MUCH SOFT COAL[1]

Malcolm Keir

Too much coal, too many miners, too little storage—these nine words tell the story of our soft coal-industry.

Beginning every December and continuing through January and February a flood of orders calling for forty millions of tons of coal per month pours in upon coal operators. Unprepared for such an avalanche of business, the operators raise the price of coal at the mine sometimes as much as two dollars a ton over the November figures. This begins the evil of too much coal. More than thirty of our forty-eight states boast workable coal deposits, many of which are so near the surface that anyone can mine them as easily as digging sand. The high winter price tempts scores of owners of coal banks into the mining business. Unfortunately they cannot go out of the industry when the demand and price of coal drops in the spring and summer. Expensive machinery has been installed, the interest on which runs regardless of coal output; pumping of gas, water, and air must be continued without reference to the number of men in the mine; a new tax rating has been incurred payable only in coal mined; and men have been hired, who, being skilled and hard to get, must be maintained. Hence the coal industry equipped to carrying the peak winter demand keeps on getting out coal haphazardly during the spring and summer. There are more than 5000 soft-coal operators in the country and their average output fluctuates around 400 tons per day, while sixty per cent of the operators employ less than twenty men. The yearly capacity of these 5000 operators is

[1] An editorial in the *Boston Herald*, March 24, 1922.

250,000,000 tons of coal in excess of the normal yearly consumption. In other words, the country could get all the coal it needs a year with a third less mining capacity provided the mines operated regularly week by week.

5   We cannot drain off the surplus coal in foreign trade as Great Britain does because our deep-sea traffic is differently organized. She imports heavy, bulky raw materials, and uses her coal as a counterbalancing outbound cargo. On the other hand, our imports are small, light and valuable, while our
10 exports are too much of the bulky sort, such as grain, cotton and oil. To export coal would add to our already unbalanced foreign trade. Furthermore our coal mines are from 150 to 375 miles inland, while none of the British mines are more than twenty miles from the coast. Neither our coal nor
15 our shipping industry is organized to take care of an extensive international coal traffic. In proportion to coal mines, the British foreign trade in coal is twelve times ours. Hence our excessive coal capacity has almost no outlet except the domestic market. This means that it is impossible to work
20 all of our mines all the time. Last year there were thirty-three weeks when the mines ran only forty per cent of full time, and at no time was the operation more than seventy per cent of full time.

   Since the mines are manned to carry the winter peak de-
25 mand, it follows that every miner suffers from slack work through a third or more of every working year. If each mine put in eight hours for six days during fifty weeks, our normal coal consumption could be supplied by 175,000 fewer miners, which indicates how extravagant in labor power our mining
30 industry is. The miners have lost an average of ninety-three days in the last thirty years; in 1919 they lost 113 days, in 1920 they lost 84 days, and last year 138 days. Wages per day worked therefore must be high. In Illinois, where the average mine wage is $9.76 per day, the yearly income is
35 less than $1000. Against the advice of their leaders and their scale committee the miners voted their demand for a five-day

week of thirty hours, which is intended to distribute the job more completely over the year, and to "make work" for many thousands of excess miners.

The railroads also suffer from existing conditions. For the enormous winter demand they are a third under-equipped, and the strain falls upon them at just the season when transportation is most hampered by weather. For the light coal traffic of the summer, the railroads are a third over-equipped, cars standing idly on sidings wasting capital. Since soft coal is the largest single item in railroad freight revenue, these things are vital.

Regularization is what the soft-coal industry needs. Of all the means of getting regularity, storage is that most often suggested; not at the mine, where there is no room for it, nor intermediately, because that would not solve winter transportation, but vast storage at the point of consumption. That a technical problem to overcome spontaneous fires in coal piles is involved should prove no permanent obstacle to a necessary reform. Until the soft-coal industry is reorganized we may expect trouble to breed within it.

It is, however, a difficulty not yet solved, and no dealer will undertake to carry any great amounts of bituminous coal in storage until it is solved.

The soft-coal industry is over-developed and overmanned. A strike will not help at all to bring about that reconstruction on an efficiency basis which the industry needs.

AMERICA'S RAILWAY FALLACY[1]

Samuel Orace Dunn

The present policy of Government regulation of railroads
and other public utilities is firmly established in the United
States. Most people strongly believe in it. Therefore, they
will react unfavorably to an indictment charging that it is
5 based mainly on a gross fallacy; that for this reason it has
done great and unnecessary harm; and that unless it is re-
built on a sound foundation it will in time do incalculable
injury to every kind of business and every class of people
in this country. It is, however, the purpose of the present
10 article to draw and to prove an indictment making these
very charges.

I do not attack all Government regulation of railroads and
public utilities; but I do attack the prevalent policy of regulation as being based mainly on a wholly unsound principle,
15 and as being not only not in the interest of the public, but a
menace to the welfare of the people of the United States.

Persons and concerns in business in this country are
divided by our law, as interpreted by the courts, into two
classes—one composed of those that are held to render serv-
20 ices which are "affected with a public use"; the other composed of those whose businesses are not "affected with a
public use."

Nobody questions the soundness of the distinction made
by the courts. But a legal principle, and a principle of eco-
25 nomics or public policy, are two entirely different things.
Our lawmakers and administrative commissions and the public have ignored the wide difference between them; and this

[1] From the *North American Review* (June, 1922), Vol. 215, No. 6, pp. 721 ff.

it is which has caused the upbuilding of our present huge
system of Government regulation of public service concerns
upon the shifting sands of fallacy. What is this gross fallacy
on which it is founded? To answer that question it will first
be necessary to review certain decisions of our courts.   5

The Supreme Court of the United States in the "Granger"
cases of the 'seventies established the principle that the States
had power to regulate the rates charged by a concern engaged
in a business "affected with a public use." It was later settled that the Federal Government had like power if the   10
concern did an interstate business. No court has attempted
to enumerate all the kinds of concerns that render a "public service" and whose business is "affected with a public
use," but, of course, railroads and public utilities are the
principal ones.   15

The courts made clear in these early decisions that the
power of Government to regulate the rates of public service
concerns grew out of the fact that these concerns were monopolistic or quasi-monopolistic in their nature, and therefore, in the absence of regulation, could and probably would   20
charge the public excessive rates, and make exorbitant profits. The principle that Government could regulate was established to protect the public from such extortion.

The States in succeeding years passed laws drastically
reducing the rates of railways and other public service con-   25
cerns. The courts then established another important principle which was intended to protect public service concerns
themselves from extortion by the public. They found that the
rates fixed in certain instances rendered the companies unable to earn any return upon their investment. They held   30
that this was in violation of the constitutional provisions
which forbid private property to be taken for public use
without due process of law or just compensation. They
laid down the principle that while the rates of concerns engaged in rendering a public service were subject to regula-   35
tion, they could not constitutionally be so regulated as to

deprive the owners of a fair return upon the fair value of
their existing property, because this would be confiscation.

Now, these decisions of the courts settled only the legal
question of what the State and National Governments had
5 power to do. They did not settle, or say, or imply, what, in
the public interest, it would be wise for the Governments to
do. They settled what could be done with property already
in existence. They had no relation whatever to what ought
to be or must be done to induce private capital to bring more
10 of the same kind of property into existence. Courts determine questions of law, not questions of public expediency;
and what ought to be done to further the interests of the
public was and is a question, not of law, but of economics
and public policy.

15 Nevertheless, most of the public and most public men,
apparently without detecting any fallacy in their reasoning,
jumped to the conclusion that what the courts had held was
the extreme limit beyond which Government regulation of
public service concerns could not constitutionally be carried,
20 was also the very limit to which, in the public interest, it
ought to be pressed. The courts had held that the rates and
net return of a railway, for example, could constitutionally
be reduced to the very lowest level which would not involve
actual confiscation of its existing property, but no further.
25 Our lawmakers and regulating commissions, with the sanc-
tion of public sentiment, proceeded rapidly, as a matter of
public policy, to establish and build up a system of regulation, the main purpose and effect of which have been and are
now to restrict the net returns of railroads to the lowest level
30 which will not involve confiscation.

When one criticizes this policy he is invariably met with
the answer that railways are engaged in rendering a public
service and, therefore, ought to be so regulated. That statement expresses the great American fallacy. The courts may
35 hold that rates which yield a net return of five or six per cent
upon the valuation of a concern do not involve confiscation

of its existing property. That settles the law; rates that will yield only five or six per cent may then legally be fixed and enforced. But it does not settle or have anything to do with the question of what return it is to the public interest that the concern should be allowed to earn. The Government is held by the courts to have many powers. It is held, for example, to have a practically unlimited power to tax. But nobody ever uses the fallacious argument that because the Government's power to tax is practically unlimited it ought to impose practically unlimited taxes. Why then, say, that because the Government has the constitutional power to reduce the rates and net returns of public service concerns to a level where confiscation will be barely avoided, it is the Government's duty to the public to do this?

It is the Government's duty to the owners of the existing property of a public service concern not to confiscate it. But it is also the Government's duty to the public to follow a policy which will permit and encourage such improvement and enlargement of a public service concern's property as will enable it to render as much better and as much more service as the public needs. Now, the measure of what return will not confiscate the existing property is not, never was and never will be the measure of what return the company must earn to be able adequately to improve and enlarge its property. A return of five or six per cent may not be confiscatory of the existing property; but at the same time a return of eight or ten per cent may be necessary to enable it to raise enough additional capital to provide necessary additional service. In that case, for the Government to restrict it to five or six per cent directly injures the public, by preventing the concern from providing needed service. The fact, however, that, as a matter of public policy, any limit except that of confiscation should ever be set to regulation, has never been recognized in any regulatory law passed in this country except the Transportation Act. This act requires the Interstate Commerce Commission in fixing rates to consider the public's need for adequate transportation; but strenuous efforts are now being made to repeal even this provision on the ground that it tends to make rates high.

Let us now take up the very practical question of what effects actually have been and are being produced because those who have passed and administered our regulating laws have failed to recognize the broad distinction between (1) the way the courts have held the Government can regulate public service concerns, and (2) the way sound principles of economics and public policy dictate that it should regulate them.

On one side we have that large class of persons and concerns that are engaged in agricultural, mining, manufacturing, mercantile and financial pursuits, and that are held not to be engaged in rendering public services, and, therefore, not subject to regulation. Many of them produce commodities or render services that are necessary; but they include all those that provide us with luxuries. They include those that build passenger automobiles, those that provide "movies" and cigarettes, those that make silk shirts, jewelry, cosmetics and chewing gum. I do not mention these particular industries of luxury in any spirit of depreciation or criticism whatever, but merely as specific illustrations that throw light on our governmental policy. All these concerns that are held not to render any public service are free to add to the capitalizations of their actual investments as much water as they like. Neither Government nor public sentiment will protest. They are free to make any profit they can. It may be six per cent, or it may be 600 per cent. The more it is, the more the public admires and applauds. Some of the very largest fortunes in the country have been built up from nothing in a very few years in these industries of luxury.

Concerns not engaged in rendering a public service may pay any salaries they please. A Postmaster-General of the United States recently has accepted from the moving picture industry a salary twice as large as that paid to any railroad

president in this country. One of our larger steel companies
pays its president a salary greater than the combined salaries
of any dozen of our railway presidents. Does not the public,
when it buys·the product or service of a concern that is not
engaged in a public service, pay the profits it makes or the
salaries of its officers, just as truly as it pays those of concerns held to be engaged in a public service?

We have looked upon that picture; now look upon this.
On this side we have all those enterprises that are engaged in
rendering what are called "public services": railroads, street
railways, electric light and power companies, gas companies,
etc. The courts held that because of their monopolistic or
quasi-monopolistic nature they might charge the public excessive rates and make exorbitant profits, and that therefore
they were subject to regulation of their charges. On this
foundation we have built a system of regulation which has
made public service concerns, and especially railway and
traction companies, the Ishmaels of the business world. We
jumped to the utterly fallacious conclusion that the only way
to make sure their rates would always be reasonable was to
restrict their net returns as much as the courts would allow.
It was decided that in order adequately to control their net
returns, they must be prevented from issuing any securities
except those representing actual investment. Knowing that
in many instances the outstanding securities do not represent
actual investment, we have developed elaborate engineering
and accounting methods of evaluating their physical properties; and we exhaust our ingenuity in devising means of so
regulating their rates as to keep their net returns on these
valuations just as low as the courts will not hold confiscatory.

In the case of the railroads, regulation originally intended
merely to protect the public from extortion has been extended
to almost every detail of their business, including the wages
and working conditions of their employees. It has not yet
reached the salaries of their higher officers; but these, although small compared with the incomes of men of equal

ability and responsibilities connected with other large concerns, have become the objects of constant attack; and recently a bill was introduced in Congress to fix a maximum for
railway salaries of $15,000.

5   Ever since this system of regulation was put into full effect
the railways and most public utilities have been earning relatively lower and lower net returns as compared with those
of other important industries. Between 1910 and 1915 the
net income (after paying interest and all Government taxes)
10 of all the corporations in the United States increased one-
half, while the net income of the railways declined one-third.
In 1917, the last year of private operation before Government
control, although the railways handled the largest business
in their history to that time—a business more than one-half
15 greater than in 1910—their net income was but one per cent
greater than in 1910, and the net income of all the corporations of the United States was 160 per cent greater than in
1910! Could any statistics show more strikingly the difference in the tendencies of profits in the railway and in other
20 businesses both before the war and during the war years?
And to-day, with the war behind us over three years, on the
pretense that it is regulation in the public interest, the railways are being forced to give their employees working conditions more favorable, and wages relatively higher than
25 those obtaining in almost any other industry, or even than
obtained during the war, although at this very time the railways as a whole are earning returns much smaller than in
former years and much smaller than any court ever held fair
and reasonable.

30   What has been the effect upon the welfare of the public
itself of the incorporation in our public policy of this remarkable distinction between these two classes of concerns? We
have seen within recent years a remarkable expansion of
concerns not engaged in rendering public services. Our min-
35 ing, manufacturing and mercantile businesses have grown
fully as much in proportion as in earlier years. We have seen

the manufacture of automobiles grow from almost nothing
into one of the largest industries in the country. A few
months ago I made a careful compilation of statistics which
seemed to show that in the year 1920 the people of the United
States, without including their investment in highways, spent 5
more for automobile transportation than for all their railroad
transportation.

While great expansion, resulting from vastly increased investment, has been the rule in the class of industries held by
the courts not to render any public service, the tendency in 10
practically all industries which are held to render such service, and which are, therefore, subjected to Government regulation, has been in exactly the opposite direction. In the
four years ending with 1912 railroad and traction companies
issued four billion dollars in securities, and industrial com- 15
panies less than three billions. In the four years ending with
1920 railroad and traction companies issued one and three
quarter billions of securities, and industrial companies over
seven billions. In consequence, there is agitation and outcry
in almost every city in the country because the development 20
of street railway lines has utterly failed to keep pace with the
growth of population and traffic. Almost everywhere the cars
during rush hours are overcrowded to the point of indecency
and of danger to the public health.

The most striking example of all is afforded by the rail- 25
roads. Their development kept pace with that of the other
industries of the country until about 1910, when the present
system of regulation began to be applied with its full rigor.
Since that time the percentage of net return earned by them
on the investment in property shown by their books has gone 30
steadily downward; in 1921 it was the smallest in any year
in the more than thirty years that the statistics of the Interstate Commerce Commission have been kept—less even than
in 1894. Their development has gone steadily downward
with their net return. Divide the last sixteen years into four 35
periods of four years each, and you will find that the de-

velopment of the railroads has been less in each period than in the preceding period; and in the last four years they tore up more miles of line and "scrapped" more locomotives and cars than they built.

5   What does all this mean? It means that as a result of the legally sound, but economically unsound, distinction that we make between concerns which do and concerns which do not render a public service, we are directly encouraging the development of many industries which are highly desirable but 10 relatively non-essential, and directly discouraging the development of industries which are absolutely essential. As a matter of public policy,—to state the facts in their baldest form,—we are encouraging the manufacture of chewing gum and discouraging the provision of electric lights and power. 15 As a matter of public policy we are encouraging the manufacture of cosmetics and silk shirts and discouraging the provision of good and adequate street railway service. As a matter of public policy we are encouraging the increase of "movie" shows and discouraging and actually making im- 20 possible the adequate development of railways.

Could anything be more fantastic, and even mad, than a governmental policy which permits unlimited profits and large fortunes to be made in, and thereby encourages the vast growth of, industries which are relatively non-essential, and 25 which at the same time restricts to the lowest limit permitted by constitutional limitations the profits that can be earned in, and consequently discourages or actually prevents the development of, concerns that render services that are absolutely essential to the public welfare? Or am I wrong, and 30 is it more essential to the public welfare for the people to have plenty of chewing gum, cosmetics, "movies," cigarettes, and silk shirts than for them to have enough street cars to ride to and from their work, enough lights for their homes, and enough railways on which to ship their goods?

35   The country already has felt in inadequate public utility and railroad service some of the effects of the stupid distinc-

tion our Governments, for at least ten years, have been making in dealing with different classes of industries. But the effects the public has thus far felt have been negligible compared with the effects it will feel in future, unless a different policy is adopted. We are overlooking the fact that there is a vital interdependence between all classes of industries, and that no large group of industries can long prosper and develop unless all other large groups prosper and develop also.

The volume of commerce possible depends upon the volume of production; and the volume of production possible depends upon the amount of transportation that can be furnished. The policy I am criticizing has resulted in facilities of production and commerce expanding far more than means of transportation. Our almost unbroken experience in the four years ending with 1920 clearly demonstrated, however, to those who carefully studied the matter, that the time when our production and commerce could increase more in proportion than our means of transportation had passed. There never was a time from the beginning of the year 1917 to the end of the year 1920, except during a few months in 1919, when the railways did or could handle all the freight offered to them. The productive capacity of our industries is greater now than ever before. When general business revives our industries will offer the railways more freight to transport than ever before. Unless there is speedily an expansion of our railways much greater than now seems probable, or even possible, the railways will not be able to handle anywhere near all this business; and the amount of production and commerce we can carry on will be correspondingly restricted.

What any manufacturing plant can produce depends on the amount of fuel and raw materials that can be taken to it and the amount of finished products that can be taken away. The size of the crops the farmers can grow is limited by the amount they can market; and they cannot market any larger crops than our means of transportation can move. As the available means of transportation determine the amount of production that can be carried on, they likewise indirectly determine the amount of commerce that can be carried on. You cannot buy and sell what cannot be produced.

5 Now, of course, in the long run, the amount of profits that can be made in industry and commerce depends upon the amount of things that can be produced and bought and sold. If you limit the amount of things that can be produced and bought and sold, you necessarily limit the profits that can be
10 made in producing, and in buying and selling. The conclusion to which this reasoning leads is plain. *The governmental policy of strictly limiting the profits allowed to be made by railroads and public utilities must inevitably result, sooner or later, in limiting correspondingly the profits that can be*
15 *made in all lines of industry and commerce.* The present policy of regulation is intended to enable the farmer, the manufacturer, the jobber, the merchant, to increase their profits at the expense of the railways and public utilities, and thus far it has had that result. But its ultimate effect must
20 be to limit the profits of all these other concerns and persons as drastically as those of the railways and public utilities themselves.

Labor union leaders and persons of Socialistic tendency may not feel deep concern over this conclusion. They may
25 fancy that the general curtailment of profits will result in higher wages and other benefits for labor. But nothing could be farther from the truth. Increases in employment and in the real wages of labor are dependent upon the expansion of production, commerce and transportation. Since this policy
30 tends directly to restrict the expansion of production, commerce and transportation, it tends directly to reduce both the demand for labor and its real wages.

It may be said I paint too gloomy a picture—that the good sense of the American people will prevent this policy of un-
35 due discrimination by the Government between concerns rendering a public service and concerns not rendering a pub-

lic service from being pursued until it has produced such
results as I have anticipated. But history is replete with
examples of public sentiment and statesmen regarded as
great having persistently given effect to policies intended to
benefit the public which finally produced ruinous effects. I
maintain that our present policy of so regulating railways
and public utilities as to restrict them to the lowest net
return that will avoid confiscation of their properties for
the ostensible purpose of promoting the public welfare is
one of the most flagrant examples of economic and political
quackery that the world has ever seen.

I wish to emphasize again that what I have discussed is
not an attack upon any class of industries or upon all Government regulation of railroads and public utilities. In
some important respects railroads and public utilities are a
peculiar class of business concerns; and they should be regulated to deprive them of opportunity and ability to practice
extortion upon the public. What I attack is the utterly unsound theory that they should be so regulated as to prevent
them from being managed according to the same general business principles as other business concerns and as to prevent
them from earning ordinary business profits. The fact that
they render a peculiar service and are properly subject to
regulation does not in the least alter the fact that if they are
to be economically and efficiently managed, their managers
must be highly paid men of ability and must be allowed that
wide scope for initiative and freedom of action which is
essential to the successful management of every other kind
of concern. The fact that they are properly subject to Government regulation does not in the least alter the fact that
when other classes of business concerns must pay 6, or 7, or
10 per cent to raise new capital, railways and public utilities
cannot raise new capital for a scintilla less than 6, or 7, or
10 per cent; and if they are not allowed to earn enough to
pay the market rate of return they cannot raise new capital.
The fact that they are properly subject to regulation does

not give them any more power than other concerns to provide improved or increased service without raising and investing additional capital.

In other words, full recognition of the principle that these
5 concerns render a service affected with a public use and are properly subject to regulation does not give them the least immunity from any of those economic conditions, or necessities, or disabilities, to which other kinds of business concerns are subject; and, therefore, it will always be an
10 economic impossibility for them to increase and improve the service they render the public, unless the public allows them year by year to enjoy as great prosperity on the average as other classes of concerns.

But, it may be said, as it often is said, these concerns in
15 rendering a public service really perform a function of government. If the Government owned and operated them it would not be under the economic necessity of deriving as large net returns from their ownership and operation as those earned by other kinds of concerns. Therefore, either their
20 present owners should willingly accept smaller returns than those earned in other businesses, or the Government should take over their ownership and operation.

This argument for Government ownership and management has been made and answered many times, and I shall
25 not try to answer it here, except to say that, economically speaking, it is just as good an argument for Government ownership of all industries as for Government ownership of some. One thing, however, is certain. If our policy of Government regulation is to be successful and not drive us into
30 Government ownership, we must throw overboard forever the glaring fallacy that concerns engaged in a public service should be regulated to the point of confiscation, simply because it is not unconstitutional to do so. The constitutional power to tax is the power to destroy, but we do not therefore
35 conclude that in the public interest the power to tax should be used to destroy legitimate businesses. The power to regu-

late railroads and public utilities is the power so to restrict their profits as, without confiscating their present properties, to make further expansion of these properties, and increase and improvement of the service rendered with them impossible; but the public welfare plainly demands, not that the power of Government shall continue to be so used to this end, but that it shall cease to be so used.

THE OPEN SHOP[1]

Lyman Abbott

Our object in this article is, first, to define the issue joined between the "open shop" and the "closed shop"; and, secondly, to give our judgment on that issue and the reasons upon which it is based.

5 An open shop is one in which union men and non-union men may work side by side upon equal terms. A closed shop is one from which either union men are excluded by the employer, or non-union men are excluded by the union; but, ordinarily, the term is applied only to those shops which are
10 closed against non-union men by the refusal of union men to work with them. It is in that sense we use the phrase in this article. Are trades-unions justified in insisting upon the closed shop—in insisting, that is, upon the exclusion from the industry in which they are engaged of all workingmen
15 who do not belong to the union?

The arguments for the closed shop deserve careful consideration; they may be briefly stated thus: Workingmen have a right to choose *with* whom they shall work, as well as *under* whom they shall work. Sometimes the industry is
20 made extra-hazardous by the employment of an incompetent workingman; often it is made extra-difficult. For this reason a fireman has a right to refuse to work with a green locomotive engineer, or a locomotive engineer with a green fireman. But a workman has a right to protect not only his
25 life, but also his feeling. He has the right to refuse to work in the intimacy of a common employment with a man who is *persona non grata*; and there is a real reason why the non-

[1] From the *Outlook* (July 16, 1904), Vol. LXXVII, pp. 630 ff.

union man is *persona non grata* to the union man. Without
sharing the expenses or the obligations of the union, he gets
—in improved conditions, better wages, and shorter hours
—all the benefits which the union secures from the employer.
The union man has a right to refuse to work with a com- 5
panion who takes all the advantages of the union without
sharing its burdens. Moreover, if the shop is open on equal
terms to both union men and non-union men, the employer
will be apt gradually to supplant the union men with non-
union men, because it is easy to increase the hours and reduce 10
the wages where there is no union to interpose organized
resistance to such industrial injustice. Finally, the object of
the union is not merely to get larger wages, lessened hours,
and better conditions. The workingman denies the assumed
right of the employer to manage his business as he pleases. 15
He insists that the employer and employed are partners in
a common enterprise, and that the employee has a right to be
consulted as to the conditions of the work, and to share in
its prosperity when it is prosperous, as he is certain to share
in its adversity when it is unprosperous. The object of the 20
union is to secure a real co-operation for the workingman
with the employer, on something like equal terms. This can
be done only by "collective bargaining"; that is, by an agreement entered into by a body of workingmen acting together
as a union, with the employer, who is generally a body of 25
capitalists acting together in a corporation. Only thus can
democratization of industry be secured and the autocracy of
industry be ended; and this result is indispensable in order
to bring the industrial organization of America into harmony
with its political, educational, and religious organizations. 30

These considerations seem to us to furnish very good reasons for the organization of labor. But do they also furnish
good reasons for compelling workingmen to join organizations of labor against their will? For the real question at
issue between the closed shop and the open shop is not, Shall 35
labor organize in order to deal on terms of greater equality

with organized capital? but, Shall the laborer be compelled
to join such organization in order to get opportunity to
labor?

This question is really two questions: Is the closed shop
5 illegal? If not illegal, is it against the public interest, and
therefore and to that extent immoral?

In a recent case in Illinois the closed shop has been
adjudged illegal. From the decision, rendered in June last,
an appeal has been taken to the Supreme Court of the State,
10 and pending that appeal the decision cannot be regarded as
conclusive. In this case a draft agreement was proposed by
a trades-union, which provided that only men of the union
should be employed, and, this agreement being rejected by
the employer, a strike was declared, and picketing was in-
15 stituted to reinforce the strike. The Court held not only that
the picketing was unlawful because it involved a suggestion
of violence, but that the strike was unlawful because it was
an endeavor to coerce an employer to make a contract against
his will, and that the contract itself would have been illegal
20 because it would have tended to create a monopoly. This
decision does not appear to us to accord with either fundamental principles of justice or with the precedents set by
decisions of other courts in England and in this country.
Those precedents sustain the decision that picketing is illegal
25 if it employs or suggests forcible interference with the rights
of free labor; but those precedents also affirm the right of
laborers to organize for the purpose of entering into collective bargaining with the employers, and to refuse to enter
into such a collective bargain with the employer except on
30 terms acceptable to the laborers. That a strike may be so
organized as to be in the nature of an illegal conspiracy
against persons and property we do not doubt, but a mere
combination to stop work except upon terms proposed by the
combination surely is not such a conspiracy. If it were, there
35 would be an end to the right of free collective bargaining;
for there can be no free bargaining if both parties are not free

to refuse to enter into the bargain. Nor can an agreement
by one employer to employ only men belonging to a specified
organization be said to tend to monopoly. A monopoly is
"such an exclusive privilege to carry on a traffic, or deal in
or control a given class of articles, as will enable the holder 5
to raise prices materially above what they would be if the
traffic or dealing were free to citizens generally." An agreement by *The Outlook* to buy all its paper of a particular mill
does not tend to give that mill a monopoly of paper manufacture. No more does an agreement by *The Outlook* to get 10
all the employees in its composing-room from a particular
labor organization tend to give that labor organization a
monopoly. Such exclusive contracts in articles of commerce
are very common. It is difficult to see why they should be
illegal when labor, not the product of labor, is the commodity 15
dealt in. Whether Judge Adams's decision is sustained by
the Supreme Court of Illinois or not, we do not believe that
the principles enunciated in that decision will be sustained
generally by the courts in this country. In a country where
labor is free, an employer has the legal right to refuse to 20
employ any union labor, and equally the legal right to refuse
to employ any non-union labor. We do not believe that the
closed shop is illegal, though, of course, violence, threats of
violence, or even remote suggestions and intimations of violence, in order to enforce the closed shop, are illegal, and 25
ought to receive far more serious penalty than is ordinarily
inflicted.

But, if not illegal, is the closed shop against public policy,
and therefore and to that extent immoral? Our answer to
this question is in the affirmative.   30

The collective bargaining is an advantage to workingmen.
It will, we believe, eventually prove an advantage to the
entire community. It tends to give the workingmen some
share in the control of the industry to which they contribute;
and some share in that control they ought to possess. The 35
organization of labor and consequent collective bargaining

are a necessary consequence of the organization of capital, whose bargains are collective. The only possible remedy for an industrial autocracy is labor organization; and industrial autocracy is unendurable in a free commonwealth.

5　　But if collective bargaining can be obtained only by sacrificing free bargaining, the price paid would be too great for the benefits secured. The very object of collective bargaining is to secure freedom, which is practically, though not theoretically, denied if the individual workingman must 10 make his contract single-handed with a great collective capitalistic organization. But to deny him the liberty to make his contract single-handed if he wishes is not to secure him freedom of contract, but to transfer him from one autocracy to another. And this, in fact, is what has taken place in some 15 trades, in which men are no longer free, but have the question whether they shall work, when they shall work, and on what terms they shall work determined for them, sometimes by a small body of men acting in secret, sometimes by a mob of men swayed by their passions or their prejudices. If the 20 only remedy for the autocracy of capital is the possibility of collective bargaining, the only remedy for the autocracy of a labor union is the possibility of individual bargaining.

Freedom of bargaining is not only thus essential to the community, and especially to the workingmen; it is also 25 essential to the best interests of the trades-unions. The trade-union, to be permanently efficient, must be an organization of free men; it must be composed of members who believe in unionism and are loyal to it; it must be an industrial army of volunteers, not of drafted men; it must make 30 its way in the labor world by persuading the laborers that it is for their interest to join it and be loyal to it, not by coercing them to join it by threats of violence on the one hand or of starvation on the other. There is only one organization which in a free community men may be compelled to join whether they will or not—namely, the State. They are born 35 into the State, are members of the State, must obey the laws enacted by the State, in time of danger must come to the defense of the State, must, if necessary, hazard their lives for the State. This is true of no other organism. If they are coerced into the church, as they were in the Middle Ages, the same process which deprives them of their freedom deprives the church of its spiritual vitality. If they are coerced into a labor organization, as some labor leaders would have them in this twentieth century, the same process which deprives them of their freedom deprives the labor organizations of that spirit of brotherhood which is at once the justification for its existence and the inspiration of its power. The right of labor to organize rests upon the right of the individual to labor. Whoever denies this right of the individual denies the foundation on which the right of organized labor rests.

If any man is inclined to say that a free labor union is the dream of an idealist, and is quite impracticable in a world of selfish and sordid men, the answer is to be found in the fact that some of the greatest and most successful of the labor organizations have always adhered to the principle of the open shop. We believe that all the railroad labor organizations are free organizations. In the Pennsylvania coal-mines union and non-union miners labored together in the same mine and reaped the same benefits from the collective bargaining carried on for them by John Mitchell. In the recent anarchy in Colorado, the one mine which went on with its work peacefully, prosperously, and without disturbance, until it was closed by military orders, was a mine which maintained the principle of the open shop, and in which union and non-union men worked peacefully together.

Our conclusion, then, is that collective bargaining in most organized industries is for the interest of employer, of employed, and of the general community; that this collective bargaining will be more speedily and permanently secured by the maintenance of free labor unions than by swelling the ranks of labor unions through processes of compulsion; that the closed shop is not and ought not to be illegal; but that

it is against the interests of workingmen, of labor organizations, and of the general community; and, whether closed by the employer against union men, or by organized labor against non-union men, is alike inconsistent with the funda-
5 mental principles and the essential spirit of free American institutions.

STUDENT'S BRIEF AND ARGUMENT

On the following pages the brief appears not as it would ordinarily be presented, but so printed with reference to the finished argument that the relation of the two can more conveniently be studied.

STUDENT'S BRIEF

RESOLVED: That the Smith Bill (H. R. 12466), providing for
the Falls River Meadows Reservoir in the southwest corner of the Yellowstone National Park, should be passed
by Congress and become operative.

INTRODUCTION TO THE BRIEF

I. The question of allowing the Idaho farmers to use the
Falls River Basin as a reservoir site has aroused national interest, in that
   A. The Smith Bill, providing for such a reservoir, has
   been repeatedly delayed in Congress.
   B. Private expeditions have been sent out to investigate the true conditions prevalent in this region, for
   example:
      1. Investigation by Mr. William C. Gregg of Hack-
      ensack, N. J. (August, 1920).
      2. Investigation by Mr. Harris A. Reynolds under
      the auspices of the Appalachian Mountain Club
      (summer of 1920).
   C. Public agitation against the bill has been shown by
      1. The fact that more than two hundred witnesses
      appeared opposing the granting of the easement
      at the inquiry at Washington last spring.
      2. The large amounts of space devoted to the subject
      in recent periodicals and pamphlets.[1]

[1] For an extended list of periodicals and pamphlets, see the bibliography
on page 247.

STUDENT'S ARGUMENT[1]

RECLAMATION OR DESECRATION?[2]

Preserve our National Monuments! Keep our Parks free from the taint of commercialism! Such are the startling warnings which have been brought to public view during the past year. Chief among the questions which have aroused such a widespread display of feeling is that of allowing the Eastern Idaho farmers to utilize the Falls River Basin in the southwest corner of the Yellowstone National Park as a reservoir site. The so-called "Smith Bill," providing for the granting of the easement, has been repeatedly delayed in Congress. Numerous private expeditions, notable among which was the party conducted by Mr. William C. Gregg of Hackensack, New Jersey, have been sent out to investigate the true conditions of the region under discussion. Mr. Harris A. Reynolds of the Appalachian Mountain Club headed one of these expeditions to the Falls River country in the summer of 1920. Indeed, the fact that over two hundred witnesses appeared at the Congressional hearings in Washington in the spring of 1920, and the large amount of space recently devoted to the subject, not only in periodicals, but in pamphlets widely circulated over the country, indicate the interest and importance of the question.

[1] To avoid repetition, the footnotes in this argument, which duplicate those in the brief, have been omitted.

[2] Written in April, 1921.

II. The following definitions will facilitate a clear under-
standing of the facts and the particular features of the
Falls River Basin region:
   A. The Falls River Basin is located
      1. Very close to the Wyoming and Idaho boundaries
         of Yellowstone National Park.
      2. At the junction of the Bechler and Falls Rivers
         in the southwestern corner of the Park, in the
         region partly drained by the Bechler River, which
         flows into the North Fork of the Snake River in
         Eastern Idaho.
   B. The area of the proposed reservoir site is 8190 acres.
   C. The proposed site is at present inaccessible by any
      wagon road, although rough trails permit entrance
      from the southern boundary.

III. A brief summary of the developments leading to the
present situation follows:
   A. The Yellowstone National Park was established by
      an Act of Congress in 1872 out of portions of the
      territories of Wyoming, Idaho, and Montana.[1]

   B. Under this Act of 1872 and the Protective Laws en-
      acted in 1894, the use of natural features of the Park
      for industrial purposes was prohibited.
   C. In 1919 the Fremont-Madison Reservoir Company
      adopted a resolution declaring the need of a reser-
      voir in the Falls River Basin.[2]

[1] *Hearings before the Committee on Rules, H. R., May 25, 1920*, p. 31.
[2] Resolution of stockholders of the Fremont-Madison Reservoir Company, a corporation, adopted at a meeting held on the 18th day of July,
1919. Quoted in *Hearing before the Committee on the Public Lands, H. R.,
March 20 and 23, 1920*, p. 12.

The Falls River Basin, in which the proposed reservoir is to be located, may be found on the topographical map of the United States Geological Survey in the extreme southwestern corner of the Yellowstone National Park, very close to the Wyoming and Idaho boundaries. The Basin itself is at the junction of the Bechler and Falls Rivers, in the region partly drained by the Bechler, which flows into the North Fork of the Snake River in Eastern Idaho. It is this basin which the irrigationists propose to flood as a storage reservoir, making a lake of 8190 acres, or approximately $\frac{1}{267}$ of the entire area of the Park. The lake would lie about five miles from the southern boundary and four miles from the western boundary of the Park, with its sides nearly parallel to these boundaries. The site is at present inaccessible by any wagon road, and has been seen by very few tourists, as only rough trails permit entrance from the southern boundary of the Park.

It may be of interest, and it will certainly facilitate an accurate insight into the question, to summarize the developments from which the present situation has arisen. Records show that the Yellowstone National Park was established by Act of Congress in 1872 out of portions of the territories of Wyoming, Montana, and Idaho, "dedicated and set aside as a public park and pleasure ground for the benefit and enjoyment of the people." Under this authorization act and the Protection Laws enacted in 1894, the use of natural features of the Park for industrial purposes was prohibited. Therefore, when the farmers of Fremont and Madison Counties, Idaho, who had formed the Fremont-Madison Reservoir Company, "whose stockholders are all canal companies and individuals having the source of their supply of water from the North Fork of the Snake River and its tributaries," desired an additional supply of water for irrigation and domestic purposes, they adopted a resolution on July 18, 1919, declaring briefly as follows: that the waters of the Snake River and its tributaries had been insufficient to supply their

D. A bill providing for this reservoir was introduced into Congress.

E. The bill passed the Senate in the spring of 1920.

F. The bill was never voted on in the House, and it lapsed with the adjournment of Congress on March 4, 1921.

IV. Both sides agree to limit the present discussion to the Smith Bill as such.

needs; that, owing to the enlargement of canals, the greater
diversity of farming, and the more intensive methods of
farming in use, the need was becoming greater and greater
each year; that an additional 200,000 acre-feet of water
would be required to supply irrigation needs alone; that by 5
far the most advantageous site for a reservoir existed in the
Falls River Meadows; and finally that an effort to secure
this site through Congressional action would be made. Since
the general Right of Way Law for public lands did not apply to the Yellowstone National Park, a bill was drawn up 10
providing for the granting of the easement, under the advice
of the Superintendent of the Park Service, by the legal officers of the Department of the Interior. The bill, known at
present as the Smith Bill, was introduced into the Senate
(where it passed in the spring of 1920) by Senator Nugent 15
of Idaho, and into the House of Representatives by Addison T. Smith of Idaho. A few weeks later, the Secretary of
the Interior, Franklin K. Lane, and Acting Secretary Alexander T. Vogelsang, both declared themselves heartily in favor
of the measure in letters to Representative Smith (Feb. 3 and 20
March 4, 1920). On March 20, the House took up the bill
for consideration, referring it, after several subsequent sit-
tings, to the Committee on Rules, where violent opposition
was evidenced by numerous witnesses at the hearings. It was
at this time that public agitation started against the Smith 25
Bill. Probably owing to such opposition, the bill was never
voted upon in the House, and it lapsed with the adjournment
of Congress on March 4, 1921. If the project urged by the
irrigationists is desirable from every standpoint, the measure
undoubtedly should be passed and become operative; if not, 30
every means should be taken to secure its defeat.

It must be made perfectly clear that the present discussion will be limited to the Smith Bill as such. The bill simply gives the discretionary power to the Secretary of the
Interior in regard to easements in the Falls River Basin. It 35
refers to no other section of the Park.

V. The opposing contentions are as follows:

    A. The Affirmative maintains that

        1. Approximately 5000 farms in Fremont and Madison Counties, Idaho, which are in a high state of development, are in dire need of additional water to secure the maximum crops.

        2. The proposed reservoir site in the Falls River Basin is the only site which can be utilized in providing an additional water supply for the land in question.

        3. On account of the peculiar conditions prevalent around this site, the reservoir can be constructed and operated without any interference whatever with the Park.

        4. This immediate vicinity contains no unusual scenery or other interesting features.

        5. The highway to be constructed by the Fremont-Madison Reservoir Company, as provided in the bill, would serve as a means of access to the Park for fire protection.

        6. The proposed reservoir would not involve expense to the Government.

    B. The Negative contends that

        1. There is not a great need for an additional water supply for irrigation and domestic purposes on the farms of Fremont and Madison Counties, drained by the North Fork of the Snake River and its tributaries.

        2. There are other sites outside of the Park which would be superior to the proposed site.

        3. If such a reservoir were built, it would scar the natural beauty of the scenery.

        4. The proposed reservoir would be a nuisance to the Park.

        5. The proposed reservoir would involve expense to the Government.

A sound, impartial consideration of the merits or demerits of the measure may be entered upon only after a brief statement of the opposing contentions and the issues to be decided. Advocates of the Smith Bill urge that there are approximately 5000 highly developed farms in Fremont and Madison Counties, Idaho, in dire need of an additional water supply for the irrigation of their crops; that the proposed site in the Falls River Basin is the only one practicable of utilization in providing it; that special local conditions permit both construction and operation of the reservoir without injury to the Park; that there is no unusual scenery in this region; that the proposed highway would reduce the risk of fires in the Park; and that no expense to the Government is involved. On the other hand, the opponents of the bill can see no vital need for the additional water supply, and moreover, maintain that there are several reservoir sites outside of the Park, superior to the one proposed. The scenic beauty of the region, declare these opponents, would be defaced by the construction of a storage reservoir in the Basin, and the reservoir itself, when completed, would be both a nuisance to the Park and an expense to the Government.

VI. The question then resolves itself into the following main issues:

    A. Is the need of an additional water supply vital?

    B. Is the proposed site the only one practicable?

    C. Would the proposed reservoir involve expense to the Government?

    D. Would the construction of the reservoir be a detriment to the Park?

BRIEF PROPER

I. The need of an additional water supply for the irrigation of approximately 5000 farms in Fremont and Madison Counties, Idaho, is vital, for

    A. The waters of the North Fork of the Snake River, the only immediate source, have been insufficient for several years past to supply the needs of these farms, for

        1. Thousands of cattle have actually starved in this section of the country, because the farmers could not raise or obtain sufficient hay.[1]

        2. The losses in crops to the farmers of this section due to water shortage have been tremendous, for

            a. The Ashton Commercial Club of Ashton, Idaho, estimates the aggregate loss in crop failures due to shortage of water during 1919 at more than $15,000,000.[2]

[1] *Hearings before the Committee on Rules, H. R., May 25, 1920,* p. 6.
[2] *H. R. Report No. 767,* Representative Addison T. Smith of Idaho, March 25, 1920, p. 3.

Obviously, then, from a short summary of the conflicting arguments, we must decide whether the need of an additional water supply for irrigation and domestic purposes on the Fremont and Madison County farms is vital; whether the proposed site is the only one practicable; whether the proposed reservoir would involve expense to the Government; and whether the construction of a reservoir there would be a detriment to the Park.

My own consideration of this reclamation question has placed me unreservedly in favor of the contentions of the irrigationists. Perhaps it is merely the cause of the "under dog." It may be more.

Although we may find, if inclined toward statistics, that the land drained by the North Fork of the Snake River is devoted in some measure to grazing,—for thousands of cattle and sheep have actually starved in this section of the country because the farmers could neither raise nor obtain from outside sufficient hay,—the main industry of the region is agriculture. Sugar beets and wheat constitute the two most important crops of the section, although an impartial book on the subject mentions a dozen or more minor products of the soil—potatoes and rye wheat being of note.

The Commercial Club of Ashton, Idaho, a small community in the heart of the region under discussion, endeavored in 1919 to determine the actual facts in regard to the alleged shortage of water on Fremont and Madison County farms. Their report, issued in 1920, estimates the aggregate loss in crop failures due to water shortage during 1919, on the land which would be additionally irrigated from the proposed reservoir (not including the loss in cattle, sheep, and other live stock), at more than fifteen millions of dollars! Of course, industries such as sugar factories, pea canneries, and flour mills, necessarily allied to the agricultural pursuits of the region, have become established during recent years in the section covered by the present canal system, all of them requiring considerable water supply; but when we consider

  b. The sugar beet crop, one of the most important in this section of the country, was not more than 40 per cent of the normal during 1919, the estimated loss being approximately $5,000,000.[1]

  c. There was an estimated loss of 2,500,000 bushels of wheat in 1919, and similar losses in other dry years.

  d. Sworn testimony from experienced farmers and reputable citizens of this region indicates a deplorable shortage of water in recent years, for

   (1) Mr. R. J. Comstock, president of the First National Bank of Rexburg, Madison County, a resident of that county for 19 years and personally well acquainted with irrigating conditions there, testifies to this fact.[2]

   (2) Mr. G. A. Fitzpatrick, manager of the St. Anthony Flour Mills, Madison County, for the past six years, gives similar testimony.[2]

[1] *H. R. Report No. 767*, Representative Addison T. Smith of Idaho, March 25, 1920, pp. 3–4.
[2] Ibid. pp. 5–9.

that the sugar beet crop in Madison and Fremont Counties
was less than 40 per cent of the theoretical yield during 1919
(the estimated loss hovering about the five-million mark),
and that 2,500,000 bushels of wheat were lost during the
same year, with similar losses in other dry years, certainly a   5
few hundred thousand acre-feet of water in reserve would be
desirable.

When, furthermore, experienced farmers and reputable
citizens—for there are honest men even in Idaho—declare
themselves willing to swear before God to the deplorable   10
shortage of water, indeed the matter will bear investigation.
Testimony, when presented second-hand, is at best only mild
evidence to the average man; however, perhaps a few of my
readers are open to conviction and will tolerate a very limited
number of quotations from persons held in high esteem by   15
the rather unsophisticated populace of Eastern Idaho. For
instance, Mr. R. H. Comstock, a resident of Madison County
for nineteen years and president of the First National Bank
of Rexburg, who should be personally well acquainted with
irrigating conditions—for the bankers out there have a habit   20
of keeping closely in touch with the financial turmoils, and
incidentally the agricultural troubles of the farmers—states
in part that "the farmers . . . during this time . . . have
sustained material losses through failure to secure necessary
water for irrigation purposes. This has been especially the   25
case during the year 1919, and all of said lands (80,000
acres) have suffered from lack of water. . . . I would estimate the general loss at more than $40 per acre." Likewise
Mr. G. A. Fitzpatrick, manager of the St. Anthony Flour
Mills, Madison County, for the past six years, who has had   30
occasion, owing to the nature and interests of his business, to
observe the irrigation conditions in that vicinity, affirms
briefly that "during the growing season of 1919 there was
such a shortage of irrigating water in this part of Idaho that
only about 15 per cent of a normal crop was grown, which   35
condition could have been avoided if the proper facilities

(3) Mr. Joseph E. Romrell, president of the
Wilford Irrigation Company, of Wilford,
Fremont County, affirms that this is the
case.[1]

B. The need of water for the purposes mentioned is
growing greater and greater each year, for
   1. The canal system is constantly being extended.[2]
   2. More intensive farming is constantly being prac-
      tised.[2]
   3. The crops are becoming more and more varied.[2]

[1] *H. R. Report No. 767*, Representative Addison T. Smith of Idaho,
March 25, 1920, pp. 5–9.
[2] *Hearing before the Committee on the Public Lands, H. R., March 20
and 23, 1920*, pp. 12–13. Also *H. R. Report No. 767*, p. 4.

were provided to take care of the flood waters in the spring
of the year." Lastly, Mr. Joseph E. Romrell, president of the
Wilford Irrigation Company of Wilford, Fremont County, a
non-speculative corporation operated solely for the purpose
of irrigating the lands owned by its members (over 2000
acres, valued at $125 to $200 per acre), states that "due to
scarcity of water during the present year (1919), the farmers
comprising this company have lost $150,500 worth of crops.
. . . We suffer yearly a shortage of water, and extremely so
in such years as 1914, 1915, 1918, and the present year."
Perhaps, as the opponents of the Smith Bill are now urging,
"there has been only one crop failure in twenty years" in
this section of the country, and perhaps the dry-farmers in
the hilly country, who use no irrigating water, have not suffered greatly from a shortage of it in the valley land, but
an unbiased man, in view of existing conditions, might be
persuaded to admit a need for an additional storage of water
for the Fremont and Madison County farms.

It seems that the necessity for an additional water supply
is becoming greater and greater each year. For one thing,
the canal system which furnishes the present supply from the
Snake River is constantly being extended and the canals are
being enlarged to meet the demands of an increased population and new industries. Furthermore, the water users are
constantly practising more intensive farming methods, stimulated by the University Extension of the Agricultural School
at Moscow, Idaho. Owing to the diversity of farming and
the more intensive methods being put into practice, the crops
grown are becoming more and more varied each year, requiring a much more extensive system of irrigation than is at
present available.

Granting a vital need for further storage of spring flood
waters to serve as an additional supply for irrigation of the
farms in Fremont and Madison Counties, the most advantageous reservoir site must now be found. It is surely worthy
of note that a dam on the Falls River Basin site previously

II. The proposed reservoir site in the Falls River Basin is the only one practicable, for

    A. A dam on this site could be completed from three to five years sooner than one elsewhere.[1]

    B. It has been demonstrated by the engineers of the United States Reclamation Service that the nine available reservoir sites outside of the Park would together furnish less than one fifth the quantity of water that could be conserved in the Falls River Basin by simply building one dam.[1]

    C. The proposed site in the Falls River Basin is the only one which can be utilized in providing an additional supply for the land in question,[2] for

        1. A careful examination of the watershed made by the officials of the State of Idaho proves this.

    D. Although the opponents of the present bill assert that other sites have been found outside the Park which can be used in supplying the needed water, none of their investigations are based on accurate surveys, for

        1. Mr. William C. Gregg of Hackensack, N. J., bases his assertions merely on personal observations.[3]

        2. Other similar expeditions are unable to give useful data.[4]

[1] *Hearing before the Select Committee on Water Power, H. R.,* January 6, *1921,* p. 16.

[2] *H. R. Report No. 767,* March 25, 1920, p. 3.

[3] William C. Gregg, "Cornering Cascades," *Saturday Evening Post,* November 20, 1920. Also *Hearing before the Select Committee on Water Power, H. R., January 6, 1921,* p. 61.

[4] Emerson Hough, "Pawning the Heirlooms," *Saturday Evening Post,* September 25, 1920. Also *Hearing before the Select Committee on Water Power, H. R.,* pp. 17–73. See also the bibliography.

described could be completed from three to five years sooner than one upon any other known available site; moreover, at the present time there are hosts of unemployed laborers in the vicinity, who could well be used in the construction of the dam and other works. Time is certainly one of the most important elements in the construction of such a dam, because of the losses annually sustained by the water users. Opponents of the Smith Bill, however, notably Mr. William C. Gregg of Hackensack, N. J., assert that they have found nine or ten superior sites outside of the boundaries of the Park. Accurate surveys by the engineers of the United States Reclamation Service conclusively show that there actually *are* nine reservoir sites outside, but that the quantity of water capable of conservation in these nine sites is only 37,000 acre-feet, whereas in the Falls River Basin, 200,000 acre-feet could be conserved by simply building one dam. A further examination of the watershed was conducted by the officials of the State of Idaho, confirming in detail the reports of the Reclamation Engineers. Although a few of the opponents of the present measure claim to have personally investigated the "superior sites outside of the Park," none of their investigations are based on accurate surveys. For example, Mr. William C. Gregg, whose expedition to the Basin undoubtedly constituted their most thorough-going examination of the available watershed, bases none of his assertions on more than an aneroid barometer and his own observation. Other expeditions are unable to present any useful data concerning the "superior sites outside of the Park." In view of such facts, we may logically conclude that the proposed site in the Falls River Basin is the only one practicable of utilization in providing an additional storage of water.

III. The proposed reservoir involves no expense to the Government, for

   A. The farmers of Fremont and Madison Counties request no aid whatsoever from the Federal Government.[1]

   B. The Smith Bill provides only for the granting of necessary easements within the Falls River Basin.[2]

   C. The bill further provides that all timber removed from the site is to be paid for by the grantee in such amounts as the Secretary of the Interior shall see fit.[2]

   D. Any Government inspectors required to insure the safety and sightliness of the finished construction would be paid for by the farmers.[1]

IV. The construction of the proposed Falls River Basin Reservoir would not be a detriment to the Park, for

   A. The Falls River Basin has very little value for Park purposes, for

      1. It contains no features of scenic value, for

         a. Director Davis of the United States Reclamation Service, who visited the site in 1919, states that the Basin is of a swampy nature and without any scenic or economic value.[3]

         b. The official United States Government pamphlet, *Yellowstone National Park, 1920,* issued by the Department of the Interior, contains no reference to features in the Falls River Basin.[4]

[1] *Hearing before the Committee on the Public Lands, H. R., March 20 and 23, 1920,* p. 8.

[2] Text of the Smith Bill. Appendix to *Hearing before the Committee on the Public Lands, H. R., March 20 and 23, 1920.*

[3] *Hearing before the Committee on the Public Lands, H. R., March 20 and 23, 1920,* p. 6.

[4] *Yellowstone National Park, 1920.* Department of the Interior, Washington, 1920.

With regard to the alleged undesirability of the Falls River
site from the standpoint of Government expense, it must be
pointed out that the farmers of Fremont and Madison Counties have requested no Federal aid whatsoever in the proposed undertaking, desiring only the privilege of putting the
reservoir in that part of the Park. They have already raised
a sum of nearly one million dollars for the purpose of constructing and maintaining such a reservoir. Moreover, the
Smith Bill itself provides only for the granting of such necessary easements within the Falls River Basin as involve no
Governmental expenditure, and further that all timber removed from the site is to be paid for by the grantee in such
amounts as the Secretary of the Interior shall see fit. Although Congress or the Department of the Interior might
consider it desirable to place Government inspectors on the
work to insure the safety and sightliness of the finished construction, they would be paid for by the farmers, unless
Congress otherwise provided. The matter of financing the
undertaking is therefore fully provided for, and involves no
expense to the people of the United States.

Notwithstanding the beauty of certain features of the Yellowstone within perhaps two hours' walk from the Basin,
there seems to be evidence tending to prove that the Falls
River Meadows, as the Basin is locally known, possess in
themselves very little value for Park purposes. Indeed,
Director Davis of the United States Reclamation Service,
who visited the site in 1919, states as part of his report:
"I do not consider even the surrounding country especially
scenic . . . that is, not up to the average mountain country
in the West. The land that would be submerged by the lake
is of a swampy nature and without any scenic or economic
value." More notable is the fact that the official Government pamphlet, *Yellowstone National Park* (100 pages),
issued by the Department of the Interior, the stated purpose
of which is to give accurate and detailed information concerning all features of scenic or other interest, contains no

    c. Several of the photographs shown by the op-
ponents of the measure, purporting to demonstrate the "beauties of the Falls River
Meadows" are deceptive, for
      (1) Some of the views have been identified
as scenes on the Warm River in Idaho, at
least 40 miles from the intended site.[1]

  2. The Falls River Basin is unsuitable for camping
during the summer season, for
    a. The land is of swampy character, for
      (1) The Ashton Commercial Club, in its re-
port of prevalent conditions in the Falls
River Basin, states this fact.[1]
      (2) The Report of the United States Geologi-
cal Survey of 1878 so testifies.[2]
      (3) Director Davis of the Reclamation Serv-
ice adds his testimony.[3]
      (4) Representative Addison T. Smith of
Idaho agrees with the report of the
Geological Survey of 1878.[2]
    b. Swarms of mosquitoes in the Basin add to the
tourist's discomfort, for
      (1) Representative Addison T. Smith gives
his experience.[2]
      (2) The report of the Ashton Commercial
Club contains testimony.[1]

[1] "Need of Yellowstone Water to reclaim Rich District in Eastern Idaho
Counties." A report of conditions by the Ashton Commercial Club of
Ashton, Idaho. In *Idaho Daily Statesman*, December 25, 1920.

[2] *Hearing before the Select Committee on Water Power, H. R.,* January 6, 1921, p. 57.

[3] *Hearing before the Committee on the Public Lands, H. R., March 20
and 23, 1920,* p. 6.

reference whatsoever to such features in the Falls River
Basin. Moreover, several of the photographs shown by the
opponents of the Smith Bill, purporting to demonstrate the
"beauties of the Falls River Meadows," are deceptive, either
in themselves or the titles appended to them. For example, 5
some of the views have been identified by citizens of Ashton,
the nearest town to the intended reservoir location, as scenes
on the Warm River in Idaho, fully forty miles from the
proposed site! One picture used to show the luxuriant
grazing fields in the Meadows has been identified as Horse- 10
shoe Flats.

Aside from the fact that the Basin is in itself of little or
no scenic value, it is significant to note that the greater part
of the so-called meadow is unsuitable for camping during the
summer season. The Ashton Commercial Club reports that 15
"the proposed reservoir is situated on a swampy piece of
ground. In ordinary seasons, it is not until late in August
that the tourist can cross the 'meadows' with any degree
of safety. Then the mosquitoes are so numerous that the
campers find themselves unable to linger in the vicinity." 20
The report of the United States Geological Survey of 1878,
which covers this territory, refers to the "swampy, springy
nature of the soil in the Falls River Basin." The statement
of the Director of the Reclamation Service, whose inspection
of the site in 1919 was for the same purpose as proposed in 25
the present bill, that "the major portion of the land that
would be flooded is now swamp," fully bears out this assertion; while Representative Addison T. Smith of Idaho, who
visited the Basin in August, 1920, was convinced from his
personal observations that the report of the Geological Sur- 30
vey was correct. He also says in part, with reference to the
desirability of the spot for camping: "In the Falls River
Basin, on the 7th of August, the mosquitoes bit me so badly
that the lumps on my neck as a result did not disappear for
several weeks after the trip. The same was true of the other 35
men. . . . After we left the Basin we found no mosquitoes."

3. The vegetation in the proposed site is of little value, for

    a. The Ashton Commercial Club reports that there are very few trees on the location.[1]

    b. Director Davis of the Reclamation Service says that there is "more or less scattering timber, but none of it merchantable."[2]

    c. The Director of the Geological Survey reports that the "timber consists of small, straggling trees of no commercial value."[3]

4. The argument advanced by the Negative, contending that the construction of the proposed reservoir will destroy an invaluable feeding ground for moose, is unfounded, for

    a. According to Mr. Stephen T. Mather, Director of the National Park Service, the habitat of the moose in the Park is at the upper end of Lake Yellowstone.[4]

    b. There would remain in the vicinity of the Basin at least 100,000 acres of excellent feeding ground.[1]

B. The proposed reservoir will not be a scenic detriment to the Park, for

  1. It will destroy no scenic features of the Park, for

    a. The Falls River Basin itself contains no scenic features (see IV, *A*, 1).

---

[1] "Need of Yellowstone Water to reclaim Rich District in Eastern Idaho Counties." A report of conditions by the Ashton Commercial Club of Ashton, Idaho, in *Idaho Daily Statesman*, December 25, 1920.

[2] *Hearing before the Committee on the Public Lands, H.R., March 20 and 23, 1920*, p. 6.

[3] *Hearings before the Committee on Rules, H.R., May 25, 1920*, p. 13.

[4] Ibid. p. 8.

When the report of the Director of the Geological Survey, stating that the timber within the Basin "consists of small, straggling trees of no commercial value," is upheld in full by Director Davis, who says that there is "more or less scattering timber, but none of it merchantable," and by the 5 Ashton Commercial Club, which reports that "there are very few trees on the location," we are inclined to believe that the only possible value which the Falls River Meadows might have for Park purposes is that of providing a feeding ground for herds of moose or elk. According to Mr. Stephen T. 10 Mather, however, Superintendent of the National Park Service, the habitat of the native moose in the Park is at the upper end of Lake Yellowstone, where abundant feeding grounds are located. Thus the use of the Falls River Basin for irrigation will not interfere materially with the wild 15 game. Since it is estimated by the Ashton Commercial Club in their report that there would remain at least 100,000 acres of luxuriant feeding ground in that vicinity after the construction of the proposed reservoir, there is no reason to suppose that the moose or elk would suffer more than at 20 present by the flooding of the Basin. We may conclude, then, that the Falls River Basin, as such, actually has no value, scenic or other, for the avowed purposes of the Yellowstone Park.

The question remains, however, as to whether the con- 25 struction of the proposed reservoir in the Basin would be detrimental to the Park, either by being in itself a blot upon the landscape, or by destroying any features known to exist in the vicinity. In the first place, as far as the Basin itself is concerned, it has been proved that there are no valuable 30 scenic features, timber lands, or camping spots inside the limits of the intended reservoir, and that such grazing lands as may be flooded do not constitute an important feeding ground for wild animals. Furthermore, the Smith Bill provides "only for such necessary easements within the Falls 35 River Basin as may, in the judgment of the Secretary of the

  b. The proposed reservoir can harm none of the
scenic features of the Park which are located
outside of the Falls River Basin, for
   (1) The Smith Bill prohibits detriment to and
interference with the use of the land for
Park purposes.[1]
   (2) Engineers state that no water will be
backed up over other portions of the
Park.[2]

 2. The proposed reservoir on the Falls River Basin
site will be in itself a scenic feature rather than
a detriment, for
  a. The provisions of the Smith Bill insure this
result.

  b. Director Davis of the Reclamation Service
says that the proposed work will be a distinct
improvement in the appearance of the region.[3]

[1] Text of the Smith Bill.
[2] *Hearings before the Committee on Rules, H. R., May 25, 1920,* p. 17.
[3] *H. R. Report No. 767,* p. 4.

Interior, be required for the purposes of this act, and may be granted without detriment or interference with the occupation and use of the land for Park purposes." The engineers of the United States Reclamation Service and the engineers of the State of Idaho, who have surveyed the proposed site, state positively that the reservoir will be limited to the Falls River Basin at all seasons of the year, no water being backed up over other portions of the Park. Thus the argument often advanced by opponents of the proposition, maintaining that the scenic beauty of such features of the Yellowstone as Colonnade and other waterfalls would be marred by the construction of the reservoir, is most certainly unfounded.

It seems, in fact, from the text of the Smith Bill, that the dam and artificial lake will actually be in themselves scenic features rather than unsightly scars. One provision states that "all reservoirs, dams, conduits and other works constructed by the grantee, not of a temporary character, shall be sightly and of suitable exterior design and finish so as to harmonize with the surrounding landscape and the use of the land as a park." The bill further provides that "all timber within the limits of any reservoir, canal, ditch, road, or other works constructed by the grantee, shall be cut and removed under the supervision of the Secretary of the Interior and paid for by the grantee; Provided: that no other timber or other things or objects in said Park, outside of such rights-of-way, shall be cut, removed, destroyed or damaged by the grantee." Thus no tree trunks or limbs will protrude from the lake to mar the attractiveness of the project. A final and general provision of the bill requires that "all plans and specifications shall be submitted to and approved by the Secretary of the Interior, . . . and the Secretary . . . is further authorized . . . to protect and preserve . . . the beauty and purposes of said Park." Director Davis of the Reclamation Service says: "The lake that would be formed would be more pleasing to the eye than the natural swamp and would eliminate a considerable area of mosquito-breeding

    c. Arguments as advanced by the Negative, con-
        tending that unsightly mud flats and back-
        water areas will be produced by the proposed
        reservoir, are unfounded, for
        (1) Competent engineers who have surveyed
            the site declare that such will not be the
            case.[1]

    d. The argument advanced by the Negative,
        maintaining that the scenic beauty of such
        features of the Park as Colonnade Falls and
        other waterfalls in the vicinity of the Basin
        will be marred by the construction of the
        Reservoir, is unfounded, for
        (1) Testimony given above (*B*, 1, *b*) proves
            this.
    e. Photographs which have been published with
        captions which lead the reader to infer that
        the construction of the proposed reservoir
        would damage the scenic beauty of other
        features of the Park are deceptive.[2]

[1] *Hearings before the Committee on Rules, H. R., May 25, 1920*, p. 17.
[2] *Hearing before the Select Committee on Water Power, H. R., January 6, 1921*, p. 58.

territory. . . . The proposed work will be a distinct improvement in the appearance of the region."

Opponents of the bill often see an analogy between the unsightly mud-flats on the shores of Jackson Lake in the Tetons—once admittedly the fairest lake in the country, but now marred by the construction of a storage dam to impound flood waters—and the proposed Falls River Reservoir lake. Any supposition that similar flats and back-water areas will be produced in the present project is unfounded, for competent engineers have surveyed the site and state that such will not be the case.

An examination of certain periodicals and pamphlets published in the winter of 1920–1921 will disclose the fact that numerous photographs have been placed before the public under deceptive captions, leading the reader to infer that the construction of the Falls River Reservoir would damage the scenic beauty of other features of the Yellowstone. For instance, Mr. William C. Gregg's article, "Cornering Cascades," in the *Saturday Evening Post* for November 20, 1920, is illustrated with some wonderfully attractive photographs of beautiful waterfalls, no doubt intended to leave the impression upon the readers that, if the reservoir were constructed, these falls would be destroyed or marred. Similar photographs appeared in an article concerning this region in the *Boston Transcript* for November 20, 1920, and in other large metropolitan newspapers; while in a print by the president of the National Association of Audubon Societies may be found a photograph of Colonnade Falls—at least five miles up the river from the Basin and five hundred feet higher in altitude—with the following caption appended: "National Parks to be destroyed unless quick action is taken. Colonnade Falls, Bechler River, Yellowstone Park,—one of the forty or more waterfalls, cascades, and hot springs beautifying the territory designed to be used by an unsightly reservoir for commercial purposes." Small wonder that the American public has become agitated and Congressmen

CONCLUSION

I. Since the need of an additional water supply is vital,

II. Since the proposed site is the only one practicable,

III. Since the proposed reservoir would involve no expense to the Government,

IV. Since the reservoir as proposed would not be a detriment to the Park,

Therefore, be it resolved, that the Smith Bill (H. R. 12466), providing for the Falls River Meadows Reservoir in the southwest corner of the Yellowstone National Park, should be passed by Congress and become operative.

alarmed, when such glaring depredations are about to be
committed upon our sacred National monuments by a few
unscrupulous Western irrigationists! Save the Parks!

Sound thinking, not panic, will decide this question—and
it is a question of reclamation, not of sentiment. Reclama- 5
tion has been one of the tremendously vital movements in
the gradual conquering of our last frontier—the desert. As I
have already made clear, I am unreservedly in favor of the
contentions of the irrigationists. The cause of the "under
dog" is at least supported by some interesting evidence: 10
the need for more water is *vital*; there is no practicable site
for a storage reservoir other than the one proposed, in the
Falls River Basin in Yellowstone Park; the construction of
such a reservoir in this location would not involve expense
to the Government; and it would not be a detriment to 15
the Park.

Does the Smith Bill provide for Desecration or Reclamation?

BIBLIOGRAPHY

*Hearing before the Committee on the Public Lands, H.R., March 20 and
        23, 1920.*

*Hearing before the Select Committee on Water Power, H.R., January 6,
        1921.*

Hearings before the Committee on Rules, H.R., May 25, 1920.

H.R. Report No. 767. Representative Addison T. Smith of Idaho, March
        25, 1920. In *House Reports, 66th Congress, 2d Session.*

History of Idaho, by C. J. Brosnan. New York, 1918.

Yellowstone National Park, 1920. Pamphlet issued by the Department of
        the Interior. Washington, 1920.

The Idaho Daily Statesman:
    "Need of Yellowstone Water to reclaim Rich District in Eastern Idaho
        Counties." December 25, 1920.
    "Governor Carey (Wyoming) takes his Stand for Reclamation." Jan-
        uary, 1921. Article on the Smith Bill.

Saturday Evening Post:
    "Pawning the Heirlooms," by Emerson Hough. September 25, 1920.
    "Cornering Cascades," by William C. Gregg. November 20, 1920.

Text of the Smith Bill. Appendix to No. 1.

Boston Evening Transcript:

   "Yellowstone Rediscovered," by Allen Chamberlain. November 20, 1920.

Annual Report of the Massachusetts Forestry Association, 1920.

Circular from the Office of the American Civic Association. January 31,
   1921.

Pamphlet issued by the New England Conference for Protection of
   National Parks, 1920.

MODELS OF DESCRIPTION

A STABLE–YARD ON A RAINY DAY[1]

Washington Irving

It was a rainy Sunday in the gloomy month of November.
I had been detained, in the course of a journey, by a slight
indisposition, from which I was recovering; but was still
feverish, and obliged to keep within doors all day, in an inn
of the small town of Derby. A wet Sunday in a country inn! 5
—whoever has had the luck to experience one can alone judge
of my situation. The rain pattered against the casements;
the bells tolled for church with a melancholy sound. I went
to the windows in quest of something to amuse the eye; but
it seemed as if I had been placed completely out of the reach 10
of all amusement. The windows of my bedroom looked out
among tiled roofs and stacks of chimneys, while those of my
sitting-room commanded a full view of the stable-yard. I
know of nothing more calculated to make a man sick of this
world than a stable-yard on a rainy day. The place was lit- 15
tered with wet straw that had been kicked about by travellers
and stable-boys. In one corner was a stagnant pool of water,
surrounding an island of muck; there were several half-
drowned fowls crowded together under a cart, among which
was a miserable, crest-fallen cock, drenched out of all life 20
and spirit; his drooping tail matted, as it were, into a single
feather, along which the water trickled from his back; near
the cart was a half-dozing cow, chewing the cud, and standing
patiently to be rained on, with wreaths of vapor rising from

[1] From "The Stout Gentleman," in *Bracebridge Hall* (Author's Revised
Edition), pp. 75–76. G. P. Putnam's Sons, New York, 1861.

her reeking hide; a wall-eyed horse, tired of the loneliness
of the stable, was poking his spectral head out of a window,
with the rain dripping on it from the eaves; an unhappy cur,
chained to a dog-house hard by, uttered something every now
and then, between a bark and a yelp; a drab of a kitchen
wench tramped backwards and forwards through the yard in
pattens, looking as sulky as the weather itself; everything in
short was comfortless and forlorn, excepting a crew of hardened ducks, assembled like boon companions round a puddle,
and making a riotous noise over their liquor.

TREASURE ISLAND[1]

Robert Louis Stevenson

The appearance of the island when I came on deck next morning was altogether changed. Although the breeze had now utterly ceased, we had made a great deal of way during the night, and were now lying becalmed about half a mile to the south-east of the low eastern coast. Grey-coloured woods covered a large part of the surface. This even tint was indeed broken up by streaks of yellow sand-break in the lower lands, and by many tall trees of the pine family, out-topping the others—some singly, some in clumps; but the general colouring was uniform and sad. The hills ran up clear above the vegetation in spires of naked rock. All were strangely shaped, and the Spy-glass, which was by three or four hundred feet the tallest on the island, was likewise the strangest in configuration, running up sheer from almost every side, and then suddenly cut off at the top like a pedestal to put a statue on.

The *Hispaniola* was rolling scuppers under in the ocean swell. The booms were tearing at the blocks, the rudder was banging to and fro, and the whole ship creaking, groaning, and jumping like a manufactory. I had to cling tight to the backstay, and the world turned giddily before my eyes; for though I was a good enough sailor when there was way on, this standing still and being rolled about like a bottle was a thing I never learned to stand without a qualm or so, above all in the morning, on an empty stomach.

Perhaps it was this—perhaps it was the look of the island,

[1] From *Treasure Island* (Thistle Edition), pp. 97–98. Charles Scribner's Sons, New York, 1895.

with its grey, melancholy woods, and wild stone spires, and the surf that we could both see and hear foaming and thundering on the steep beach—at least, although the sun shone bright and hot, and the shore birds were fishing and crying all
5 around us, and you would have thought any one would have been glad to get to land after being so long at sea, my heart sank, as the saying is, into my boots; and from that first look onward, I hated the very thought of Treasure Island.

NOON IN THE PLAZA[1]

FRANK NORRIS

It was high noon, and the rays of the sun, that hung poised
directly overhead in an intolerable white glory, fell straight
as plummets upon the roofs and streets of Guadalajara. The
adobe walls and sparse brick sidewalks of the drowsing town
radiated the heat in an oily, quivering shimmer. The leaves 5
of the eucalyptus trees around the Plaza drooped motionless,
limp and relaxed under the scorching, searching blaze. The
shadows of these trees had shrunk to their smallest circum-
ference, contracting close about the trunks. The shade had
dwindled to the breadth of a mere line. The sun was every- 10
where. The heat exhaling from brick and plaster and metal
met the heat that steadily descended blanketwise and smoth-
ering, from the pale, scorched sky. Only the lizards—they
lived in chinks of the crumbling adobe and in interstices of
the sidewalk—remained without, motionless, as if stuffed, 15
their eyes closed to mere slits, basking, stupefied with heat.
At long intervals the prolonged drone of an insect developed
out of the silence, vibrated a moment in a soothing, somnolent, long note, then trailed slowly into the quiet again.
Somewhere in the interior of one of the 'dobe houses a guitar 20
snored and hummed sleepily. On the roof of the hotel a
group of pigeons cooed incessantly with subdued, liquid mur-
murs, very plaintive; a cat, perfectly white, with a pink nose
and thin, pink lips, dozed complacently on a fence rail,
full in the sun. In a corner of the Plaza three hens wal- 25
lowed in the baking hot dust, their wings fluttering, clucking
comfortably.

[1] From *The Octopus*, chap. vi, pp. 212–213. Doubleday, Page & Company, New York, 1901. Copyright, 1901, by Doubleday, Page & Company.

RUNNING BEFORE THE WIND[1]

JOHN MASEFIELD

It is at such times that I remember the good days, the exciting days, the days of vehement and spirited living. One day stands out, above nearly all my days, as a day of joy.

We were at sea off the River Plate, running south like a stag. The wind had been slowly freshening for twenty-four hours, and for one whole day we had whitened the sea like a battleship. Our run for the day had been 271 knots, which we thought a wonderful run, though it has, of course, been exceeded by many ships. For this ship it was an exceptional run. The wind was on the quarter, her best point of sailing, and there was enough wind for a glutton. Our captain had the reputation of being a "cracker-on," and on this one occasion he drove her till she groaned. For that one wonderful day we staggered and swooped, and bounded in wild leaps, and burrowed down and shivered, and anon rose up shaking. The wind roared up aloft and boomed in the shrouds, and the sails bellied out as stiff as iron. We tore through the sea in great jumps—there is no other word for it. She seemed to leap clear from one green roaring ridge to come smashing down upon the next. I have been in a fast steamer—a very fast turbine steamer—doing more than twenty knots, but she gave me no sense of great speed. In this old sailing ship the joy of the hurry was such that we laughed and cried aloud. The noise of the wind booming, and the clack, clack, clack of the sheet-blocks, and the ridged seas roaring past us, and the groaning and whining of every block and plank, were like

[1] From *A Tarpaulin Muster*, pp. 180–182. Dodd, Mead & Company, New York, 1919. Originally published in 1907.

tunes for a dance. We seemed to be tearing through it at
ninety miles an hour. Our wake whitened and broadened,
and rushed away aft in a creamy fury. We were running
here, and hurrying there, taking a small pull of this, and getting another inch of that, till we were weary. But as we 5
hauled we sang and shouted. We were possessed of the spirits
of the wind. We could have danced and killed each other.
We were in an ecstasy. We were possessed. We half believed
that the ship would leap from the waters and hurl herself into
the heavens, like a winged god. Over her bows came the 10
sprays in showers of sparkles. Her foresail was wet to the
yard. Her scuppers were brooks. Her swing-ports spouted
like cataracts. Recollect, too, that it was a day to make your
heart glad. It was a clear day, a sunny day, a day of brightness and splendour. The sun was glorious in the sky. The 15
sky was of a blue unspeakable. We were tearing along across
a splendour of sea that made you sing. Far as one could see
there was the water shining and shaking. Blue it was, and
green it was, and of a dazzling brilliance in the sun. It rose
up in hills and in ridges. It smashed into a foam and roared. 20
It towered up again and toppled. It mounted and shook in
a rhythm, in a tune, in a music. One could have flung one's
body to it as a sacrifice. One longed to be in it, to be a part
of it, to be beaten and banged by it. It was a wonder and a
glory and a terror. It was a triumph, it was royal, to see 25
that beauty.

THE HOUSE OF USHER[1]

Edgar Allan Poe

During the whole of a dull, dark, and soundless day in the autumn of the year, when the clouds hung oppressively low in the heavens, I had been passing alone, on horseback, through a singularly dreary tract of country; and at length
5 found myself, as the shades of the evening drew on, within view of the melancholy House of Usher. I know not how it was—but, with the first glimpse of the building, a sense of insufferable gloom pervaded my spirit. I say insufferable; for the feeling was unrelieved by any of that half-pleasurable,
10 because poetic, sentiment with which the mind usually receives even the sternest natural images of the desolate or terrible. I looked upon the scene before me—upon the mere house, and the simple landscape features of the domain, upon the bleak walls, upon the vacant eye-like windows, upon a
15 few rank sedges, and upon a few white trunks of decayed trees—with an utter depression of soul which I can compare to no earthly sensation more properly than to the after-dream of the reveller upon opium: the bitter lapse into every-day life, the hideous dropping off of the veil. There was an
20 iciness, a sinking, a sickening of the heart, an unredeemed dreariness of thought which no goading of the imagination could torture into aught of the sublime. What was it—I paused to think—what was it that so unnerved me in the contemplation of the House of Usher? It was a mystery all
25 insoluble; nor could I grapple with the shadowy fancies that crowded upon me as I pondered. I was forced to fall back

[1] From "The Fall of the House of Usher," in *Poe's Works* (ed. Stedman and Woodberry), Vol. I, pp. 131 ff. Chicago, 1894.

upon the unsatisfactory conclusion, that while, beyond doubt, there *are* combinations of very simple natural objects which have the power of thus affecting us, still the analysis of this power lies among considerations beyond our depth. It was possible, I reflected, that a mere different arrangement of the particulars of the scene, of the details of the picture, would be sufficient to modify, or perhaps to annihilate, its capacity for sorrowful impression; and acting upon this idea, I reined my horse to the precipitous brink of a black and lurid tarn that lay in unruffled lustre by the dwelling, and gazed down —but with a shudder even more thrilling than before— upon the remodelled and inverted images of the gray sedge, and the ghastly tree-stems, and the vacant and eye-like windows.

IN THE LUXEMBOURG GARDENS[1]

WILLIAM JOHN LOCKE

Everything wore a startlingly fresh appearance, after the
heavy rains. The gravel walk had the prim neatness of a
Peter de Hoogh garden path. The white balustrades and
flights of steps around the great circle, the statuary and the
5 fountains in the middle lake, flashed pure. The enormous
white caps of nurses, their gay silk streamers fluttering behind them, the white-clad children, the light summer dresses
of women; the patches of white newspaper held by other
loungers on the seats; a dazzling bit of cirro-cumulus scud-
10 ding across the clear Paris sky; the pale dome of the Pan-
théon rising to the east; the background of the Luxembourg
itself in which one was only conscious of the high lights on
the long bold cornices; all set the key of the picture and gave
it symphonic value. The eye rejected everything but the
15 whites and the pearl greys, subordinating all other tones to
its impression of fantastic purity.

[1] From *The Belovéd Vagabond*, pp. 176–177. Dodd, Mead & Company,
New York. Originally published in 1900.

THE PRISON DOOR[1]

Nathaniel Hawthorne

A throng of bearded men, in sad-colored garments, and gray, steeple-crowned hats, intermixed with women, some wearing hoods and others bareheaded, was assembled in front of a wooden edifice, the door of which was heavily timbered with oak, and studded with iron spikes. 5

The founders of a new colony, whatever Utopia of human virtue and happiness they might originally project, have invariably recognized it among their earliest practical necessities to allot a portion of the virgin soil as a cemetery, and another portion as the site of a prison. In accordance with 10 this rule, it may safely be assumed that the forefathers of Boston had built the first prison-house somewhere in the vicinity of Cornhill, almost as seasonably as they marked out the first burial-ground, on Isaac Johnson's lot, and round about his grave, which subsequently became the nucleus 15 of all the congregated sepulchres in the old churchyard of King's Chapel. Certain it is, that, some fifteen or twenty years after the settlement of the town, the wooden jail was already marked with weather-stains and other indications of age, which gave a yet darker aspect to its beetle-browed and 20 gloomy front. The rust on the ponderous iron-work of its oaken door looked more antique than anything else in the New World. Like all that pertains to crime, it seemed never to have known a youthful era. Before this ugly edifice, and between it and the wheel-track of the street, was a grass-plot, 25 much overgrown with burdock, pigweed, apple-peru, and such unsightly vegetation, which evidently found something

---

[1] From *The Scarlet Letter*, chap. i.

congenial in the soil that had so early borne the black flower of civilized society, a prison. But, on one side of the portal, and rooted almost at the threshold, was a wild rose-bush, covered, in this month of June, with its delicate gems, which
5 might be imagined to offer their fragrance and fragile beauty to the prisoner as he went in, and to the condemned criminal as he came forth to his doom, in token that the deep heart of Nature could pity and be kind to him.

This rose-bush, by a strange chance, has been kept alive
10 in history; but whether it had merely survived out of the stern old wilderness, so long after the fall of the gigantic pines and oaks that originally overshadowed it,—or whether, as there is fair authority for believing, it had sprung up under the footsteps of the sainted Ann Hutchinson, as she entered
15 the prison-door,—we shall not take upon us to determine. Finding it so directly on the threshold of our narrative, which is now about to issue from that inauspicious portal, we could hardly do otherwise than pluck one of its flowers, and present it to the reader. It may serve, let us hope, to symbolize some
20 sweet moral blossom, that may be found along the track, or relieve the darkening close of a tale of human frailty and sorrow.

THE WATER OF LEITH[1]

Robert Louis Stevenson

I have named, among many rivers that make music in my memory, that dirty Water of Leith. Often and often I desire to look upon it again; and the choice of a point of view is easy to me. It should be at a certain water-door, embowered in shrubbery. The river is there dammed back for 5 the service of the flour-mill just below, so that it lies deep and darkling, and the sand slopes into brown obscurity with a glint of gold; and it has but newly been recruited by the borrowings of the snuff-mill just above, and these, tumbling merrily in, shake the pool to its black heart, fill it with 10 drowsy eddies, and set the curded froth of many other mills solemnly steering to and fro upon the surface. Or so it was when I was young; for change, and the masons, and the pruning-knife, have been busy; and if I could hope to repeat a cherished experience, it must be on many and impossible 15 conditions. I must choose, as well as the point of view, a certain moment in my growth, so that the scale may be exaggerated, and the trees on the steep opposite side may seem to climb to heaven, and the sand by the water-door, where I am standing, seem as low as Styx. And I must choose the 20 season also, so that the valley may be brimmed like a cup with sunshine and the songs of birds;—and the year of grace, so that when I turn to leave the riverside I may find the old manse and its inhabitants unchanged.

[1] From "The Manse," in *Memories and Portraits* (Thistle Edition), pp. 241–242. Charles Scribner's Sons, New York, 1895.

THE GRAND CAÑON OF THE YELLOWSTONE[1]

RUDYARD KIPLING

I followed with the others round the corner to arrive at the
brink of the cañon: we had to climb up a nearly perpendicu-
lar ascent to begin with, for the ground rises more than the
river drops. Stately pine woods fringe either lip of the
gorge, which is—the Gorge of the Yellowstone.

All I can say is that without warning or preparation I
looked into a gulf seventeen hundred feet deep with eagles
and fish-hawks circling far below. And the sides of that gulf
were one wild welter of colour—crimson, emerald, cobalt,
ochre, amber, honey splashed with port-wine, snow-white,
vermilion, lemon, and silver-grey, in wide washes. The sides
did not fall sheer, but were graven by time and water and air
into monstrous heads of kings, dead chiefs, men and women
of the old time. So far below that no sound of its strife
could reach us, the Yellowstone River ran—a finger-wide
strip of jade-green. The sunlight took those wondrous walls
and gave fresh hues to those that nature had already laid
there. Once I saw the dawn break over a lake in Rajputana
and the sun set over the Oodey Sagar amid a circle of Holman
Hunt hills. This time I was watching both performances
going on below me—upside down, you understand—and the
colours were real! The cañon was burning like Troy town;
but it would burn for ever.

[1] From *From Sea to Sea*, Vol. II, chap. xxxi. Doubleday, Page & Company, New York, 1899. By special permission of Mr. Kipling and of the
publisher.

© J. E. Haynes, St. Paul

THE GRAND CAÑON OF THE YELLOWSTONE FROM ARTIST POINT

EL CAPITAN, YOSEMITE VALLEY
From the photograph by A. C. Pillsbury

EL CAPITAN[1]

John Burroughs

What an impression of mass and of power and of grandeur
in repose filters into you as you walk along! El Capitan
stands there showing its simple sweeping lines through the
trees as you approach, like one of the veritable pillars of the
firmament. How long we are nearing it and passing it! It 5
is so colossal that it seems near while it is yet far off. It is
so simple that the eye takes in its naked grandeur at a
glance. It demands of you a new standard of size which you
cannot at once produce. It is as clean and smooth as the
flank of a horse, and as poised and calm as a Greek statue. 10
It curves out toward the base as if planted there to resist
the pressure of worlds—probably the most majestic single
granite column or mountain buttress on the earth.

[1] From "The Spell of the Yosemite," in *Time and Change*. By permission of, and by special arrangement with, Houghton Mifflin Company, Boston, 1912.

A LOAMSHIRE LANDSCAPE[1]

GEORGE ELIOT

The Green lay at the extremity of the village, and from it the road branched off in two directions, one leading farther up the hill by the church, and the other winding gently down towards the valley. On the side of the Green that led towards the church, the broken line of thatched cottages was continued nearly to the churchyard gate; but on the opposite, northwestern side, there was nothing to obstruct the view of gently-swelling meadow, and wooded valley, and dark masses of distant hill. That rich undulating district of Loamshire to which Hayslope belonged, lies close to a grim outskirt of Stonyshire, overlooked by its barren hills as a pretty blooming sister may sometimes be seen linked in the arm of a rugged, tall, swarthy brother; and in two or three hours' ride the traveller might exchange a bleak treeless region, intersected by lines of cold grey stone, for one where his road wound under the shelter of woods, or up swelling hills, muffled with hedgerows and long meadow-grass and thick corn; and where at every turn he came upon some fine old country-seat nestled in the valley or crowning the slope, some homestead with its long length of barn and its cluster of golden ricks, some grey steeple looking out from a pretty confusion of trees and thatch and dark-red tiles. It was just such a picture as this last that Hayslope Church had made to the traveller as he began to mount the gentle slope leading to its pleasant uplands, and now from his station near the Green he had before him in one view nearly all the other typical features of this pleasant land. High up against the

---

[1] From *Adam Bede*, chap. ii.

horizon were the huge conical masses of hill, like giant
mounds intended to fortify this region of corn and grass
against the keen and hungry winds of the north; not distant
enough to be clothed in purple mystery, but with sombre
greenish sides visibly specked with sheep, whose motion was 5
only revealed by memory, not detected by sight; wooed
from day to day by the changing hours, but responding with
no change in themselves—left for ever grim and sullen after
the flush of morning, the winged gleams of the April noon-
day, the parting crimson glory of the ripening summer sun. 10
And directly below them the eye rested on a more advanced
line of hanging woods, divided by bright patches of pasture
or furrowed crops, and not yet deepened into the uniform
leafy curtains of high summer, but still showing the warm
tints of the young oak and the tender green of the ash and 15
lime. Then came the valley, where the woods grew thicker,
as if they had rolled down and hurried together from the
patches left smooth on the slope, that they might take the
better care of the tall mansion which lifted its parapets and
sent its faint blue summer smoke among them. Doubtless 20
there was a large sweep of park and a broad glassy pool in
front of that mansion, but the swelling slope of meadow
would not let our traveller see them from the village green.
He saw instead a foreground that was just as lovely—the
level sunlight lying like transparent gold among the gently- 25
curving stems of the feathered grass and the tall red sorrel,
and the white umbels of the hemlocks lining the bushy hedgerows. It was that moment in summer when the sound of the
scythe being whetted makes us cast more lingering looks at
the flower-sprinkled tresses of the meadows.   30

THE RIVER DART[1]

Eden Phillpotts

From the rapt loneliness of her cradle, from her secret
fountains, where the red sundew glimmers and cotton grasses
wave unseen, Dart comes wandering southward with a song.
Her pools and silent places mirror the dawn; noontide sunshine glitters along the granite aprons of her thousand falls;
the wind catches her volume leaping downward, and flings it
aloft into rainbows by day and moonlit veils by night. Beneath the echoing hills she passes; under the grey rain or
silver mist she takes her most musical course; and presently,
the richer by many a little sister river, grows into adult
beauty of being, swells to the noblest stream in all the West
Country, descends from her high places and winds, full
fraught with mystery and loveliness, into the lives of men.
Thereupon legends arise from her crystal depths; stories,
sinister enough, are whispered; romance awakens to brood
by her deep reaches and hanging woods. Henceforth humanity grows concerned with Dart, and, even as man pollutes her
current with drosses and accretions from caldron or vat, so
by him is her character clouded, her fair name maligned.

A mother of old story, with haunted pools; a flowing
record of the past, whose silvery scroll is written close with
chronicles of joy and grief, Dart hides many a deep grave
beneath her bosom, yet still takes the little children to her
heart, that they may play there and shine like pink pearls
upon her amber shallows. From happiest memory to darkest
sorrow, ever rolling, ever changing, the river strays; and the

[1] From *The River*, pp. 3–7. Copyright, 1902, by Frederick A. Stokes
Company, New York.

266

nature of mankind is reflected in her many moods, in her
peaceful and sunlit summer-time, in her autumn torrents and
winter darkness banked with snow. To-day she glides and
swirls in sleepy backwaters, and twinkles in a thousand separate threads over the great rocks; to-morrow she leaps and 5
thunders cherry-red, with a storm message from the mountains; to-day the sub-aqueous mosses gasp as her receding
stream leaves them shrunken under full blaze of light; to-
morrow she foams in freshet, tosses her wild locks on high,
shouts hoarsely, with echoing reverberations in deep gorges 10
and old secret caves, drowns half a fathom deep the little
flower that has budded and bloomed with trust beside her
brink.

  Innocent as yet of all story—a stream unblessed, uncursed
—this virgin river shall be found winding upon Dartmoor's 15
bosom. Untamed she riots here among the everlasting hills;
untrammelled she leaps down her stairways, and rejoices to
run her course. She brings goodness to the green things,
light and flashing fire to the stone, life to the sequestered
dwellers that throng her banks. As yet no bridge, save a 20
rainbow on the mist, has ever spanned her stream, no wheel
has stolen her strength, no keel has ridden her, no oar has
struck. Younger than the young noon, older than the whole
life of man, she passes from solitude to solitude; slides onward in sheets and twined threads of glassy crystal; mirrors 25
the dark peat and shining gravel, the rush and thistle and
cushions of pale ling bloom; she cuddles tiny islets where
small rats dwell; she dimples into laughter when the trout
rise; she smiles with a tremor of bubbles and shining wake as
the flat-nosed otter paddles up stream and leads her cubs to 30
their hidden nursery. Out of the wilderness she passes onward and downward, with many a pause and acceleration,
with many a curve and sweep and soft round conflexure, over
marsh and peat tye and hollow to the land of ancient bridges,
of forests, and placid water-meadows. Here red cattle come 35
and little calves drink; in spring-time the sallows make a

dawn of sudden pale gold; gorse and broom flame beside the great salmon pools; and bluebells bring down a gleam of sky to the verdant earth.

But there is a region near her sources, where the river winds
5 under huge hills crowned and scattered as to their grassy undulations with stone. The high lands clamber round about to a wild horizon that is roughly hurled upward in mighty confusion against the sky; and from the deep channels of the river's passage her music lulls or throbs at the will of the
10 wind, and wakes or ceases suddenly as the breezes blow. Here, beneath the conical mitre of Longaford Tor, in Dartmoor's central waste and fastness, she sweeps along the fringes of a primeval forest. Upon the steep foot-hills of the tor, crooked, twisted, convulsed by centuries of western winds
15 and bitter winters, like a regiment of old, chained and tortured ghosts, stands an ancient assemblage of dwarf oaks: that wonder of the Moor named Wistman's Wood. Grey lichens shroud each venerable bough, and heavy mosses— bronze and black—drip like wet hair from the joints and
20 elbows of the trees, climb aloft within a span of the new year's leaves and fruit. In the deep laps of these shattered oaks, where rot and mould have built up rich root-room, grow whortle-berries that hang out red bells in spring and ripen their purple fruit beside the acorn harvest in autumn;
25 ivy strangles the sturdy dwarfs; the chaos of fern and boulders from which they grow swallows their fallen limbs and carcasses, but still they endure and still stoutly obey the call of the seasons. Their amber buds cast sheath at each new-born April; their lemon catkins powder the leaves again
30 in May. After a thousand years life moves yet in their knotty hearts, and the young green of them is as fair as the fresh spike of the wild wood rush renewed beneath their shadows, or the dream-like corydalis, that here passes her brief summer at their feet.

35 Transcendent age marks this ancestral wood and each hoary stock and stone within it broods abstracted, breathes

the heavy air of eld. Here ancient meets with ancient and
fashions a home and a resting-place for night. Night, indeed,
by taper of star and moon, moves familiarly through these
dim glades, knows each stem and bough for a friend, wakens
her secret pensioners in holt and den. Now red foxes dwell
in Wistman's Wood, and yesterday a mother wolf suckled
her litter there. Here Time shall be surprised asleep; here
the unchanging serpent, roughly wakened, shall uncoil her
wheel, curled like a woman's necklet, and flow away over the
rocks, in a sudden rivulet of ebony and silver and olive
brown. The trees laugh at their frail footstools of granite,
for the transparent egg they hold aloft in a pigeon's nest is
stronger than the stone. One bears the eternal, but these
crystalline giants of quartz, felspar, and mica are playthings
for winter and the latter rain. The years nibble and gnaw
each monstrous boulder; the frost stabs them; the ages wait
their attrition with patience. Yet this wood of Wistman in-
dues its youth like a garment, and the second spring of the
oak annually bedecks each leafy crown with rosettes of car-
mine foliage that glow against dark summer green. Acorns
also yearly feed the doves, or, sinking into earth, rise again
and take the places of their fathers. Rowans are scattered
through the grove, and their berries, lighting autumn-time,
weave scarlet into the foliage of the oaks. Then, the last
leaf fallen, this forest sprawls in hibernal nakedness, like a
grey web flung over the sere or snow of the wintry hills.
Descended from trees that formed the bygone Chase of
Dartmoor, these old oaks still flourish and defy death. It
has been conjectured that from the Celtic springs their name,
for Wistman's Wood may haply have been *uisg-maen-coed*,
"the stony wood by the water"—a description of the spot
most just and perfect. Here, at least, these two immortals
—the stream and the forest—continue to survey each other
through the centuries, and, still flourishing in the proper
polity of green wood and living water, preserve a melodious
and eternal tryst with time.

A TROPICAL RIVER[1]

Joseph Conrad

The white man, leaning with both arms over the roof of the little house in the stern of the boat, said to the steersman: "We will pass the night in Arsat's clearing. It is late."

The Malay only grunted, and went on looking fixedly at the river. The white man rested his chin on his crossed arms and gazed at the wake of the boat. At the end of the straight avenue of forests cut by the intense glitter of the river, the sun appeared unclouded and dazzling, poised low over the water that shone smoothly like a band of metal. The forests, sombre and dull, stood motionless and silent on each side of the broad stream. At the foot of the big, towering trees, trunkless nipa palms rose from the mud of the bank, in bunches of leaves enormous and heavy, that hung unstirring over the brown swirl of eddies. In the stillness of the air every tree, every leaf, every bough, every tendril of creeper, and every petal of minute blossoms seemed to have been bewitched into an immobility perfect and final. Nothing moved on the river but the eight paddles that rose flashing regularly, dipped together with a single splash; while the steersman swept right and left with a periodic and sudden flourish of his blade describing a glinting semi-circle above his head. The churned-up water frothed alongside with a confused murmur. And the white man's canoe, advancing up stream in the short-lived disturbance of its own making, seemed to enter the portals of a land from which the very memory of motion had for ever departed.

The white man, turning his back upon the setting sun,

[1] From "The Lagoon," in *Tales of Unrest*, pp. 319–323. Charles Scribner's Sons, New York, 1898.

looked along the empty and broad expanse of the sea-reach. For the last three miles of its course the wandering, hesitating river, as if enticed irresistibly by the freedom of an open horizon, flows straight into the sea, flows straight to the east—to the east that harbours both light and darkness. Astern of the boat the repeated call of some bird, a cry discordant and feeble, skipped along over the smooth water and lost itself, before it could reach the other shore, in the breathless silence of the world.

The steersman dug his paddle into the stream, and held hard with stiffened arms, his body thrown forward. The water gurgled aloud; and suddenly the long straight reach seemed to pivot on its center, the forests swung in a semicircle, and the slanting beams of sunset touched the broadside of the canoe with a fiery glow, throwing the slender and distorted shadows of its crew upon the streaked glitter of the river. The white man turned to look ahead. The course of the boat had been altered at right-angles to the stream, and the carved dragon-head of its prow was pointing now at a gap in the fringing bushes of the bank. It glided through, brushing the overhanging twigs, and disappeared from the river like some slim and amphibious creature leaving the water for its lair in the forests.

The narrow creek was like a ditch: tortuous, fabulously deep; filled with gloom under the thin strip of pure and shining blue of the heaven. Immense trees soared up, invisible behind the festooned draperies of creepers. Here and there, near the glistening blackness of the water, a twisted root of some tall tree showed amongst the tracery of small ferns, black and dull, writhing and motionless, like an arrested snake. The short words of the paddlers reverberated loudly between the thick and sombre walls of vegetation. Darkness oozed out from between the trees, through the tangled maze of the creepers, from behind the great fantastic and unstirring leaves; the darkness, mysterious and invincible; the darkness scented and poisonous of impenetrable forests.

The men poled in the shoaling water. The creek broadened, opening out into a wide sweep of a stagnant lagoon. The forests receded from the marshy bank, leaving a level strip of bright green, reedy grass to frame the reflected blueness of the sky. A fleecy pink cloud drifted high above, trailing the delicate colouring of its image under the floating leaves and the silvery blossoms of the lotus. A little house, perched on high piles, appeared black in the distance. Near it, two tall nibong palms, that seemed to have come out of the forests in the background, leaned slightly over the ragged roof, with a suggestion of sad tenderness and care in the droop of their leafy and soaring heads.

The steersman, pointing with his paddle, said: "Arsat is there. I see his canoe fast between the piles."

THE LITTLE HOUSE[1]

Coningsby Dawson

I am a London house and a very little house, standing in a fashionable square near Hyde Park. I have known my ups and downs. Once was the time when I was almost in the country and the link-boys used to make a fuss at having to escort my lady so far in her sedan-chair. It's a long way to 5 the country now, for the city has spread out miles beyond me. Within sight through the trees at the end of the square, red motor-buses pass, bumping their way rowdily down to Hammersmith and Kew. In my young days these places were villages, but I am told they are full of noises now. I 10 have at least escaped that, for our square is a backwater of quiet and leads to nowhere, having an entrance only at one end. All the houses in the square were built at the same time as I was, which makes things companionable. We all look very much alike, with tiny areas, three stone steps leading 15 up from the pavement, one window blinking out from the ground-floor, two blinking out from each of the other floors and a verandah running straight across us. In summer-time the verandah is gay with flowers. Our only difference is the colour we are painted, especially the colour of our doors. 20 Mine is white; but some of our neighbors' are blue, some green, some red. We're very proud of the front-doors in our square. In the middle stands a railed-in garden, to which none but our owners have access. Its trees are as ancient as ourselves. Behind us, so hidden that it is almost forgotten, 25 stands the grey parish-church, surrounded by a graveyard in which many of the people who have been merry in us rest.

[1] From *The Little House*, pp. 13–14. Dodd, Mead & Company, New York, 1922.

LONDON[1]

ARTHUR SYMONS

English air, working upon London smoke, creates the real London. The real London is not a city of uniform brightness, like Paris, nor of savage gloom, like Prague; it is a picture continually changing, a continual sequence of pic-
5 tures, and there is no knowing what mean street corner may not suddenly take on a glory not its own. The English mist is always at work like a subtle painter, and London is a vast canvas prepared for the mist to work on. The especial beauty of London is the Thames, and the Thames is so wonderful
10 because the mist is always changing its shapes and colours, always making its lights mysterious, and building palaces of cloud out of mere Parliament Houses with their jags and turrets. When the mist collaborates with night and rain, the masterpiece is created.

15 Most travellers come into London across the river, sometimes crossing it twice. The entrance, as you leave the country behind you, is ominous. If you come by night, and it is never wise to enter any city except by night, you are slowly swallowed up by a blank of blackness, pierced by holes and
20 windows of dingy light; foul and misty eyes of light in the sky; narrow gulfs, in which lights blink; blocks and spikes of black against grey; masts, as it were, rising out of a sea of mist; then a whole street suddenly laid bare in bright light; shoulders of dark buildings; and then black shiny rails, and
25 then the river, a vast smudge, dismal and tragic; and, as one crosses it again, between the vast network of the bridge's bars, the impossible fairy peep-show of the Embankment.

[1] From *Cities and Sea-Coasts and Islands*. Brentano's, New York, 1918.

All this one sees in passing, in hardly more than a series of
flashes; but if you would see London steadily from the point
where its aspect is finest, go on a night when there has been
rain to the footpath which crosses Hungerford Bridge by the
side of the railway-track. The river seems to have suddenly 5
become a lake; under the black arches of Waterloo Bridge
there are reflections of golden fire, multiplying arch beyond
arch, in a lovely tangle. The Surrey side is dark, with tall
vague buildings rising out of the mud on which a little water
crawls: is it the water that moves or the shadows? A few 10
empty barges or steamers lie in solid patches on the water
near the bank; and a stationary sky-sign, hideous where it
defaces the night, turns in the water to wavering bars of
rosy orange. The buildings on the Embankment rise up,
walls of soft greyness with squares of lighted windows, which 15
make patterns across them. They tremble in the mist, their
shapes flicker; it seems as if a breath would blow out their
lights and leave them bodiless husks in the wind. From one
of the tallest chimneys a reddish smoke floats and twists like
a flag. Below, the Embankment curves towards Cleopatra's 20
Needle: you see the curve of the wall, as the lamps light it,
leaving the obelisk in shadow, and falling faintly on the
grey mud in the river. Just that corner has a mysterious air,
as if secluded, in the heart of a pageant; I know not what
makes it quite so tragic and melancholy. The aspect of the 25
night, the aspect of London, pricked out in points of fire
against an enveloping darkness, is as beautiful as any sunset
or any mountain; I do not know any more beautiful aspect.
And here, as always in London, it is the atmosphere that
makes the picture, an atmosphere like Turner, revealing 30
every form through the ecstasy of its colour.

It is not only on the river that London can make absolute
beauty out of the material which lies so casually about in its
streets. A London sunset, seen through vistas of narrow
streets, has a colour of smoky rose which can be seen in no 35
other city, and it weaves strange splendours, often enough,

on its edges and gulfs of sky, not less marvellous than Venice
can lift over the Giudecca, or Siena see stretched beyond its
walls. At such a point as the Marble Arch you may see con-
flagrations of jewels, a sky of burning lavender, tossed abroad
5 like a crumpled cloak, with broad bands of dull purple and
smoky pink, slashed with bright gold and decked with grey
streamers; you see it through a veil of moving mist, which
darkens downwards to a solid block, coloured like lead,
where the lighted road turns, meeting the sky.

   .   .   .   .

10   If the Thames is the soul of London, and if the parks are
its eyes, surely Trafalgar Square may well be reckoned its
heart. There is no hour of day or night when it is not admirable, but for my part I prefer the evening, just as it
grows dusk, after a day of heavy rain. How often have I
15 walked up and down, for mere pleasure, for a pleasure which
quickened into actual excitement, on that broad, curved platform from which you can turn to look up at the National
Gallery, like a frontispiece, and from which you can look
down over the dark stone pavement, black and shining with
20 rain, on which the curved fountains stand with their inky
water, while two gas-lamps cast a feeble light on the granite
base of the Nelson monument and on the vast sulky lions at
the corners. The pedestal goes up straight into the sky,
diminishing the roofs, which curve downwards to the white
25 clock-face, alone visible on the clock-tower at Westminster.
Whitehall flows like a river, on which vague shapes of traffic
float and are submerged. The mist and the twilight hide the
one harmonious building in London, the Banqueting Hall.
You realise that it is there, and that beyond it are the Abbey
30 and the river, with the few demure squares and narrow frugal
streets still left standing in Westminster.

TRAFALGAR SQUARE, LONDON

The National Gallery   St. Martin's-in-the-Fields   Nelson's Monument   The Strand

PARIS

Looking toward Notre Dame from the Louvre

PARIS[1]

SIR PHILIP GIBBS

Only those who have known Paris and loved her beauty
can understand the thrill that came to us on that morning in
September [1914] when we had expected to hear the roar of
great guns around her, and to see the beginning of a ghastly
destruction. Paris was still safe! By some kind of miracle 5
the enemy had not yet touched her beauty nor tramped into
her streets. How sharp and clear were all the buildings
under that cloudless sky! Spears of light flashed from the
brazen-winged horses above Alexander's bridge, and the dome
of the Invalides was a golden crown above a snow-white 10
palace. The Seine poured in a burnished stream beneath all
the bridges, and far away beyond the houses and the island
trees and all the pictures of Paris etched by a master hand
through long centuries of time the towers of Notre Dame
were faintly penciled in the blue screen of sky. Oh, fair 15
dream-city, in which the highest passions of the spirit have
found a dwelling-place,—with the rankest weeds of vice,—in
which so many human hearts have suffered and strived and
starved for beauty's sake, in which always there have lived
laughter and agony and tears, where Liberty was cherished 20
as well as murdered, and where Love has redeemed a thousand crimes, I, though an Englishman, found tears in my
eyes because on that day of history your beauty was still
unspoiled.

[1] From *The Soul of the War*, pp. 103–104. Copyright, 1915, by Robert
M. McBride & Co., New York. Quoted with the permission of the
publishers.

THE WHEAT PIT[1]

FRANK NORRIS

It was a vast enclosure, lighted on either side by great
windows of coloured glass, the roof supported by thin iron
pillars elaborately decorated. To the left were the bulletin
blackboards, and beyond these, in the northwest angle of
5 the floor, a great railed-in space where the Western Union
Telegraph was installed. To the right, on the other side of
the room, a row of tables, laden with neatly arranged paper
bags half full of samples of grains, stretched along the east
wall from the doorway of the public room at one end to the
10 telephone room at the other.

The centre of the floor was occupied by the pits. To the
left and to the front of Landry the provision pit, to the right
the corn pit, while further on at the north extremity of the
floor, and nearly under the visitors' gallery, much larger than
15 the other two, and flanked by the wicket of the official re-
corder, was the wheat pit itself.

Directly opposite the visitors' gallery, high upon the south
wall, a great dial was affixed, and on the dial a marking hand
that indicated the current price of wheat, fluctuating with
20 the changes made in the Pit. Just now it stood at ninety-
three and three-eighths, the closing quotation of the preceding day.

As yet all the pits were empty. It was some fifteen minutes after nine. Landry checked his hat and coat at the coat-
25 room near the north entrance, and slipped into an old tennis
jacket of striped blue flannel. Then, hatless, his hands in his
pockets, he leisurely crossed the floor, and sat down in one of

[1] From *The Pit*, pp. 91 ff. Doubleday, Page & Company, New York,
1903. Copyright, 1903, by Doubleday, Page & Company.

the chairs that were ranged in files upon the floor in front of
the telegraph enclosure. He scrutinised again the despatches
and orders that he held in his hands ; then, having fixed them
in his memory, tore them into very small bits, looking
vaguely about the room, developing his plan of campaign for 5
the morning.

.   .   .   .

Meanwhile the floor was beginning to fill up. Over in the
railed-in space, where the hundreds of telegraph instruments
were in place, the operators were arriving in twos and threes.
They hung their hats and ulsters upon the pegs in the wall 10
back of them, and in linen coats, or in their shirt-sleeves,
went to their seats, or, sitting upon their tables, called back
and forth to each other, joshing, cracking jokes. Some few
addressed themselves directly to work, and here and there
the intermittent clicking of a key began, like a diligent 15
cricket busking himself in advance of its mates.

From the corridors on the ground floor up through the
south doors came the pit traders in increasing groups. The
noise of footsteps began to echo from the high vaulting of
the roof.   20

The groups of traders gradually converged upon the corn
and wheat pits, and on the steps of the latter, their arms
crossed upon their knees, two men, one wearing a silk skull
cap all awry, conversed earnestly in low tones.

.   .   .   .

But by now it was near to half-past nine. From the 25
Western Union desks the clicking of the throng of instruments rose into the air in an incessant staccato stridulation.
The messenger boys ran back and forth at top speed, dodging
in and out among the knots of clerks and traders, colliding
with one another, and without interruption intoning the 30
names of those for whom they had despatches. The throng
of traders concentrated upon the pits, and at every moment
the deep-toned hum of the murmur of many voices swelled
like the rising of a tide.

·   ·   ·   ·   ·   ·   ·   ·   ·   ·

The official reporter climbed to his perch in the little cage on the edge of the Pit, shutting the door after him. By now the chanting of the messenger boys was an uninterrupted chorus. From all sides of the building, and in every direc-
5 tion, they crossed and recrossed each other, always running, their hands full of yellow envelopes. From the telephone alcoves came the prolonged, musical rasp of the call bells. In the Western Union booths the keys of the multitude of instruments raged incessantly. Bare-headed young men hur-
10 ried up to one another, conferred an instant comparing des-patches, then separated, darting away at top speed. Men called to each other halfway across the building. Over by the bulletin boards clerks and agents made careful memo-randa of primary receipts, and noted down the amount of
15 wheat on passage, the exports and the imports.

And all these sounds, the chatter of the telegraph, the in-toning of the messenger boys, the shouts and cries of clerks and traders, the shuffle and trampling of hundreds of feet, the whirring of telephone signals rose into the troubled air,
20 and mingled overhead to form a vast note, prolonged, sus-tained, that reverberated from vault to vault of the airy roof, and issued from every doorway, every opened window in one long roll of interrupted thunder. In the Wheat Pit the bids, no longer obedient of restraint, began one by one to burst
25 out, like the first isolated shots of a skirmish line.

·   ·   ·   ·   ·   ·   ·   ·   ·   ·

Then suddenly, cutting squarely athwart the vague cre-scendo of the floor, came the single incisive stroke of a great gong. Instantly a tumult was unchained. Arms were flung upward in strenuous gestures, and from above the crowding
30 heads in the Wheat Pit a multitude of hands, eager, the fingers extended, leaped into the air. All articulate expres-sion was lost in the single explosion of sound as the traders surged downwards to the centre of the Pit, grabbing each other, struggling towards each other, tramping, stamping,

charging through with might and main. Promptly the hand
on the great dial above the clock stirred and trembled, and
as though driven by the tempest breath of the Pit moved
upward through the degrees of its circle. It paused, wavered,
stopped at length, and on the instant the hundreds of tele- 5
graph keys scattered throughout the building began clicking
off the news to the whole country, from the Atlantic to the
Pacific and from Mackinac to Mexico, that the Chicago
market had made a slight advance and that May wheat,
which had closed the day before at ninety-three and three- 10
eighths, had opened that morning at ninety-four and a half.

.   .   .   .

By degrees the clamour died away, ceased, began again
irregularly, then abruptly stilled. Here and there a bid was
called, an offer made, like the intermittent crack of small
arms after the stopping of the cannonade.   15

"'Sell five May at one-eighth."

"'Sell twenty at one-quarter."

"'Give one-eighth for May."

For an instant the shoutings were renewed. Then suddenly
the gong struck. The traders began slowly to leave the 20
Pit. One of the floor officers, an old fellow in uniform and
vizored cap, appeared, gently shouldering towards the door
the groups wherein the bidding and offering were still
languidly going on. His voice full of remonstration, he repeated continually: "Time's up, gentlemen. Go on now and 25
get your lunch. Lunch time now. Go on now, or I'll have
to report you. Time's up."

The tide set toward the doorways. In the gallery the few
visitors rose, putting on coats and wraps. Over by the check
counter, to the right of the south entrance to the floor, a 30
throng of brokers and traders jostled each other, reaching
over one another's shoulders for hats and ulsters. In steadily
increasing numbers they poured out of the north and south
entrances, on their way to turn in their trading cards to
the offices.   35

Little by little the floor emptied. The provision and grain
pits were deserted, and as the clamour of the place lapsed
away the telegraph instruments began to make themselves
heard once more, together with the chanting of the mes-
5 senger boys.

Swept clean in the morning, the floor itself, seen now
through the thinning groups, was littered from end to end
with scattered grain—oats, wheat, corn, and barley, with
wisps of hay, peanut shells, apple parings, and orange peel,
10 with torn newspapers, odds and ends of memoranda, crushed
paper darts, and above all with a countless multitude of yellow telegraph forms, thousands upon thousands, crumpled
and muddied under the trampling of innumerable feet. It
was the débris of the battle-field, the abandoned impedi-
15 menta and broken weapons of contending armies, the detritus
of conflict, torn, broken, and rent, that at the end of each
day's combat encumbered the field.

At last even the click of the last of telegraph keys died
down. Shouldering themselves into their overcoats, the oper-
20 ators departed, calling back and forth to one another, making
"dates," and cracking jokes. Washerwomen appeared with
steaming pails; porters pushing great brooms before them
began gathering the refuse of the floor into heaps.

.   .   .   .

A cat, grey and striped, and wearing a dog collar of nickel
25 and red leather, issued from the coat-room and picked her
way across the floor. Evidently she was in a mood of the
most ingratiating friendliness, and as one after another of
the departing traders spoke to her, raised her tail in the air
and arched her back against the legs of the empty chairs.
30 The janitor put in an appearance, lowering the tall colored
windows with a long rod. A noise of hammering and the
scrape of saws began to issue from a corner where a couple
of carpenters tinkered about one of the sample tables.

Then at last even the settlement clerks took themselves
35 off. At once there was a great silence, broken only by the

harsh rasp of the carpenters' saws and the voice of the janitor exchanging jokes with the washerwomen. The sound of footsteps in distant quarters re-echoed as if in a church.

The washerwomen invaded the floor, spreading soapy and steaming water before them. Over by the sample tables a negro porter in shirt-sleeves swept entire bushels of spilled wheat, crushed, broken, and sodden, into his dust pans.

The day's campaign was over. It was past two o'clock. On the great dial against the eastern wall the indicator stood —sentinel fashion—at ninety-three. Not till the following morning would the whirlpool, the great central force that spun the Niagara of wheat in its grip, thunder and bellow again.

Later on even the washerwomen, even the porter and janitor, departed. An unbroken silence, the peacefulness of an untroubled calm, settled over the place. The rays of the afternoon sun flooded through the west windows in long parallel shafts full of floating golden motes. There was no sound; nothing stirred. The floor of the Board of Trade was deserted. Alone, on the edge of the abandoned Wheat Pit, in a spot where the sunlight fell warmest—an atom of life, lost in the immensity of the empty floor—the grey cat made her toilet, diligently licking the fur on the inside of her thigh, one leg, as if dislocated, thrust into the air above her head.

TENNYSON[1]

Thomas Carlyle

Alfred is the son of a Lincolnshire Gentleman Farmer, I
think; indeed, you see in his verses that he is a native of
"moated granges," and green, fat pastures, not of mountains
and their torrents and storms. He had his breeding at Cambridge, as if for the Law or Church; being master of a small
annuity on his Father's decease, he preferred clubbing with
his Mother and some Sisters, to live unpromoted and write
Poems. In this way he lives still, now here, now there; the
family always within reach of London, never in it; he himself making rare and brief visits, lodging in some old comrade's rooms. I think he must be under forty, not much
under it. One of the finest-looking men in the world. A
great shock of rough dusty-dark hair; bright-laughing hazel
eyes; massive aquiline face, most massive yet most delicate;
of sallow-brown complexion, almost Indian-looking; clothes
cynically loose, free-and-easy;—smokes infinite tobacco. His
voice is musical metallic,—fit for loud laughter and piercing
wail, and all that may lie between; speech and speculation
free and plenteous: I do not meet, in these late decades, such
company over a pipe!

[1] From *The Carlyle-Emerson Correspondence* (ed. C. E. Norton), Vol. II,
pp. 66–67. Houghton Mifflin Company, Boston, 1892.

ALFRED, LORD TENNYSON
From the photograph by Julia Margaret Cameron

DANIEL WEBSTER

DANIEL WEBSTER[1]

Thomas Carlyle

Not many days ago I saw at breakfast the notablest of all
your Notabilities, Daniel Webster. He is a magnificent
specimen; you might say to all the world, This is your
Yankee Englishman, such Limbs *we* make in Yankeeland!
As a Logic-fencer, Advocate, or Parliamentary Hercules, one 5
would incline to back him at first sight against all the extant
world. The tanned complexion, that amorphous crag-like
face; the dull black eyes under their precipice of brows, like
dull anthracite furnaces, needing only to be *blown*; the
mastiff-mouth, accurately closed:—I have not traced as 10
much of *silent Berserkir-rage*, that I remember of, in any
other man.

[1] From *The Carlyle-Emerson Correspondence* (ed. C. E. Norton), Vol. I,
pp. 260–261. Houghton Mifflin Company, Boston, 1892.

TWO PORTRAITS BY RAEBURN[1]

ROBERT LOUIS STEVENSON

I

One interesting portrait was that of Duncan of Camperdown. He stands in uniform beside a table, his feet slightly straddled with the balance of an old sailor, his hand poised upon a chart by the finger tips. The mouth is pursed, the nostril spread and drawn up, the eye-brows very highly arched. The cheeks lie along the jaw in folds of iron, and have the redness that comes from much exposure to salt sea winds. From the whole figure, attitude and countenance, there breathes something precise and decisive, something alert, wiry, and strong. You can understand, from the look of him, that sense, not so much of humour, as of what is grimmest and driest in pleasantry, which inspired his address before the fight at Camperdown. He had just overtaken the Dutch fleet under Admiral de Winter. "Gentlemen," says he, "you see a severe winter approaching; I have only to advise you to keep up a good fire." Somewhat of this same spirit of adamantine drollery must have supported him in the days of the mutiny at the Nore, when he lay off the Texel with his own flagship, the *Venerable*, and only one other vessel, and kept up active signals, as though he had a powerful fleet in the offing, to intimidate the Dutch.

[1] From "Some Portraits by Raeburn," in *Virginibus Puerisque* (Thistle Edition), pp. 129–131. Charles Scribner's Sons, New York, 1895.

ADMIRAL DUNCAN OF CAMPERDOWN
From the portrait by Raeburn in Trinity House, Leith

ROBERT M'QUEEN, LORD BRAXFIELD
From the portrait by Raeburn in Parliament House, Edinburgh

II

Another portrait which irresistibly attracted the eye, was the half-length of Robert M'Queen, of Braxfield, Lord Justice-Clerk. If I know gusto in painting when I see it, this canvas was painted with rare enjoyment. The tart, rosy, humorous look of the man, his nose like a cudgel, his face resting squarely on the jowl, has been caught and perpetuated with something that looks like brotherly love. A peculiarly subtle expression haunts the lower part, sensual and incredulous, like that of a man tasting good Bordeaux with half a fancy it has been somewhat too long uncorked. From under the pendulous eyelids of old age, the eyes look out with a half-youthful, half-frosty twinkle. Hands, with no pretence to distinction, are folded on the judge's stomach. So sympathetically is the character conceived by the portrait painter, that it is hardly possible to avoid some movement of sympathy on the part of the spectator.

BEATRIX ESMOND[1]

William Makepeace Thackeray

In the hall of Walcote House . . . is a staircase that leads
from an open gallery, where are the doors of the sleeping
chambers: and from one of these, a wax candle in her hand,
and illuminating her, came Mistress Beatrix—the light fall-
5 ing indeed upon the scarlet riband which she wore, and upon
the most brilliant white neck in the world.

Esmond had left a child and found a woman, grown beyond the common height; and arrived at such a dazzling
completeness of beauty, that his eyes might well show surprise
10 and delight at beholding her. In hers there was a brightness
so lustrous and melting, that I have seen a whole assembly
follow her as if by an attraction irresistible: and that
night the great Duke was at the playhouse after Ramillies,
every soul turned and looked (she chanced to enter at the
15 opposite side of the theatre at the same moment) at her, and
not at him. She was a brown beauty: that is, her eyes, hair,
and eyebrows and eyelashes were dark: her hair curling with
rich undulations, and waving over her shoulders; but her
complexion was as dazzling white as snow in sunshine: ex-
20 cept her cheeks, which were a bright red, and her lips, which
were of a still deeper crimson. Her mouth and chin, they
said, were too large and full, and so they might be for a
goddess in marble, but not for a woman whose eyes were
fire, whose look was love, whose voice was the sweetest low
25 song, whose shape was perfect symmetry, health, decision,
activity, whose foot as it planted itself on the ground was
firm but flexible, and whose motion, whether rapid or slow,

[1] From *The History of Henry Esmond, Esq.*, Bk. II, chap. vii.

288

was always perfect grace—agile as a nymph, lofty as a queen
—now melting, now imperious, now sarcastic—there was no
single movement of hers but was beautiful. As he thinks
of her, he who writes feels young again, and remembers a
paragon.   5

So she came holding her dress with one fair rounded arm,
and her taper before her, tripping down the stair to greet
Esmond.

A PORTRAIT[1]

Robert Louis Stevenson

He went boldly to the door and knocked with an assured hand. On both previous occasions, he had knocked timidly and with some dread of attracting notice; but now when he had just discarded the thought of a burglarious entry, knock-
5 ing at a door seemed a mighty simple and innocent proceeding. The sound of his blows echoed through the house with thin, phantasmal reverberations, as though it were quite empty; but these had scarcely died away before a measured tread drew near, a couple of bolts were withdrawn, and one
10 wing was opened broadly, as though no guile or fear of guile were known to those within. A tall figure of a man, muscular and spare but a little bent, confronted Villon. The head was massive in bulk, but finely sculptured; the nose blunt at the bottom, but refining upward to where it joined a pair of
15 strong and honest eyebrows; the mouth and eyes surrounded with delicate markings, and the whole face based upon a thick white beard, boldly and squarely trimmed. Seen as it was by the light of a flickering hand-lamp, it looked perhaps nobler than it had a right to do; but it was a fine face, hon-
20 ourable rather than intelligent, strong, simple, and righteous.

[1] From "A Lodging for the Night," in *New Arabian Nights* (Thistle Edition), p. 303. Charles Scribner's Sons, New York, 1895.

CAFÉ DES EXILÉS[1]

GEORGE WASHINGTON CABLE

That which in 1835—I think he said thirty-five—was a reality in the Rue Burgundy—I think he said Burgundy—is now but a reminiscence. Yet so vividly was its story told me, that at this moment the old Café des Exilés appears before my eye, floating in the clouds of revery, and I doubt not I 5 see it just as it was in the old times.

An antiquated story-and-a-half Creole cottage sitting right down on the banquette, as do the Choctaw squaws who sell bay and sassafras and life-everlasting, with a high, close board-fence shutting out of view the diminutive garden on 10 the southern side. An ancient willow droops over the roof of round tiles, and partly hides the discolored stucco, which keeps dropping off into the garden as though the old café was stripping for the plunge into oblivion—disrobing for its execution. I see, well up in the angle of the broad side gable, 15 shaded by its rude awning of clapboards, as the eyes of an old dame are shaded by her wrinkled hand, the window of Pauline. Oh, for the image of the maiden, were it but for one moment, leaning out of the casement to hang her mocking-bird and looking down into the garden,—where, above the 20 barrier of old boards, I see the top of the fig-tree, the pale green clump of bananas, the tall palmetto with its jagged crown, Pauline's own two orange-trees holding up their hands toward the window, heavy with the promises of autumn; the broad, crimson mass of the many-stemmed oleander, and the 25 crisp boughs of the pomegranate loaded with freckled apples, and with here and there a lingering scarlet blossom.

[1] From *Old Creole Days*, pp. 85–88. Copyright, 1879, 1883, 1897, by Charles Scribner's Sons, New York.

The Café des Exilés, to use the figure, flowered, bore fruit, and dropped it long ago—or rather Time and Fate, like some uncursed Adam and Eve, came side by side and cut away its clusters, as we sever the golden burden of the banana from
5 its stem; then, like a banana which has borne its fruit, it was razed to the ground and made way for a newer, brighter growth. I believe it would set every tooth on edge should I go by there now,—now that I have heard the story,—and see the old site covered by the "Shoo-fly Coffee-house." Pleas-
10 anter far to close my eyes and call to view the unpretentious portals of the old café, with her children—for such those exiles seem to me—dragging their rocking-chairs out, and sitting in their wonted group under the long, out-reaching eaves which shaded the banquette of the Rue Burgundy.

15 It was in 1835 that the Café des Exilés was, as one might say, in full blossom. Old M. D'Hemecourt, father of Pauline and host of the café, himself a refugee from San Domingo, was the cause—at least the human cause—of its opening. As its white-curtained, glazed doors expanded, emitting a little
20 puff of his own cigarette smoke, it was like the bursting of catalpa blossoms, and the exiles came like bees, pushing into the tiny room to sip its rich variety of tropical sirups, its lemonades, its orangeades, its orgeats, its barley-waters, and its outlandish wines, while they talked of dear home—that
25 is to say, of Barbadoes, of Martinique, of San Domingo, and of Cuba.

There were Pedro and Benigno, and Fernandez and Francisco, and Benito. Benito was a tall, swarthy man, with immense gray moustachios, and hair as harsh as tropical grass
30 and gray as ashes. When he could spare his cigarette from his lips, he would tell you in a cavernous voice, and with a wrinkled smile, that he was "a t-thorty-seveng."

There was Martinez of San Domingo, yellow as a canary, always sitting with one leg curled under him, and holding
35 the back of his head in his knitted fingers against the back of his rocking-chair. Father, mother, brother, sisters, all,

had been massacred in the struggle of '21 and '22; he alone was left to tell the tale, and told it often, with that strange, infantile insensibility to the solemnity of his bereavement so peculiar to Latin people.

But, besides these, and many who need no attention, there were two in particular, around whom all the story of the Café des Exilés, of old M. D'Hemecourt and of Pauline, turns as on a double center. First, Manuel Mazaro, whose small, restless eyes were as black and bright as those of a mouse, whose light talk became his dark girlish face, and whose redundant locks curled so prettily and so wonderfully black under the fine white brim of his jaunty Panama. He had the hands of a woman, save that the nails were stained with the smoke of cigarettes. He could play the guitar delightfully, and wore his knife down behind his coat-collar.

The second was "Major" Galahad Shaughnessy. I imagine I can see him, in his white duck, brass-buttoned roundabout, with his sabreless belt peeping out beneath, all his boyishness in his sea-blue eyes, leaning lightly against the door-post of the Café des Exilés as a child leans against his mother, running his fingers over a basketful of fragrant limes, and watching his chance to strike some solemn Creole under the fifth rib with a good old Irish joke.

VILLON AND HIS CREW[1]

ROBERT LOUIS STEVENSON

It was late in November, 1456. The snow fell over Paris with rigorous, relentless persistence; sometimes the wind made a sally and scattered it in flying vortices; sometimes there was a lull, and flake after flake descended out of the 5 black night air, silent, circuitous, interminable. To poor people, looking up under moist eyebrows, it seemed a wonder where it all came from. Master Francis Villon had propounded an alternative that afternoon, at a tavern window: was it only Pagan Jupiter plucking geese upon Olympus? or 10 were the holy angels moulting? He was only a poor Master of Arts, he went on; and as the question somewhat touched upon divinity, he durst not venture to conclude. A silly old priest from Montargis, who was among the company, treated the young rascal to a bottle of wine in honour of the jest and 15 grimaces with which it was accompanied, and swore on his own white beard that he had been just such another irreverent dog when he was Villon's age.

The air was raw and pointed, but not far below freezing; and the flakes were large, damp, and adhesive. The whole 20 city was sheeted up. An army might have marched from end to end and not a footfall given the alarm. If there were any belated birds in heaven, they saw the island like a large white patch, and the bridges like slim white spars, on the black ground of the river. High up overhead the snow settled 25 among the tracery of the cathedral towers. Many a niche was drifted full; many a statue wore a long white bonnet on

---

[1] From "A Lodging for the Night," in *New Arabian Nights* (Thistle Edition), pp. 287–290. Charles Scribner's Sons, New York, 1895.

its grotesque or sainted head. The gargoyles had been trans-
formed into great false noses, drooping towards the point.
The crockets were like upright pillows swollen on one side.
In the intervals of the wind, there was a dull sound of dripping about the precincts of the church.   5

The cemetery of St. John had taken its own share of
the snow. All the graves were decently covered; tall white
housetops stood around in grave array; worthy burghers
were long ago in bed, be-nightcapped like their domiciles;
there was no light in all the neighborhood but a little peep 10
from a lamp that hung swinging in the church choir, and
tossed the shadows to and fro in time to its oscillations. The
clock was hard on ten when the patrol went by with halberds
and a lantern, beating their hands; and they saw nothing
suspicious about the cemetery of St. John.   15

Yet there was a small house, backed up against the cemetery wall, which was still awake, and awake to evil purpose,
in that snoring district. There was not much to betray it
from without; only a stream of warm vapor from the chimney-
top, a patch where the snow melted on the roof, and a few 20
half-obliterated footprints at the door. But within, behind
the shuttered windows, Master Francis Villon the poet, and
some of the thievish crew with whom he consorted, were
keeping the night alive and passing round the bottle.

A great pile of living embers diffused a strong and ruddy 25
glow from the arched chimney. Before this straddled Dom
Nicolas, the Picardy monk, with his skirts picked up and
his fat legs bared to the comfortable warmth. His dilated
shadow cut the room in half; and the firelight only escaped
on either side of his broad person, and in a little pool between 30
his outspread feet. His face had the beery, bruised appearance of the continual drinker's; it was covered with a network of congested veins, purple in ordinary circumstances,
but now pale violet, for even with his back to the fire the cold
pinched him on the other side. His cowl had half fallen 35
back, and made a strange excrescence on either side of his

bull neck. So he straddled, grumbling, and cut the room in
half with the shadow of his portly frame.

On the right, Villon and Guy Tabary were huddled together over a scrap of parchment; Villon making a ballade
5 which he was to call the "Ballade of Roast Fish," and Tabary
spluttering admiration at his shoulder. The poet was a rag
of a man, dark, little, and lean, with hollow cheeks and
thin black locks. He carried his four-and-twenty years with
feverish animation. Greed had made folds about his eyes,
10 evil smiles had puckered his mouth. The wolf and pig struggled together in his face. It was an eloquent, sharp, ugly,
earthly countenance. His hands were small and prehensile,
with fingers knotted like a cord; and they were continually
flickering in front of him in violent and expressive panto-
15 mime. As for Tabary, a broad, complacent, admiring imbecility breathed from his squash nose and slobbering lips:
he had become a thief, just as he might have become the most
decent of burgesses, by the imperious chance that rules the
lives of human geese and human donkeys.

20 At the monk's other hand, Montigny and Thevenin Pensete
played a game of chance. About the first there clung some
flavour of good birth and training, as about a fallen angel;
something long, lithe, and courtly in the person; something
aquiline and darkling in the face. Thevenin, poor soul, was
25 in great feather: he had done a good stroke of knavery that
afternoon in the Faubourg St. Jacques, and all night he had
been gaining from Montigny. A flat smile illuminated his
face; his bald head shone rosily in a garland of red curls;
his little protuberant stomach shook with silent chucklings
30 as he swept in his gains.

THE FARGUS FAMILY[1]

Arthur Stuart Menteth Hutchinson

Mr. Fargus, who lived next door down the Green, and outside whose gate the bicycle had made its celebrated shortage
record, was a grey little man with grey whiskers and always
in a grey suit. He had a large and very red wife and six thin
and rather yellowish daughters. Once a day, at four in sum- 5
mer and at two in winter, the complete regiment of Farguses
moved out in an immense mass and proceeded in a dense
crowd for a walk. The female Farguses, having very long
legs, walked very fast, and the solitary male Fargus, having
very short legs, walked very slowly, and was usually, there- 10
fore, trotting to keep up with the pack. He had, moreover,
not only to keep pace but also to keep place. He was forever
getting squeezed out from between two tall Farguses and
trotting agitatedly around the heels of the battalion to recover a position in it. He always reminded Sabre of a grey old 15
Scotch terrier toddling along behind and around the flanks
of a company of gaunt, striding mastiffs. He returned from
those walks panting slightly and a little perspiring, and at
the door gave the appearance of being dismissed, and trotted
away rather like a little grey old Scotch terrier toddling off 20
to the stables. The lady Farguses called this daily walk
"exercise"; and it certainly was exercise for Mr. Fargus.

The eldest Miss Fargus was a grim thirty-nine and the
youngest Miss Fargus a determined twenty-eight. They
called their father "Papa" and used the name a good deal. 25
When Sabre occasionally had tea at the Farguses' on a Sun-

[1] From *If Winter Comes*, pp. 64–66. Copyright, 1921, by Little, Brown
& Company, Boston.

day afternoon, Mr. Fargus always appeared to be sitting at
the end of an immense line of female Farguses. Mrs. Fargus
would pour out a cup and hand it to the Miss Fargus at her
end of the line with the loud word "Papa!" and it would
5 whiz down the chain from daughter to daughter to the clamorous direction, each to each, "Papa!—Papa!—Papa!—
Papa!" The cup would reach Mr. Fargus at the speed of a
thunderbolt, and Mr. Fargus, waiting for it with agitated
hands as a nervous fielder awaits a rushing cricket ball, would
10 stop it convulsively and usually drop and catch at and miss
the spoon, whereupon the entire chain of Farguses would give
together a very loud "*Tchk!*" and immediately shoot at their
parent a plate of buns with "Buns—Buns—Buns—Buns" all
down the line. Similarly when Mr. Fargus's grey little face
15 would sometimes appear above the dividing wall to Sabre in
the garden there would come a loud cry of "Papa, the
plums!" and from several quarters of the garden this would
be echoed "Papa, the plums!" "Papa, the plums!" and the
grey little head, in the middle of a sentence, would disappear
20 with great swiftness.

The Farguses kept but one servant, a diminutive and
startled child with one hand permanently up her back in
search of an apron shoulder string, and permanently occupied in frantically pursuing loud cracks, like pistol shots, of
25 "Kate!—Kate!—Kate!" Each Miss Fargus "did" something in the house. One "did" the lamps, another "did" the
silver, another "did" the fowls. And whatever it was they
"did" they were always doing it. Each Miss Fargus, in
addition, "did" her own room, and unitedly they all "did"
30 the garden. Every doing was done by the clock; and at any
hour of the day any one Miss Fargus could tell a visitor
precisely what, and at what point of what, every other
Miss Fargus was doing.

In this well-ordered scheme of things what Mr. Fargus
35 principally "did" was to keep out of the way of his wife and
daughters, and this duty took him all his time and ingenuity.

From the back windows of Sabre's house the grey little figure
was frequently to be seen fleeting up and down the garden
paths in wary evasion of daughters "doing" the garden, and
there was every reason to suppose that, within the house, the
grey figure similarly fleeted up and down the stairs and
passages. "Where *is* Papa?" was a constant cry from mouth
to mouth of the female Farguses; and fatigue parties were
constantly being detached from their duties to skirmish in
pursuit of him.

In his leisure from these flights Mr. Fargus was intensely
absorbed in chess, in the game of Patience, and in the solution of acrostics.

THE ARMY OF FRANCE[1]

GUY WETMORE CARRYL

Oh, it was all very well, the wonderful French army, all
very well if one could have been a marshal or a general, or
even a soldier of the line in time of war. There was a chance
for glory, bon sang! But to be a drummer—a drummer one
5 metre seventy in height, with flaming red hair and a freckled
face—a drummer who was called Little Tapin; and to have,
for one's most important duty, to drum the loungers out of a
public garden! No, evidently he would desert.

"But why?" said a grave voice beside him. Little Tapin
10 was greatly startled. He had not thought he was saying the
words aloud. And his fear increased when, on turning to
see who had spoken, he found himself looking into the eyes
of one who was evidently an officer, though his uniform was
unfamiliar. He was plain-shaven and very short, almost as
15 short, indeed, as Little Tapin himself, but about him there
was a something of dignity and command which could not
fail of its effect. He wore a great black hat like a gendarme's,
but without trimming, and a blue coat with a white plastron,
the tails lined with scarlet, and the sleeves ending in red and
20 white cuffs. White breeches, and knee-boots carefully pol-
ished, completed the uniform, and from over his right shoulder a broad band of crimson silk was drawn tightly across his
breast. A short sword hung straight at his hip, and on his
left breast were three orders on red ribbons,—a great star,
25 with an eagle in the centre, backed by a sunburst studded
with brilliants; another eagle, this one of white enamel, pend-

[1] From "Little Tapin," in *Zut*, pp. 294–303. Houghton Mifflin Company, Boston, 1903.

ant from a jeweled crown, and a smaller star of enameled white and green, similar to the large one.

Little Tapin had barely mastered these details when the other spoke again.

"Why art thou thinking to desert?" he said.

"Monsieur is an officer?" faltered the drummer,—"a general, perhaps. Pardon, but I do not know the uniform."

"A corporal, simply—a soldier of France, like thyself. Be not afraid, my little one. All thou sayest shall be held in confidence. Tell me thy difficulties."

His voice was very kind, the kindest Little Tapin had heard in three long months, and suddenly the barrier of his Breton reserve gave and broke. The nervous strain had been too great. He must have sympathy and advice—yes, even though it meant confiding in a stranger and the possible discovery and failure of his dearly cherished plans.

"A soldier of France!" he exclaimed, impulsively. "Ah, monsieur, there you have all my difficulty. What a thing it is to be a soldier of France! And not even that, but a drummer, a drummer who is called Little Tapin because he is the smallest and weakest in the corps. To be taken from home, from the country he loves, from Brittany, and made to serve among men who despise him, who laugh at him, who avoid him in the hours of leave, because he is not bon camarade. To wear a uniform that has been already worn. To sleep in a dormitory where there are bêtes funestes. To have no friends. To know that he is not to see Plougastel, and the sweetheart, and the Little Mother for three years. Never to fight, but, at best, to drum voyous out of a garden! That, monsieur, is what it is to be a soldier of France!"

There were tears in Little Tapin's eyes now, but he was more angry than sad. The silence of months was broken, and the hoarded resentment and despair of his long martyrdom, once given rein, were not to be checked a second time. He threw back his narrow shoulders defiantly, and said a hideous thing:—

"Conspuez l'armée française!"

There was an instant's pause, and then the other leaned forward, and with one white-gloved hand touched Little Tapin on the eyes.

. . . .

5 Before them a great plain, sloping very gradually upward in all directions, like a vast, shallow amphitheatre, spread away in a long series of low terraces to where, in the dim distance, the peaks of a range of purple hills nicked and notched a sky of palest turquoise. From where they stood,
10 upon a slight elevation, the details of even the farthest slopes seemed singularly clean-cut and distinct,—the groups of grey willows; the poplars, standing stiffly in twos and threes; the short silver reaches of a little river, lying in the hollows where the land occasionally dipped; at long intervals, a
15 white-washed cottage, gleaming like a sail against this sea of green; even, on the most distant swell of all, a herd of ruddy cattle, moving slowly up toward the crest,—each and all of these, although in merest miniature, as clear and vivid in form and color as if they had been the careful creations of a
20 Claude Lorrain.

Directly before the knoll upon which they were stationed, a wide road, dazzling white in the sunlight, swept in a superb full curve from left to right, and on its further side the ground was covered with close-cropped turf, and com-
25 pletely empty for a distance of two hundred metres. But beyond! Beyond, every hectare of the great semicircle was occupied by dense masses of cavalry, infantry, and artillery, regiment upon regiment, division upon division, corps upon corps, an innumerable multitude, motionless, as if carved out
30 of many-colored marbles!

In some curious, unaccountable fashion, Little Tapin seemed to know all these by name. There, to the left, were the chasseurs à pied, their huge bearskins flecked with red and green pompons, and their white cross-belts slashed like
35 capital X's against the blue of their tunics; there, beside

them, the foot artillery, a long row of metal collar plates, like dots of gold, and gold trappings against dark blue; to the right, the Garde Royale Hollandaise, in brilliant crimson and white; in the centre, the infantry of the Guard, with tall, straight pompons, red above white, and square black shakos, trimmed with scarlet cord.

Close at hand, surrounding Little Tapin and his companion, were the most brilliant figures of the scene, and these, too, he seemed to know by name. None was missing. Prince Murat, in a cream-white uniform blazing with gold embroidery, and with a scarlet ribbon across his breast; a group of marshals, Ney, Oudinot, Duroc, Macdonald, Augereau, and Soult, with their yellow sashes, and cocked hats laced with gold; a score of generals, Larouche, Durosnel, Marmont, Letort, Henrion, Chasteller, and the rest, with white instead of gold upon their hats,—clean-shaven, severe of brow and lip-line, they stood without movement, their gauntleted hands upon their sword-hilts, gazing straight before them.

Little Tapin drew a deep breath.

Suddenly from somewhere came a short, sharp bugle note, and instantly the air was full of the sound of hoofs, and the ring of scabbards and stirrup-irons, and the wide white road before them alive with flying cavalry. Squadron after squadron, they thundered by: mounted chasseurs, with pendants of orange-colored cloth fluttering from their shakos, and plaits of powdered hair bobbing at their cheeks; Polish light horse, with metal sunbursts gleaming on their square-topped helmets, and crimson and white pennons snapping in the wind at the points of their lances; Old Guard cavalry, with curving helmets like Roman legionaries; Mamelukes, with full red trousers, white and scarlet turbans, strange standards of horsehair surmounted by the imperial eagle, brazen stirrups singularly fashioned, and horse trappings of silver with flying crimson tassels; Horse Chasseurs of the Guard, in hussar tunics and yellow breeches, their sabretaches swinging as they rode; and Red Lancers, in gay uniforms of green and scarlet. Like a whirlwind they went past,—each squadron, in turn, wheeling to the left, and coming to a halt in the open space beyond the road, until the last lancer swept by.

5 A thick cloud of white dust, stirred into being by the flying horses, now hung between the army and the knoll, and through this one saw dimly the mounted band of the 20th Chasseurs, on gray stallions, occupying the centre of the line, and heard, what before had been drowned by the thun-
10 der of the hoofs, the strains of "Partant pour la Syrie."

Slowly, slowly, the dust cloud thinned and lifted, so slowly that it seemed as if it would never wholly clear. But, on a sudden, a sharp puff of wind sent it whirling off in arabesques to the left, and the whole plain lay revealed.

15 "Bon Dieu!" said Little Tapin.

The first rank of cavalry was stationed within a metre of the further border of the road, the line sweeping off to the left and right until details became indistinguishable. And beyond, reaching away in a solid mass, the vast host dwindled
20 and dwindled, back to where the ascending slopes were broken by the distant willows and the reaches of the silver stream. With snowy white of breeches and plastrons, with lustre of scarlet velvet and gold lace, with sparkle of helmet and cuirass, and dull black of bearskin and smoothly groomed
25 flanks, the army blazed and glowed in the golden sunlight like a mosaic of a hundred thousand jewels. Silent, expectant, the legions flashed crimson, emerald, and sapphire, rolling away in broad swells of light and color, motionless save for a long, slow heave, as of the ocean, lying, vividly irides-
30 cent, under the last rays of the setting sun. Then, without warning, as if the touch of a magician's wand had roused the multitude to life, a myriad sabres swept twinkling from their scabbards, and, by tens of thousands, the guns of the infantry snapped with a sharp click to a present arms. The bugles
35 sounded all along the line, the tricolors dipped until their golden fringes almost swept the ground, the troopers stood

upright in their stirrups, their heads thrown back, their bronzed faces turned toward the knoll, their eyes blazing. And from the farthest slopes inward, like thunder that growls afar, and, coming nearer, swells into unbearable volume, a hoarse cry ran down the massed battalions and broke in a stupendous roar upon the shuddering air,—

"Vive l'empereur!"

.   .   .   .

Little Tapin rubbed his eyes.

"I am ill," he murmured. "I have been faint. I seemed to see—"

"Thou hast seen," said the voice of his companion, very softly, very solemnly,—"thou hast seen simply what it is to be a soldier of France!"

AUTUMN ON CAPE COD[1]

HENRY DAVID THOREAU

Before sunset, having already seen the mackerel fleet returning into the Bay, we left the seashore on the north of
Provincetown, and made our way across the desert to the
eastern extremity of the town. From the first high sand-hill,
5 covered with beach-grass and bushes to its top, on the edge
of the desert, we overlooked the shrubby hill and swamp
country which surrounds Provincetown on the north, and
protects it, in some measure, from the invading sand. Notwithstanding the universal barrenness, and the contiguity of
10 the desert, I never saw an autumnal landscape so beautifully
painted as this was. It was like the richest rug imaginable
spread over an uneven surface; no damask nor velvet, nor
Tyrian dye of stuffs, nor the work of any loom, could ever
match it. There was the incredibly bright red of the Huckle-
15 berry, and the reddish brown of the Bayberry, mingled with
the bright and living green of small Pitch-Pines, and also the
duller green of the Bayberry, Boxberry, and Plum, the yellowish green of the Shrub-Oaks, and the various golden and
yellow and fawn-colored tints of the Birch and Maple and
20 Aspen,—each making its own figure, and, in the midst, the
few yellow sand-slides on the sides of the hills looked like
the white floor seen through rents in the rug. Coming from the
country as I did, and many autumnal woods as I had seen,
this was perhaps the most novel and remarkable sight that I
25 saw on the Cape. Probably the brightness of the tints was
enhanced by contrast with the sand which surrounded this

[1] From *Cape Cod* (Riverside Edition), pp. 232–234. Houghton Mifflin
Company, Boston, 1894.

306

tract. This was a part of the furniture of Cape Cod. We had for days walked up the long and bleak piazza which runs along her Atlantic side, then over the sanded floor of her halls, and now we were being introduced into her boudoir. The hundred white sails crowding round Long Point into Provincetown Harbor, seen over the painted hills in front, looked like toy ships upon a mantel-piece.

The peculiarity of this autumnal landscape consisted in the lowness and thickness of the shrubbery, no less than in the brightness of the tints. It was like a thick stuff of worsted or a fleece, and looked as if a giant could take it up by the hem, or rather the tasseled fringe which trailed out on the sand, and shake it, though it needed not to be shaken. But no doubt the dust would fly in that case, for not a little has accumulated underneath it. Was it not such an autumnal landscape as this which suggested our high-colored rugs and carpets? Hereafter when I look on a richer rug than usual, and study its figures, I shall think, there are the huckleberry hills, and there the denser swamps of boxberry and blueberry; there the shrub-oak patches and the bayberries, there the maples and the birches and the pines.

LIGHT ON THE CAMPAGNA[1]

JOHN RUSKIN

It had been wild weather when I left Rome, and all across the Campagna the clouds were sweeping in sulphurous blue, with a clap of thunder or two, and breaking gleams of sun along the Claudian aqueduct, lighting up the infinity of its
5 arches like the bridge of chaos. But as I climbed the long slope of the Alban Mount, the storm swept finally to the north, and the noble outlines of the domes of Albano, and graceful darkness of its ilex grove, rose against pure streaks of alternate blue and amber; the upper sky gradually flush-
10 ing through the last fragments of rain-cloud in deep, palpitating azure, half ether and half dew. The noon-day sun came slanting down the rocky slopes of La Riccia, and its masses of entangled and tall foliage, whose autumnal tints were mixed with the wet verdure of a thousand evergreens, were pene-
15 trated with it as with rain. I cannot call it color; it was conflagration. Purple and crimson and scarlet, like the curtains of God's tabernacle, the rejoicing trees sank into the valley in showers of light, every separate leaf quivering with buoyant and burning life; each, as it turned to reflect or to
20 transmit the sunbeam, first a torch and then an emerald. Far up into the recesses of the valley, the green vistas arched like the hollows of mighty waves of some crystalline sea, with the arbutus flowers dashed along their flanks for foam, and silver flakes of orange spray tossed into the air around
25 them, breaking over the grey walls of rock into a thousand separate stars, fading and kindling alternately as the weak wind lifted and let them fall. Every glade of grass burned

[1] From *Modern Painters*, Vol. I, Part II, sect. 2, chap. ii.

like the golden floor of heaven, opening in sudden gleams as
the foliage broke and closed above it, as sheet-lightning opens
in a cloud at sunset; the motionless masses of dark rock,—
dark though flushed with scarlet lichen,—casting their quiet
shadows across its restless radiance, the fountain underneath 5
them filling its marble hollow with blue mist and fitful sound,
and over all—the multitudinous bars of amber and rose, the
sacred clouds that have no darkness, and only exist to illume,
were seen in fathomless intervals between the solemn and
orbed repose of the stone pines, passing to lose themselves in 10
the last, white, blinding lustre of the measureless line where
the Campagna melted into the blaze of the sea.

THE VOICE OF THE PACIFIC[1]

ROBERT LOUIS STEVENSON

The one common note of all this country is the haunting presence of the ocean. A great faint sound of breakers follows you high up into the inland cañons; the roar of water dwells in the clean, empty rooms of Monterey as in a shell
5 upon the chimney; go where you will, you have but to pause and listen to hear the voice of the Pacific. You pass out of the town to the southwest, and mount the hill among pine woods. Glade, thicket, and grove surround you. You follow winding sandy tracks that lead nowhither. You see a deer;
10 a multitude of quail arises. But the sound of the sea still follows you as you advance, like that of wind among the trees, only harsher and stranger to the ear; and when at length you gain the summit, out breaks on every hand and with freshened vigour, that same unending, distant, whisper-
15 ing rumble of the ocean; for now you are on the top of Monterey peninsula, and the noise no longer only mounts to you from behind along the beach towards Santa Cruz, but from your right also, round by Chinatown and Pinos light-house, and from down before you to the mouth of the Car-
20 mello river. The whole woodland is begirt with thundering surges. The silence that immediately surrounds you where you stand is not so much broken as it is haunted by this distant, circling rumour. It sets your senses upon edge; you strain your attention; you are clearly and unusually con-
25 scious of small sounds near at hand; you walk listening like an Indian hunter; and that voice of the Pacific is a sort of disquieting company to you in your walk.

[1] From "The Old Pacific Capital" in *Across the Plains* (Thistle Edition), p. 151. Charles Scribner's Sons, New York, 1895.

NIGHT SOUNDS IN THE FOREST[1]

Stewart Edward White

About once in so often you are due to lie awake at night.
Why this is so I have never been able to discover. It apparently comes from no predisposing uneasiness of indiges-
tion, no rashness in the matter of too much tea or tobacco,
no excitation of unusual incident or stimulating conversa- 5
tion. In fact, you turn in with the expectation of rather a
good night's rest. Almost at once the little noises of the
forest grow larger, blend in the hollow bigness of the first
drowse; your thoughts drift idly back and forth between
reality and dream; when—*snap!*—you are broad awake! 10

Perhaps the reservoir of your vital forces is full to the
overflow of a little waste; or perhaps, more subtly, the great
Mother insists thus that you enter the temple of her larger
mysteries.

For, unlike mere insomnia, lying awake at night in the 15
woods is pleasant. The eager, nervous straining for sleep
gives way to a delicious indifference. You do not care. Your
mind is cradled in an exquisite poppy-suspension of judgment and of thought. Impressions slip vaguely into your
consciousness and as vaguely out again. Sometimes they 20
stand stark and naked for your inspection; sometimes they
lose themselves in the mist of half-sleep. Always they lay
soft velvet fingers on the drowsy imagination, so that in their
caressing you feel the vaster spaces from which they have
come. Peaceful-brooding your faculties receive. Hearing, 25
sight, smell—all are preternaturally keen to whatever of

[1] From *The Forest*, pp. 53–57. Doubleday, Page & Company, New York.
Originally published in 1903.

sound and sight and woods perfume is abroad through the night; and yet at the same time active appreciation dozes, so these things lie on it sweet and cloying like fallen rose-leaves.

In such circumstances you will hear what the *voyageurs* call the voices of the rapids. Many people never hear them at all. They speak very soft and low and distinct beneath the steady roar and dashing, beneath even the lesser tinklings and gurglings whose quality superimposes them over the louder sounds. They are like the tear-forms swimming across the field of vision, which disappear so quickly when you concentrate your sight to look at them, and which reappear so magically when again your gaze turns vacant. In the stillness of your hazy half-consciousness they speak; when you bend your attention to listen, they are gone, and only the tumults and the tinklings remain.

But in the moments of their audibility they are very distinct. Just as often an odor will wake all a vanished memory, so these voices, by the force of a large impressionism, suggest whole scenes. Far off are the cling-clang-cling of chimes and the swell-and-fall murmur of a multitude *en fête*, so that subtly you feel the gray old town, with its walls, the crowded market-place, the decent peasant crowd, the booths, the mellow church building with its bells, the warm, dust-moted sun. Or, in the pauses between the swish-dash-dashings of the waters, sound faint and clear voices singing intermittently, calls, distant notes of laughter, as though many canoes were working against the current—only the flotilla never gets any nearer, nor the voices louder. The *voyageurs* call these mist people the Huntsmen; and look frightened. To each is his vision, according to his experience. The nations of the earth whisper to their exiled sons through the voices of the rapids. Curiously enough, by all reports, they suggest always peaceful scenes—a harvest-field, a street fair, a Sunday morning in a cathedral town, careless travelers—never the turmoils and struggles. Perhaps this is the great Mother's compensation in a harsh mode of life.

Nothing is more fantastically unreal to tell about, nothing more concretely real to experience, than this undernote of the quick water. And when you do lie awake at night, it is always making its unobtrusive appeal. Gradually its hypnotic spell works. The distant chimes ring louder and nearer as you cross the borderland of sleep. And then outside the tent some little woods noise snaps the thread. An owl hoots, a whippoorwill cries, a twig cracks beneath the cautious prowl of some night creature—at once the yellow sunlit French meadows puff away—you are staring at the blurred image of the moon spraying through the texture of your tent.

The voices of the rapids have dropped into the background, as have the dashing noises of the stream. Through the forest is a great silence, but no stillness at all. The whippoorwill swings down and up the short curve of his regular song; over and over an owl says his rapid *whoo, whoo, whoo*. These, with the ceaseless dash of the rapids, are the web on which the night traces her more delicate embroideries of the unexpected. Distant crashes, single and impressive; stealthy footsteps near at hand; the subdued scratching of claws; a faint *sniff! sniff! sniff!* of inquiry; the sudden clear tin-horn *ko-ko-ko-óh* of the little owl; the mournful, long-drawn-out cry of the loon, instinct with the spirit of loneliness; the ethereal call-note of the birds of passage high in the air; a *patter, patter, patter*, among the dead leaves, immediately stilled; and then at the last, from the thicket close at hand, the beautiful silver purity of the white-throated sparrow— the nightingale of the North—trembling with the ecstasy of beauty, as though a shimmering moonbeam had turned to sound; and all the while the blurred figure of the moon mounting to the ridge-line of your tent—these things combine subtly, until at last the great Silence of which they are a part overarches the night and draws you forth to contemplation.

THE RIDE OF LITTLE TOOMAI[1]

Rudyard Kipling

The elephant turned without a sound, took three strides back to the boy in the moonlight, put down his trunk, swung him up to his neck, and almost before Little Toomai had settled his knees slipped into the forest.

5 There was one blast of furious trumpeting from the lines, and then the silence shut down on everything, and Kala Nag began to move. Sometimes a tuft of high grass washed along his sides as a wave washes along the sides of a ship, and sometimes a cluster of wild-pepper vines would scrape
10 along his back, or a bamboo would creak where his shoulder touched it; but between those times he moved absolutely without any sound, drifting through the thick Garo forest as though it had been smoke. He was going up-hill, but though Little Toomai watched the stars in the rifts of the
15 trees, he could not tell in what direction.

Then Kala Nag reached the crest of the ascent and stopped for a minute, and Little Toomai could see the tops of the trees lying all speckled and furry under the moonlight for miles and miles, and the blue-white mist over the river in the
20 hollow. Toomai leaned forward and looked, and he felt that the forest was awake below him—awake and alive and crowded. A big brown fruit-eating bat brushed past his ear; a porcupine's quills rattled in the thicket; and in the darkness between the tree-stems he heard a hog-bear digging
25 hard in the moist, warm earth, and snuffing as it digged.

Then the branches closed over his head again, and Kala Nag began to go down into the valley—not quietly this time,

[1] From "Toomai of the Elephants," in *The Jungle Book*, pp. 244–246. By special permission of Mr. Kipling and Doubleday, Page & Company.

but as a runaway gun goes down a steep bank—in one rush.
The huge limbs moved as steadily as pistons, eight feet to
each stride, and the wrinkled skin of the elbow-points rustled.
The undergrowth on either side of him ripped with a noise
like torn canvas, and the saplings that he heaved away right 5
and left with his shoulders sprang back again, and banged
him on the flank, and great trails of creepers, all matted together, hung from his tusks as he threw his head from side
to side and plowed out his pathway. Then Little Toomai
laid himself down close to the great neck, lest a swinging 10
bough should sweep him to the ground, and he wished that
he were back in the lines again.

SWIMMING THE WHIRLPOOL[1]

Henry Milner Rideout

He was off, running to the beach, and along it northward,
to make his start as far as possible above the line where the
whirlpool might appear. Ripping off his clothes, he ran
naked down to the water's edge, doused the oil over his body,
5 and rubbed hastily till the great white muscles glistened in
the sun. He felt hollow from lack of food and sleep; the
water stretched hopelessly far to the mainland; but the excitement as he ran splashing out, and the cold shock of the
plunge, set his heart thumping stoutly. His first thought was
10 one of despair, "It's too cold." But he shut his mind to that,
and clove his way ahead through the bright green water,
swimming with a powerful side stroke. That lowness of
vision over a flat surface which is peculiar to swimming made
colors and lines abnormally distinct. With his cheek goug-
15 ing through the water, he could see the ruddy cliffs retreating
behind him, the greenness and the black shadows of little
trees that clung in crevices, the pink curve of the beach, the
shining, shifting lines of the water, his own legs, distorted by
refraction till they looked ridiculously pale and green and
20 thin, kicking away like alien marine things in pursuit of his
body and of the big, glistening deltoid that capped his shoulder, strongly contracting and relaxing. Ahead, as he shot his
arm forward, appeared his first distance mark, a white can-
buoy two thirds of the way across the channel; beyond that,
25 a broad eddy of the tide, a slightly raised surface, smooth
and yellowish-white, like a sheet of ice, where hundreds of

[1] From "Blue Peter," in *Beached Keels*, pp. 92–98. Houghton Mifflin
Company, Boston, 1906.

316

white gulls wheeled or floated in search of breakfast; and beyond these again, the wharves and meagre shipping of the town,—the square-rigged shapely tangle of his own ship, the Elizabeth Fanning.

The numbness began to leave him, though an ice-cold ring circled his neck where wind and water met. Like all swimmers, he grew confused in his sense of time, and had strange thoughts. Halfway to the can-buoy now; no longer slack water; must hurry. A half-eaten apple came bobbing peacefully toward him on the young flood. He wondered who had eaten it, and whether it were sweet or sour. But where the devil had all his Latin gone to? Her father had said "enaviganda." Did that mean it could be swum through, or it couldn't? He suffered a morbid worry over the meaning of this word, as if it contained the secret of his present fate. The thing had been done—that fellow in '56. At all events, he shifted his stroke again, and swam on tediously.

Of a sudden he noticed that the apple was bearing rapidly down,—was alongside, on a little raised rim of water like a moving flaw in glass. Next instant he had spun about and was facing seaward. Something below twirled his legs violently.

"Hello!" he sputtered aloud. "Good Lord!" he thought. "This is bad. I must get out of this."

But the running ocean was stronger. The water hissed, curved on a slant, boiled upward, regurgitated in patches white as with melting snow-flakes. A submarine force, gigantic and appalling, spun him round and round and whirled him downward. He wrestled frantically. His head sank inside a wide cylinder of smooth green glass, laced about spirally with running silver threads. His ears, long deafened by the noise of swimming, were filled with a strange roar. "Whirlpool! It's all up. I'll see where it goes to, anyway," he thought insanely, and strained for a last breath as he shot under. In a green light he was slatted about dreadfully, spinning upright, then horizontal, his useless arms and legs

flying wide and shaken. A giant weight, a personal, hateful weight, began pressing on his back, pressing him slowly down into the dark. Acute worry seized him because this thing was unfair—would not give him a chance to get just one
5 more breath—was squeezing him down into a funnel, and he did not think the bore at the end was big enough to let him through. "Why," he thought, "why, this is It! This is dying. What they call Death!—I'm very sorry for them all up there." And then he thought, as suddenly, "Hold on! I
10 can't yet, because before this sort of thing I'm due to come back to the island,—I've drunk from her spring—Helen— that was the agreement—" But still he was pressed down- ward, and the pain grew heavy and dull. No one would ever tell her of the cold, the dark, the loneliness. It was all years
15 ago, anyway, and very deep.

Slowly he was rising. "Where next?" he thought cyn- ically. Perhaps it was over now, and this was just the fel- low's soul going up, up. "No, by golly, there's too much pain about it. It's lighter— The sun— It's me, and I'm
20 out— Air!"

He struck out in leaden imitation of swimming, just to take it up where he had left off; then stopped; then began again. He was more interested in a pale thing that accom- panied him, large and speckled, like a potato, but twitching
25 round the edges, round the nostrils. "Why, it's my nose, and I've got one eye shut. How silly!" The humor of this woke him up, and now he really swam. "I've wasted a lot of time down there," he mourned.

Something large, white, and round came rushing at him
30 through the water. The can-buoy,—the tide was carrying him past, he mustn't lose that. He lashed out for it blindly, and managed to be flung against the slope. Though it dipped, swayed, and rolled, he slowly climbed up, over barnacles and painted sheet-iron, to where he could grasp the iron ring at
35 the top. It must have been for a long time that he clung there. The tiny knives of the barnacles had sliced his legs,

and blood ran in slow, red streams through the hair on his shins. "It's all up," he reflected, watching the tide race by. "I've come through the upper tip-edge of the whirlpools, off there. Just a baby one that got me; but it's done the trick. This is a mighty poor exhibition. What will Peter say, and Helen?" The only answer was despair; he grew colder and weaker, his aching fingers loosened, time dragged on, and he longed to go to sleep.

THE TIME OF NEW TALK[1]

Rudyard Kipling

In an Indian Jungle the seasons slide one into the other almost without division. There seem to be only two—the wet and the dry; but if you look closely below the torrents of rain and the clouds of char and dust you will find all four
5 going round in their regular ring. Spring is the most wonderful, because she has not to cover a clean, bare field with new leaves and flowers, but to drive before her and to put away the hanging-on, over-surviving raffle of half-green things which the gentle winter has suffered to live, and to
10 make the partly-dressed stale earth feel new and young once more. And this she does so well that there is no spring in the world like the Jungle spring.

There is one day when all things are tired, and the very smells, as they drift on the heavy air, are old and used. One
15 cannot explain this, but it feels so. Then there is another day—to the eye nothing whatever has changed—when all the smells are new and delightful, and the whiskers of the Jungle People quiver to their roots, and the winter hair comes away from their sides in long, draggled locks. Then, perhaps, a
20 little rain falls, and all the trees and the bushes and the bamboos and the mosses and the juicy-leaved plants wake with a noise of growing that you can almost hear, and under this noise runs, day and night, a deep hum. *That* is the noise of the spring—a vibrating boom which is neither bees, nor fall-
25 ing water, nor the wind in tree-tops, but the purring of the warm, happy world.

[1] From "The Spring Running," in *The Second Jungle Book*, pp. 290–292. By special permission of Mr. Kipling and of Doubleday, Page & Company.

Up to this year Mowgli had always delighted in the turn of the seasons. It was he who generally saw the first Eye-of-the-Spring deep down among the grasses, and the first bank of spring clouds, which are like nothing else in the Jungle. His voice could be heard in all sorts of wet, star-lighted, blossoming places, helping the big frogs through their choruses, or mocking the little up-side-down owls that hoot through the white nights. Like all his people, spring was the season he chose for his flittings—moving, for the mere joy of rushing through the warm air, thirty, forty, or fifty miles between twilight and the morning star, and coming back panting and laughing and wreathed with strange flowers. The Four did not follow him on these wild ringings of the Jungle, but went off to sing songs with other wolves. The Jungle People are very busy in the spring, and Mowgli could hear them grunting and screaming and whistling according to their kind. Their voices then are different from their voices at other times of the year, and that is one of the reasons why spring in the Jungle is called the Time of New Talk.

THE JUNGLE AT NIGHT[1]

RUDYARD KIPLING

It was a perfect white night, as they call it. All green
things seemed to have made a month's growth since the
morning. The branch that was yellow-leaved the day before
dripped sap when Mowgli broke it. The mosses curled deep
5 and warm over his feet, the young grass had no cutting edges,
and all the voices of the Jungle boomed like one deep harp-
string touched by the moon—the Moon of New Talk, who
splashed her light full on rock and pool, slipped it between
trunk and creeper, and sifted it through a million leaves.
10 Forgetting his unhappiness, Mowgli sang aloud with pure
delight as he settled into his stride. It was more like flying
than anything else, for he had chosen the long downward
slope that leads to the Northern Marshes through the heart
of the main Jungle, where the springy ground deadened the
15 fall of his feet. A man-taught man would have picked his
way with many stumbles through the cheating moonlight,
but Mowgli's muscles, trained by years of experience, bore
him up as though he were a feather. When a rotten log or a
hidden stone turned under his foot he saved himself, never
20 checking his pace, without effort and without thought. When
he tired of ground-going he threw up his hands monkey-
fashion to the nearest creeper, and seemed to float rather
than to climb up into the thin branches, whence he would
follow a tree-road till his mood changed, and he shot down-
25 ward in a long, leafy curve to the levels again. There were
still, hot hollows surrounded by wet rocks where he could

[1] From "The Spring Running," in *The Second Jungle Book*, pp. 297–299.
By special permission of Mr. Kipling and of Doubleday, Page & Company.

hardly breathe for the heavy scents of the night flowers and
the bloom along the creeper buds; dark avenues where the
moonlight lay in belts as regular as checkered marbles in a
church aisle; thickets where the wet young growth stood
breast-high about him and threw its arms around his waist; 5
and hilltops crowned with broken rock, where he leaped
from stone to stone above the lairs of the frightened little
foxes. He would hear, very faint and far off, the *chug-drug*
of a boar sharpening his tusks on a bole; and would come
across the great gray brute all alone, scribing and rending 10
the bark of a tall tree, his mouth dripping with foam, and
his eyes blazing like fire. Or he would turn aside to the
sound of clashing horns and hissing grunts, and dash past a
couple of furious sambhur, staggering to and fro with lowered
heads, striped with blood that showed black in the moon- 15
light. Or at some rushing ford he would hear Jacala the
Crocodile bellowing like a bull, or disturb a twined knot of
the Poison People, but before they could strike he would be
away and across the glistening shingle, deep in the Jungle
again.   20

So he ran, sometimes shouting, sometimes singing to himself, the happiest thing in all the Jungle that night, till the
smell of the flowers warned him that he was near the marshes,
and those lay far beyond his furthest hunting-grounds.

STUDENTS' THEMES: DESCRIPTION

I

Were you ever brave or foolish enough to venture into the kitchen just before dinner was served? You remember, then, as you opened the door, the heat that struck your face, and the savory smells of soup, roast, vegetables, and spicy dessert that greeted you all at once. Disorder everywhere! The stove, crowded with saucepans whose lids are popping to let out little jets of steam, is going full blast. The kitchen table is a confusion of platters, teapots, pans and butter-tubs. Drops of water trickle down the vapor-clouded windows. There is a thump, thump, thump of potatoes being vigorously mashed, a sizzle and crackle of roasting meat, and a clatter of china. Puss, with an eye to filching a chop, sniffs expectantly round the oven, while the cook, red and perspiring, rushes like a mad thing between stove and table, plunging her big fork into this, peeping at that, stirring, sampling, seasoning, and stumbling over that "divil of a cat."

II

The numberless heat waves fairly sprang into the air from the chip-and-splinter-strewn opening before the cabin. The tall hardwood growth stood motionless and baking, while the small ground plants withered up under the scorching heat. Even the brook moving quietly along under the edge of the shade seemed visibly to diminish in size. A match lighted to start a pipe burned listlessly, even seeming to go out in the fierce sunlight. Yet we knew that if that match were thrown aside, the whole clearing would break into flame. The absolutely motionless air resounded with the buzz of hundreds of deer flies, unpleasantly shiny and active in the quivering atmosphere.

III

Ahead the great lights throw their blinding gleam, picking out each detail of the dusty road and etching a picture out of the black of night. The motor purrs to itself contentedly as it conquers distance; the grass by the side of the way stands starkly fixed as if petrified; the blackness on each side, out of which lean reaching arms of leafy boughs, creeps toward us and slips harmlessly to the rear. Above, the deep blue velvet pathway of the sky lies ever open, marked out by twinkling pearls and diamonds that move on with us. A rabbit pauses in wonder on the road ahead, and then leaps off into the cool forest away from the blinding eyes so strange. The trees murmur softly above the wind that throws its mimic roar into our ears. Behind, reigns the night-calm undisturbed by the dust that settles slowly back to earth.

IV

While you are showing your pass to the man at the door of the timekeeper's office, you hear a steady rumble which you not only hear, but feel. When you open the door into the shop, an avalanche of noise, pure noise, completely smothers you and at first bewilders you. As your ears become tuned to the wild melody of the machines, you are able to pick out a note here and there. The shrill shriek of a belt over your head, as it is thrown into tension, startles you at first, but as you listen, the same shriek comes continually from all directions. A big planer starts; and its harsh, crunching, irresistible grind seems to turn your bones end for end. That is the bass part of the symphony. The air is made up of many things, the careless rattle of loose pulleys, the monotonous drone of a whip saw, and the biting rasp of

an emery wheel. What at first seemed like a harsh jangle of noise now seems like a great melodious whirl. You have a queer, vague sensation about the back of your ears. You look around—to find the foreman shouting in them to tell
5 you of some new machine.

V

When I was first introduced to my surroundings in my present place of employment, I glanced out of the window at the red-brick wall next door, and thought, "How *can* any-one bear to sit near this spiritless view!" Now my seat has
10 been changed, and I am next that window. Gradually I have learned to love the scene, and to watch for the effect in different kinds of weather; and I derive great benefit from stealing a moment now and then to glance out.

On clear, windy mornings the solid red chimneys rise
15 sharply against a bold blue sky; spurts of fitful smoke go hurrying off; and the chimney-pots whizz gaily. In the bricked-up back yard bravely struggles a wash; while high in air, against vigorous white clouds, exult birds on sweeping wings.

20 At noon the sun pours generously upon the mellow bricks. Pigeons strut above the gutter in undisputed sovereignty, and chat with one another peaceably. You would not recognize these benignant birds for those which at other times crouch, dreary and forlorn, under a drizzling rain. Their
25 purple and green necklaces glisten as they ramble along their chosen promenade. Their feathers harmonize well with the gray of slate which slants downward to meet the red of brick. There are two shades of the slate. Across the darker gray extend two strips of lighter, which contain considerable
30 green; and in the gutter just below, this light green is again observable, mingled with the harsh brown of rust. Rarely can I see inhabitants of the house, but at the window opposite mine, a squat red pitcher remains, a faithful friend.

In the afternoon the sun glances on the bricks in mottled richness, and toward sunset delightful clouds pass over the roof—clouds gold-tipped or shadowy. Then, when darkness envelops details, the whole—except a luminous window or two—is a dark blot outside my window; but the chimney-pots still revolve, now against a deepening sky.

VI

The baby that grew to be I myself experienced in the first two years of life a mixed assemblage of sensations. The Chinese nurse with dry-skinned hands that dressed and bathed and fed her; Chinese faces thrust close to hers saying Chinese words; loose-sleeved, padded Chinese garments—always faded blue in color; gray brick courtyards, gray tiled, peaked roof edges; wooden beams across the ceilings; coolies squatting on their heels in doorways; bound feet of women hobbling agilely about their duties; women sitting cross-legged on their ovens, kneading pastry; women gossiping in high-pitched Chinese voices, sitting on their brick kangs sewing; little naked Chinese babies sprawling on the kangs beside them; smells of Chinese food a-cooking; savory smells of Chinese sauces; smell of garments worn all winter; the peculiar smell of Chinese bodies; the click of chopsticks on the rice bowls; the loud sucking up of hot food; the smacking of moist lips; the warm steam filling the room; the gray-blue smoke curling from long-stemmed pipes; the shiny black look of the pipe stems; the long yellow finger nails; the fascination of nails protruding beyond the fingers turning over the leaves of books; the fastidiousness of the well-groomed hands of a Chinese scholar; the horrid touch of dry, rough skin; sleekly smoothed black hair; long pig-tails; sounds of sing-song intonations; distant sounds of street-way traffic; barking dogs; the whine of beggars.

VII

A pale, fat little woman opened a door in the row of dark houses that all looked alike, and called something in a merry, inarticulate voice that suggested false teeth. Thereupon a fat white dog rose slowly from the sidewalk. He took a step
5 or two forward, and then stood perfectly still, with his head and his stub of a tail dejected, as if he were loath to leave the warm sun that sank into his back. As the old lady kept on calling, the dog shoved himself painfully along until he reached the steps, then he waited a long time, with his front
10 paws on the first step, wiggling heavily. When I last saw him, he was dragging his hind feet slowly, reluctantly, from the second to the third step.

AN OLD SEA-DOG

I saw him first laboriously hauling to her moorings a heavy fishing dory, which had come broadside on to a rather heavy sea, and consequently was as unmanageable as a skittish colt. His garments flapping in the wind; his chin whiskers and "sou'wester" glistening with ocean spray, which constantly washed over him; his back bent, and every muscle straining at its work—he was indeed an unusual and picturesque sight to one not accustomed to life on the sea-coast.

Having placed the green and white dory to his complete satisfaction, the old man condescended to notice me; although I am fully convinced that, had his boat required his further attention, though I were the admiral of the British Navy, I might have stood there all night and never have received so much as a glance from him. With a cheery, "Wal, some wind, eh?" and a grip that brought tears to my eyes, he shook my hand. Then, without replying to my profuse explanations of my delay, he led the way briskly up the beach to the cottage where he and his mate had spent their summers for the past forty years.

Slatting his sou'wester against the piazza post to remove the water that clung to it, he preceded me into the house. Once indoors, he threw his streaming hat into a closet, and, removing his rubber coat and heavy boots of the same material, put them beside the roaring stove to dry. Then, drawing on a pair of felt slippers, he half sat, half threw himself into an ancient cane rocker by the window, gazing absently out over the stormy waters as he leisurely took from one pocket an old, blackened clay pipe, from another a huge plug of black, poisonous-looking tobacco and a perfectly murderous knife, and, still disregarding my presence, loaded the old, broken-stemmed thing whose companionship was so much more valued than my own.

While he was thus engaged I had an excellent opportunity to study him unobserved. His grizzly grey hair and beard, still damp with the salt spray, from the midst of which peeked two bright eyes, blue as the ocean; a weather-beaten, sinewy neck and chest, protruding from the open collar of a soiled flannel shirt, told eloquently of a life of exposure to all climates; while firm lips and a protruding jaw, combined with a steely gleam in the eyes, spoke of a master, yes, a commander of men. His brown, brawny arms, which were never sheltered from the sun of summer or cold of winter by a shirt sleeve—save when he was occasionally persuaded to struggle into a "Sunday-go-to-meetin' suit"—and large, scarred hands explained why he had been the champion oarsman of the fleet in his younger days.

In rather pleasing contrast to this general appearance of bold, self-reliant man of the deep was a tattooed anchor standing out boldly in blue and scarlet against the tan of his left forearm. Cannot you imagine the young, reckless boy, proud to overflowing of the fact that he was at last a real sailor, hastening to show a pretty little damsel of some sea-coast town this latest testimony of his calling, and to tell her of bold deeds done, and yet to be accomplished? Ah, if you could only have seen him as I did, that stormy afternoon, looking back, through the thin smoke of the old pipe, on the days and deeds that had toughened his skin and swollen his knuckles, then you would have felt with me the magic of the sea and the poetry of those who live by the sea.

MARBLEHEAD HARBOR

I awoke shortly after daylight and remained in my bunk a moment, trying to guess what the weather was. The annual cruise of the Eastern Yacht Club was to start at seven. I heard the slow, steady drip, drip, of the water on the deck. I knew that it was thick fog outside. But I jumped up, put 5 on my damp clothes, and went on deck. The cold fog struck me full in the face as I stepped out. Water trickled from spars and rigging, and moisture seemed to ooze from every piece of wood. Drops falling on my head sent cold shivers along my spine and kept me miserably aware of the clammy 10 atmosphere about me. I could see nothing except this white blanket of mist. I had completely lost my bearings. Where the other yachts were, or the town, I did not know. I went to the cockpit and took off the drenched cover of the compass and got my bearings. At that moment the little white ferry 15 came from the direction of the town. I could see it for an instant, then it glided off into the whiteness again, and all that I could make out was the shroud of white, and the ripples from the ferry. I went below, disgusted with the weather. 20

In half an hour I came up on deck again. Still the fog was everywhere, but it seemed thinner and less depressing. I smelt some soft-coal smoke. I looked up to see whence the west wind was blowing the smoke and saw nothing but a line of black in the white. Yet on all sides I heard sounds. 25 From somewhere to the starboard came the familiar rattle of a windlass—someone weighing anchor. And from astern came the clicking of blocks as a sail was being hoisted. Up forward the crew were tumbling out of the fo'castle and were starting to take the covers off the sails. The deck was still 30

damp, but no longer did water drip from mast and rigging. The sun seemed trying to break through the fog and the white almost dazzled my eyes. I looked again at the trail of smoke. I saw nothing. Then, as I was about to turn
5 away, a white steam yacht suddenly appeared. I looked again. Sure enough, there it was, as large and as clear as could be. I was surprised that I had not seen it before. And there was the shore beyond at the head of the harbor. One after another the yachts grew visible. The west wind,
10 rippling the water, sent the fog scurrying out of the harbor. In a moment I was standing in the glorious sunshine. It was as though some great being were shoving the fog away with his hand.

I stood on deck and watched the fog disappear from the
15 harbor. It went out in a solid wall, leaving behind it the bay full of yachts and boats of all kinds. The smooth white sides of the yachts glistened and the varnished upper work sparkled like diamonds in the sunshine. The crews were dressed in their white uniforms and everywhere were hustling
20 about their work. The clank of chains, the ropes and blocks striking each other, the sails flapping in the breeze, bespoke the eagerness of the crews to get started. Then the great yachts spread their wings and sailed out of the harbor.

AUBIÈRE

One does not find the true France in its great cities. Paris
is beautiful, scintillating, mad, but it is superficial. I have
promenaded the Rue des Italiens and rubbed elbows with
the world, but I have looked down from my balcony window
in Aubière and glimpsed the soul of France.   5

Aubière is an insignificant dot on the map. It is a little
village of scarcely a thousand peasants, tucked comfortably
away among the grape-laden uplands of southern France. In
the near west are the Monts Dore, a chain of rugged, volcanic
ranges, mellow gold by day and cloud-kissed at night. A   10
great plain stretches towards the north, but on every other
side Aubière gazes abruptly up at the rounded hills that roll
away to the sky line. The village has the air of being very
old, as though years of sunlight had painted the red tiled roof
tops, and centuries of rain had weathered the concrete houses 15
to an ancient brown.

My balcony window looked down upon the Place du Jour,
an open square that was the principal rendezvous of the
town. Just beneath, a little rivulet faltered by, and here the
women folk came to scrub their clothes. A band stand, 20
shaded by two stripling trees, occupied the exact centre of
the square, and on every side there were cafés, butcher shops,
and bakeries. Aged peasants clattered by in their wooden
shoes, loose frocks, and broad brimmed hats, driving the
cows in from pastures. The town crier beat his drum and 25
shouted the latest *avis* of the mayor. Comely matrons, in
voluminous black dresses and quaint little bonnets, rode into
market in their two-wheeled gigs. There was a bright mixture of Allied uniforms. When the regimental band came
here to play, one had the sense of looking upon a very color- 30
ful and highly realistic musical comedy.

The streets wandered away from the Place in apparent disorder. One might discover all sorts of little shops hidden in their shadowy recesses, or come suddenly upon the great church that always seemed about to tumble to the ground. Each of these winding, aimless streets possessed a personality, differing distinctly from each other. The Rue de Jeanne d'Arc, for instance, was much dirtier than the Rue de Champlon, and the Rue de Cemetière was much gloomier than the ill-paved Rue de Liam. I loved to stroll in those puzzling streets, to discover some new café, to breathe in their ancient atmosphere, and to learn the real France from the lips of some friendly shop-keeper.

How huddled and cramped the little town seemed at first! It was like the crowded dwelling section of a great city. The door steps almost ran into each other, and there was hardly a back yard or a garden plot in the entire village. The children played in the streets; the café tables were placed almost in the gutters; neighbors talked and worked together outside their kitchen doors. Here was the very spirit of friendly, life-loving France. The empty plains and the open hills were the workshops for these simple peasant folk, but the streets were their playgrounds, their dining rooms, and their theatres. The French are too sociable to build their houses apart. A sort of national passion for fraternity crowds them together in their picturesque villages, and a national love of candid expression brings them out on the street, where the passer-by may share their wine, and observe their artless, open ways.

REYNARD THE FOX

Did you ever meet a fox face to face, surprising him quite as much as yourself? If so, you were deeply impressed, no doubt, by his perfect dignity and self-possession. Such a meeting comes about thus.

It is a late winter afternoon. You are swinging rapidly over pastures, or loitering along the winding old road through the woods. The color deepens in the west; the pines grow black against it; the rich brown of the oak leaves seems to glow in the last soft light; and the mystery that is always on the watch begins to rustle in the thickets. You are busy with your own thoughts, seeing nothing in particular, till a flash of yellow passes before your eyes, and a fox stands in the path, one foot uplifted, the fluffy brush swept aside in graceful curves, the bright eyes looking straight into yours, looking through them, to read the intent which gives the eyes their expression. That is the way with a fox; he seems to be looking at your thoughts.

Surprise and eagerness are all in your face on the instant; but the beautiful creature before you draws himself together with quiet self-possession. Dropping his head, he turns to the left, and trots slowly past you. There is no hurry,—not the shadow of suspicion or uneasiness. His eyes are cast down; his brow wrinkled, as if in deep thought; he seems to have forgotten your existence. You watch him curiously as he reënters the path behind you and disappears over the hill.

You did not watch sharply enough. You did not see, as he circled past, that cunning side glance of his yellow eyes, which understood your attitude perfectly. Had you stirred, he would have vanished like a flash. If you ran to the top

335

of the hill where he disappeared, you would see him burst into speed the instant he was out of your sight.

Reynard, wherever you meet him, impresses you as an animal of dignity and calculation. He never seems surprised, much less frightened; never loses his head; never does things hurriedly, on the spur of the moment. You meet him as he leaves the warm rock on the south slope of some hill, where he has been curled up asleep all the winter afternoon. Now he is off on his nightly hunt; he is trotting along, head down, brows wrinkled, planning it all out.

"Let me see," he is thinking. "Last night I hunted the oak woods. To-night I'll cross the brook and take a look into that pasture-corner among the junipers. There's a rabbit that plays around there on fine nights; I'll have him presently. Then I'll go down to the meadow after mice. I haven't been there for a week; last time I got six. If I don't find mice, there's that chicken coop of old Smith. Only"—he stops, with his foot up, and listens as the far-away bark of a dog floats in through the woods—"only he locks the coop and leaves the dog loose ever since I took the big rooster. On the way—Hi! there!"

In the midst of his planning he gives a grasshopper jump aside, and brings both paws down hard on a bit of green moss that quivered as he passed. He spreads his paws cautiously, thrusts his nose between them, drags a young wood mouse from under the moss, eats him, licks his chops, and goes on planning as if nothing had happened.

MODELS OF NARRATION

SIR EDWARD AT THE CARNIVAL[1]

Lord Frederic Hamilton

As in most countries of Spanish origin, the Carnival was kept at Buenos Ayres in the old-fashioned style. In my time, on the last day of the Carnival, Shrove Tuesday, the traditional water-throwing was still allowed in the streets. Everyone going into the streets must be prepared for being drenched 5 with water from head to foot. My new Chief, whom I will call Sir Edward (though he happened to have a totally different name), had just arrived in Buenos Ayres. He was quite unused to South American ways. On Shrove Tuesday I came down to breakfast in an old suit of flannels and a 10 soft shirt and collar, for from my experiences of the previous year I knew what was to be expected in the streets. Sir Edward, a remarkably neat dresser, appeared beautifully arrayed in a new suit, the smartest of bow-ties, and a yellow jean waistcoat. I pointed out to my Chief that it was water- 15 throwing day, and suggested the advisability of his wearing his oldest clothes. Sir Edward gave me to understand that he imagined that few people would venture to throw water over her Britannic Majesty's representative.

Off we started on foot for the Chancery of the Legation, 20 which was situated a good mile from our house. I knew what was coming. In the first five minutes we got a bucket of water from the top of a house, plumb all over us, soaking us both to the skin. Sir Edward was speechless with rage for a

[1] From *The Vanished Pomps of Yesterday*, pp. 249–253. Copyright, 1921, by George H. Doran Company, New York, Publishers.

minute or so, after which I will not attempt to reproduce his language. Men were selling everywhere in the streets the large squirts ("*pomitos*" in Spanish) which are used on these occasions. I equipped myself with a perfect Woolwich
5 Arsenal of *pomitos*, but Sir Edward waved them all disdainfully away. Soon two girls darted out of an open doorway, armed with *pomitos*, and caught us each fairly in the face, after which they giggled and ran into their house, leaving the front door open. Sir Edward fairly danced with rage on the
10 pavement, shouting out the most uncomplimentary opinions as to the Argentine Republic and its inhabitants. The front door having been left open, I was entitled by all the laws of Carnival time to pursue our two fair assailants into their house, and I did so, in spite of Sir Edward's remonstrances.
15 I chased the two girls into the drawing-room, where we experienced some little difficulty in clambering over sofas and tables, and I finally caught them in the dining-room, where a venerable lady, probably their grandmother, was reposing in an armchair. I gave the two girls a thorough good soaking
20 from my *pomitos*, and bestowed the mildest sprinkling on their aged relative, who was immensely gratified by the attention. "Oh! my dears," she cried in Spanish to the girls, "you both consider me so old. You can see that I am not too old for this young man to enjoy paying me a little
25 compliment."

Autres pays, autres mœurs! Just conceive the feelings of an ordinary British middle-class householder, residing, let us say, at Balham or Wandsworth, at learning that the sanctity of "The Laurels" or "Ferndale" had been invaded
30 by a total stranger; that his daughters had been pursued round the house, and then soaked with water in his own dining-room, and that even his aged mother's revered white hairs had not preserved her from a like indignity. I cannot imagine him accepting it as a humorous everyday incident.
35 Our progress to the Chancery was punctuated by several more interludes of a similar character, and I was really pained

on reaching the shelter of our official sanctuary to note how Sir Edward's spotless garments had suffered. Personally, on a broiling February day (corresponding with August in the northern hemisphere) I thought the cool water most re-freshing. Our Chancery looked on to the fashionable Calle Florida, and a highly respectable German widow who had lived for thirty years in South America acted as our house-keeper. Sir Edward, considerably ruffled in his temper, sat down to continue a very elaborate memorandum he was drawing up on the new Argentine Customs tariff. The sub-ject was a complicated one, there were masses of figures to deal with, and the work required the closest concentration. Presently our housekeeper, Frau Bauer, entered the room demurely, and made her way to Sir Edward's table.

"Wenn Excellenz so gut sein werden um zu entschuldigen," began Frau Bauer with downcast eyes, and then suddenly with a discreet titter she produced a large *pomito* from under her apron and, secure in the licence of Carnival time, she thrust it into Sir Edward's collar, and proceeded to squirt half a pint of cold water down his back, retiring swiftly with elderly coyness amid an explosion of giggles. I think that I have seldom seen a man in such a furious rage. I will not attempt to reproduce Sir Edward's language, for the printer would have exhausted his entire stock of "blanks" before I had got halfway through. The Minister, when he had eased his mind sufficiently, snapped out, "It is obvious that with all this condemned (that was not quite the word he used) foolery going on, it is impossible to do any serious work to-day. Where . . . where . . . can one buy the infernal squirts these condemned idiots use?"

"Anywhere in the streets. Shall I buy you some, Sir Edward?"

"Yes, get me a lot of them, and the biggest you can find." So we parted.

Returning home after a moist but enjoyable afternoon, I saw a great crowd gathered at the junction of two streets, engaged in a furious water-fight. The central figure was a most disreputable-looking individual with a sodden wisp of linen where his collar should have been; remnants of a tie trailed dankly down, his soaked garments were shapeless, and his head was crowned with a sort of dripping poultice. He was spouting water in all directions like the Crystal Palace fountains in their heyday, with shouts of "Take that, you foolish female; and that, you fat feminine Argentine!" With grief I recognised in this damp reveller her Britannic Majesty's Minister Plenipotentiary.

HOW I CAUGHT SALMON IN THE CLACKAMAS[1]

RUDYARD KIPLING

Imagine a stream seventy yards broad divided by a pebbly island, running over seductive riffles, and swirling into deep, quiet pools where the good salmon goes to smoke his pipe after meals. Set such a stream amid fields of breast-high crops surrounded by hills of pines, throw in where you please 5 quiet water, log-fenced meadows, and a hundred-foot bluff just to keep the scenery from growing too monotonous, and you will get some faint notion of the Clackamas.

Portland had no rod. He held the gaff and the whisky. California sniffed upstream and downstream across the rac- 10 ing water, chose his ground, and let the gaudy spoon drop in the tail of a riffle. I was getting my rod together when I heard the joyous shriek of the reel and the yells of California, and three feet of living silver leaped into the air far across the water. The forces were engaged. The salmon tore up- 15 stream, the tense line cutting the water like a tide-rip behind him, and the light bamboo bowed to breaking. What happened after I cannot tell. California swore and prayed, and Portland shouted advice, and I did all three for what appeared to be half a day, but was in reality a little over a 20 quarter of an hour, and sullenly our fish came home with spurts of temper, dashes head-on, and sarabands in the air; but home to the bank came he, and the remorseless reel gathered up the thread of his life inch by inch. We landed him in a little bay, and the spring-weight checked at eleven 25

[1] From *From Sea to Sea*, Vol. II, pp. 37–41. By special permission of Mr. Kipling and of Doubleday, Page & Company, New York, 1899.

and a half pounds. Eleven and one-half pounds of fighting
salmon! We danced a war-dance on the pebbles, and California caught me round the waist in a hug that went near to
breaking my ribs while he shouted: "Partner! Partner!
5 This *is* glory! Now you catch your fish! Twenty-four years
I've waited for this!"

I went into that icy-cold river and made my cast just
above a weir, and all but foul-hooked a blue and black water-
snake with a coral mouth who coiled herself on a stone and
10 hissed maledictions. The next cast—ah, the pride of it, the
regal splendour of it! the thrill that ran down from finger-
tip to toe! The water boiled. He broke for the fly and got
it! There remained enough sense in me to give him all he
wanted when he jumped not once but twenty times before
15 the upstream flight that ran my line out to the last half-dozen
turns, and I saw the nickeled reel-bar glitter under the thinning green coils. My thumb was burned deep when I strove
to stopper the line, but I did not feel it till later, for my soul
was out in the dancing water praying for him to turn ere he
20 took my tackle away. The prayer was heard. As I bowed
back, the butt of the rod on my left hip-bone and the top
joint dipping like unto a weeping-willow, he turned, and I accepted each inch of slack that I could by any means get in as
a favour from on High. There be several sorts of success in
25 this world that taste well in the moment of enjoyment, but
I question whether the stealthy theft of line from an able-
bodied salmon who knows exactly what you are doing and
why you are doing it is not sweeter than any other victory
within human scope. Like California's fish, he ran at me
30 head-on and leaped against the line, but the Lord gave me
two hundred and fifty pairs of fingers in that hour. The
banks and the pine trees danced dizzily round me, but I only
reeled—reeled as for life—reeled for hours, and at the end of
the reeling continued to give him the butt while he sulked
35 in a pool. California was farther up the reach, and with the
corner of my eye I could see him casting with long casts and

much skill. Then he struck, and my fish broke for the weir in the same instant, and down the reach we came, California and I; reel answering reel even as the morning stars sung together.

The first wild enthusiasm of capture had died away. We were both at work now in deadly earnest to prevent the lines fouling, to stall off a downstream rush for deep water just above the weir, and at the same time to get the fish into the shallow bay downstream that gave the best practicable landing. Portland bade us both be of good heart, and volunteered to take the rod from my hands. I would rather have died among the pebbles than surrender my right to play and land my first salmon, weight unknown, on an eight-ounce rod. I heard California, at my ear it seemed, gasping: "He's a fighter from Fightersville sure!" as his fish made a fresh break across the stream. I saw Portland fall off a log-fence, break the overhanging bank, and clatter down to the pebbles, all sand and landing-net, and I dropped on a log to rest for a moment. As I drew breath the weary hands slackened their hold, and I forgot to give him the butt. A wild scutter in the water, a plunge and a break for the headwaters of the Clackamas was my reward, and the hot toil of reeling in with one eye under the water and the other on the top joint of the rod was renewed. Worst of all, I was blocking California's path to the little landing-bay aforesaid, and he had to halt and tire his prize where he was. "The Father of all Salmon!" he shouted. "For the love of Heaven, get your *trout* to bank, Johnny Bull!" But I could no more. Even the insult failed to move me. The rest of the game was with the salmon. He suffered himself to be drawn, skipping with pretended delight at getting to the haven where I would fain have him. Yet no sooner did he feel shoal water under his ponderous belly than he backed like a torpedo-boat, and the snarl of the reel told me that my labour was in vain. A dozen times at least this happened ere the line hinted he had given up that battle and would be towed in. He was towed. The

landing-net was useless for one of his size, and I would not
have him gaffed. I stepped into the shallows and heaved
him out with a respectful hand under the gill, for which kindness he battered me about the legs with his tail, and I felt
5 the strength of him and was proud. California had taken
my place in the shallows, his fish hard held. I was up the
bank lying full length on the sweet-scented grass, and gasping in company with my first salmon caught, played and
landed on an eight-ounce rod. My hands were cut and bleed-
10 ing. I was dripping with sweat, spangled like harlequin
with scales, wet from the waist down, nose-peeled by the sun,
but utterly, supremely, and consummately happy. He, the
beauty, the darling, the daisy, my Salmon Bahadur, weighed
twelve pounds, and I had been seven-and-thirty minutes
15 bringing him to bank! He had been lightly hooked on the
angle of the right jaw, and the hook had not wearied him.
That hour I sat among princes and crowned heads—greater
than them all.

AN ELK HUNT[1]

Theodore Roosevelt

One day Merrifield and I went out together and had a
rather exciting chase after some bull elk. The previous evening, toward sunset, I had seen three bulls trotting off across
an open glade toward a great stretch of forest and broken
ground, up near the foot of the rocky peaks. Next morning 5
early we started off to hunt through this country. The walking was hard work, especially up and down the steep cliffs,
covered with slippery pine needles; or among the windfalls,
where the rows of dead trees lay piled up across one another
in the wildest confusion. We saw nothing until we came to 10
a large patch of burnt ground, where we at once found the
soft, black soil marked up by elk hoofs; nor had we penetrated into it more than a few hundred yards before we came
to tracks made but a few minutes before, and almost instantly afterward saw three bull elk, probably those I had 15
seen on the preceding day. We had been running briskly
up-hill through the soft, heavy loam, in which our feet made
no noise but slipped and sank deeply; as a consequence, I
was all out of breath and my hand so unsteady that I missed
my first shot. Elk, however, do not vanish with the in- 20
stantaneous rapidity of frightened deer, and these three
trotted off in a direction quartering to us. I doubt if I ever
went through more violent exertion than in the next ten
minutes. We raced after them at full speed, opening fire; I
wounded all three, but none of the wounds were immediately 25
disabling. They trotted on and we panted afterwards, slip-

[1] From *Hunting Trips of a Ranchman* (Medora Edition), pp. 286-289.
G. P. Putnam's Sons, New York, 1885.

ping on the wet earth, pitching headlong over charred stumps,
leaping on dead logs that broke beneath our weight, more
than once measuring our full length on the ground, halting
and firing whenever we got a chance. At last one bull fell;
5 we passed him by after the others which were still running
up-hill. The sweat streamed into my eyes and made furrows
in the sooty mud that covered my face, from having fallen
full length down on the burnt earth; I sobbed for breath as
I toiled at a shambling trot after them, as nearly done out
10 as could well be. At this moment they turned down-hill. It
was a great relief; a man who is too done up to go a step up-
hill can still run fast enough down; with a last spurt I closed
in near enough to fire again; one elk fell; the other went off
at a walk. We passed the second elk and I kept on alone
15 after the third, not able to go at more than a slow trot myself, and too much winded to dare risk a shot at any distance.
He got out of the burnt patch, going into some thick timber
in a deep ravine; I closed pretty well, and rushed after him
into a thicket of young evergreens. Hardly was I in when
20 there was a scramble and bounce among them and I caught
a glimpse of a yellow body moving out to one side; I ran out
toward the edge and fired through the twigs at the moving
beast. Down it went, but when I ran up, to my disgust I
found that I had jumped and killed, in my haste, a black-tail
25 deer, which must have been already roused by the passage of
the wounded elk. I at once took up the trail of the latter
again, but after a little while the blood grew less, and ceased,
and I lost the track; nor could I find it, hunt as hard as I
might. The poor beast could not have gone five hundred
30 yards; yet we never found the carcass.

Then I walked slowly back past the deer I had slain by so
curious a mischance, to the elk. The first one shot down was
already dead. The second was only wounded, though it
could not rise. When it saw us coming it sought to hide from
35 us by laying its neck flat on the ground, but when we came
up close it raised its head and looked proudly at us, the heavy

mane bristling up on the neck, while its eyes glared and its teeth grated together. I felt really sorry to kill it. Though these were both well-grown elks, their antlers, of ten points, were small, twisted, and ill-shaped; in fact hardly worth preserving, except to call to mind a chase in which during a few minutes I did as much downright hard work as it has often fallen to my lot to do.

FIGHT RAGES ON DECK OF LOST SCHOONER ONATO AS RESCUE SHIP BEARS DOWN[1]

OFFICERS, BY TORCHES' GLARE, SEE SKIPPER'S DEAD BODY—
CHARGE SURVIVORS WITH MUTINY AND MURDER OF CAPTAIN
AND MATE

[Special Dispatch to the Herald]

PHILADELPHIA, Oct. 16—A vivid description of mutiny and murder aboard the schooner Onato, as seen by the glare of the sailing vessel's distress flares from the bridge of the American line freighter Zirkel, while both vessels pitched and tossed in the trough of a high running sea in the darkness of early morning, was given by the Zirkel's officers on her arrival here late today with four rescued survivors of the Onato.

The four rescued men were taken off the Zirkel at quarantine by the revenue cutter Guthrie and charged with mutiny on the high seas, the penalty of which is death. They are held at the Gloucester detention house to await the investigation and action of the British consul, who has jurisdiction in the strange tragedy of the sea, as the dead officers were Newfoundlanders and subjects of Great Britain and the surviving seamen come from the same island.

WITNESSES OF FIGHT

The four accused men are Douglas Nicholl, 24, seaman, of Carbonear, N.F.; Lorenzo Ash, 24, cook, also of Carbonear; Thomas Moulton, 29, seaman, of Burin; and Ernest Fizzard, 19, seaman, also of Burin, which was the home of

---

[1] From the *Boston Herald*, October 17, 1919. These newspaper dispatches were the source of the story "To Windward of the Truth," p. 355. For the relation between the story and its source, see note, p. 501.

Capt. Brushett and his brother, the mate, and the port of the
two-masted schooner, now adrift on the high seas, with the
dead bodies of her murdered officers on her deck. The rescue
took place 300 miles off Newfoundland.

TELLS TALE OF DEEP

Seated in the cabin of the Zirkel on her arrival here today, 5
Capt. Daniel A. Sullivan, who directed the rescue of the
Onato's survivors, and preferred charges of mutiny against
the four men, unfolded the strange tale of the deep, which
might have been taken from the fiction of Jack London, or
Stevenson, or Robertson.   10

Exhausted after virtually going without sleep during the
eight days and nights following the rescue and storm, during
which the Zirkel's steering gear was disabled, the captain described the tragedy, clearing the mystery of the Onato's fate.

"I have been up ever since it happened," he said. "We 15
had been a week out of Rotterdam, proceeding to Philadelphia on the northerly route. On the afternoon of Oct. 8, the
wind, which had been east of south, began to strengthen, and
the sea to rise. The sky clouded and the barometer fell,
indicating a blow.   20

"About 10:45 that night, Robert F. Fremont, 2d mate,
who was on watch, sighted a white light and flare two points
off the starboard bow. At first, he thought it was a lifeboat, but as we drew nearer, he thought he discovered the
schooner's two masts, and called to me. The sea was running 25
very high and it was dangerous for a lifeboat to be out.

BRINGS SHIP ASTERN

"Again we saw a flare, and decided that it was some one in
distress. We altered our course, and made out definitely that
the other vessel was a two-masted schooner, with three sails
up, crossing our course at right angles less than half a mile 30
away. The night was very dark. I brought our ship close

astern to see if the sailing vessel was in distress or simply in need of provisions. My first impression was that she might be in need of fresh water, as is frequently the case with schooners.

5 "As we crossed her stern I took my night glasses. We were 300 yards away, and I saw a man standing aft of a white light.

"At that moment they launched another flare, and in the light of this flare there was a free-for-all fight on the poop of 10 the sailing-ship.

"The flare went overboard. I tried to swing my vessel to circle the schooner and bear down on her, when my steering gear broke down. We hove to for four hours. The gear broke down at 11 o'clock and we were disabled until 3 in 15 the morning.

"While we were wallowing in the trough of the sea the schooner sailed around and came up on our starboard quarter, passed our port side, and appeared in fairly good condition. She had plenty of buoyancy and rode the sea as is 20 customary with the type. I hailed her, but received no response. At this time it was necessary for me to leave the bridge and supervise repairs to the steering gear. J. O. Bailey, supercargo, took my place, and I instructed him under no circumstances to lose sight of that ship.

TROUBLE ABOARD

25 "I knew there was trouble aboard and was determined to go to her aid as soon as we were able. While I was aft a rain squall came up. Watching the schooner at intervals, we saw her change her course. She headed straight for our ship and crossed close to our stern. I hailed again, and this time they 30 responded and said they were leaking badly, were sinking and couldn't last through the night. They begged us to save their lives. When repairs to our gear were effected I did go to their aid.

"About 3 A.M., I launched a lifeboat, in charge of E. Sims,

chief officer, and a crew of six men. At this time, the sea was
running very high and it was blowing a gale, making the
attempt extremely dangerous. As our lifeboat was battered
in launching, and completely smashed while hoisting in, it
was abandoned.   5

"Sims proceeded to the schooner and asked how many
were aboard. 'Four left,' came back the reply. He called to
the four men, and they jumped over the sides. As they
landed in the boat he inquired which one was the captain.
They told him that the captain and mate had been killed 10
when the schooner's cargo of salt shifted.

"Sims brought the lifeboat alongside, and with difficulty
and danger (our vessel was rolling 30 degrees) we brought
the men aboard.

"After I launched the lifeboat, we had drifted out of posi- 15
tion, as it was necessary to manœuvre the ship to bring her
alongside of the lifeboat again.

BODY ON HATCH

"In this manœuvre, I wanted to go very close to the
schooner, and we passed alongside, at a distance of 30 feet,
just close enough that when we rolled we would clear 20
each other.

"My first impression was that the men were not all off,
and we hailed. I received no reply. We then flashed every
electric torch on the deck of the schooner. She was in ele-
gant condition, and lying across a hatch, between the fore- 25
mast and the mainmast was a man's body. He was in blue
uniform, with rubber boots, no hat, and lying face downward,
with hands outstretched. His body could be plainly made
out, and was seen by three officers of the Zirkel standing on
the bridge. One ran along our deck flashing his torch on the 30
body trying to get an answer.

"After ordering the men up for statements, Bailey, the
supercargo, testified that while the sailing vessel was on our
beam, he distinctly heard two shots at 30-second intervals.

"The crew of the schooner declared that their vessel was leaking and had been in a southwest gale four days. Our logs and radios showed good weather until we met the Onato. They claimed that the captain and mate had dug a hole in the cargo of salt, and were bailing the water out when the vessel keeled over, and the cargo shifted, burying them on Oct. 4. They said they made no effort to dig the captain and mate out until Oct. 8, when they buried them at sea.

"Ash, the cook, showed hard usage. He had fresh bruises under each eye. He boasted he had the watches of the dead captain and mate and told conflicting stories."

ACQUIT ONATO'S CREW OF MUTINY[1]

FOUR SEAMEN RESCUED BY AMERICAN STEAMER TO BE SENT TO THEIR HOMES .

No Evidence Found of Fight on Vessel

PHILADELPHIA, Oct. 19—The four survivors of the crew of the British schooner Onato, who were charged with mutiny by Capt. Sullivan of the American steamship Zirkel, were exonerated today by T. P. Porter, the British consul, after an inquiry into the charges. They will be sent to their 5 homes in Newfoundland in a few days as shipwrecked seamen.

KILLED BY SHIFTING CARGO

After the inquiry Mr. Porter stated he was satisfied there were no grounds for the allegation of foul play and that the testimony had convinced him that Capt. Brushett and his brother were killed while working in the hold of the vessel 10 on Oct. 5, in an effort to free the pumps. The little craft was battling against a heavy gale, he said, and the cargo of salt shifted and buried the captain and mate. Nicholls also was buried to his waist, but managed to extricate himself. Three days later, according to the testimony, the four members of 15 the crew opened the hatches and found the bodies under seven feet of salt. They were buried at sea.

MISJUDGED SURVIVORS' ACTIONS

As to the supposed fight, Capt. Sullivan claimed to have seen when he was approaching the disabled schooner, the survivors testified that they believed the Zirkel, which had 20

[1] From the *Boston Herald*, October 20, 1919.

broken its steering gear, was going to abandon them and that their frantic efforts to attract the attention of the steamer probably had the appearance of a fight. All four men said they had been close friends of Capt. Brushett and his brother 5 for years.

Mr. Porter has sent a letter of thanks to Capt. Sullivan and other members of the Zirkel crew for rescuing the sailors.

TO WINDWARD OF THE TRUTH[1]

KENNETH PAYSON KEMPTON

Red Purvis and I were tallying a car load of Canadian deals.

At ten o'clock of a breathless August night the longshore-men and freight handlers are likely to show a waning enthusiasm for the stern tasks before them, and to ask fre- 5 quently for the time. This particular breathless August night was no exception. But he who tallies Canadian deals is favored by the gods of the dock; for the only proper method is to sit down somewhere, wait until the car is empty—then rise and count. Red and I, therefore, felt neither hot nor 10 sleepy. Arrayed in almost nothing, we sprawled upon the cool planking and watched the gang make specious pretense at labor. The harbor water licked the piles beneath us with little crackling noises; through the wide doorway overhead a red scimitar moon was struggling feebly with the murk of 15 the city. Red spoke:

"Wan thing I knows: it pays t' make shure. Always count thim lumber piles twice. Chalk the ends wit' white, cross-chalk 'em wit' blue. An' count like wan wrong meant the Boss wit' a hatchit—as sometimes it does. Since the day av 20 Adam wise burds like me here has told the wurrld t' make shure. An' since the day av Eve 'tis the wurrld has told us where we gets off—an' *jumped*. I mind me—"

Red paused. Listening to the endless low rumble of trucks along the dock, I waited. 25

"I mind me av the tanker *Gulfleet*. Her skipper wuz ol' Martin Price, a God-fearin' man and an able navigat'r—but

[1] From *The Open Road*, August, 1920.

355

hasty like. I wuz supercargo aboard av the *Gulfleet*—
that wuz before I got me a game leg an' the fambly. We wuz
a matter av eight days out from Tampico, bound fur New
York wit' fifty thousand barr'ls av crude oil, an' makin' knots
5 in heavy weather. Price wuz the drivin' sort. Gale 'r calm,
he aimed t' get there quick. Always a-pesterin' the engine
room: 'More steam, more steam there, Mister Oakes, if ye
please. The log's gone ta sleep.' 'More steam me eye,' the
Chief wud observe t' his piston rings, an' turrn the page av
10 last week's Bridgeport *Gazette*.

"So we wuz wallerin' along . . . I mind me the time wuz
late October an' cold fur them latitoods. The mate wuz
poorly, an' I, bein' an obligin' sort, wuz takin' his midnight
trick on the bridge fur him. Ol' Price didn't shine t' the
15 idea. He wuz fur iveryman doin' his dooty, dead or alive.
An' fur the fust hour 'r two he kep' a-dodgin' up on the bridge
t' squint at the binnacle an' see if Oakes wuz a-doin' his
dooty by speed an' I mine by navigatin'. An irritatin'
man. . . .

20 "In the course av time the Skipper turrned into his bunk.
A nasty night, thinks I t' meself, as the bows av the *Gulfleet*
went a-rarin' into them Hatteras ripples; a mischievious
evenin', thinks I agin, as she come down *Zoom!* on the trough
an' hung a-quiverin'. But a smart helmsman I had that
25 watch. North b'east half east I gave him at eight bells, an'
north b'east half east he wuz to a hair ivery time I conned
him. So pretty soon I found me a corner an' braced meself
on the railin's an' stuck me chin in the collar av me oil-
skin. 'Make yerself snug, Purvus,' sez I. ''Tis no bit av use
30 worryin' ol' Father Time?'

"I will not swear that I went asleep on the bridge av the
Gulfleet. I will not swear that I did not. But all av a sudden I took notice av a red like flare off t' the eastward. 'Twuz
low on the water an' hidden now and agin by the seaway,
35 which as I told ye wuz wicked. An' I climbs over t' the
wheel an' puts up t' me helmsman's ear.

"'What d'ye make av that, Quartermaster?' sez I pointin'
t' eastard.

"''Twuz what I wuz askin' meself,' sez he.

"'A ship in distress most like,' sez I.

"'Ye may be right,' he sez 'z he.   5

"At the call av his bell ol' Price come a-bouncin' an'
a-boomin' onto the bridge. 'Now Supercargo Purvus, an'
what have ye done t' me ship?' sez he. 'Somebody in distress, eh! Good,' sez he. 'Ease her off a mite, Whalen.
Now hold her there. We must look into this,' sez he.   10

"So we heads her off an' bears down on them red flares
which shows up now and agin t' eastard. An' pretty soon
''Tis a schooner!' sez the ol' man 'z he, peerin' through his
night glasses into the muck. 'Call all hands, Supercargo
Purvus,' sez he, an' rings down fur Slow Ahead on both   15
engines.

"After I'd turrned out bos'n an' told him how things stood
I hops on the bridge again. Fur this show wuz worth losin'
sleep fur. An' climbin' the companion I looks out an' seen
the little vessel close under our bows. In the gatherin' dawn   20
she wuz only a shadow like. But av a sudden wan av them
flares goes off on her deck an' as plain as day I seen her from
stem t' starn. An' split me eyes if they wuzn't a little bunch
av men a-rarin' round in a scrap along her decks. An' av a
sudden two shots cracks in me ears, an' s' help me I sees two   25
corpses layin' over the schooner's after hatch coamin'. Plain
as day I seen 'em stretched stiff in blue clothes an' rubber
boots in that fearsome red light av the signal flare. An' like
the wink av an eye that flare went out an' the schooner wuz
a-wallerin' shadow like under our bows.   30

"''Tis mutiny!' screeches Martin Price behind me.

"An' so it looked as shure as the Day av Judgment.

"Though the sea wuz roilin' as I've said, we launched
the starb'd boat, an' the second mate puts off in her. An'
the ol' man an' I stood on the bridge an' waited. Pretty   35
soon we sees four little shadows drop off'n the schooner's

rail int' the boat. Ol' Price he wuz a-champin' an' chawin'
wit' impatience. ''Twas luck a God-fearin' man shud come
along,' sez he. ''Tis a-hangin' by the neck the four av them
should be, fur layin' hands on their sooperiors,' the Skipper
sez 'z he.

"When that there starboard boat got back we bust her t'
flinders in that brawlin' sea. But down the deck come four
limp shadows, stumblin' like.

"'Put 'em in irons, put 'em in irons, Mister Beech,' sez
the ol' man 'z he. An' we lay the *Gulfleet* on her course as
the dawn come gray in the east. The thurrd mate took the
bridge. I seen the little schooner a-flappin' an' a-bangin'
astern av us. Then I tucks below t' get a sight av the
mutineers.

"The Skipper had 'em in his cabin aft. Ol' Price wuz
a-settin' at his big table wit' the log before him. T'wan side
av him stood Beech, the second mate, t' the other wuz Quartermaster Whalen. The four stood acrost the table in their
irons all proper, lookin' ashamed an' sad.

"'Cap'n, cap'n, 'tis I can explain the whole av it,' wan av
them wuz sayin'. But 'Hold yer tongue there!' sez Martin
Price 'z he. 'Hold yer tongue, Mister Mutineer,' sez he.
''Tis the truth I'm after all right an' proper, an' ye can bide
yer time till yer called on,' sez he. An' he hops up an'
handles the four av 'em a bit so's they whams agin the bulk-
head an' the irons on 'em jangles. 'I'll be after larnin' ye
manners in me cabin,' sez the Skipper 'z he. An evil lot,
thinks I, an' slips in quiet like. But ol' Price he sees me
quick.

"'An' what may you be doin' in me cabin, Mister Supercargo Purvus?' sez he majestic.

"'Bein' a witness av the tragedy, Sur,' sez I, 'I thinks as
how me testimony shud be av some assistance.'

"'True, Purvus, true, me man,' sez he. 'Ye can bear us a
hand in bringin' these miscreants t' justice,' sez he. 'Stand
by until yer wanted.'

"So I sets me down t'wan side av the big table an' took another look at them miscreants. Wan av the four wuz a mere boy, ye might say, at all odds not gone seventeen. Bein' a slim lad an' white as spindrift, he stared like it wuz a child dreamin'; an' him it wuz, too, that looked uncommon sad and whipped like. The shaver takes it hard, thinks I, 'tis the youth av him. And I turrns me gaze t' his partners in crime. They wuz usual lookin' burds but wretched like an' seemin'ly underfed. From wan fut t' the other they shifted, while them irons jingled faint. Their eyes they kep' on the deck, but now and agin one 'd cast a look at the boy. A sinful lot an' deep in crime, thinks I.

"Though all hands wuz as still 's the grave, ol' Price he raps hard on the table. Solemn as a judge wuz the Skipper an' twice as important.

"'Quartermaster Whalen!'

"'Sur?' sez he.

"'You will tell what ye know av the present durrty bizness.'

"An' Whalen tells as how him an' me noticed red flares t' the eastard, goin' on four bells av the midnight watch, our course bein' north b' east half east. Iverythin' right an' proper he tells it just as I give ye t' understand before. Only in the cabin ivery last thing seems important. Fur ol' Price bends his heavy eye on him an' writes down ivery wurrd in the log. An' I sees the sweat stand out on Whalen's forehead an' his hands go wranglin' an' twistin'. Fur I'm tellin' ye this Price wuz an aggravatin' man—he shud av been a lawyer. An' Whalen wuz after tellin' me when it wuz all over that before he'd fair started he got t' thinkin' 'twas him did the murder instid av them in irons.

"'An' what did ye see just after all hands wuz called?' sez the Skipper t' Whalen.

"''Tis a red flare I seen, Sur, that light'ns her decks the like av high noon,' sez he.

"'An' what did ye hear an' what more did ye see?'

"'I hears some shots an' I sees a scrabble av men on her

decks an' a coupla lifeless corpses layin' atop the after hatch coamin',' sez Whalen 'z he.

"'An' will ye swear it is the truth, Quartermaster Whalen?' sez the Skipper.

5   "'That I will, Sur,' sez Whalen a-shakin' in every limb.

"'D'ye hear that now, ye murrderers!' roars ol' Price at them four, rubbin' his hands an' glowerin' an' scowlin'.

"'But, Cap'n, I—'

"'*Hold yer peace, ye scum!*' sez he.

10   "Then Whalen gets through an' the Skipper turrns t' me an' sez:

"'Supercargo Purvus, wuz you in command av the deck at the time aforementioned?'

"'Yes, Sur,' sez I, an' feels me sins overtakin' me.

15   "'An' wuz ye awake an' in yer senses about the time av four bells aforementioned?'

"'I wuz, Sur,' sez I. Fur so help me, wakin' an' dozin' 'tis much the same thing t' me an' always wuz.

"'An' can ye testify that Quartermaster Whalen has spoke 20 the truth in ivery detail?'

"'I can, Sur,' sez I.

"Ol' Price fair glowers at me then, feelin' no doubt I shud av told Whalen he lied on a few minor points, as makin' the sin more complicatin'. But I cud not oblige him. So he 25 turrns t' Beech, the second mate.

"'Mister Beech,' sez he, 'ye will recount yer experiences from the time the starb'd boat shoved off t' the time she returrned.'

"An' Beech tells as how he made the best av bad water 30 between the ship's side an' the schooner. How two or three times he thought they wuz done fur in that peanut shell, but managed t' keep top side up till they wuz under the schooner's starn.

"'What wuz the schooner's crew a-doin' when ye lay along- 35 side?' sez ol' Price sharp like.

"'They wuz hangin' over the rail an' wavin',' sez Beech.

"'An' wuz they anything av a struggle goin' on?' sez Price.

"'No, Sur,' sez he.

"The Skipper looks like the mate's chances fur salvation wuz a-peterin'. Ivery wurrd he writes in the log. Then he sez:

"'An' what did ye see layin' atop the after hatch coamin', Beech?' sez he.

"'When that the schooner rolled we seen two lifeless corpses, Sur. They wuz stretched stiff in blue clothes an' sea boots. We took 'em fur the vessel's officers,' sez Beech 'z he.

"Ol' Price rubs his hands t'gether an' fair growls at them four acrost the table. An' 'Aha!' sez the Skipper, the God-fearin' man. 'An' d'ye hear that now,' sez he.

"Niver a wurrd sez the three av 'em but looks t' the boy an' he looks on the deck. Then the Skipper begins agin on Beech.

"'An' what did ye do?' sez he.

"'I hollered at them four, askin' wuz they anybody but them aboard. An' this wan,' sez Beech indicatin' the young 'un, 'this wan hollered back there ain't. Then I tells 'em t' jump fur it, there bein' no chance t' board her in that howlin' sea. An' they jumps wan by wan, near breakin' they necks in the job, an' we makes back alongside.'

"Martin Price writes this all down proper, gnawin' his whiskers an' scowlin' at them four. Then he lays down his pen an' leans back in his chair. An' he fixes his heavy eye on them four an' sez:

"'An' now what have you four men got ter say fur yer-selves,' sez he. 'I've enough evidence here,' sez ol' Price slappin' the log layin' there before him. 'I've got enough right here t' convict ye av mutiny an' murrder on the high seas, the penalty fur which bein' death. But I'm a fair minded man,' sez he. 'An' I'll give y' a chance fur t' speak fur yerselves. Come now,' sez he, 'come now. Is they any

reason why I shud not take ye to New York an' turrn y'
over t' the authorities av the law? Speak up an' tell me yer
story,' sez the Skipper 'z he. 'But be careful what ye say.'

"Then the three old 'uns av them four shifts from wan
foot t' the other an' jangles them irons jest a mite in the
stillness av that cabin. An' the three av 'em they looks t'
the young 'un like that he shud do the talkin'. An' this young
'un standin' there white an' tired like a boy, he heaves a
great sigh, castin' down his eyes t' the deck, an' begins
like this:

"'Me name is ——'

"''Tis not yer name I'm wantin'!' screeches the Skipper in
a rage. An' he beats on the table wit' his two fists. ''Tis
yer comin's an' yer goin's on the high seas wit' a fight an'
two dead men on deck that I needs t' have explained. 'Tis
the truth I'm after, tell me that,' 'z he.

"So the young 'un heaves another sigh an' begins wance
more:

"'We left Oporto, Spain, on the twentieth av August,' sez
he, 'wit' a cargo av salt fur the fishin' trade av Newfoundland. West av the Canaries we run into heavy weather an'
had it bad all the way acrost,' sez he. 'The schooner wuz
down by the head wit' salt, an' bein' an old boat anyways she
wallered an' pounded pretty bad. About a week back we
found her seams had started wit' the poundin', an' we had
two men t' the pumps night an' day from then on. It wuz
day before yestiddy—'

"He stops here an' looks up at them three like as he wuz
askin' their opinion in the matter av the day before yestiddy,
an' they all nods quick like, follerin' him very eager.

"'It wuz the day before yestiddy that we wuz runnin'
free-an'-by, an' rollin' fearsomely, when the salt in 'midships
hold shifted wit' the rollin' an' laid her hard down so's we
cud nather wurrk the pumps nur bring the ship about. Then
the Skipper he sez him an' the mate will go down 'midships
wit' shovels an' dig a hole in the salt down t' the bilges so's

we can start the pumps an' then mebbe light'n her so's the
cargo will shift back an' set her on an even keel. They wuz
some on us didn't want them both t' go—but them two wuz
afeard av nothin'—an' they went. An' we heard 'em a-
shovelin' an' a-singin' away down there like they had not 5
a care in the wurrld.'

"The boy stops here an' coughs a mite an' clears out his
throat. If he's actin' he shud be on the Hippydrome, thinks
I. Ye cud hear a pin drop in the Skipper's cabin.

"'Pretty soon we seen the pumps wuz free an' we pumped 10
fur might an' main t' light'n her. An' all av a sudden a wave
come under her lee an' lifted her over an' we heard the salt
a-rushin' an' a-whistlin' under her decks. An' we run t' midships hatch an' found the salt flush wit' the coamin'—an'
them two below.' 15

"Here he stops agin an' coughs all choked up like. He
shud be a noospaper man, thinks I t' meself. Ol' Price niver
sez wan wurrd, but glowers somethin' fearful an' chaws his
whiskers.

"'They wuz but wan shovel beside them two buried, but 20
we fetched it an' made scoops av boards an' we dug in that
salt all day yestiddy. An' last night we found 'em, wit' they
mouths an' ears an' eyes full av salt, an' salt stuffed up they
nostrils—stone dead. An' we laid 'em out on the after hatch
coamin' an' looked t' each other, not knowin' what t' do. 25
Fur only them two knew the vessel's position an' none av us
bein' skilled in figgers an' rackonin'. Then we got out red
flares an' signal pistol t' show we wuz in distress.'

"'We lit them flares up most av the night tho near dead we
wuz wit' cold an' want av food. An' goin' on four bells av the 30
midnight watch we seen a ship a-bearin' down on us. I wuz
at the wheel keepin' her hove-to, an' I yelled t' them for'd t'
light the red light an' set off the gun, an' I seen them scramble
an' fight t' get the signals up before that the ship cud get
away in the muck without a-seein' us. Pretty soon we seen 35
the boat under our starn. An' the rest ye knows.'

"So the young lad gets through his story an' the other three they looks at him an' nods an' looks t' the Skipper.

"But ol' Martin Price, the God-fearin' sail'rman, he gets up quick on his two feet an' stands over the boy an' shakes
5 his fist at him.

"'Now Heaven be me witness yer a liar!' sez the Skipper 'z he. 'An' d' ye expect a jury av twelve good men t' believe a wild cavort like that,' he sez, 'when I meself seen ye fightin' on the decks av that schooner, when I stood on me bridge an'
10 heard ye shootin' an' seen the bluecoated corpses ye killed,' sez he. 'What proof have ye four rascals an' murrderers that will be after savin' yer blighted necks. 'Tis proof I want, not fairy tales,' sez ol' Price, the God-fearin', hasty man. ''Tis the truth I'm after,' 'z he.

15 "At that the young 'un stands straight on his two legs an' stares the Skipper in the eye.

"'Ef ye would av let me tell ye me name in the fust place,' sez he, ''tis all av this broilin' would have ben saved. They is no need av proof,' he sez. 'These men will back me wurrd,
20 an' the ship's papers an' me burth certificate 'll be doin' the rest. Fur indeed an' t'would be you that should bring proof that I 'r any av us here brought death t' the Skipper av that schooner,' sez he. '*The man wuz me father*,' sez the boy 'z he.

25 "The other three av 'em nods quick an' looks t' ol' Price, standin' there stone still as that he sees the banshee. But at them wurrds the young lad slops down over the table an' sobs like his young heart wud crack."

.   .   .   .

The car was empty. From somewhere across the harbor a
30 clock tolled eleven. Red Purvis scrambled to his feet and started chalking the ends of the deals piled before us. Ten minutes later we checked out the big gate and plunged into the night.

"We'll be after countin' them deals in the marnin' agin,"
35 said Red Purvis, "*t' make shure*."

THE HOUSE OPPOSITE[1]

Sir Anthony Hope Hawkins

We were talking over the sad case of young Algy Groom;
I was explaining to Mrs. Hilary exactly what had happened.

"His father gave him," said I, "a hundred pounds, to keep
him for three months in Paris while he learned French."

"And very liberal too," said Mrs. Hilary.   5

"It depends where you dine," said I. "However, that question did not arise, for Algy went to the Grand Prix the day
after he arrived—"

"A *horse race?*" asked Mrs. Hilary, with great contempt.

"Certainly the competitors are horses," I rejoined. "And   10
there he, most unfortunately, lost the whole sum, without
learning any French to speak of."

"How disgusting!" exclaimed Mrs. Hilary, and little
Miss Phyllis gasped in horror.

"Oh, well," said Hilary, with much bravery (as it struck   15
me), "his father's very well off."

"That doesn't make it a bit better," declared his wife.

"There's no mortal sin in a little betting, my dear. Boys
will be boys—"

"And even that," I interposed, "wouldn't matter if we   20
could only prevent girls from being girls."

Mrs. Hilary, taking no notice whatever of me, pronounced
sentence. "He grossly deceived his father," she said, and
took up her embroidery.

"Most of us have grossly deceived our parents before   25
now," said I. "We should all have to confess to something
of the sort."

[1] From *The Dolly Dialogues*, chap. xv. Henry Holt and Company, New
York, 1894.

365

"I hope you're speaking for your own sex," observed Mrs. Hilary.

"Not more than yours," said I. "You used to meet Hilary on the pier when your father wasn't there—you told me so."

5   "Father had authorized my acquaintance with Hilary."

"I hate quibbles," said I.

There was a pause. Mrs. Hilary stitched: Hilary observed that the day was fine.

"Now," I pursued, carelessly, "even Miss Phyllis here has
10 been known to deceive her parents."

"Oh, let the poor child alone, anyhow," said Mrs. Hilary.

"Haven't you?" said I to Miss Phyllis.

I expected an indignant denial. So did Mrs. Hilary, for she remarked with a sympathetic air:

15   "Never mind his folly, Phyllis, dear."

"Haven't you, Miss Phyllis?" said I.

Miss Phyllis grew very red. Fearing that I was causing her pain, I was about to observe on the prospects of a Dissolution, when a shy smile spread over Miss Phyllis's face.

20   "Yes, once," said she, with a timid glance at Mrs. Hilary, who immediately laid down her embroidery.

"Out with it," I cried, triumphantly. "Come along, Miss Phyllis. We won't tell, honor bright!"

Miss Phyllis looked again at Mrs. Hilary. Mrs. Hilary is
25 human:

"Well, Phyllis, dear," said she, "after all this time I shouldn't think it my duty—"

"It only happened last summer," said Miss Phyllis.

Mrs. Hilary looked rather put out.

30   "Still," she began—

"We must have the story," said I.

Little Miss Phyllis put down the sock she had been knitting.

"I was very naughty," she remarked. "It was my last
35 term at school."

"I know that age," said I to Hilary.

"My window looked out toward the street. You're sure you won't tell? Well, there was a house opposite—"

"And a young man in it," said I.

"How did you know that?" asked Miss Phyllis, blushing immensely.

"No girls' school can keep up its numbers without one," I explained.

"Well, there was, anyhow," said Miss Phyllis. "And I and two other girls went to a course of lectures at the Town Hall, on literature or something of that kind. We used to have a shilling given us for our tickets."

"Precisely," said I. "A hundred pounds!"

"No, a shilling," corrected Miss Phyllis. "A hundred pounds! How absurd, Mr. Carter! Well, one day, I—I—"

"You're sure you wish to go on, Phyllis?" asked Mrs. Hilary.

"You're afraid, Mrs. Hilary," said I, severely.

"Nonsense, Mr. Carter. I thought Phyllis might—"

"I don't mind going on," said Miss Phyllis, smiling. "One day I—I lost the other girls."

"The other girls are always easy to lose," I observed.

"And on the way there—oh, you know, he went to the lectures."

"The young dog," said I, nudging Hilary. "I should think he did!"

"On the way there it became rather—rather foggy."

"Blessings on it!" I cried; for little Miss Phyllis's demure but roguish expression delighted me.

"And he—he found me in the fog."

"What are you doing, Mr. Carter?" cried Mrs. Hilary.

"Nothing, nothing," said I. I believe I had winked at Hilary.

"And—and we couldn't find the Town Hall."

"Oh, Phyllis!" groaned Mrs. Hilary.

Little Miss Phyllis looked alarmed for a moment. Then she smiled.

"But we found the confectioner's," said she.

"The *Grand Prix*," said I, pointing my forefinger at Hilary.

"He had no money at all," said Miss Phyllis.

"It's ideal!" said I.

5 "And—and we had tea on—on—"

"The shilling?" I cried, in rapture.

"Yes," said little Miss Phyllis, "on the shilling. And he saw me home."

"Details, please," said I.

10 Little Miss Phyllis shook her head.

"And left me at the door."

"Was it still foggy?" I asked.

"Yes. Or he wouldn't have—"

"Now what did he—?"

15 "Come to the door, Mr. Carter," said Miss Phyllis, with obvious wariness. "Oh, and it was such fun!"

"I'm sure it was."

"No, I mean when we were examined in the lectures. I bought the local paper, you know, and read it up, and I got

20 top marks easily, and Miss Green wrote to mother to say how well I had done."

"It all ended most satisfactorily," I observed.

"Yes, didn't it?" said little Miss Phyllis.

Mrs. Hilary was grave again.

25 "And you never told your mother, Phyllis?" she asked.

"N—no, Cousin Mary," said Miss Phyllis.

I rose and stood with my back to the fire. Little Miss Phyllis took up her sock again, but a smile still played about the corners of her mouth.

30 "I wonder," said I, looking up at the ceiling, "what happened at the door."

Then, as no one spoke, I added:

"Pooh! I know what happened at the door."

"I'm not going to tell you anything more," said Miss

35 Phyllis.

"But I should like to hear it in your own—"

Miss Phyllis was gone! She had suddenly risen and run from the room!

"It did happen at the door," said I.

"Fancy Phyllis!" mused Mrs. Hilary.

"I hope," said I, "that it will be a lesson to you." 5

"I shall have to keep my eye on her," said Mrs. Hilary.

"You can't do it," said I in easy confidence. I had no fear of little Miss Phyllis being done out of her recreations. "Meanwhile," I pursued, "the important thing is this: my parallel is obvious and complete." 10

"There's not the least likeness," said Mrs. Hilary, sharply.

"As a hundred pounds are to a shilling, so is the Grand Prix to the young man opposite," I observed, taking my hat, and holding out my hand to Mrs. Hilary.

"I am very angry with you," she said. "You've made the 15 child think there was nothing wrong in it."

"Oh! nonsense," said I. "Look how she enjoyed telling it."

Then, not heeding Mrs. Hilary, I launched into an apostrophe. 20

"Oh, divine House Opposite!" I cried. "Charming House Opposite! What is a man's own dull, uneventful home compared with that Glorious House Opposite? If only I might dwell forever in the House Opposite!"

"I haven't the least notion what you mean," remarked 25 Mrs. Hilary, stiffly. "I suppose it's something silly—or worse."

I looked at her in some puzzle.

"Have you no longing for the House Opposite?" I asked.

Mrs. Hilary looked at me. Her eyes ceased to be abso- 30 lutely blank. She put her arm through Hilary's and answered, gently:

"I don't want the House Opposite."

"Ah," said I, giving my hat a brush, "but maybe you remember the House—when it was Opposite?" 35

Mrs. Hilary, one arm still in Hilary's, gave me her hand.

She blushed and smiled.

"Well," said she, "it was your fault; so I won't scold Phyllis."

"No, don't, my dear," said Hilary, with a laugh.

5   As for me, I went down-stairs, and, in absence of mind, bid my cabman drive to the House Opposite. But I have never got there.

THE STORY OF MUHAMMAD DIN[1]

Rudyard Kipling

Who is the happy man? He that sees in his own house at home little children crowned with dust, leaping and falling and crying.—*Munichandra*, translated by Professor Peterson.

The polo-ball was an old one, scarred, chipped, and dinted. It stood on the mantelpiece among the pipe-stems which Imam Din, *khitmatgar*, was cleaning for me.

"Does the Heaven-born want this ball?" said Imam Din deferentially. 5

The Heaven-born set no particular store by it; but of what use was a polo-ball to a *khitmatgar*?

"By Your Honour's favour, I have a little son. He has seen this ball, and desires it to play with. I do not want it for myself." 10

No one would for an instant accuse portly old Imam Din of wanting to play with polo-balls. He carried out the battered thing into the verandah; and there followed a hurricane of joyful squeaks, a patter of small feet, and the *thud-thud-thud* of the ball rolling along the ground. Evidently 15 the little son had been waiting outside the door to secure his treasure. But how had he managed to see that polo-ball?

Next day, coming back from office half an hour earlier than usual, I was aware of a small figure in the dining-room —a tiny, plump figure in a ridiculously inadequate shirt 20 which came, perhaps, half-way down the tubby stomach. It wandered round the room, thumb in mouth, crooning to itself as it took stock of the pictures. Undoubtedly this was the "little son."

[1] From *Plain Tales from the Hills*, pp. 288–292. By special permission of Mr. Kipling and of Doubleday, Page & Company.

He had no business in my room, of course; but was so
deeply absorbed in his discoveries that he never noticed me
in the doorway. I stepped into the room and startled him
nearly into a fit. He sat down on the ground with a gasp.
His eyes opened, and his mouth followed suit. I knew what
was coming, and fled, followed by a long, dry howl which
reached the servants' quarters far more quickly than any
command of mine had ever done. In ten seconds Imam Din
was in the dining-room. Then despairing sobs arose, and I
returned to find Imam Din admonishing the small sinner,
who was using most of his shirt as a handkerchief.

"This boy," said Imam Din judicially, "is a *budmash*—
a big *budmash*. He will, without doubt, go to the *jail-khana*
for his behaviour." Renewed yells from the penitent, and
an elaborate apology to myself from Imam Din.

"Tell the baby," said I, "that the Sahib is not angry, and
take him away." Imam Din conveyed my forgiveness to the
offender, who had now gathered all his shirt around his neck,
stringwise, and the yell subsided into a sob. The two set off
for the door. "His name," said Imam Din, as though the
name were part of the crime, "is Muhammad Din, and he is
a *budmash*." Freed from present danger, Muhammad Din
turned round in his father's arms, and said gravely, "It is
true that my name is Muhammad Din, Tahib, but I am not
a *budmash*. I am a *man!*"

From that day dated my acquaintance with Muhammad
Din. Never again did he come into my dining-room, but
on the neutral ground of the garden we greeted each other
with much state, though our conversation was confined to
"*Talaam*, Tahib" from his side, and "*Salaam*, Muhammad
Din" from mine. Daily, on my return from office, the little
white shirt and the fat little body used to rise from the shade
of the creeper-covered trellis where they had been hid; and
daily I checked my horse here, that my salutation might not
be slurred over or given unseemly.

Muhammad Din never had any companions. He used to

trot about the compound, in and out of the castor-oil bushes, on mysterious errands of his own. One day I stumbled upon some of his handiwork far down the grounds. He had half buried the polo-ball in the dust, and stuck six shrivelled old marigold flowers in a circle round it. Outside that circle 5 again was a rude square, traced out in bits of red brick alternating with fragments of broken china; the whole bounded by a little bank of dust. The water-man from the well-curb put in a plea for the small architect, saying that it was only the play of a baby and did not much disfigure my garden. 10

Heaven knows that I had no intention of touching the child's work then or later; but, that evening, a stroll through the garden brought me unawares full on it; so that I trampled, before I knew, marigold-heads, dust-bank, and fragments of broken soap-dish into confusion past all hope of mending. 15 Next morning, I came upon Muhammad Din crying softly to himself over the ruin I had wrought. Some one had cruelly told him that the Sahib was very angry with him for spoiling the garden, and had scattered his rubbish, using bad language the while. Muhammad Din laboured for an hour at 20 effacing every trace of the dust-bank and pottery fragments, and it was with a tearful and apologetic face that he said, "*Talaam*, Tahib," when I came home from office. A hasty inquiry resulted in Imam Din informing Muhammad Din that, by my singular favour, he was permitted to disport him- 25 self as much as he pleased. Whereat the child took heart and fell to tracing the ground-plan of an edifice which was to eclipse the marigold-polo-ball creation.

For some months the chubby little eccentricity revolved in his humble orbit among the castor-oil bushes and in the 30 dust; always fashioning magnificent palaces from stale flowers thrown away by the bearer, smooth water-worn pebbles, bits of broken glass, and feathers pulled, I fancy, from my fowls—always alone, and always crooning to himself.

A gaily-spotted sea-shell was dropped one day close to the 35 last of his little buildings; and I looked that Muhammad

Din should build something more than ordinarily splendid on the strength of it. Nor was I disappointed. He meditated for the better part of an hour, and his crooning rose to a jubilant song. Then he began tracing in the dust. It would certainly be a wondrous palace, this one, for it was two yards long and a yard broad in ground-plan. But the palace was never completed.

Next day there was no Muhammad Din at the head of the carriage-drive, and no "*Talaam*, Tahib" to welcome my return. I had grown accustomed to the greeting, and its omission troubled me. Next day Imam Din told me that the child was suffering slightly from fever and needed quinine. He got the medicine, and an English Doctor.

"They have no stamina, these brats," said the Doctor, as he left Imam Din's quarters.

A week later, though I would have given much to have avoided it, I met on the road to the Mussulman buryingground Imam Din, accompanied by one other friend, carrying in his arms, wrapped in a white cloth, all that was left of little Muhammad Din.

THE KING OF BOYVILLE[1]

WILLIAM ALLEN WHITE

Boys who are born in a small town are born free and equal.
In the big city it may be different; there are doubtless good
little boys who disdain bad little boys, and poor little boys
who are never to be noticed under any circumstances. But
in a small town, every boy, good or bad, rich or poor, stands 5
among boys on his own merits. The son of the banker who
owns a turning-pole in the back yard, does homage to the
baker's boy who can sit on the bar and drop and catch by his
legs; while the good little boy, who is kept in wide collars
and cuffs by a mistaken mother, gazes through the white 10
paling of his father's fence at the troop headed for the swimming hole, and pays all the reverence which his dwarfed
nature can muster to the sign of the two fingers. In the
social order of boys who live in country towns, a boy is
measured by what he can do, and not by what his father is. 15
And so, Winfield Hancock Pennington, whose boy name was
Piggy Pennington, was the King of Boyville. For Piggy
could walk on his hands, curling one foot gracefully over his
back, and pointing the other straight in the air; he could
hang by his heels on a flying trapeze; he could chin a pole so 20
many times that no one could count the number; he could
turn a somersault in the air from the level ground, both backwards and forwards; he could "tread" water and "lay" his
hair; he could hit any marble in any ring from "taws" and
"knucks down,"—and better than all, he could cut his initials 25
in the ice on skates, and whirl around and around so many

[1] From *The Real Issue*, Chicago, 1897. By permission of McClure,
Phillips & Company.

times that he looked like an animated shadow, when he
would dart away up the stream, his red "comfort" flapping
behind him like a laugh of defiance. In the story books such
a boy would be the son of a widowed mother, and turn out
5 very good or very bad, but Piggy was not a story book boy,
and his father kept a grocery store, from which Piggy used
to steal so many dates that the boys said his father must
have cut up the almanac to supply him. As he never gave
the goodies to the other boys, but kept them for his own use,
10 his name of "Piggy" was his by all the rights of Boyville.

There was one thing Piggy Pennington could not do, and
it was the one of all things he most wished he could do: he
could not under any circumstances say three consecutive and
coherent words to any girl under fifteen and over nine. He
15 was invited with nearly all of the boys of his age in town, to
children's parties. And while any other boy, whose only ac-
complishment was turning a cart wheel, or skinning the cat
backwards, or, at most, hanging by one leg and turning a
handspring, could boldly ask a girl if he could see her home,
20 Piggy had to get his hat and sneak out of the house when the
company broke up. He would comfort himself by walking
along on the opposite side of the street from some couple,
while he talked in monosyllables about a joke which he and
the boy knew, but which was always a secret to the girl.
25 Even after school Piggy could not join the select coterie of
boys who followed the girls down through town to the postoffice. He could not tease the girls about absent boys at
such times and make up rhymes like

"First the cat and then her tail;
30   Jimmie Sears and Maggie Hale,"

and shout them out for the crowd to hear. Instead of joining this courtly troupe Piggy Pennington went off with the
boys who really didn't care for such things, and fought, or
played "tracks up," or wrestled his way leisurely home in
35 time to get in his "night wood." But his heart was not in

these pastimes; it was with a red shawl of a peculiar shade, that was wending its way to the postoffice and back to a home in one of the few two-story houses in the little town. Time and again had Piggy tried to make some sign to let his feelings be known, but every time he had failed. Lying in wait for her at corners, and suddenly breaking upon her with a glory of backward and forward somersaults did not convey the state of his heart. Hanging by his heels from an apple tree limb over the sidewalk in front of her, unexpectedly, did not tell the tender tale for which his lips could find no words. And the nearest he could come to an expression of the longing in his breast, was to cut her initials in the ice beside his own when she came weaving and wobbling past on some other boy's arm. But she would not look at the initials, and the chirography of his skates was so indistinct that it required a key; and everything put together, poor Piggy was no nearer a declaration at the end of the winter than he had been at the beginning of autumn. So only one heart beat with but a single thought, and the other took motto candy and valentines and red apples and picture cards and other tokens of esteem from other boys, and beat on with any number of thoughts, entirely immaterial to the uses of this narrative. But Piggy Pennington did not take to the enchantment of corn silk cigarettes and rattan and grape vine cigars; he tried to sing, and wailed dismal ballads about the "Gypsy's Warning," and "The Child in the Grave With Its Mother," and "She's a Daisy, She's a Darling, She's a Dumpling, She's a Lamb," whenever he was in hearing distance of his Heart's Desire, in the hope of conveying to her some hint of the state of his affections; but it was useless. Even when he tried to whistle plaintively as he passed her house in the gloaming, his notes brought forth no responsive echo.

One morning in the late spring, he spent half an hour before breakfast among his mother's roses, which were just in first bloom. He had taken out there all the wire from an old broom, and all his kite string. His mother had to call three

times before he would leave his work. The youngster was the first to leave the table, and by eight o'clock he was at his task again. Before the first school bell had rung, Piggy Pennington was bound for the schoolhouse with a strange look-
5 ing parcel under his arm. He tried to put his coat over it, but it stuck out, and the newspaper that was wrapped around it bulged into so many corners that it looked like a home-tied bundle of laundry.

"What you got?" asked the freckle-faced boy, who was
10 learning at Piggy's feet how to do the "muscle grind" on the turning-pole.

But Piggy Pennington was the King of Boyville, and he had a right to look straight ahead of him, as if he did not hear the question, and say:

15 "Lookie here, Mealy, I wish you would go and tell Abe I want him to hurry up, for I want to see him."

"Abe" was Piggy's nearest friend. His other name was Carpenter. Piggy only wished to be rid of the freckle-faced boy. But the freckle-faced boy was not used to royalty and
20 its ways, so he pushed his inquiry.

"Say, Piggy, have you got your red ball-pants in that bundle?"

There was no reply. The freckle-faced boy grew tired of tattooing with a stick, as they walked beside a paling fence,
25 so he began touching every tree on the other side of the path with his fingers. They had gone a block when the freckle-faced boy could stand it no longer and said:

"Say, Piggy, you needn't be so smart about your old bundle; now honest, Piggy, what have you got in that
30 bundle?"

"Aw—soft soap, take a bite—good fer yer appetite," said the King, as he faced about and drew up his left cheek and lower eye-lid pugnaciously. The freckle-faced boy saw he would have to fight if he stayed, so he turned to go, and said,
35 as though nothing had happened, "Where do you suppose old Abe is, anyhow?"

Just before school was called Piggy Pennington was play-ing "scrub" with all his might, and a little girl—his Heart's Desire—was taking out of her desk a wreath of roses, tied to a shaky wire frame. There was a crowd of girls around her admiring it, and speculating about the possible author of the gift; but to these she did not show the patent medicine card, on which was scrawled, over the druggist's advertisement: "Yours truly, W. H. P."

When the last bell rang, Piggy Pennington was the last boy in, and he did not look toward the desk, where he had put the flowers, until after the singing.

Then he stole a sidewise glance that way, and his Heart's Desire was deep in her geography. It was an age before she filed past him with the "B" class in geography, and took a seat directly in front of him, where he could look at her all the time, unobserved by her. Once she squirmed in her place and looked toward him, but Piggy Pennington was head over heels in the "Iser rolling rapidly." When their eyes did at last meet, just as Piggy, leading the marching around the room, was at the door to go out for recess, the thrill amounted to a shock that sent him whirling in a pin wheel of hand-springs toward the ball ground, shouting "scrub—first bat, first bat, first bat," from sheer, bubbling joy. Piggy made four tallies that recess, and the other boys couldn't have put him out if they had used a hand-grenade or a Babcock fire extinguisher.

He received four distinct shots that day from the eyes of his Heart's Desire, and the last one sent him home on the run, tripping up every primary urchin whom he found tag-ging along by the way, and whooping at the top of his voice. When his friends met in his barn, some fifteen minutes later, Piggy tried to turn a double somersault from his spring board, to the admiration of the crowd, and was only calmed by falling with his full weight on his head and shoulders at the edge of the hay, with the life nearly jolted out of his little body.

The next morning, Piggy Pennington astonished his friends
by bringing a big armful of red and yellow and pink and
white roses to school.

He had never done this before, and when he had run the
gauntlet of the big boys, who were not afraid to steal them
from him, he made straight for his schoolroom, and stood
holding them in his hands while the girls gathered about him
teasing for the beauties. It was nearly time for the last bell
to ring, and Piggy knew that his Heart's Desire would be in
the room by the time he got there. He was not mistaken.
But Heart's Desire did not clamor with the other girls for
one of the roses. Piggy stood off their pleadings as long as
he could with "Naw," "Why naw, of course I won't," "Naw,
what I want to give you one for," and "Go way from here,
I tell you," and still Heart's Desire did not ask for her
flowers. There were but a few moments left before school
would be called to order, and in desperation Piggy gave one
rose away. It was not a very pretty rose, but he hoped she
would see that the others were to be given away, and ask for
one. But she—his Heart's Desire—stood near a window,
talking to the freckle-faced boy. Then Piggy gave away one
rose after another. As the last bell began to ring he gave
them to the boys, as the girls were all supplied. And still
she came not. There was one rose left, the most beautiful
of all. She went to her desk, and as the teacher came in, bell
in hand, Piggy surprised himself, the teacher, and the school
by laying the beautiful flower without a word on the teacher's
desk. That day was a dark day. When a new boy, who
didn't belong to the school, came up at recess to play, Piggy
shuffled over to him and asked gruffly:

"What's your name?"

"Puddin' 'n' tame, ast me agin an' I'll tell you the same,"
said the new boy, and then there was a fight. It didn't
soothe Piggy's feelings one bit that he whipped the new boy,
for the new boy was smaller than Piggy. And he dared not
turn his flushed face towards his Heart's Desire. It was al-

most four o'clock when Piggy Pennington walked to the master's desk to get him to work out a problem, and as he passed the desk of Heart's Desire he dropped a note in her lap. It read:

"Are you mad?" 5

But he dared not look for the answer, as they marched out that night, so he contented himself with punching the boy ahead of him with a pin, and stepping on his heels, when they were in the back part of the room, where the teacher would not see him. The King of Boyville walked home alone 10 that evening. The courtiers saw plainly that his majesty was troubled.

So his lonely way was strewn with broken stick-horses, which he took from the little boys, and was marked by trees adorned with the string, which he took from other young- 15 sters, who ran across his pathway playing horse. In his barn he sat listlessly on a nail keg, while Abe and the freckle-faced boy did their deeds of daring, on the rings and the trapeze. Only when the new boy came in, did Piggy arouse himself to mount the flying bar, and, swinging in it to the very 20 rafters, drop and hang by his knees, and again drop from his knees, catching his ankle in the angle of the rope where it meets the swinging bar. That was to awe the new boy.

After this feat the King was quiet.

At dusk, when the evening chores were done, Piggy Pen- 25 nington walked past the home of his Heart's Desire and howled out a doleful ballad which began:

> "You ask what makes this darkey wee-eep,
> Why he like others am not gay."

But a man on the sidewalk passing said, "Well, son, that's 30 pretty good, but wouldn't you just as lief sing as to make that noise?" So the King went to bed with a heavy heart.

He took that heart to school with him, the next morning, and dragged it over the school ground, playing crack the whip and "stink-base." But when he saw Heart's Desire 35

wearing in her hair one of the white roses from his mother's garden—the Penningtons had the only white roses in the little town—he knew it was from the wreath which he had given her, and so light was his boyish heart, that it was with
5 an effort that he kept it out of his throat. There were smiles and smiles that day. During the singing they began, and every time she came past him from a class, and every time he could pry his eyes behind her geography, or her grammar, a flood of gladness swept over his soul. That night Piggy
10 Pennington followed the girls from the schoolhouse to the postoffice, and in a burst of enthusiasm, he walked on his hands in front of the crowd, for nearly half a block. When his Heart's Desire said:

"Oh, ain't you afraid you'll hurt yourself, doing that?"
15 Piggy pretended not to hear her, and said to the boys:

"Aw, that ain't nothin'; come down to my barn, an' I'll do somepin that'll make yer head swim."

He was too exuberant to contain himself, and when he left the girls he started to run after a stray chicken, that hap-
20 pened along, and ran till he was out of breath. He did not mean to run in the direction his Heart's Desire had taken, but he turned a corner, and came up with her suddenly.

Her eyes beamed upon him, and he could not run away as he wished. She made room for him on the sidewalk, and he
25 could do nothing but walk beside her. For a block they were so embarrassed that neither spoke.

It was Piggy who broke the silence. His words came from his heart. He had not yet learned to speak otherwise.

"Where's your rose?" he asked, not seeing it.
30 "What rose?" said the girl, as though she had never in her short life heard of such an absurd thing as a rose.

"Oh, you know," returned the boy, stepping irregularly, to make the tips of his toes come on the cracks of the sidewalk. There was another pause, during which Piggy picked
35 up a pebble, and threw it at a bird in a tree. His heart was sinking rapidly.

"Oh, that rose?" said his Heart's Desire, turning full upon him with the enchantment of her childish eyes. "Why, here it is in my grammar. I'm taking it to keep with the others. Why?"

"Oh, nuthin' much," replied the boy. "I bet you can't 5 do this," he added, as he glowed up into her eyes from an impulsive handspring.

And thus the King of Boyville first set his light little foot upon the soil of an unknown country.

TOBIN'S PALM[1]

O. HENRY

Tobin and me, the two of us, went down to Coney one day, for there was four dollars between us, and Tobin had need of distractions. For there was Katie Mahorner, his sweetheart, of County Sligo, lost since she started for America three months before with two hundred dollars, her own savings, and one hundred dollars from the sale of Tobin's inherited estate, a fine cottage and pig on the Bog Shannaugh. And since the letter that Tobin got saying that she had started to come to him not a bit of news had he heard or seen of Katie Mahorner. Tobin advertised in the papers, but nothing could be found of the colleen.

So, to Coney me and Tobin went, thinking that a turn at the chutes and the smell of the popcorn might raise the heart in his bosom. But Tobin was a hard-headed man, and the sadness stuck in his skin. He ground his teeth at the crying balloons; he cursed the moving pictures; and, though he would drink whenever asked, he scorned Punch and Judy, and was for licking the tintype men as they came.

So I gets him down a side way on a board walk where the attractions were some less violent. At a little six by eight stall Tobin halts, with a more human look in his eye.

"'Tis here," says he, "I will be diverted. I'll have the palm of me hand investigated by the wonderful palmist of the Nile, and see if what is to be will be."

Tobin was a believer in signs and the unnatural in nature. He possessed illegal convictions in his mind along the sub-

[1] From *The Four Million*. Doubleday, Page & Company, New York. Originally published in 1906.

jects of black cats, lucky numbers, and the weather predictions in the papers.

We went into the enchanted chicken coop, which was fixed mysterious with red cloth and pictures of hands with lines crossing 'em like a railroad centre. The sign over the door says it is Madame Zozo the Egyptian Palmist. There was a fat woman inside in a red jumper with pothooks and beasties embroidered upon it. Tobin gives her ten cents and extends one of his hands. She lifts Tobin's hand, which is own brother to the hoof of a drayhorse, and examines it to see whether 'tis a stone in the frog or a cast shoe he has come for.

"Man," says this Madame Zozo, "the line of your fate shows—"

"'Tis not me foot at all," says Tobin, interrupting. "Sure, 'tis no beauty, but ye hold the palm of me hand."

"The line shows," says the Madame, "that ye've not arrived at your time of life without bad luck. And there's more to come. The mount of Venus—or is that a stone bruise?—shows that ye've been in love. There's been trouble in your life on account of your sweetheart."

"'Tis Katie Mahorner she has references with," whispers Tobin to me in a loud voice to one side.

"I see," says the palmist, "a great deal of sorrow and tribulation with one whom ye cannot forget. I see the lines of designation point to the letter K and the letter M in her name."

"Whist!" says Tobin to me; "do ye hear that?"

"Look out," goes on the palmist, "for a dark man and a light woman; for they'll both bring ye trouble. Ye'll make a voyage upon the water very soon, and have a financial loss. I see one line that brings good luck. There's a man coming into your life who will fetch ye good fortune. Ye'll know him when ye see him by his crooked nose."

"Is his name set down?" asks Tobin. "'Twill be convenient in the way of greeting when he backs up to dump off the good luck."

"His name," says the palmist, thoughtful looking, "is not spelled out by the lines, but they indicate 'tis a long one, and the letter 'o' should be in it. There's no more to tell. Good-evening. Don't block up the door."

5 "'Tis wonderful how she knows," says Tobin as we walk to the pier.

As we squeezed through the gates a nigger man sticks his lighted segar against Tobin's ear, and there is trouble. Tobin hammers his neck, and the women squeal, and by presence 10 of mind I drag the little man out of the way before the police comes. Tobin is always in an ugly mood when enjoying himself.

On the boat going back, when the man calls "Who wants the good-looking waiter?" Tobin tried to plead guilty, feel-15 ing the desire to blow the foam off a crock of suds, but when he felt in his pocket he found himself discharged for lack of evidence. Somebody had disturbed his change during the commotion. So we sat, dry, upon the stools, listening to the Dagoes fiddling on deck. If anything, Tobin was lower in 20 spirits and less congenial with his misfortunes than when we started.

On a seat against the railing was a young woman dressed suitable for red automobiles, with hair the colour of an un-smoked meerschaum. In passing by Tobin kicks her foot 25 without intentions, and, being polite to ladies when in drink, he tries to give his hat a twist while apologising. But he knocks it off, and the wind carries it overboard.

Tobin came back and sat down, and I began to look out for him, for the man's adversities were becoming frequent. He 30 was apt, when pushed so close by hard luck, to kick the best dressed man he could see, and try to take command of the boat.

Presently Tobin grabs my arm and says, excited: "Jawn," says he, "do ye know what we're doing? We're taking a voyage upon the water."

35 "There now," says I; "subdue yeself. The boat'll land in ten minutes more."

"Look," says he, "at the light lady upon the bench. And have ye forgotten the nigger man that burned me ear? And isn't the money I had gone—a dollar sixty-five it was?"

I thought he was no more than summing up his catastrophes so as to get violent with good excuse, as men will do, and I tried to make him understand such things was trifles.

"Listen," says Tobin. "Ye've no ear for the gift of prophecy or the miracles of the inspired. What did the palmist lady tell ye out of me hand? 'Tis coming true before your eyes. 'Look out,' says she, 'for a dark man and a light woman; they'll bring ye trouble.' Have ye forgot the nigger man, though he got some of it back from me fist? Can ye show me a lighter woman than the blonde lady that was the cause of me hat falling in the water? And where's the dollar sixty-five I had in me vest when we left the shooting gallery?"

The way Tobin put it, it did seem to corroborate the art of prediction, though it looked to me that these accidents could happen to any one at Coney without the implication of palmistry.

Tobin got up and walked around on deck, looking close at the passengers out of his little red eyes. I asked him the interpretation of his movements. Ye never know what Tobin has in his mind until he begins to carry it out.

"Ye should know," says he, "I'm working out the salvation promised by the lines in me palm. I'm looking for the crooked-nose man that's to bring the good luck. 'Tis all that will save us. Jawn, did ye ever see a straighter-nosed gang of hellions in the days of your life?"

'Twas the nine-thirty boat, and we landed and walked up-town through Twenty-second Street, Tobin being without his hat.

On a street corner, standing under a gas-light and looking over the elevated road at the moon, was a man. A long man he was, dressed decent, with a segar between his teeth, and I saw that his nose made two twists from bridge to end, like the wriggle of a snake. Tobin saw it at the same time, and

I heard him breathe hard like a horse when you take the saddle off. He went straight up to the man, and I went with him.

"Good-night to ye," Tobin says to the man. The man takes out his segar and passes the compliments, sociable.

5 "Would ye hand us your name," asks Tobin, "and let us look at the size of it? It may be our duty to become acquainted with ye."

"My name," says the man, polite, "is Friedenhausman— Maximus G. Friedenhausman."

10 "'Tis the right length," says Tobin. "Do you spell it with an 'o' anywhere down the stretch of it?"

"I do not," says the man.

"*Can* ye spell it with an 'o'?" inquires Tobin, turning anxious.

15 "If your conscience," says the man with the nose, "is indisposed toward foreign idioms ye might, to please yourself, smuggle the letter into the penultimate syllable."

"'Tis well," says Tobin. "Ye're in the presence of Jawn Malone and Daniel Tobin."

20 "'Tis highly appreciated," says the man, with a bow. "And now since I cannot conceive that ye would hold a spelling bee upon the street corner, will ye name some reasonable excuse for being at large?"

"By the two signs," answers Tobin, trying to explain, 25 "which ye display according to the reading of the Egyptian palmist from the sole of me hand, ye've been nominated to offset with good luck the lines of trouble leading to the nigger man and the blonde lady with her feet crossed in the boat, besides the financial loss of a dollar sixty-five, all so far 30 fulfilled according to Hoyle."

The man stopped smoking and looked at me.

"Have ye any amendments," he asks, "to offer to that statement, or are ye one too? I thought by the looks of ye ye might have him in charge."

35 "None," says I to him, "except that as one horseshoe resembles another so are ye the picture of good luck as pre-

dicted by the hand of me friend. If not, then the lines of
Danny's hand may have been crossed, I don't know."

"There's two of ye," says the man with the nose, looking
up and down for the sight of a policeman. "I've enjoyed
your company immense. Good-night."

With that he shoves his segar in his mouth and moves
across the street, stepping fast. But Tobin sticks close to
one side of him and me at the other.

"What!" says he, stopping on the opposite sidewalk and
pushing back his hat; "do ye follow me? I tell ye," he says,
very loud, "I'm proud to have met ye. But it is my desire
to be rid of ye. I am off to me home."

"Do," says Tobin, leaning against his sleeve. "Do be off
to your home. And I will sit at the door of it till ye come out
in the morning. For the dependence is upon ye to obviate
the curse of the nigger man and the blonde lady and the
financial loss of the one-sixty-five."

"'Tis a strange hallucination," says the man, turning to me
as a more reasonable lunatic. "Hadn't ye better get him
home?"

"Listen, man," says I to him. "Daniel Tobin is as sensible
as he ever was. Maybe he is a bit deranged on account of
having drink enough to disturb but not enough to settle his
wits, but he is no more than following out the legitimate
path of his superstitions and predicaments, which I will explain to you." With that I relates the facts about the palmist
lady and how the finger of suspicion points to him as an instrument of good fortune. "Now, understand," I concludes,
"my position in this riot. I am the friend of me friend Tobin,
according to me interpretations. 'Tis easy to be a friend to
the prosperous, for it pays; 'tis not hard to be a friend to the
poor, for ye get puffed up by gratitude and have your picture printed standing in front of a tenement with a scuttle of
coal and an orphan in each hand. But it strains the art of
friendship to be true friend to a born fool. And that's what
I'm doing," says I, "for, in my opinion, there's no fortune

to be read from the palm of me hand that wasn't printed there with the handle of a pick. And, though ye've got the crookedest nose in New York City, I misdoubt that all the fortune-tellers doing business could milk good luck from 5 ye. But the lines of Danny's hand pointed to ye fair, and I'll assist him to experiment with ye until he's convinced ye're dry."

After that the man turns, sudden, to laughing. He leans against a corner and laughs considerable. Then he claps me 10 and Tobin on the backs of us and takes us by an arm apiece.

"'Tis my mistake," says he. "How could I be expecting anything so fine and wonderful to be turning the corner upon me? I came near being found unworthy. Hard by," says he, "is a café, snug and suitable for the entertainment of 15 idiosyncrasies. Let us go there and have drink while we discuss the unavailability of the categorical."

So saying, he marched me and Tobin to the back room of a saloon, and ordered the drinks, and laid the money on the table. He looks at me and Tobin like brothers of his, and 20 we have the segars.

"Ye must know," says the man of destiny, "that me walk in life is one that is called the literary. I wander abroad be night seeking idiosyncrasies in the masses and truth in the heavens above. When ye came upon me I was in contempla- 25 tion of the elevated road in conjunction with the chief lumi- nary of night. The rapid transit is poetry and art: the moon but a tedious, dry body, moving by rote. But these are pri- vate opinions, for, in the business of literature, the conditions are reversed. 'Tis me hope to be writing a book to explain 30 the strange things I have discovered in life."

"Ye will put me in a book," says Tobin, disgusted; "will ye put me in a book?"

"I will not," says the man, "for the covers will not hold ye. Not yet. The best I can do is to enjoy ye meself, for the 35 time is not ripe for destroying the limitations of print. Ye would look fantastic in type. All alone by meself must I

drink this cup of joy. But, I thank ye, boys; I am truly
grateful."

"The talk of ye," says Tobin, blowing through his mous-
tache and pounding the table with his fist, "is an eyesore to
me patience. There was good luck promised out of the crook
of your nose, but ye bear fruit like the bang of a drum. Ye
resemble, with your noise of books, the wind blowing through
a crack. Sure, now, I would be thinking the palm of me hand
lied but for the coming true of the nigger man and the blonde
lady and—"

"Whist!" says the long man; "would ye be led astray by
physiognomy? Me nose will do what it can within bounds.
Let us have these glasses filled again, for 'tis good to keep
idiosyncrasies well moistened, they being subject to deterio-
ration in a dry moral atmosphere."

So, the man of literature makes good, to my notion, for he
pays, cheerful, for everything, the capital of me and Tobin
being exhausted by prediction. But Tobin is sore, and drinks
quiet, with the red showing in his eye.

By and by we moved out, for 'twas eleven o'clock, and
stands a bit upon the sidewalk. And then the man says he
must be going home, and invites me and Tobin to walk that
way. We arrives on a side street two blocks away where
there is a stretch of brick houses with high stoops and iron
fences. The man stops at one of them and looks up at the
top windows, which he finds dark.

"'Tis me humble dwelling," says he, "and I begin to perceive by the signs that me wife has retired to slumber. Therefore I will venture a bit in the way of hospitality. 'Tis me
wish that ye enter the basement room, where we dine, and
partake of a reasonable refreshment. There will be some
fine cold fowl and cheese and a bottle or two of ale. Ye will
be welcome to enter and eat, for I am indebted to ye for
diversions."

The appetite and conscience of me and Tobin was congenial to the proposition, though 'twas sticking hard in

Danny's superstitions to think that a few drinks and a cold
lunch should represent the good fortune promised by the
palm of his hand.

"Step down the steps," says the man with the crooked
5 nose, "and I will enter by the door above and let ye in.
I will ask the new girl we have in the kitchen," says he, "to
make ye a pot of coffee to drink before ye go. 'Tis fine coffee
Katie Mahorner makes for a green girl just landed three
months. Step in," says the man, "and I'll send her down
10 to ye."

THE RED–HEADED LEAGUE[1]

Sir Arthur Conan Doyle

I had called upon my friend, Mr. Sherlock Holmes, one
day in the autumn of last year, and found him in deep conversation with a very stout, florid-faced, elderly gentleman,
with fiery red hair. With an apology for my intrusion, I was
about to withdraw, when Holmes pulled me abruptly into the 5
room and closed the door behind me.

"You could not possibly have come at a better time, my
dear Watson," he said, cordially.

"I was afraid that you were engaged."

"So I am. Very much so."   10

"Then I can wait in the next room."

"Not at all. This gentleman, Mr. Wilson, has been my
partner and helper in many of my most successful cases, and
I have no doubt that he will be of the utmost use to me in
yours also."   15

The stout gentleman half-rose from his chair and gave a
bob of greeting, with a quick little questioning glance from
his small, fat-encircled eyes.

"Try the settee," said Holmes, relapsing into his arm-chair
and putting his finger-tips together, as was his custom when 20
in judicial moods. "I know, my dear Watson, that you share
my love of all that is bizarre and outside the conventions and
humdrum routine of every-day life. You have shown your
relish for it by the enthusiasm which has prompted you to
chronicle, and, if you will excuse my saying so, somewhat 25
to embellish, so many of my own little adventures."

[1] From *Adventures of Sherlock Holmes*. Harper & Brothers, New
York, 1892.

"Your cases have indeed been of the greatest interest to me," I observed.

"You will remember that I remarked the other day, just before we went into the very simple problem presented by Miss Mary Sutherland, that for strange effects and extraordinary combinations we must go to life itself, which is always far more daring than any effort of the imagination."

"A proposition which I took the liberty of doubting."

"You did, doctor, but none the less you must come round to my view, for otherwise I shall keep on piling fact upon fact on you, until your reason breaks down under them and acknowledges me to be right. Now, Mr. Jabez Wilson here has been good enough to call upon me this morning, and to begin a narrative which promises to be one of the most singular which I have listened to for some time. You have heard me remark that the strangest and most unique things are very often connected not with the larger but with the smaller crimes, and occasionally, indeed, where there is room for doubt whether any positive crime has been committed. As far as I have heard, it is impossible for me to say whether the present case is an instance of crime or not, but the course of events is certainly among the most singular that I have ever listened to. Perhaps, Mr. Wilson, you would have the great kindness to recommence your narrative. I ask you, not merely because my friend Dr. Watson has not heard the opening part, but also because the peculiar nature of the story makes me anxious to have every possible detail from your lips. As a rule, when I have heard some slight indication of the course of events, I am able to guide myself by the thousands of other similar cases which occur to my memory. In the present instance I am forced to admit that the facts are, to the best of my belief, unique."

The portly client puffed out his chest with an appearance of some little pride, and pulled a dirty and wrinkled newspaper from the inside pocket of his great-coat. As he glanced down the advertisement column, with his head thrust forward, and the paper flattened out upon his knee, I took a good look at the man, and endeavored, after the fashion of my companion, to read the indications which might be presented by his dress or appearance.

I did not gain very much, however, by my inspection. Our visitor bore every mark of being an average commonplace British tradesman, obese, pompous, and slow. He wore rather baggy gray shepherd's check trousers, a not over-clean black frock-coat, unbuttoned in the front, and a drab waistcoat with a heavy brassy Albert chain, and a square pierced bit of metal dangling down as an ornament. A frayed top-hat and a faded brown overcoat with a wrinkled velvet collar lay upon a chair beside him. Altogether, look as I would, there was nothing remarkable about the man save his blazing red head, and the expression of extreme chagrin and discontent upon his features.

Sherlock Holmes's quick eye took in my occupation, and he shook his head with a smile as he noticed my questioning glances. "Beyond the obvious facts that he has at some time done manual labor, that he takes snuff, that he is a Freemason, that he has been in China, and that he has done a considerable amount of writing lately, I can deduce nothing else."

Mr. Jabez Wilson started up in his chair, with his forefinger upon the paper, but his eyes upon my companion.

"How, in the name of good fortune, did you know all that, Mr. Holmes?" he asked. "How did you know, for example, that I did manual labor. It's as true as gospel, for I began as a ship's carpenter."

"Your hands, my dear sir. Your right hand is quite a size larger than your left. You have worked with it, and the muscles are more developed."

"Well, the snuff, then, and the Freemasonry?"

"I won't insult your intelligence by telling you how I read that, especially as, rather against the strict rules of your order, you use an arc-and-compass breastpin."

"Ah, of course, I forgot that. But the writing?"

"What else can be indicated by that right cuff so very shiny for five inches, and the left one with the smooth patch near the elbow where you rest it upon the desk."

5 "Well, but China?"

"The fish that you have tattooed immediately above your right wrist could only have been done in China. I have made a small study of tattoo marks, and have even contributed to the literature of the subject. That trick of staining the fishes'
10 scales of a delicate pink is quite peculiar to China. When, in addition, I see a Chinese coin hanging from your watch-chain, the matter becomes even more simple."

Mr. Jabez Wilson laughed heavily. "Well, I never!" said he. "I thought at first that you had done something clever,
15 but I see that there was nothing in it, after all."

"I begin to think, Watson," said Holmes, "that I make a mistake in explaining. 'Omne ignotum pro magnifico,' you know, and my poor little reputation, such as it is, will suffer shipwreck if I am so candid. Can you not find the advertise-
20 ment, Mr. Wilson?"

"Yes, I have got it now," he answered, with his thick, red finger planted half-way down the column. "Here it is. This is what began it all. You just read it for yourself, sir."

I took the paper from him, and read as follows:

25 "To the Red-headed League: On account of the bequest of the late Ezekiah Hopkins, of Lebanon, Pa., U.S.A., there is now another vacancy open which entitles a member of the League to a salary of £4 a week for purely nominal services. All red-headed men who are sound in body and mind, and
30 above the age of twenty-one years, are eligible. Apply in person on Monday, at eleven o'clock, to Duncan Ross, at the offices of the League, 7 Pope's Court, Fleet Street."

"What on earth does this mean?" I ejaculated, after I had twice read over the extraordinary announcement.

Holmes chuckled, and wriggled in his chair, as was his habit when in high spirits. "It is a little off the beaten track, isn't it?" said he. "And now, Mr. Wilson, off you go at scratch, and tell us all about yourself, your household, and the effect which this advertisement had upon your fortunes. You will first make a note, doctor, of the paper and the date."

"It is *The Morning Chronicle*, of April 27, 1890. Just two months ago."

"Very good. Now, Mr. Wilson?"

"Well, it is just as I have been telling you, Mr. Sherlock Holmes," said Jabez Wilson, mopping his forehead; "I have a small pawnbroker's business at Coburg Square, near the city. It's not a very large affair, and of late years it has not done more than just give me a living. I used to be able to keep two assistants, but now I only keep one; and I would have a job to pay him, but that he is willing to come for half wages, so as to learn the business."

"What is the name of this obliging youth?" asked Sherlock Holmes.

"His name is Vincent Spaulding, and he's not such a youth, either. It's hard to say his age. I should not wish a smarter assistant, Mr. Holmes; and I know very well that he could better himself, and earn twice what I am able to give him. But, after all, if he is satisfied, why should I put ideas in his head?"

"Why, indeed? You seem most fortunate in having an *employé* who comes under the full market price. It is not a common experience among employers in this age. I don't know that your assistant is not as remarkable as your advertisement."

"Oh, he has his faults, too," said Mr. Wilson. "Never was such a fellow for photography. Snapping away with a camera when he ought to be improving his mind, and then diving down into the cellar like a rabbit into its hole to develop his pictures. That is his main fault; but, on the whole, he's a good worker. There's no vice in him."

"He is still with you, I presume?"

"Yes, sir. He and a girl of fourteen, who does a bit of simple cooking, and keeps the place clean—that's all I have in the house, for I am a widower, and never had any family. We live very quietly, sir, the three of us; and we keep a roof over our heads, and pay our debts, if we do nothing more.

"The first thing that put us out was that advertisement. Spaulding, he came down into the office just this day eight weeks, with this very paper in his hand, and he says:

"'I wish to the Lord, Mr. Wilson, that I was a red-headed man.'

"'Why that?' I asks.

"'Why,' says he, 'here's another vacancy on the League of the Red-headed Men. It's worth quite a little fortune to any man who gets it, and I understand that there are more vacancies than there are men, so that the trustees are at their wits' end what to do with the money. If my hair would only change color, here's a nice little crib all ready for me to step into.'

"'Why, what is it, then?' I asked. You see, Mr. Holmes, I am a very stay-at-home man, and as my business came to me instead of my having to go to it, I was often weeks on end without putting my foot over the door-mat. In that way I didn't know much of what was going on outside, and I was always glad of a bit of news.

"'Have you never heard of the League of the Red-headed Men?' he asked, with his eyes open.

"'Never.'

"'Why, I wonder at that, for you are eligible yourself for one of the vacancies.'

"'And what are they worth?' I asked.

"'Oh, merely a couple of hundred a year, but the work is slight, and it need not interfere very much with one's other occupations.'

"Well, you can easily think that that made me prick up my ears, for the business has not been over-good for some years, and an extra couple of hundred would have been very handy.

"'Tell me all about it,' said I.

"'Well,' said he, showing me the advertisement, 'you can see for yourself that the League has a vacancy, and there is the address where you should apply for particulars. As far as I can make out, the League was founded by an American millionaire, Ezekiah Hopkins, who was very peculiar in his ways. He was himself red-headed, and he had a great sympathy for all red-headed men; so, when he died, it was found that he had left his enormous fortune in the hands of trustees, with instructions to apply the interest to the providing of easy berths to men whose hair is of that color. From all I hear it is splendid pay, and very little to do.'

"'But,' said I, 'there would be millions of red-headed men who would apply.'

"'Not so many as you might think,' he answered. 'You see it is really confined to Londoners, and to grown men. This American had started from London when he was young, and he wanted to do the old town a good turn. Then, again, I have heard it is no use your applying if your hair is light red, or dark red, or anything but real bright, blazing, fiery red. Now, if you cared to apply, Mr. Wilson, you would just walk in; but perhaps it would hardly be worth your while to put yourself out of the way for the sake of a few hundred pounds.'

"Now, it is a fact, gentlemen, as you may see for yourselves, that my hair is of a very full and rich tint, so that it seemed to me that, if there was to be any competition in the matter, I stood as good a chance as any man that I had ever met. Vincent Spaulding seemed to know so much about it that I thought he might prove useful, so I just ordered him to put up the shutters for the day, and to come right away with me. He was very willing to have a holiday, so we shut the business up, and started off for the address that was given us in the advertisement.

"I never hope to see such a sight as that again, Mr. Holmes. From north, south, east, and west every man who had a shade of red in his hair had tramped into the city to answer the advertisement. Fleet Street was choked with red-headed
5 folk, and Pope's Court looked like a coster's orange barrow. I should not have thought there were so many in the whole country as were brought together by that single advertisement. Every shade of color they were—straw, lemon, orange, brick, Irish-setter, liver, clay; but, as Spaulding said, there
10 were not many who had the real vivid flame-colored tint. When I saw how many were waiting, I would have given it up in despair; but Spaulding would not hear of it. How he did it I could not imagine, but he pushed and pulled and butted until he got me through the crowd, and right up to the steps
15 which led to the office. There was a double stream upon the stair, some going up in hope, and some coming back dejected; but we wedged in as well as we could, and soon found ourselves in the office."

"Your experience has been a most entertaining one," re-
20 marked Holmes, as his client paused and refreshed his memory with a huge pinch of snuff. "Pray continue your very interesting statement."

"There was nothing in the office but a couple of wooden chairs and a deal table, behind which sat a small man, with a
25 head that was even redder than mine. He said a few words to each candidate as he came up, and then he always managed to find some fault in them which would disqualify them. Getting a vacancy did not seem to be such a very easy matter, after all. However, when our turn came, the little man
30 was much more favorable to me than to any of the others, and he closed the door as we entered, so that he might have a private word with us.

"'This is Mr. Jabez Wilson,' said my assistant, 'and he is willing to fill a vacancy in the League.'
35 "'And he is admirably suited for it,' the other answered. 'He has every requirement. I cannot recall when I have seen

anything so fine.' He took a step backward, cocked his head on one side, and gazed at my hair until I felt quite bashful. Then suddenly he plunged forward, wrung my hand, and congratulated me warmly on my success.

"'It would be injustice to hesitate,' said he. 'You will, however, I am sure, excuse me for taking an obvious precaution.' With that he seized my hair in both his hands, and tugged until I yelled with the pain. 'There is water in your eyes,' said he, as he released me. 'I perceive that all is as it should be. But we have to be careful, for we have twice been deceived by wigs and once by paint. I could tell you tales of cobbler's wax which would disgust you with human nature.' He stepped over to the window, and shouted through it at the top of his voice that the vacancy was filled. A groan of disappointment came up from below, and the folk all trooped away in different directions, until there was not a red head to be seen except my own and that of the manager.

"'My name,' said he, 'is Mr. Duncan Ross, and I am myself one of the pensioners upon the fund left by our noble benefactor. Are you a married man, Mr. Wilson? Have you a family?'

"I answered that I had not.

"His face fell immediately.

"'Dear me!' he said, gravely, 'that is very serious indeed! I am sorry to hear you say that. The fund was, of course, for the propagation and spread of the red-heads as well as for their maintenance. It is exceedingly unfortunate that you should be a bachelor.'

"My face lengthened at this, Mr. Holmes, for I thought that I was not to have the vacancy after all; but, after thinking it over for a few minutes, he said that it would be all right.

"'In the case of another,' said he, 'the objection might be fatal, but we must stretch a point in favor of a man with such a head of hair as yours. When shall you be able to enter upon your new duties?'

"'Well, it is a little awkward, for I have a business already,' said I.

"'Oh, never mind about that, Mr. Wilson!' said Vincent Spaulding. 'I shall be able to look after that for you.'

5 "'What would be the hours?' I asked.

"'Ten to two.'

"Now a pawnbroker's business is mostly done of an evening, Mr. Holmes, especially Thursday and Friday evening, which is just before pay-day; so it would suit me very well 10 to earn a little in the mornings. Besides, I knew that my assistant was a good man, and that he would see to anything that turned up.

"'That would suit me very well,' said I. 'And the pay?'

"'Is £4 a week.'

15 "'And the work?'

"'Is purely nominal.'

"'What do you call purely nominal?'

"'Well, you have to be in the office, or at least in the building, the whole time. If you leave, you forfeit your 20 whole position forever. The will is very clear upon that point. You don't comply with the conditions if you budge from the office during that time.'

"'It's only four hours a day, and I should not think of leaving,' said I.

25 "'No excuse will avail,' said Mr. Duncan Ross; 'neither sickness nor business nor anything else. There you must stay, or you lose your billet.'

"'And the work?'

"'Is to copy out the "Encyclopædia Britannica." There 30 is the first volume of it in that press. You must find your own ink, pens, and blotting-paper, but we provide this table and chair. Will you be ready to-morrow?'

"'Certainly,' I answered.

"'Then, good-bye, Mr. Jabez Wilson, and let me congratu-35 late you once more on the important position which you have been fortunate enough to gain.' He bowed me out of the room, and I went home with my assistant, hardly knowing what to say or do, I was so pleased at my own good fortune.

"Well, I thought over the matter all day, and by evening I was in low spirits again; for I had quite persuaded myself that the whole affair must be some great hoax or fraud, 5 though what its object might be I could not imagine. It seemed altogether past belief that any one could make such a will, or that they would pay such a sum for doing anything so simple as copying out the 'Encyclopædia Britannica.' Vincent Spaulding did what he could to cheer me up, but 10 by bedtime I had reasoned myself out of the whole thing. However, in the morning I determined to have a look at it anyhow, so I bought a penny bottle of ink, and with a quill-pen, and seven sheets of foolscap paper, I started off for Pope's Court. 15

"Well, to my surprise and delight, everything was as right as possible. The table was set out ready for me, and Mr. Duncan Ross was there to see that I got fairly to work. He started me off upon the letter A, and then he left me; but he would drop in from time to time to see that all was right 20 with me. At two o'clock he bade me good-day, complimented me upon the amount that I had written, and locked the door of the office after me.

"This went on day after day, Mr. Holmes, and on Satur-day the manager came in and planked down four golden sov- 25 ereigns for my week's work. It was the same next week, and the same the week after. Every morning I was there at ten, and every afternoon I left at two. By degrees Mr. Duncan Ross took to coming in only once of a morning, and then, after a time, he did not come in at all. Still, of course, I 30 never dared to leave the room for an instant, for I was not sure when he might come, and the billet was such a good one, and suited me so well, that I would not risk the loss of it.

"Eight weeks passed away like this, and I had written about Abbots and Archery and Armor and Architecture and 35 Attica, and hoped with diligence that I might get on to the

B's before very long. It cost me something in foolscap, and
I had pretty nearly filled a shelf with my writings. And then
suddenly the whole business came to an end."

"To an end?"

5   "Yes, sir. And no later than this morning. I went to my
work as usual at ten o'clock, but the door was shut and
locked, with a little square of card-board hammered on to the
middle of the panel with a tack. Here it is, and you can
read for yourself."

10   He held up a piece of white card-board about the size of a
sheet of note-paper. It read in this fashion:

"THE RED-HEADED LEAGUE

IS

DISSOLVED.

October 9, 1890."

15

Sherlock Holmes and I surveyed this curt announcement
and the rueful face behind it, until the comical side of the
affair so completely overtopped every other consideration
that we both burst out into a roar of laughter.

20   "I cannot see that there is anything very funny," cried
our client, flushing up to the roots of his flaming head. "If
you can do nothing better than laugh at me, I can go elsewhere."

"No, no," cried Holmes, shoving him back into the chair
25 from which he had half risen. "I really wouldn't miss your
case for the world. It is most refreshingly unusual. But
there is, if you will excuse my saying so, something just a
little funny about it. Pray what steps did you take when
you found the card upon the door?"

30   "I was staggered, sir. I did not know what to do. Then
I called at the offices round, but none of them seemed to
know anything about it. Finally, I went to the landlord,
who is an accountant living on the ground-floor, and I asked
him if he could tell me what had become of the Red-headed
35 League. He said that he had never heard of any such body.

Then I asked him who Mr. Duncan Ross was. He answered that the name was new to him.

"'Well,' said I, 'the gentleman at No. 4.'

"'What, the red-headed man?'

"'Yes.'   5

"'Oh,' said he, 'his name was William Morris. He was a solicitor, and was using my room as a temporary convenience until his new premises were ready. He moved out yesterday.'

"'Where could I find him?'

"'Oh, at his new offices. He did tell me the address. Yes, 10 17 King Edward Street, near St. Paul's.'

"I started off, Mr. Holmes, but when I got to that address it was a manufactory of artificial knee-caps, and no one in it had ever heard of either Mr. William Morris or Mr. Duncan Ross."   15

"And what did you do then?" asked Holmes.

"I went home to Saxe-Coburg Square, and I took the advice of my assistant. But he could not help me in any way. He could only say that if I waited I should hear by post. But that was not quite good enough, Mr. Holmes. I did not 20 wish to lose such a place without a struggle, so, as I had heard that you were good enough to give advice to poor folk who were in need of it, I came right away to you."

"And you did very wisely," said Holmes. "Your case is an exceedingly remarkable one, and I shall be happy to look 25 into it. From what you have told me I think that it is possible that graver issues hang from it than might at first sight appear."

"Grave enough!" said Mr. Jabez Wilson. "Why, I have lost four pound a week."   30

"As far as you are personally concerned," remarked Holmes, "I do not see that you have any grievance against this extraordinary league. On the contrary, you are, as I understand, richer by some £30, to say nothing of the minute knowledge which you have gained on every subject which 35 comes under the letter A. You have lost nothing by them."

"No, sir. But I want to find out about them, and who they are, and what their object was in playing this prank—if it was a prank—upon me. It was a pretty expensive joke for them, for it cost them two and thirty pounds."

5 "We shall endeavor to clear up these points for you. And, first, one or two questions, Mr. Wilson. This assistant of yours who first called your attention to the advertisement— how long had he been with you?"

"About a month then."

10 "How did he come?"

"In answer to an advertisement."

"Was he the only applicant?"

"No, I had a dozen."

"Why did you pick him?"

15 "Because he was handy, and would come cheap."

"At half-wages, in fact."

"Yes."

"What is he like, this Vincent Spaulding?"

"Small, stout-built, very quick in his ways, no hair on his 20 face, though he's not short of thirty. Has a white splash of acid upon his forehead."

Holmes sat up in his chair in considerable excitement. "I thought as much," said he. "Have you ever observed that his ears are pierced for earrings?"

25 "Yes, sir. He told me that a gypsy had done it for him when he was a lad."

"Hum!" said Holmes, sinking back in deep thought. "He is still with you?"

"Oh yes, sir; I have only just left him."

30 "And has your business been attended to in your absence?"

"Nothing to complain of, sir. There's never very much to do of a morning."

"That will do, Mr. Wilson. I shall be happy to give you an opinion upon the subject in the course of a day or two. 35 To-day is Saturday, and I hope that by Monday we may come to a conclusion."

"Well, Watson," said Holmes, when our visitor had left us, "what do you make of it all?"

"I make nothing of it," I answered, frankly. "It is a most mysterious business."

"As a rule," said Holmes, "the more bizarre a thing is the less mysterious it proves to be. It is your commonplace, featureless crimes which are really puzzling, just as a commonplace face is the most difficult to identify. But I must be prompt over this matter."

"What are you going to do, then?" I asked.

"To smoke," he answered. "It is quite a three-pipe problem, and I beg that you won't speak to me for fifty minutes." He curled himself up in his chair, with his thin knees drawn up to his hawk-like nose, and there he sat with his eyes closed and his black clay pipe thrusting out like the bill of some strange bird. I had come to the conclusion that he had dropped asleep, and indeed was nodding myself, when he suddenly sprang out of his chair with the gesture of a man who has made up his mind, and put his pipe down upon the mantel-piece.

"Sarasate plays at the St. James's Hall this afternoon," he remarked. "What do you think, Watson? Could your patients spare you for a few hours?"

"I have nothing to do to-day. My practice is never very absorbing."

"Then put on your hat and come. I am going through the city first, and we can have some lunch on the way. I observe that there is a good deal of German music on the programme, which is rather more to my taste than Italian or French. It is introspective, and I want to introspect. Come along!"

We travelled by the Underground as far as Aldersgate; and a short walk took us to Saxe-Coburg Square, the scene of the singular story which we had listened to in the morning. It was a pokey, little, shabby-genteel place, where four lines of dingy two-storied brick houses looked out into a small railed-in enclosure, where a lawn of weedy grass and a

few clumps of faded laurel-bushes made a hard fight against
a smoke-laden and uncongenial atmosphere. Three gilt balls
and a brown board with "JABEZ WILSON" in white letters,
upon a corner house, announced the place where our red-
5 headed client carried on his business. Sherlock Holmes
stopped in front of it with his head on one side, and looked
it all over, with his eyes shining brightly between puckered
lids. Then he walked slowly up the street, and then down
again to the corner, still looking keenly at the houses. Finally
10 he returned to the pawnbroker's, and, having thumped vigorously upon the pavement with his stick two or three times,
he went up to the door and knocked. It was instantly opened
by a bright-looking, clean-shaven young fellow, who asked
him to step in.

15 "Thank you," said Holmes, "I only wished to ask you how
you would go from here to the Strand."

"Third right, fourth left," answered the assistant, promptly,
closing the door.

"Smart fellow, that," observed Holmes, as we walked
20 away. "He is, in my judgment, the fourth smartest man in
London, and for daring I am not sure that he has not a claim
to be third. I have known something of him before."

"Evidently," said I, "Mr. Wilson's assistant counts for a
good deal in this mystery of the Red-headed League. I am
25 sure that you inquired your way merely in order that you
might see him."

"Not him."

"What then?"

"The knees of his trousers."

30 "And what did you see?"

"What I expected to see."

"Why did you beat the pavement?"

"My dear doctor, this is a time for observation, not for
talk. We are spies in an enemy's country. We know some-
35 thing of Saxe-Coburg Square. Let us now explore the parts
which lie behind it."

The road in which we found ourselves as we turned round the corner from the retired Saxe-Coburg Square presented as great a contrast to it as the front of a picture does to the back. It was one of the main arteries which convey the traffic of the city to the north and west. The roadway was blocked with the immense stream of commerce flowing in a double tide inward and outward, while the foot-paths were black with the hurrying swarm of pedestrians. It was difficult to realize as we looked at the line of fine shops and stately business premises that they really abutted on the other side upon the faded and stagnant square which we had just quitted.

"Let me see," said Holmes, standing at the corner, and glancing along the line, "I should like just to remember the order of the houses here. It is a hobby of mine to have an exact knowledge of London. There is Mortimer's, the tobacconist, the little newspaper shop, the Coburg branch of the City and Suburban Bank, the Vegetarian Restaurant, and McFarlane's carriage-building depot. That carries us right on to the other block. And now, doctor, we've done our work, so it's time we had some play. A sandwich and a cup of coffee, and then off to violin-land, where all is sweetness and delicacy and harmony, and there are no red-headed clients to vex us with their conundrums."

My friend was an enthusiastic musician, being himself not only a very capable performer, but a composer of no ordinary merit. All the afternoon he sat in the stalls wrapped in the most perfect happiness, gently waving his long, thin fingers in time to the music, while his gently smiling face and his languid, dreamy eyes were as unlike those of Holmes, the sleuthhound, Holmes the relentless, keen-witted, ready-handed criminal agent, as it was possible to conceive. In his singular character the dual nature alternately asserted itself, and his extreme exactness and astuteness represented, as I have often thought, the reaction against the poetic and contemplative mood which occasionally predominated in him. The swing

of his nature took him from extreme languor to devouring
energy; and, as I knew well, he was never so truly formidable as when, for days on end, he had been lounging in his
arm-chair amid his improvisations and his black-letter edi-
5 tions. Then it was that the lust of the chase would suddenly
come upon him, and that his brilliant reasoning power would
rise to the level of intuition, until those who were unac-
quainted with his methods would look askance at him as on
a man whose knowledge was not that of other mortals. When
10 I saw him that afternoon so enwrapped in the music at St.
James's Hall I felt that an evil time might be coming upon
those whom he had set himself to hunt down.

"You want to go home, no doubt, doctor," he remarked,
as we emerged.

15 "Yes, it would be as well."

"And I have some business to do which will take some
hours. This business at Coburg Square is serious."

"Why serious?"

"A considerable crime is in contemplation. I have every
20 reason to believe that we shall be in time to stop it. But to-
day being Saturday rather complicates matters. I shall want
your help to-night."

"At what time?"

"Ten will be early enough."

25 "I shall be at Baker Street at ten."

"Very well. And, I say, doctor, there may be some little
danger, so kindly put your army revolver in your pocket."
He waved his hand, turned on his heel, and disappeared in
an instant among the crowd.

30 I trust that I am not more dense than my neighbors, but I
was always oppressed with a sense of my own stupidity in
my dealings with Sherlock Holmes. Here I had heard what
he had heard, I had seen what he had seen, and yet from his
words it was evident that he saw clearly not only what had
35 happened, but what was about to happen, while to me the
whole business was still confused and grotesque. As I drove

home to my house in Kensington I thought over it all, from the extraordinary story of the red-headed copier of the "Encyclopædia" down to the visit to Saxe-Coburg Square, and the ominous words with which he had parted from me. What was this nocturnal expedition, and why should I go armed? Where were we going, and what were we to do? I had the hint from Holmes that this smooth-faced pawnbroker's assistant was a formidable man—a man who might play a deep game. I tried to puzzle it out, but gave it up in despair, and set the matter aside until night should bring an explanation.

It was a quarter past nine when I started from home and made my way across the Park, and so through Oxford Street to Baker Street. Two hansoms were standing at the door, and, as I entered the passage, I heard the sound of voices from above. On entering his room I found Holmes in animated conversation with two men, one of whom I recognized as Peter Jones, the official police agent, while the other was a long, thin, sad-faced man, with a very shiny hat and oppressively respectable frock-coat.

"Ha! our party is complete," said Holmes, buttoning up his pea-jacket, and taking his heavy hunting crop from the rack. "Watson, I think you know Mr. Jones, of Scotland Yard? Let me introduce you to Mr. Merryweather, who is to be our companion in to-night's adventure."

"We're hunting in couples again, doctor, you see," said Jones, in his consequential way. "Our friend here is a wonderful man for starting a chase. All he wants is an old dog to help him to do the running down."

"I hope a wild goose may not prove to be the end of our chase," observed Mr. Merryweather, gloomily.

"You may place considerable confidence in Mr. Holmes, sir," said the police agent, loftily. "He has his own little methods, which are, if he won't mind my saying so, just a little too theoretical and fantastic, but he has the makings of a detective in him. It is not too much to say that once or twice, as in that business of the Sholto murder and the Agra treasure, he has been more nearly correct than the official force."

"Oh, if you say so, Mr. Jones, it is all right," said the stranger, with deference. "Still, I confess that I miss my rubber. It is the first Saturday night for seven-and-twenty years that I have not had my rubber."

"I think you will find," said Sherlock Holmes, "that you will play for a higher stake to-night than you have ever done yet, and that the play will be more exciting. For you, Mr. Merryweather, the stake will be some £30,000; and for you, Jones, it will be the man upon whom you wish to lay your hands."

"John Clay, the murderer, thief, smasher, and forger. He's a young man, Mr. Merryweather, but he is at the head of his profession, and I would rather have my bracelets on him than on any criminal in London. He's a remarkable man, is young John Clay. His grandfather was a royal duke, and he himself has been to Eton and Oxford. His brain is as cunning as his fingers, and though we meet signs of him at every turn, we never know where to find the man himself. He'll crack a crib in Scotland one week, and be raising money to build an orphanage in Cornwall the next. I've been on his track for years, and have never set eyes on him yet."

"I hope that I may have the pleasure of introducing you to-night. I've had one or two little turns also with Mr. John Clay, and I agree with you that he is at the head of his profession. It is past ten, however, and quite time that we started. If you two will take the first hansom, Watson and I will follow in the second."

Sherlock Holmes was not very communicative during the long drive, and lay back in the cab humming the tunes which he had heard in the afternoon. We rattled through an endless labyrinth of gas-lit streets until we emerged into Farringdon Street.

"We are close there now," my friend remarked. "This fellow Merryweather is a bank director, and personally interested in the matter. I thought it as well to have Jones with us also. He is not a bad fellow, though an absolute imbecile in his profession. He has one positive virtue. He is as brave as a bull-dog, and as tenacious as a lobster if he gets his claws upon any one. Here we are, and they are waiting for us." 5

We had reached the same crowded thoroughfare in which we had found ourselves in the morning. Our cabs were dismissed, and, following the guidance of Mr. Merryweather, we passed down a narrow passage and through a side door, which he opened for us. Within there was a small corridor, which 10 ended in a very massive iron gate. This also was opened, and led down a flight of winding stone steps, which terminated at another formidable gate. Mr. Merryweather stopped to light a lantern, and then conducted us down a dark, earth-smelling passage, and so, after opening a third door, into a 15 huge vault or cellar, which was piled all round with crates and massive boxes.

"You are not very vulnerable from above," Holmes remarked, as he held up the lantern and gazed about him.

"Nor from below," said Mr. Merryweather, striking his 20 stick upon the flags which lined the floor. "Why, dear me, it sounds quite hollow!" he remarked, looking up in surprise.

"I must really ask you to be a little more quiet," said Holmes, severely. "You have already imperilled the whole success of our expedition. Might I beg that you would have 25 the goodness to sit down upon one of those boxes, and not to interfere?"

The solemn Mr. Merryweather perched himself upon a crate, with a very injured expression upon his face, while Holmes fell upon his knees upon the floor, and, with the lan- 30 tern and a magnifying lens, began to examine minutely the cracks between the stones. A few seconds sufficed to satisfy him, for he sprang to his feet again, and put his glass in his pocket.

"We have at least an hour before us," he remarked; "for 35 they can hardly take any steps until the good pawnbroker is

safely in bed. Then they will not lose a minute, for the
sooner they do their work the longer time they will have for
their escape. We are at present, doctor—as no doubt you
have divined—in the cellar of the city branch of one of the
5 principal London banks. Mr. Merryweather is the chairman
of directors, and he will explain to you that there are reasons
why the more daring criminals of London should take a considerable interest in this cellar at present."

"It is our French gold," whispered the director. "We
10 have had several warnings that an attempt might be made
upon it."

"Your French gold?"

"Yes. We had occasion some months ago to strengthen
our resources, and borrowed, for that purpose, 30,000 napo-
15 leons from the Bank of France. It has become known that
we have never had occasion to unpack the money, and that
it is still lying in our cellar. The crate upon which I sit
contains 2000 napoleons packed between layers of lead foil.
Our reserve of bullion is much larger at present than is
20 usually kept in a single branch office, and the directors have
had misgivings upon the subject."

"Which were very well justified," observed Holmes. "And
now it is time that we arranged our little plans. I expect
that within an hour matters will come to a head. In the
25 mean time, Mr. Merryweather, we must put the screen over
that dark lantern."

"And sit in the dark?"

"I am afraid so. I had brought a pack of cards in my
pocket, and I thought that, as we were a *partie carrée*, you
30 might have your rubber after all. But I see that the enemy's
preparations have gone so far that we cannot risk the presence of a light. And, first of all, we must choose our positions. These are daring men, and though we shall take them
at a disadvantage, they may do us some harm unless we are
35 careful. I shall stand behind this crate, and do you conceal
yourselves behind those. Then, when I flash a light upon

them, close in swiftly. If they fire, Watson, have no compunction about shooting them down."

I placed my revolver, cocked, upon the top of the wooden case behind which I crouched. Holmes shot the slide across the front of his lantern, and left us in pitch darkness—such an absolute darkness as I have never before experienced. The smell of hot metal remained to assure us that the light was still there, ready to flash out at a moment's notice. To me, with my nerves worked up to a pitch of expectancy, there was something depressing and subduing in the sudden gloom, and in the cold, dank air of the vault.

"They have but one retreat," whispered Holmes. "That is back through the house into Saxe-Coburg Square. I hope that you have done what I asked you, Jones?"

"I have an inspector and two officers waiting at the front door."

"Then we have stopped all the holes. And now we must be silent and wait."

What a time it seemed! From comparing notes afterwards it was but an hour and a quarter, yet it appeared to me that the night must have almost gone, and the dawn be breaking above us. My limbs were weary and stiff, for I feared to change my position; yet my nerves were worked up to the highest pitch of tension, and my hearing was so acute that I could not only hear the gentle breathing of my companions, but I could distinguish the deeper, heavier in-breath of the bulky Jones from the thin, sighing note of the bank director. From my position I could look over the case in the direction of the floor. Suddenly my eyes caught the glint of a light.

At first it was but a lurid spark upon the stone pavement. Then it lengthened out until it became a yellow line, and then, without any warning or sound, a gash seemed to open and a hand appeared; a white, almost womanly hand, which felt about in the centre of the little area of light. For a minute or more the hand, with its writhing fingers, protruded out of the floor. Then it was withdrawn as suddenly as it appeared, and all was dark again save the single lurid spark which marked a chink between the stones.

Its disappearance, however, was but momentary. With a rending, tearing sound, one of the broad, white stones turned
5 over upon its side, and left a square, gaping hole, through which streamed the light of a lantern. Over the edge there peeped a clean-cut, boyish face, which looked keenly about it, and then, with a hand on either side of the aperture, drew itself shoulder-high and waist-high, until one knee rested upon
10 the edge. In another instant he stood at the side of the hole, and was hauling after him a companion, lithe and small like himself, with a pale face and a shock of very red hair.

"It's all clear," he whispered. "Have you the chisel and the bags? Great Scott! Jump, Archie, jump, and I'll swing
15 for it!"

Sherlock Holmes had sprung out and seized the intruder by the collar. The other dived down the hole, and I heard the sound of rending cloth as Jones clutched at his skirts. The light flashed upon the barrel of a revolver, but Holmes's
20 hunting crop came down on the man's wrist, and the pistol clinked upon the stone floor.

"It's no use, John Clay," said Holmes, blandly. "You have no chance at all."

"So I see," the other answered, with the utmost coolness.
25 "I fancy that my pal is all right, though I see you have got his coat-tails."

"There are three men waiting for him at the door," said Holmes.

"Oh, indeed! You seem to have done the thing very completely.
30 I must compliment you."

"And I you," Holmes answered. "Your red-headed idea was very new and effective."

"You'll see your pal again presently," said Jones. "He's quicker at climbing down holes than I am. Just hold out
35 while I fix the derbies."

"I beg that you will not touch me with your filthy hands,"

remarked our prisoner, as the handcuffs clattered upon his wrists. "You may not be aware that I have royal blood in my veins. Have the goodness, also, when you address me always to say 'sir' and 'please.'"

"All right," said Jones, with a stare and a snigger. "Well, would you please, sir, march up-stairs, where we can get a cab to carry your highness to the police-station?"

"That is better," said John Clay, serenely. He made a sweeping bow to the three of us, and walked quietly off in the custody of the detective.

"Really, Mr. Holmes," said Mr. Merryweather, as we followed them from the cellar, "I do not know how the bank can thank you or repay you. There is no doubt that you have detected and defeated in the most complete manner one of the most determined attempts at bank robbery that have ever come within my experience."

"I have had one or two little scores of my own to settle with Mr. John Clay," said Holmes. "I have been at some small expense over this matter, which I shall expect the bank to refund, but beyond that I am amply repaid by having had an experience which is in many ways unique, and by hearing the very remarkable narrative of the Red-headed League."

"You see, Watson," he explained, in the early hours of the morning, as we sat over a glass of whiskey-and-soda in Baker Street, "it was perfectly obvious from the first that the only possible object of this rather fantastic business of the advertisement of the League, and the copying of the 'Encyclopædia,' must be to get this not over-bright pawnbroker out of the way for a number of hours every day. It was a curious way of managing it, but, really, it would be difficult to suggest a better. The method was no doubt suggested to Clay's ingenious mind by the color of his accomplice's hair. The £4 a week was a lure which must draw him, and what was it to them, who were playing for thousands? They put in the advertisement, one rogue has the temporary office, the other

rogue incites the man to apply for it, and together they manage to secure his absence every morning in the week. From the time that I heard of the assistant having come for half wages, it was obvious to me that he had some strong motive
5 for securing the situation."

"But how could you guess what the motive was?"

"Had there been women in the house, I should have suspected a mere vulgar intrigue. That, however, was out of the question. The man's business was a small one, and there was
10 nothing in his house which could account for such elaborate preparations, and such an expenditure as they were at. It must, then, be something out of the house. What could it be? I thought of the assistant's fondness for photography, and his trick of vanishing into the cellar. The cellar! There
15 was the end of this tangled clue. Then I made inquiries as to this mysterious assistant, and found that I had to deal with one of the coolest and most daring criminals in London. He was doing something in the cellar—something which took many hours a day for months on end. What could it be, once
20 more? I could think of nothing save that he was running a tunnel to some other building.

"So far I had got when we went to visit the scene of action. I surprised you by beating upon the pavement with my stick. I was ascertaining whether the cellar stretched out in front
25 or behind. It was not in front. Then I rang the bell, and, as I hoped, the assistant answered it. We have had some skirmishes, but we had never set eyes upon each other before. I hardly looked at his face. His knees were what I wished to see. You must yourself have remarked how worn,
30 wrinkled, and stained they were. They spoke of those hours of burrowing. The only remaining point was what they were burrowing for. I walked round the corner, saw that the City and Suburban Bank abutted on our friend's premises, and felt that I had solved my problem. When you drove home
35 after the concert I called upon Scotland Yard, and upon

the chairman of the bank directors, with the result that you have seen."

"And how could you tell that they would make their attempt to-night?" I asked.

"Well, when they closed their League offices that was a sign that they cared no longer about Mr. Jabez Wilson's presence—in other words, that they had completed their tunnel. But it was essential that they should use it soon, as it might be discovered, or the bullion might be removed. Saturday would suit them better than any other day, as it would give them two days for their escape. For all these reasons I expected them to come to-night."

"You reasoned it out beautifully," I exclaimed, in unfeigned admiration. "It is so long a chain, and yet every link rings true."

"It saved me from ennui," he answered, yawning. "Alas! I already feel it closing in upon me. My life is spent in one long effort to escape from the commonplaces of existence. These little problems help me to do so."

"And you are a benefactor of the race," said I.

He shrugged his shoulders. "Well, perhaps, after all, it is of some little use," he remarked. "'L'homme c'est rien—l'œuvre c'est tout,' as Gustave Flaubert wrote to Georges Sand."

STUDENTS' THEMES: NARRATION

IN A TANK

A sharp kick administered on the sole of my boot, followed by a gruff "Get up," brought me to the consciousness that I was about to take part in the Great Adventure, and that activities were commencing already. I climbed from under
5 the big "Mark Five Star" tank which we had brought up under cover of darkness the night before, and under which I had snatched a few hours' sleep. I stood around for a minute or two while the burly sergeant dragged the other members of the crew from restless sleep, and gazed at the narrow
10 purple thread that zigzagged over the landscape representing the Hindenburg Line, and the barely visible water of the St. Quentin Canal lying behind. The first sign of dawn made Bony, a mass of ruins, stand out like some demolished Egyptian temple.

15 I was aroused from my reverie by the rest of the men, who climbed in through the big side door and took their places. Down the line we could hear the humming of other "busses" who were warming up, and ready to start. The Lieutenant climbed in last, shut and bolted the door.

20 "Give her a spin."

Four nervous hands clutched the great crank handle, and after a few spasmodic revolutions the powerful engine purred softly. The Lieutenant climbed into his seat, as did driver and mechanic, the six-pound gunners took their stations, while
25 the machine-gunners, including myself, with trembling hands inserted the strip, an iron belt which contains the cartridges, and stood by. Then there was an interval of several minutes during which we fastened on our gas-masks and made ready

the iron-mesh masks, for the protection of the eyes against splinters of steel, but which were very rarely worn. The Lieutenant held a hasty consultation with somebody outside, and after examining his wrist-watch several times waved a signal of assent to the driver. 5

Life has few moments such as that, and I know that never again will such a feeling of utter helplessness come into my soul. What I recalled during that brief moment of starting could never be set down by human pen. Among other things the picture of the soldier in Tolstoy's *War and Peace* who 10 was lying wounded in a field and whose thoughts were of the smallness of Napoleon as compared to the great expanse of blue heaven that confronted him, struck me as being horribly true. And what a perfect nonentity I was in this great struggle. 15

With a roar and a lurch we moved forward at a slow pace. This action seemed to break the spell, for immediately I was nervous energy once more, though weeping internally with fear. I stood with my hand on the pistol-grip of my Hotchkiss, and my eyes glued to the six little perforations which 20 served as a look-out. Though I could hear the "pom-pom" of the high explosive shells, I knew that it would be six or seven minutes before we should be under real fire. A slight jar told me that we had crossed our own front-line trenches, and as I could no longer see the white tape laid down the 25 previous day by the reconnaissance men, I knew that we were in "No Man's Land." Minutes dragged eternally, and soon a sharp rattle like hail on a roof and sharp explosions to our right showed that the Boches had got our range. I could barely see their front-line trenches, and but for dark figures 30 that would occasionally come into view, no target presented itself. I let go a couple of bursts, and at the same time the other men started firing. The noise was terrific, the tap-tap-tap of the machine-guns was like a rivet-driver in your ears, while the six-pounder sent out fumes of cordite which caused 35 your head to sing like a top. I looked around to see how the

others were standing the ordeal, and the man next to me suddenly moved away from the peep-hole and clasped a hand to his face, and through his fingers ran a thin stream of blood which flowed along his forearm and onto the floor. In the
5 dim haze of the morning I could see two gray-clad figures working furiously over a machine-gun, and close by was a short, bearded individual in his shirt-sleeves, firing a huge anti-tank rifle, one of whose shots had carried away our exhaust pipe, filling the place with fumes. As I was firing at
10 them, a great tower of dirt arose in front of them, and all I could see was the man in shirt-sleeves dragging himself away on his hands and knees.

There is little more to tell: we crossed the line with great difficulty and had to return because of no reinforcements;
15 nevertheless, I think we put the fear of God into a few German souls.

A LEAF FROM A LOG

July 23, 1908

Run,—Gloucester to Isles of Shoals: 30 miles.

The sun was just showing his rim over the top of the breakwater, as, with a cheery Yo-Ho, we broke out the anchor from its bed in the bottom of Gloucester harbor, and before five minutes had passed, our yacht had rounded the jetty and was standing for the open sea. The tide was at the last of the ebb and bore us out at good speed, but the wind which had encouraged us to start seemed to go out with it, and at the turn of the tide we lay with idly flapping canvas, about two miles offshore from the Eastern Point Lighthouse. The crew of the yacht, consisting of my brother, a sailor, and myself, regarded the dispiriting scene with various expressions of disgust. For some time no word was spoken, and then, of a sudden, the sailor, with an exclamation of awe, pointed to the westward with a sweep of his hand. "What's the matter, Underwood?" I asked. "Nothin' much, sir," he replied, "only I don't like that kind o' sky this time o' day." Looking in the direction indicated, I beheld the most perfect mackerel sky that I have ever seen. "You might remember, sir," continued the old fellow, "what they say 'bout it at sea, 'mackerel sky in the mornin', sailors take warnin'.' Never seen no good come of it yet, sir. We'll ketch it 'fore we're through." "Nonsense," I exclaimed, "an old woman's saw." He looked silently at the water for a few moments, and then, "Shall I take the wheel for a spell, sir? You might like a bit o' rest. We'll not have much to-night." I relinquished the wheel to him, and went down to get a book. Through the open cabin-slide I could see the old man sitting beside the binnacle, his

423

left hand on the wheel, his right shading his eyes as he looked
intently at the sky, slowly shaking his head. Something of
the old sailor's gloom seemed to enter into us; we were a
pretty sober company.

5   Hour after hour dragged by without a breath of wind. The
sun shone with burning heat, but it was not the bright, life-
giving sun of a fine day; it seemed rather to threaten than to
cheer, and though the sky was now cloudless, the whole
aspect of the sea was sullen with a grayish tinge that became
10 more marked as the morning wore on. Toward noon, a few
cat's-paws crept out from the haze-enshrouded land and
wafted us fitfully along. At about one o'clock we were
abreast of Thatcher's Island. "Seven miles in seven hours,"
I remarked, gaily, but my companions only groaned; they
15 appeared somehow to have lost all interest.

Off the point of Cape Ann the tide, sweeping around the
deep curve of Ipswich Bay, joins the ebb from the North
Shore and flows straight out to sea with great power. We
were caught in this tide in the early part of the afternoon
20 and carried seaward at a great rate. Our course was north,
half east, and as the tide was running about northeast, we
felt that at least we were gaining something.

A dark line suddenly appeared on the sea astern. It advanced with astonishing speed. "Drop the main peak!" I
25 shouted. "Brail in the jib; jigger sheet flat!" A hot, dry
gust struck us and we lay over until the water foamed on the
deck. With a booming of canvas the yacht shot into the
wind and lay trembling. After a few wild puffs, the wind
settled to a wholesale breeze, and for the first time that day
30 we "felt the helm," as the saying goes. My spirits rose and
I broke into song. But the notes suddenly stuck in my
throat, for down in the west, but rising rapidly, was a great
bank of inky cloud, its edges tinged with yellow.

How horribly fast they rose, those clouds; already they
35 were beginning to hide the sun, now low in the west. "All
hands on deck," I cried, as merrily as possible; "we're going

to catch it this time." Our preparations were soon made. With a double reef in the mainsail and the skylight battened down, the yawl pushed bravely on over the darkening sea. "Lots o' sea room anyway," remarked the sailor, looking around. "Can't see no land anywheres." The wind grad- 5 ually failed, grew puffy, and was gone.

"In mainsail! Three stops on the boom!" I cried, for out of the heart of the darkness in the west I saw a bright green line rushing toward us. With a shriek the squall struck the yacht. For a moment, even under jib and jigger alone, we 10 lay on our beam ends, driven sidewise; then we bore away and fled through the darkness. Torn gray rags of cloud whirled by, no higher than our masthead. The lightning blazed incessantly, and the roar of thunder for whole minutes drowned the screech of the wind. How long we thus drove 15 on I knew not at the time; I have a dim impression that it rained, but my whole attention was on the steering of my boat. The lightning ceased at last and the wind moderated, but it continued as dark as ever. We gave her the mainsail, and with a sigh of weariness I handed over the helm to my 20 brother. Strange as it may seem, we had spoken no word since the first gust of wind had knocked the breath out of us. "'Bout time to get a bite ter eat." The voice roused me from a sort of dream. "Is it supper time?" I asked. "Ha' parst eight," the old fellow answered. "Go forward and see 25 if you can see anything, while I hunt up some supper," I remarked; then to my brother, "How's her head,—about right?" He nodded. "North, quarter west." "Red 'n' white flash couple o' pints orf the starboard bow," sang out the sailor from the forward deck. "Isles of Shoals light," I re- 30 marked. "Good shot that."

A couple of hours later, we passed the whistling buoy off White Island, one of the Isles of Shoals, and stood off for the Whaleback light at the entrance to Portsmouth harbor, hoping to make port at the slack of the high tide. Gently, and 35 yet more gently the wind blew, and as it failed it veered more and more to the eastward. The yacht rolled about wildly in the trough of the sea. Crash! The boom had swept across and "fetched up" with a suddenness that brought our teeth together. Again we were becalmed.

5   If there is one thing that a sailor hates more than another, it is a calm with a heavy roll. For about ten minutes we stood the slatting of sails, the creaking of cordage, and the crashing of blocks, and then, driven to desperation, we furled the sails and came to anchor in sixteen fathoms of water.
10 I sent my weary comrades down below to rest, and with a pipe for company, settled myself to watch. The night was starless and sultry. The dew was very heavy and dripped from cabin roof and spars. One could hear the breakers on the distant shore and the occasional splash of a seal. Once
15 a whale rose near at hand and blew. The sound, like escaping steam, startled me from my reverie. I sat upright and looked about. I rubbed my eyes and looked again. Where were the lights, the shore lights and the lighthouses? All had disappeared. What had happened? And then the ex-
20 planation flashed upon me,—fog. Even as I started up, a faint breath of chill air came to me; more a smell than a wind. I went below to see the barometer, and when I came again on deck, though only a moment had elapsed, the whole scene had altered. A stiff northeast wind was singing through
25 the rigging and already kicking up a sea.

    As there was nothing to be done, I crouched in the shelter of the cabin. In spite of myself, a horrid presentiment of danger crept over me. For an hour or more I remained thus with the feeling growing stronger every moment. I could
30 bear it no longer; I rose and went forward. How big the seas were! How the gale had increased! The yacht was plunging bowsprit under and bringing up on her cable with vicious jerks. Every part of her groaned and creaked under the strain, but the anchor seemed to be holding. The fog was
35 so thick that from my position forward the binnacle light was a mere blur. And then as I turned to make my way aft,

three long, clear blasts of a fog horn came down the wind to my startled ears. I scrambled aft, and dove head first into the cabin. "Vessel dead ahead, running before the wind!" I roared, and was on deck again before my crew could leap to their feet. I had snatched the fog horn from its rack, and now, with my mind intent upon getting the loudest possible blast for every breath, I was unconscious of what went on around me. It was impossible to tell how far off the ship to windward might be. At last my breath gave out, and my brother, seizing the horn, clapped it to his lips. Its hoarse notes sounded deafeningly loud to us, but would they carry far enough against the wind to warn the scudding vessel ahead in time? Three more long blasts, this time a trifle to one side; but almost instantly the sound was repeated from dead ahead. Our horn emitted one last despairing wail, and as if in answer to it we heard a deep voice, apparently coming from our bowsprit end, roar out, "Port your hellum; hard over now." There followed a great creaking and a medley of shouts, and then a bright light shone through the fog on our staring eyes. A huge indistinct shadow swept by us to starboard; and the yacht rolled scuppers under in the swell.

The rest of the night passed like an empty dream. The wind must have abated gradually, for when after what seemed like whole years of darkness it began to grow light, the seas were no longer breaking. Silently we watched the grayness creep over the scene. We could now see each other quite clearly. I looked up at the sky, and to my surprise saw a bank of shell-pink clouds. Quickly as it had come the fog was breaking away on every side. In long wavering lines, it was driven shoreward by the fresh east wind, while the rising sun chased the last straggling wisps over the water. All nature seemed to rejoice that the night of terror and storm had passed. The crisp little waves danced merrily, and the sea gulls wheeled and screamed in the clear sky of the new day.

RAILROAD TIES—AND OTHERS

A cross-continental train is a laboratory in which to study life. Here, in eight or nine little rooms being dragged by a puffing black slave for five days and nights,—here is thrown together a little of all the world. We have the rich dowager
5 and her bored—and often boring—daughter, the traveling man, the porter,—every grade of wealth, labor, or class. Many peculiar experiments take place in these laboratories; many odd solutions result.

The day was hot, stifling hot; the sand-laden air blew
10 in hot blasts through the Pullman windows. The water in the "cooler" was tepid. Sweat trickled down the various high or sloping or straight or narrow brows of the irritable passengers. Yesterday, as the train snorted out of San Francisco, these same wilted beings had been cheerful and pleas-
15 ant to their fellow passengers. A mean day like this one, however, had worn off a little of the veneer of politeness. Mrs. Robert K. Evans slapped little Robert Jr.'s hands because he insisted upon having Mr. Charles Stone, of Stone and Sons, Inc., show him his watch; Mr. Stone wasn't nearly
20 as pleased with Robert's attentions as he had been the day before. Mrs. Perry Harkins was, in no soft or unmistakable tones, giving Perry her views on a man who couldn't refrain from looking across the aisle where Miss Stella La Blanche of the Flicker Film Co. sat cross-legged and berouged.
25 In striking contrast to all this display of frayed nerves was Chuck Harlow. In all the four years that Chuck had traveled back and forth from San Francisco, Cal., to Providence, R. I., not once had he realized the dream of every commercial traveler,—that of picking up an acquaintance

428

of real importance. To be sure, he had met many people of some interest, innumerable salesmen, now and then a college man, often old ladies, but never before had he had the prospect of spending four days with such a vision of glory as was Gloria Gay. It was pure heaven-sent luck, Chuck told himself, that Miss Gay should have tripped over his grip and fallen right into his lap like a breath of the Orient whose perfume exhaled from her beautiful hair. Of course, when two young people are thus thrown together, literally and figuratively, friendship springs up rapidly. He had helped her arrange her grips under the seat, he had got her a cup of water, he had given her his comic paper. More than once he caught her glancing at him over the top of the magazine. (He had failed to note that Gloria had, unconsciously no doubt, shifted a diamond solitaire from her left to her right hand.)

So today, and all through the trip, Chuck was happy. The two had long chats together on the observation platform. At Kansas City they ran into a drug store for a soda, and had to make a dash for their train as it pulled out. By the time they reached the Mississippi, they knew each other's family history,—that is, all but a little of it. At Cincinnati, Chuck had told Gloria she was a mighty good-looking girl, and that he wished he could take her to a dance. Gloria had smiled, and looked at the diamond on her right hand.

When the day had come on which they were to end their trip, and perhaps, acquaintance, Chuck felt qualms of fear. Gloria had seemed much cooler all morning. He couldn't understand why she had refused his invitation to lunch,— goodness knows she knew enough about his family not to fear him, and goodness also knows that she'd been perfectly willing to have him buy her all her meals on the train the last two days.

"Noo Yawk! Noo Yawk next!" And there was a hustle of people arranging grips, putting on hats or coats, calling for the porter, and preparing for "disembarkation."

Chuck approached Gloria; he didn't know just how to go about it. He noticed that she seemed slightly nervous, and a little anxious to be rid of him, he thought. She had her gloves on now, but Sherlock Holmes would have noticed a
5 bulge on the third finger of her *left* hand.

"I think there will be someone to meet me at the station, so we'd better say good-bye here," Gloria was saying a little confusedly.

The train had come to a dead stop with a final groan. As
10 he looked out the window, Chuck could see the faces of many people waiting on the other side of the bars—a man was waving to Gloria. He saw other faces—and gulped. Yes, Gloria was right, they had better part in the train. He muttered good-bye to her retreating back, and went out at the
15 other end of the car.

A moment later he was clasping in his arms his little wife, who had "come down from Providence all alone just to surprise him." And she certainly had surprised him.

THE GILT CLOCK

As the office door opened slowly a long green plume first appeared, closely followed by the ample form of its wearer, Mrs. McCarthy.

"It's Lawyer Lawrence I'm after seeing," she said to the office boy; "Jimmy, you know,—not the old gent. It's Delia 5 as wants him." When Mr. Lawrence came in, she greeted him vociferously. "Sure, Jimmy, here I be, as used to wash your face no matter how you squealed. Who'd ever have thought you'd be such a foine-looking swell! I'm not after forgetting how your ma used to fight wid yez about your 10 dirty hands."

To shut out the tittering obligato of the clerks, Mr. Lawrence hastily ushered his client into his private office. Not till she had inquired for her former mistress, and had given a long account of her Jamie's latest attack of croup, did 15 Mrs. McCarthy announce the object of her call.

"It's me man," she said with solemn emphasis; "me gilt clock and me man. I'm through with him, I be."

"You mean you want a divorce?" inquired Mr. Lawrence, in astonishment. 20

"It's hoping I be it won't come to that," replied Mrs. McCarthy, dolefully. She went on to explain how her exasperation with Patrick's drinking, shiftless ways had come to a climax with his failure to produce the ticket after he had pawned her gilt clock,—a wedding gift, and the most 25 splendid of their possessions. "Can't I git me clock back without a divorce?" she concluded, anxiously.

Finally agreeing to Mr. Lawrence's suggestion that he interview Patrick about the matter the following week, Mrs. McCarthy gave directions for locating her erring 30 spouse: "Just hang round the corner by Timmy Timilty's barroom any night as the factory is after closing. Me man's the tall, red-headed one, with a false black heart, and an old brown coat of your pa's."

5 In a more cheerful frame of mind, Mrs. McCarthy returned to her dingy abode. A dull light, filtering through the soiled curtains, touched with somber gray the shabby furnishings of the kitchen. The dilapidated chairs and a rickety couch, on three legs and a packing-box, groaned under their
10 burden of papers, caps, rags, and broken toys. Along the walls kindergarten drawings and cigarette posters were incongruously mismated. The photographs of the parish priests and the patent-medicine bottles on the shelf stood out conspicuously in the clutter of trinkets. Broken bits of bread
15 and a greasy dish of butter on the table bespoke a recent hasty meal, while the soup kettle and the teapot, steaming lazily on the stove, promised better fare for the evening.

Pushing up the window, Mrs. McCarthy called across the court to her friend Mrs. Doherty. "He'll have the scare of
20 his life," she announced with conviction. "Just see if I don't git one hand on that pawn ticket and the other aholt of his collar." Several heads now appeared at their respective windows. "Yis, I seen me lawyer," continued the irate wife, carefully pitching her voice so all could hear, "me lawyer in
25 the Exchange Building. He's going to have the law on Pat."

"I'm sorry for yez," condoled Mrs. Flanagan. "A foine wait you'll have. Yer gray hairs will git around afore yer lawyer. But if you'd be more peaceable-like yerself—"

"Thank you kindly," was the quick retort. "I'm asking
30 no advice of a lady as slapped another lady in the very Church, but—" Here the Flanagan window went down with a bang. "She don't forgit how me Mikie licked her Dennie," was added as explanation to the remaining auditors.

"Well, well," murmured Mrs. Doherty, closing her win-
35 dow as the conversation was concluded. "But when the drink ain't in him, Patsy ain't the bad lad, though."

With dusk the McCarthy children trooped noisily in. Their mother, for the last hour brooding alone over her lost treasure, had been busily planning a short cut for its recovery. Wait for days while the neighbors taunted? Never! Intent on a new scheme, she left the children to dish out the soup for supper, and dashed across the court to confide in Mrs. Doherty.

"I'll have me revenge right now!" she cried, her face flushing with excitement. "It's not another day I'll wait till I gits Pat where he'll answer me questions. I'll have him arristed tonight."

Mrs. Doherty gasped in admiration. "How iver will ye do it?"

"Easy like," declared Mrs. McCarthy confidently. "Just you keep your winder up a crack, and when you hears me bawling like a banshee, run for the cop, and tell him me husband's beating me."

"Holy Mary! how—"

"Huh!" sniffed Mrs. McCarthy. "It's a fool of a woman as can't git a licking when she wants it. You'll hear me all right. The kids will help: they always yells when they hears me holler."

By midnight the little court was quiet save as an occasional reveller awakened echoes with his unsteady step and uncertain song. One of the last of the home-faring tipplers was Patrick McCarthy. Not too befuddled to dread a further fusillade of reproach, he felt his way softly along the hall, hoping to steal in unobserved. Cautiously but clumsily he fumbled at the lock. Suddenly his wife jerked open the door, greeting him noisily.

"Drunk agin, you brute! You oughter be hanged."

Patrick grinned tipsily in his desire to propitiate. Stumbling over a chair, he staggered against the wall with a thud.

"Smashing the furniture!" shrieked Mrs. McCarthy. "Stop it—help—stop!"

"Shut up," muttered Patrick, thickly, half sobered by his

fall; then, persisting in a pacific policy, he shook his fist playfully, just grazing her cheek: "Oh, wouldn't I like to be after going to your funeral!"

"Help! Murder! Help! Help!"

5   "Shut up," he snarled again, now sullenly angry.

"Help! Help!" Mrs. McCarthy continued to call lustily, circling about the room in a frenzy. Seizing a rolling-pin in one hand and a frying-pan in the other, she brandished them threateningly in her husband's face. "Don't you dare hit me 10 agin," she screamed. "Help!"

Thoroughly aroused, Mr. McCarthy lunged toward her, just in the path of the rolling-pin on its downward swing. It struck him squarely in the temple. As he dropped limply to the floor, blood streaming down his face, the door was 15 pushed in by a burly policeman.

"Murder! Murder! Murder!" Mrs. McCarthy's voice reverberated through the court. The children, tumbling from their beds, added their shrill cries.

"I've got what was coming to me, Off'cer," whimpered the 20 victim in a weak, high voice. "It served me right."

"Murder! Murder!" Mrs. McCarthy continued to shriek hysterically.

A hurry of steps pattered through the court. The policeman, enlisting the services of two sober citizens, soon bore 25 away Patrick, in a state of complete collapse, his head bound up in his wife's shawl. With his departure the gathering crowd soon scattered: the boys following the patrol wagon; the men returning to their beds, yawning in disgust at missing the knock-out blow; the women collecting in little knots, 30 each to give to another her version of the affair. Soon only Mrs. Doherty was left to comfort the rescued wife, who, throwing her apron over her head, rocked back and forth, moaning inconsolably.

The next day when Patrick McCarthy was called to the 35 dock of the Municipal Court, an anxious group pressed round the Judge. The wife, her long green plume quivering with emotion, drew her five little ones about her. "Me man don't look a third his natural size," she whispered to Mr. Lawrence, clutching the lawyer's arm. "It makes me feel half a widow for sure."

"What is the charge?" inquired the Judge. 5

"For drunk, and A and B," replied the clerk.

"Assault and battery on the wife," explained the patrolman who made the arrest. He was the first witness called.

"I heard a hollering just as I was ringing in, your Honor," testified the officer, "and a woman told me the row was at 10 McCarthy's. He'd been dragging his wife around by the hair; but just as I broke in, he fell and banged his head. He's mostly a civil chap, though,—bums a little, but I never seen him with no such jag on before."

"Is the wife here?" inquired the Judge. 15

The green plume, much agitated, made a deep obeisance. "Your Honor,—oh, your Honor—your Honor," began Mrs. McCarthy in a quavering voice.

"Speak up, lady," encouraged the clerk.

"Oh, your Honor," continued Mrs. McCarthy, gaining 20 confidence, "that man there, with his head tied up, looking so pale and so handsome,—it makes me heart bleed! If your Honor knowed what he's after doing for his family! When me Timmy had ammonia, didn't he sit up all night to give him brandy, and put two candles on the altar; and when poor 25 Timmy died, didn't he have him waked in the bist of style? And—"

"One minute, madam. Your husband is accused of assault. Tell the truth about the matter,—briefly, please."

"Yis, your Honor, it's the truth I'm after telling, every 30 time. Don't I lick me Mikie for fibbing, though boys will,— now Jimmy here,—Mr. Lawrence,—he used to lie to his ma like anything, but—"

Here Mrs. McCarthy was again admonished as to the point in question. 35

"It's not denying I'd be he has lifted his hand to me," she

admitted, shaking her head solemnly. "But thin, maybe I'd be after deserving it, and forgive him I would for one look at me gilt clock. I don't want no divorce, your Honor, but just git me that pawn ticket, and—"

5　The Judge had reached the limit of his patience. "Assault charge dismissed," he announced, shortly; "for drunkenness, five dollars or eight days."

As the group moved aside to make way for the next case, Mrs. McCarthy, fumbling with shaking fingers, brought forth
10 from its repository a roll of bills. "I keeps me money in me stocking to have it handy," she explained, somewhat unnecessarily. Carefully counting out five greenbacks, she handed over to the clerk the sum which gave her husband his liberty. As she began to fold the few remaining bills, her cry of de-
15 light startled the Court. "Mother in Heaven! the ticket,— me clock!"

"Order, order!"

Hustled out of the room by Mr. Lawrence, Mrs. McCarthy waved aloft the recovered pawn ticket. "Glory be! Its me-
20 self as had the baste all along!" She recalled how, before missing the clock, she had in rifling her husband's pockets appropriated this ticket, not realizing what it represented. "'Just one of his tools gone,' says I to meself,—but poor folks sometimes has poor since, they do!"

25　As Patrick sheepishly rejoined his wife, she greeted him with affection: "Ah, Patsy, me lad, it's a narrow escape we've had," she said, taking his arm. "It's celebrate we will wid a turkey for dinner." "I'll remember you in me prayers, Mr. Jimmy," she added, turning to her lawyer.
30 "Sure your standing by and looking so respectable-like pulled us through. For me clock and me happy home I has to thank the Lord and you, and mostly I thanks you!"

THY NEIGHBOR'S STILL

Eastern Kentucky is in the heart of the Cumberland range. For a century and a half, two families have occupied adjacent holdings on the west bank of the Big Sandy. For a century and a half, these two families have been continually at swords' points, in feuds without end. Years ago the cause of 5 the first quarrel was forgotten, but the heads of the two factions still kept the wound open by numerous unfriendly acts. The southernmost of the two families, that of Daniel Smithers, had finally tired of the useless warfare and it had nearly died out. But the other, headed by Josiah Whittel, 10 thought differently. The inaction of the Whittels had been merely for want of a feasible plan. Now, it was theirs. A coup d'état was in the making. Josiah Whittel congratulated himself.

It was a spring evening. The moon was rising over the 15 eastern hills, casting a dancing path of silver across the Big Sandy. Two hundred yards back from the river bank the Whittel homestead reared itself, white and spectral, against the black background of the mountains. The light from a parlor window silhouetted a party of seven seated on the 20 broad veranda, enjoying the evening. Small talk occupied their attention so that they did not notice a solitary figure which trudged past the house down the river road. He walked with the sidelong shuffle customary to the members of his fraternity. An unkempt stubble of beard covered his 25 face like a mask. His scarecrow costume failed to hide his elbows and toes, which had long since been bared to the light of day. He glanced at the house as he passed, hesitated, and then went on. After sidling down the road for perhaps a quarter of a mile, he struck off into a field, yet unplowed, 30

and headed back for the house. The manœuvre took him
out of sight of those on the veranda. He angled so as to
approach the house from the rear. A barbed-wire fence
separated him from the yard. He stopped and listened in-
5 tently. Was there a dog? He heard nothing and proceeded
to crawl between the wires. His tattered coat caught on a
barb and ripped with a wail of anguish. He stifled a "Damn,"
and dropped to the ground. He lay for a minute, motionless, assuring himself that the coast was clear. Then he felt
10 his way carefully toward the barn. At last he was inside.
No dewy "underneath-the-stars" for him to-night. He ended
his soliloquy forcibly against the post of a stall, from which
he rebounded against the warm body of a horse. The horse,
frightened, jumped against the opposite side of the stall,
15 kicking over a pail. "Whoa, Jenny, what's the matter?"
cried a voice from the darkness. The tramp dove into Jenny's
manger and burrowed under the hay. A man carrying a
lighted lantern stepped into the barn through the same door
that the trespasser had used half a minute before. "Whoa,
20 Jenny girl," he repeated. Jenny was straining against her
halter, ears back, eyes wild. "There, old girl," he soothed.
She became calmer under the caressing pressure of his hand.
"Jim, Harry, come on," he called, stepping away from the
stall and placing his lantern on the floor near the opposite
25 wall. As he straightened up, two younger men entered the
door. "Jim," indicating the elder and larger of the two, "toss
down the hay for each stall, and, Harry, bed them down for
the night." They seized pitchforks and set about their duties.
Josiah Whittel procured three empty soap boxes from the
30 harness room. He placed them on end around the lantern and
seated himself on one with his back toward Jenny. As he
finished, a great forkful of hay fell through the shoot and
buried the tramp more completely. When it fell on him, he
jumped apprehensively, kicking the feed box. "Whoa, Jenny,
35 it's all right," comforted Whittel again. He stepped into the
stall and stroked her neck. The man in the manger was

uncomfortable. When Whittel regained his seat, a prayer of thanksgiving wormed its way upward through the hay.

In a short time, the brothers had finished their tasks and had joined their father. They seated themselves on the boxes and looked to him to proceed. "What's the matter with that mare?" Whittel demanded. "She's been actin' skittish ever since I've been here. One of you look in her manger and see if there's a hen or a cat in it."

The hay trembled imperceptibly. The atmosphere was becoming warm in the bottom of the manger.

"I'll do it later, Paw. Get our plans made now." Josiah was satisfied. So was the tramp.

Josiah turned toward the light. He was a large bulbous man with a scarlet face and piglike eyes. The sons were both tall, but did not share his weight. Neither looked like him, nor desired to. Jim was hardly more prepossessing. His hard gray eyes, separated by a crooked nose, were formidable. Harry was better to look upon. Two missing front teeth made his amiable grin seem even more guileless.

They got down to business immediately. Josiah addressed them both. "It looks to me like we're mighty nigh ready to spring the trap. Harry, you take the note to the fool police tomorrow afternoon. Don't let 'em ketch sight of you. Everything is goin' our way, so far. Old Smithers'll see the inside of the pen before there's another Monday gone by. We've had luck on our side all the way through. If you boys hadn't happened on his old still, we'd been in for peace with 'em. It's in a good place, too, not a hundred yards from our south boundary, and well hid. The willows tend to that. They grow powerful dense on that side of the creek. The old boiler and coils are still pretty good, considerin' how many years they have been doin' nothin'. It didn't take us long to fix 'em up to look like they had been used recently. But there's one thing to fix yet. I left too much of my whisky down there. The police'll just grab what they find. There's three gallon demijohns half full. Don't know why I took so

much of it down. I'll go there in the morning and bring most
of it back. A little will be enough to cook his hash. I wish
I could see Smithers' face when they grab him. He won't
have a chance."

5　　Meanwhile, the tramp listened, mouth open, in spite of the
very successful attempts that the wisps of hay were making
to get into it. At the name Smithers, he applied his eye
even more eagerly to a crack which he had discovered in the
board front of the manger. Suddenly, while he was trying to
10 find a more comfortable position, he thrust his hand beyond
his head without encountering a partition. The manger was
continuous. The sides of the stall did not extend into it.
Here was luck! Slowly, taking care not to miss a word, he
wriggled, snake fashion, into the next stall, where there was
15 no horse, but, luckily, a sufficient covering of hay. His elbow
struck a solid object as he settled down. The object crunched,
and the "gooey" internals of an egg wet his arm. More luck!
Perhaps the egg had relatives in the vicinity. He carefully
felt around him until another smooth, hard ellipsoid en-
20 countered his hand. His supper! He jubilantly rolled onto
his back and opened his mouth with his lower jaw extended.
Holding the supper tenderly, he tapped it hard against one
of his canine teeth. The tooth protested violently. The egg
was china!

25　　As this painful operation ended, Josiah and his sons arose.
Jim took a hayfork and prodded Jenny's manger thoroughly.
"Nothing in there, old girl," he assured her. She whinnied
her thanks. Then Josiah led the way back to the house.
The tramp lumbered gratefully from his hiding place and
30 patted Jenny as he passed. "Tried to give me away? Well,
well, if it ain't just like the ladies. But I'll fool you and the
rest of the bunch yet. Spring the trap, will they?" He felt
his way to the stairway and ascended to the loft.

　　Early next morning the Whittel family was at breakfast.
35 In the loft of the big red barn a pile of hay shook from an
internal convulsion. A foot, clad in a toeless shoe, projected

suddenly from it. The pile parted in the middle, and Adonis
of the Hayloft shook the cobwebs from his senses. He ven-
tured down the stairs and across the yard toward the back
door. Inside, Josiah was finishing his meal. The "hired
girl" stuck her head in at the door. "Please, Mr. Whittel," 5
she rasped, "there's a tramp at the door wantin' to work for
his meals."

Josiah was not interested. "Tell 'im to wait." He hated
to have his meals interrupted. When he had finished, he
passed through the kitchen to the back porch. He stood in 10
the doorway, surveying the newcomer from head to foot.
"Hungry?" he demanded.

The tramp's mouth widened into a grin. "Reckon I ain't
et no food since yestiday noon, boss."

"How's your muscle?" was the encouraging rejoinder. 15
The tramp flexed his right arm, and patted it.

"See that wood pile? You know what to do if you're
hungry. Fifty logs and the breakfast's yours. And say," on
afterthought, "if you want to work here a couple of days for
your meals,—" 20

"Yer on, boss. That's me!"

"Why, you could take that sorrel stallion from the barn
after your breakfast and bring down the sheep in the north
end and pasture 'em over there," indicating an inclosed field.
"What's your handle?" 25

"They call me 'Tough-luck' Pete. Never did have any
luck, but what's the dif?"

"Stranger?"

"Oh! yessir, sure 'nough. Never been in the state before."
Pete's conscience did not reprimand him. It was all in a 30
good cause.

He assaulted the wood pile with vigor accelerated by a
void amidships. For several minutes the chips flew, until
his stomach decided that he had worked long enough and
that it was time to claim his reward. 35

When the inner man had finally been gorged into insensi-

bility, Pete issued forth, planning his campaign. He saddled
the sorrel stallion and started north, ostentatiously after the
sheep. As soon as the rolling ground hid him from sight of
the house, he turned to the left, into the foothills of the moun-
5 tains. When he reached their wooded slopes, he turned south
again, in the direction that he had come, spurring his horse
into a lope. He was completely concealed from the river
road by a low ridge. He continued on, behind this ridge,
until he struck a tiny creek which gurgled down toward the
10 Sandy. Here he tied his horse to a tree and made his way
along the stream on foot, on the southern bank. He was in
Smithers' land. The creek marked the boundary. Five hundred yards further, it ran into a dense clump of dwarf willows. Somewhere in here, he knew, was his objective. He
15 saw no evidence of the way that the Whittels had entered the
grove. He kept on toward the river, and suddenly happened
to notice a place where some heavy object had been dragged
across the creek. It had plainly marked a trail in the soft
ground. He followed it and easily succeeded in penetrating
20 the interior of the clump. He pushed a last screen of branches
aside. The still! It was situated in a small clearing, perhaps fifteen feet in diameter. A pile of recently cut branches
and a few weeds lay at one side. Opposite the entrance, what
looked like a copper wash-boiler sat upon a brick fireplace.
25 Sticks for a fire were laid beneath it. Beside the boiler was
a wooden trough the size of a small bath tub. In it rested a
long, tightly coiled spiral of copper piping. One end of the
pipe was connected with the top of the boiler, while the other
left the wooden cooling tank near the bottom, terminating in
30 a spigot. A lead pipe, issuing from the willows, passed a
constant stream of cold water into the tank. The overflow
ran away into the thicket. A number of smaller articles,
including three demijohns, half full of liquor, littered the
ground around the apparatus.
35 Pete surveyed it with interest, taking care to touch nothing. After a few minutes' consideration, he returned to the

horse, mounted, and clucked his marching orders. The horse
took the shortest way back, instead of the way that they
had come. Pete was so engrossed with his thoughts that he
did not notice that the road he was traveling would soon
bring him in full sight of the farm. When suddenly he
rounded the base of a hill, he brought up short, face to face
with Josiah. The latter looked as if he were about to suc-
cumb to a fit of apoplexy. "What th' hell you doin' down
here?" he demanded angrily, at the same time looking apprehensively at the empty demijohn that he was carrying.

"Down here?" Pete's surprise sounded genuine. "Boss,
I've been lookin' for them sheep you said was down here!"

"South? I told you they were north."

Pete was nothing if not a good liar. He opened his mouth
slowly and stared vacantly at the other. "Zasso, boss?
Well, well, I thought you said south."

Josiah shook his head perplexedly. "Get along, get it done,
pronto. Sabe?" and they separated.

The sun had crossed the zenith two hours before. Pete,
again straddling the stallion, started cautiously up the lane
toward the north. A quarter of a mile from the house, he
struck off toward the river. Six miles up the river road lay
the village of Georgeburg, crouching in the foothills. An hour
later, Pete rode along the town's main street, attentively
watching the houses on his right. Finally, he drew rein before
one, and tied his horse to the hitching block. The house was
set far back in a beech-covered lawn,—pillars, brass knocker,
unmarred by time, the same as they had been a century before. Pete bravely marched up to the porch. From a pillar
hung the legend, "Hiram Wigby, Justice of the Peace."
Pete tiptoed up the steps, realizing the shock which his appearance must have given the staid surroundings. He raised
the knocker and let it fall with a bang. A minute elapsed.
Then the heavy door swung open, disclosing the magistrate
himself. He was a funny little man who looked as if he had

been built to match his dwelling. Bald as a baby, clean
shaven, with twinkling blue eyes and a rusty, bleak looking Prince Albert. He looked his disapproval of his guest.
"What do you want? Why didn't you come to the back
5 door?"

Pete smiled. "You don't remember me, Judge?—the little
fellow you used to dance on your foot? Little Pete?"

The Judge was dumfounded. "Pete? Well, my boy, I
can't say you've changed for the better. Never mind, though.
10 Come in, come in. Tell me about yourself."

Pete followed him to a study in the rear of the house. The
Judge bade him be seated, and did so himself. Then Pete
explained in a few words what he had discovered. He was
evidently dropping his dialect for the benefit of his auditor.
15 Then he added: "They haven't an idea, Judge, what's on
foot. Of course, I can't let them know, personally. And it's
not for the police. As I just said, Whittel is going to notify
the cops this afternoon. That means that whatever is done
will have to be done in a hurry. My plan is this. Somehow,
20 I must get a note to them. I saw the still this morning.
Three men working on it for half an hour could destroy all
of the evidence so that it would be impossible for Whittel to
prove anything. It's the only way, for with the cards that
Whittel holds there isn't a chance of his not winning,—so
25 long as the still remains. I propose to tell the folks to be at
the still this evening at seven. I'll be there, and maybe—
I'll tell them who I am. We'll tear it up and turn the creek
into the willows. What say?"

"Pete, that is an act contrary to law. I can't advocate
30 anything of the kind. But you're right! It's not an affair
for the police. As an old friend of the family, I feel as you
do, that Whittel's game will have to be spoiled at the source.
I'll tell you what. You write your anonymous note, and I'll
be glad to give it to Jerry Keenan. He'll be passing Dan's
35 place this afternoon and can drop it in the mail box."

Pete wrote the note.

After his interview with the Judge, he cantered back toward Whittel's farm. Just outside town, he passed a small automobile driven by Harry. Another bad omen, he thought.

Stephen Ketchum was sleepy. His dilapidated rocking-chair creaked a weird lullaby as he oscillated slowly back and forth. Since it was spring, his thoughts naturally turned to love and the High Cost of Living. The breeze wafted an odor of earth mold and green grass in at the window. At any rate, green grass was one thing that hadn't gone up yet. What was Helen doing just then? Was she perhaps thinking of him? A tickling in his right ear assured him that she was. "Buzz," went the tickle. He instinctively "swatted" at it. The first fly of the season winged its way out of the window. His imagination wandered. Pretty deceptive old world, this. Here, a minute ago he had thought that he was seated in the little jail office without a thing to do. But now he found himself riding a bucking broncho, somewhere in Arizona. "Hang on, boy, don't pull leather! Yip, see 'im go!" The broncho left the ground and soared above the house tops. Down he came, stiff-legged, with a twist to the left. Stephen slid to the ground with a bump and opened his eyes. Back in his office again. Funny old world. The rocking-chair oscillated slowly a few inches behind him.

As he looked, a paper fluttered from the desk near the window and touched the floor within reach of his hand. Queer, there hadn't been any loose papers on the desk before. He looked at it curiously and rubbed his eyes, without unfolding it. It was a single sheet of ruled white paper, such as used to come in nickel pads before the war. It was folded once, as if it had been done hurriedly. Stephen unfolded it and regarded the contents hastily. Then he grabbed his hat and slammed the door behind him.

He hurried down the lane and turned into Main Street. Half a minute later, he paused before Magistrate Wigby's house. Another minute more, and he was seated in the study at the

back of the house, taking the letter from his pocket. "Judge,"
as he handed it over, "Helen's father is being framed."

The Judge took the note. It contained three lines of scrupulously vertical handwriting, evidently disguised. It read:

5   Dear Sir,
            Dan Smithers is running a still in the northwest
       corner of his land in the willows.
                                    A Friend of Prohibition

The Judge handed it back gravely. "I was hoping that
10 you wouldn't get it until tomorrow. Yes, don't be surprised.
Pete's back after all these years. He's been working for
Whittel. Whittel wrote that note and 'planted' the still. It's
your business to fasten the blame where it belongs. You'll
have to hurry, too."

15   Steve and the Judge consulted together for half an hour.
Then Steve took the car from the Judge's barn, and speeded
down the river road.

Supper that night at the Whittels' was a council of war.
"Boys," began Josiah, "what's your idea about this tramp?"

20   Harry spoke up. "There's somepin funny about him. I
passed him this afternoon when I was goin' in town. Wonder
what he'd been there for?"

"There is somepin funny. I met him snoopin' around near
the still, this mornin'. He had a glib story, but it didn't ring
25 true. We'd better watch him. I don't know who he is, but
he isn't here for any good. It's not Smithers or the son. We
know that. Course, he did have another son, but he disappeared years ago. They say Smithers drove him out, and
told him he'd kill him if he ever came back. It's not likely
30 him. We'd best follow him if we see him goin' anywheres."

That was how, when, at a quarter of seven, Pete started
boldly south toward the still, he was followed at a distance
by three self-constituted shadows.

At ten minutes of seven it was nearly as light as day. The
35 screen of branches separating the still from the outer world

parted, and Steve entered, followed by another man. The
police department had grown! The two concealed themselves to the right of the entrance. At three minutes of seven,
Pete glided through the passageway in the trees and concealed himself opposite the entrance. Two minutes more 5
saw the third addition to the party. Josiah, followed by Jim
and Harry in single file, stole in, where they imagined that
Pete had gone. Not seeing him, they turned, and started
back for the entrance. Two figures blocked their exit. "Put
up your hands, all of you,—and cut the noise." Steve had 10
always had a secret ambition to be a hold-up man.

Josiah was dismayed. A policeman's star? Had his plans
slipped a cog? The commands meant business, and Josiah
and his sons obeyed. At the point of his .38, Steve marched
them into concealment. His assistant snapped steel cuffs 15
on their wrists and forced them to sit down to wait the
finale. Josiah looked at Jim, and Jim looked back. What
did it mean? Did the police think they were the moon-
shiners? If so, why the secrecy? The elder Whittel opened
his mouth to speak. Steve jabbed the .38 in his ribs. Foot- 20
steps! Two men, one much older than the other, entered
the clearing. Anger and surprise were written large upon
their faces. As they turned to investigate the scene further,
a voice, that of Steve, rang from the place of concealment.
"It's all right, Mr. Smithers,—I'll bring you the culprits." 25
He issued with his prisoners, into the light. Smithers looked
at the manacled figures ominously. Steve broke the spell,
turning to Josiah. "Perhaps," he said, "you'd like to know
how I got you. In the first place, I got the dope, second hand,
I admit, from somebody who knew the whole thing. Pete, 30
where are you?" At the name Pete, Smithers looked greatly
surprised. Pete stepped from his hiding place and seated
himself nonchalantly on the edge of the cooling-trough. His
plans had missed connections, but evidently for the better.

Steve continued. "As soon as I had heard this, I came 35
down here and looked over the ground. Whittel, you made

some fatal mistakes. I admit that the plan was clever. But
you shouldn't have left your knife here. The initials are a
dead give-away. Besides, it is such an old way of getting
caught. Then, that note was a bad blunder. When you try
5 it again, wear gloves. In creasing it, you left a fine set of
finger prints. They matched up perfectly with those on the
knife. The wood," pointing to that which was laid in the
fireplace, "gave some more proof. It is perfectly simple to
see where it came from. You shouldn't have dragged it. You
10 didn't see any dead timber near here, so you brought it with
you. If you'd looked a little closer, you would have seen
that there was some a good deal nearer, and on Smithers'
land, at that. Another thing that you forgot to do was to
get the still to working. The cooling tube is stopped up
15 completely. There's one more thing I'll show you, shortly, as
soon as my other man gets here. He went up to your house,
Whittel, to get us some liquid refreshments. You didn't
leave enough in these three demijohns." Whittel glared.
The party waited. Suddenly, the other deputy broke into
20 the circle, lugging a demijohn full of whisky. He placed
it on the ground beside two tumblers which Steve had made
appear from no place in particular. Steve then poured one
glassful from the demijohn which had just been brought and
one from one of those that he had found at the still. The
25 onlookers were completely mystified. His preparations finished, Steve stood up and took a cylindrical case, six inches
long and one in diameter, from his pocket. He opened it,
and drew out a small glass tube, enlarged in the middle, with
a bulb of buckshot at the lower end. Both ends were sealed.
30 The small upper part of the tube contained a graduated
scale like that of a thermometer. He held it up. "Here's
our last piece of evidence," he announced. "I'm going to
prove that the whisky that I found here at the still is part
of the private stock of Whittel." He floated the hydrometer
35 in one of the tumblers, noting the reading to which it sank.
Then he did the same with the other. The readings were

identical. He was triumphant. "There she is, gentlemen. They have exactly the same alcohol content. Two samples that hadn't come out of the same bottle wouldn't do that. Our demonstration is ended for the evening. Mr. Smithers, I'm glad to have been of assistance. Whittel, we'll be able to accommodate you in town, this evening."

Smithers regarded the officer with a new interest. "I think I can change my opinion about having you as a son-in-law. Shake, my boy!"

Pete edged forward wearily. Smithers had not recognized him. "Don't I come in on the general felicity, dad? Won't you take me back?"

Smithers recognized the voice before the words were fairly out of his mouth. Tears rushed to his eyes and a lump rose in his throat. "Pete," he faltered, "your mother and I have missed you."

NOTES AND COMMENTS

EXPOSITION [1]

The specimens of prose composition in this book have two purposes: first, to illustrate the special elements and qualities in Exposition, Argument, Description, and Narration; and, second, to show the relations of the principles of structure to the various kinds of composition. All writing is divided into these four classes, according to the purpose of the writer. If his purpose is to explain a term or a set of facts, the result is called Exposition; if his purpose is to convince or to persuade another person of the truth of a particular set of facts, it is called Argument; if his purpose is to represent objects which appeal to the senses, it is called Description; if his purpose is to recount events in sequence of time, it is called Narration. Clearly, the first two classes appeal to the intellect, and the last two appeal to the emotions and to the imagination. Inasmuch, then, as Exposition and Argument appeal primarily to the intellect, they are in mood *analytic*; and inasmuch as Description and Narration appeal primarily to the senses and to the imagination, they are in mood *pictorial*.

In actual practice, however, all kinds of writing are so closely interrelated that a novel, for instance, may be both analytical and pictorial. Biography, again, may include analytic, narrative, and descriptive passages, but, since it aims to explain facts about a man's character and life, the union of these elements will be Exposition.

The principles of composition — Unity, Coherence, and Emphasis — are usually studied as if they applied to all kinds of writing inflexibly. The truth of the matter is, however, that they hold with equal firmness, but vary in application according as the writer's purpose is to analyze or to depict. When the mood changes, methods of structure and of style change. Let us consider how the nature of the material and the author's aim influence the way in which these principles of composition are applied to produce the intended effect. First we come to Exposition.

[1] For other introductory chapters, see Essay, p. 461; Criticism, p. 464; Biography, p. 468; Argument, p. 473; Description, p. 476; Narration, p. 496.

Unity. Unity demands that a composition shall gratify our sense of completeness. In the case of Exposition this means not only that there should be one central idea, but that this central idea should be completely developed. Half an explanation is of no value: nothing but the whole explanation will satisfy clearness. In order that an exposition may be the whole explanation, a writer should at the outset limit the field of material for the purpose of making sure that the subject is neither a fragment nor a chaos. The best device for thus assuring himself is the outline plan. A well-constructed plan is a guide which will prevent him from introducing extraneous material. When subject-matter can be reduced to an outline in which each heading and sub-heading is clearly included under the title, the whole composition will possess Unity.

A plan expresses the limits of a writer's subject-matter; it gives no hint of his attitude toward this subject-matter. Before a student can write his exposition, he must decide who his readers are to be. In analytic writing the matter of an audience is of vital importance. An exposition of the structure of a lobster may be written for an audience of zoölogists, or of working men, or of children. Although the facts remain true in any one of the explanations, the treatment will invariably change. For the chief purpose of an explanation is to be understood, and consequently clearness must be its distinguishing quality. To achieve this clearness, a writer must assume a definite attitude, or, technically speaking, adopt a mental point of view, toward his subject and toward his audience, and hold this point of view consistently. The problem, therefore, of explaining his subject, no matter how well it is planned, to a particular audience is the severest task of the writer of Exposition. An admirable example of skill in adopting a point of view is *On the Study of Zoölogy* (p. 29). This explanation is effective because Huxley has conceived — as the writer of Exposition always should conceive — the precise state of his hearers' information. He approaches the subject, familiar and comprehensible to him as a scientist, by the easy stages along which the mind of a layman would inevitably proceed. Other examples are *Taxation and Government* (p. 3) and *The Wonder-World of Atoms* (p. 42).

Though a writer may be sure of his attitude toward his subject, he is liable, in the course of his work, to commit two errors: false beginnings and digressions. False beginnings are due to the fact that an untrained writer is uncertain how much to assume his reader knows. This desire to tell all the preliminary facts is comically illustrated by Miss Bates in Jane Austen's *Emma*. The trained mind, however, ignoring all encumbering preliminaries, seizes the right moment for beginning. " I purpose," says Macaulay, in opening his *History of England*, " I purpose to write the history of England from the accession of King James the Second down to a time which is within the memory of men still living." Digressions are caused by the inability to resist the allurements of a bewildering number of associated ideas. But, though this trait may enhance the charm of the garrulous yarn of an old sailor, it is fatal to the success of the writer of Exposition.

For avoiding these dangers of false beginnings and digressions there are various devices. Most effective are short announcements of procedure, either in the beginning of an article or just before the treatment of a subdivision. An example of the first is in Professor Palmer's *Self-Cultivation in English*:

> Watch your speech, then. That is all which is needed. Only it is desirable to know what qualities of speech to watch for. I find three, — accuracy, audacity, and range, — and I will say a few words about each (p. 22, ll. 12–16).

See also *The Story of Finance and Banking* (p. 9, ll. 1–4), *On the Study of Zoölogy* (p. 30, ll. 25–30), *The Wonder-World of Atoms* (p. 42, ll. 9–15). Another valuable device is the use of summaries, which may be either intermediary or final. The former may come in the course of an article after the treatment of one or more divisions, as in *Taxation and Government* (p. 5, ll. 28–36). The latter is a brief enumeration, at the end, of the chief points that have been made, as in *Self-Cultivation in English* (p. 28, ll. 31–33):

> Such, then, are the excellences of speech. If we would cultivate ourselves in the use of English, we must make our daily talk accurate, daring, and full.

This crisp and enumerative summary may easily become, in the hands of a less skillful writer, wooden and mechanical. That final summaries may possess variety and flexibility is shown by the conclusions of *Taxation and Government* (p. 8), *On the Study of Zoölogy* (p. 41), and *John Gilley* (p. 149).

Coherence. When once we are sure that the subject-matter forms a complete unit, we must arrange the material so that the relation of part to part shall be clear. There must be an orderly sequence of facts or ideas. Just what the sequence shall be depends on the nature of the subject. In Exposition more varieties of order are possible than in other kinds of writing owing to the numerous complexities which confront explanation: (1) order of time—as in *The Story of Finance and Banking* (p. 9); (2) order of space—as in *Life in the Wilderness* (p. 52); (3) order from the simple to the complex—as in *On the Study of Zoölogy* (p. 29) and *The Story of Finance and Banking* (p. 9); (4) order from the familiar to the unfamiliar—as in *Taxation and Government* (p. 3); (5) order from cause to effect—as in *The Discovery of X-Rays and Radium* (p. 46); (6) order of division—as in *Self-Cultivation in English* (p. 21) and *On the Study of Zoölogy* (p. 29); (7) order of climax—as in *The Pleasantness of American Life* (p. 56). These modes of progression are not entirely independent of each other. Two or more may be combined, as, for example, (3) and (6) in *On the Study of Zoölogy*.

As soon as the reader understands what the mode of progression is to be, he is prepared to follow the course of the explanation. But his progress should be made easy and even pleasant by announcements of method and by transitions from part to part. Note the admirable transitions throughout *Taxation and Government* (p. 3) and *Self-Cultivation in English* (p. 21). When the subdivisions are rather extensive in themselves, the transitions between them should be ample enough to allow the reader to get his breath: a fine example occurs in *On the Study of Zoölogy* (p. 37, l. 34—p. 38, l. 18). In turn, the relations between paragraph and paragraph and between sentences within the paragraph should be clearly indicated by transitions or connective words. Coherence of thought, then, is the first concern; from that will grow Coherence of expression.

Emphasis. Emphasis of structure is a matter of position and proportion. Ordinarily, the most important ideas should be put in the most important positions—the beginning and the end. But the most important parts of an explanation are not always the beginning or the end, but often the middle. The steady unfolding of the facts and the proper stressing of the vital ones *wherever* they occur is the way to make an explanation carry. The beginning and the end, however, perform valuable functions in Exposition. The beginning is the place to arouse interest, state the subject (perhaps in a topic-sentence), and announce the method of procedure. This does not necessarily mean revealing the whole plan: sometimes it is best to give only a hint in order to keep the reader's curiosity from being dulled. Compare the beginnings of the various models of Exposition. The end is the opportunity to summarize the main ideas and enforce the central thought. Many examples of effective endings have already been mentioned under Unity. It will be seen that Unity and Emphasis go hand in hand.

Proportion means that each part of the whole should be given an amount of space appropriate to its value. Of three subdivisions one may be so important that it requires the most detailed treatment. Note, for instance, the relative amount of space given to each of the subdivisions of *On the Study of Zoölogy* (p. 29).

Structure, however, is not the only way of making Exposition forcible. The use of specific words, plenty of concrete examples to support general statements, illustrative instances drawn from matters familiar to the reader, a bright and original style — all combine to drive home the explanation.

FISKE: TAXATION AND GOVERNMENT (PAGE 3)

Biography. John Fiske (1842–1901), American philosopher and historian. After graduation from Harvard in 1863 and from the Harvard Law School in 1865, he turned his attention to writing and lecturing. Fascinated by the work of Darwin and Spencer, he applied the principles of evolution to philosophy. In this field his chief works are *Outlines of Cosmic Philosophy*, 1874; *The Destiny of Man*, 1884; *The Idea of God*, 1885. Later he devoted himself to American history, and produced volume after volume covering all our earlier history. Among them are *The Critical Period of American History, 1783–89*, 1888; *The Beginnings of New England*, 1889; *The American Revolution*, 1891; *The Discovery of America*, 1892; *Old Virginia and Her Neighbors*, 1897; *The Dutch and Quaker Colonies in America*, 1899; *The Mississippi Valley in the Civil War*, 1900. Gifted with remarkable powers of exposition, a genius for presenting facts so that everybody can understand them, he appealed to a wide audience.

Note. This is an example of the simplest kind of exposition, i.e. definition. Unity is obtained by various means. The point of view which unifies the treatment of the subject is that of a writer who endeavors to interpret a complex subject in terms of concrete and daily experience. He shows how taxes affect the individual citizen. Notice how the two divisions of the subject — taxation and government — are treated, first individually, then in their interrelations. A detailed plan will reveal the excellence of the structure.

To secure the first element of Coherence — order — the writer proceeds from the treatment of taxes, by an inevitable transition, to the treatment of government (p. 4, l. 35 to p. 5, l. 10); then, by uniting both subjects in a single definition (p. 5, ll. 34–36), he amplifies their relations. Various technical devices to secure Coherence are " transition paragraphs " (p. 4, l. 35; p. 5, l. 28), skillful transitions from paragraph to paragraph, and transitions from sentence to sentence. A valuable exercise is to underline all words and phrases which serve as connectives.

Emphasis is attained in the beginning of the article by stating in an interesting way the necessity of understanding the puzzling subject of taxation, and at the end by a hypothetical case which explains the matter poignantly. Note how excellent the proportion is. Observe the various methods of obtaining Emphasis in paragraphs and in sentences (p. 3, par. 1; p. 4, ll. 1–7). This extract illustrates many devices especially valuable in analytic writing: the skillful definition of terms, often by stating the meaning of each before giving it a technical name; and the use of concrete and homely illustration (p. 3, ll. 2–6, 16–20; p. 4, ll. 8 ff.).

FORBES: THE STORY OF FINANCE AND BANKING (Page 9)

Biography. William Cameron Forbes (1870–   ), American banker and Governor-General of the Philippines. Well known as an athlete, he gained experience in the business world both in banking and electrical engineering. From 1904 to 1909 he served in the Philippines as Secretary of Commerce and Police, and from 1909 to 1913 as Governor-General. He wrote *The Romance of Business*, 1921, to explain the vital part business plays in our lives. After reading the chapter here given, you will find it enjoyable to look up some of the others on textiles, steel, transportation, electricity, and capital and labor.

Note. The operations explained in this selection are unfamiliar to most persons because of the vast scale on which the exchange of goods and money is now carried on, and because the basis of the exchange — "credit" — is an invisible thing which we do not think much about. Clear and abundant illustrations; the use, at first, of small sums of money and small transactions in a little community; the increasing scale of operations as the chapter goes on; the sparing use of technical terms, — all these make for interest and for the success of the explanation.

With the method of this selection in mind as a model, you might attempt to explain other financial transactions: stocks, bonds, insurance, taxes, letters of credit, — any one of these might be treated. Or you might — as Mr. Forbes does in other parts of his book — take up in the same way manufacturing, transportation, or some other form of business.

PALMER: SELF-CULTIVATION IN ENGLISH (Page 21)

Biography. George Herbert Palmer (1842–   ), American writer and teacher, was for many years Professor of Philosophy at Harvard, from which chair he retired in 1913. His writings include a prose translation of the *Odyssey*, 1891; a life of *Alice Freeman Palmer*, 1908; several books on ethics; *Self-Cultivation in English*, 1897; and *The Teacher*, 1908.

Note. A mellow and winning treatment of a subject which might easily become schoolbookish. There could not be a better example of the principles here preached. Like Emerson, Professor Palmer has a way of saying striking things quietly and naturally. He also has — what Emerson was rather deficient in — great deftness in really *composing* his essay so that part follows part smoothly and naturally. Beginning, ending, and transitions, — all are exactly fitted to the purpose. The essay is full of words which impoverished speakers and writers ought to adopt; yet these words are never allowed to seem like decorations artfully displayed. Indeed, Professor Palmer modestly says (p. 27, l. 8) that "we" — he and the reader — use far too few words. It is because one feels that Professor Palmer really means to include himself among those who need to learn more about the fascinating art of gathering verbal riches that this essay is so pleasantly instructive.

22 4–5 poorest and busiest . . . leisured rich: a good example of balance disguised by a slight departure from exact grammatical correspondence between the two phrases.

HUXLEY: ON THE STUDY OF ZOÖLOGY (PAGE 29)

Biography. Thomas Henry Huxley (1825–1895), English man of science and writer, did equally distinguished work as an investigator in various fields of science — especially zoölogy — and as a writer, both technical and popular, on scientific subjects. Living at a time when the consequences of recent discoveries in science (especially Darwin's) were regarded by many as contradictory to Biblical teaching, Huxley, both by his own research and by his extraordinarily clear and skillful presentation of the results of others, exercised a profound influence upon English education and popular thought. His textbooks and laboratory manuals show that he was a pioneer in insisting that knowledge of biology, even for elementary students, must be based on the examination of typical specimens in the laboratory. Among his more popular essays (collected in nine volumes) are "Three Lectures on Evolution," "Coral and Coral Reefs," "On a Piece of Chalk," "A Liberal Education and Where to Find It," and "On the Educational Value of the Natural History Sciences."

Note. The extraordinary clearness and simplicity of Huxley's popular essays and addresses on scientific subjects should not lead us to forget the skill required to produce them, — a greater skill, probably, than is needed to write technically on similar subjects. Huxley seems to have thought so, for he says: "I found that the task of putting the truths learned in the field, the laboratory and the museum, into language which, without bating a jot of scientific accuracy shall be generally intelligible, taxed such scientific and literary faculty as I possessed to the uttermost." (*Discourses: Biological and Geological*, London, 1894, p. v.)

Clear and delightful as his style may be, however, we must not forget Huxley's insistence on the importance of laboratory work, and we must imagine his text illustrated by specimens and diagrams.

In exposition he always, as here, avoids both extremes, — dry classification and unnecessary detail. He skillfully reduces his lobster to lowest terms, and then — just as he seems in danger of simplifying too much —

he neatly brings in the argument based on the embryology of the lobster to convince us that "the doctrine of unity of plan is . . . the expression of deep-seated natural facts." Note Huxley's effective use of common and often vivid words to explain technicalities.

Possible exercises based on this essay:

1. Make a plan of the essay.
2. Make a plan of as much of zoölogy as is here sketched.

THOMSON: THE WONDER-WORLD OF ATOMS AND THE DISCOVERY OF X-RAYS AND RADIUM (Pages 42 and 46)

Biography. John Arthur Thomson (1861–   ), Scottish man of science and writer, Regius Professor of Natural History in the University of Aberdeen since 1899. Among his publications are many authoritative, yet popular works, such as *Evolution*, 1911; *Introduction to Science*, 1911; *The System of Animate Nature*, 1920. The present selection is from *The Outline of Science*, 1922.

Note. Whoever watches the new books must have been struck by the number of bird's-eye views for laymen that have recently appeared, — *The Outline of History*, by H. G. Wells; *The Story of Mankind*, by H. W. Van Loon; *The Outline of Science*, by Professor Thomson, and others. New ones are being written, and their method seems to be influencing certain college courses. It is a real chapter in popular education.

The difficulty of such writing is great: it demands not only a thorough knowledge of the subject, but also a nice sense of the layman's point of view and great skill in building upon the foundation of familiar objects and experiences. The vast stretches of time and space which are a matter of course to the geologist and the astronomer, and the minutest measurements of the physicist and the chemist are, after all, not quite inconceivable if a writer has the ability which Thomson shows in these fascinating chapters.

Even the student in an elementary course in science can make that course mean much more, and at the same time greatly increase his skill in exposition, if he will practise explaining things to someone who knows nothing whatever about the subject.

ROOSEVELT: LIFE IN THE WILDERNESS (Page 52)

Biography. Theodore Roosevelt (1858–1919), the many-sided hero of our time — statesman, soldier, hunter, naturalist, explorer, and author. On graduation from Harvard in 1880 he began his long fight for clean politics, and was successively member of the New York legislature, U. S. Civil Service Commissioner, and Police Commissioner of New York City. When in 1897 he was appointed Assistant Secretary of the Navy, he used his opportunity to perfect the gunnery marksmanship of the navy, which led to the brilliant sea victories of the Spanish-American War. On the outbreak of this war, 1898, he resigned his position to organize the famous cavalry regiment, the " Rough Riders," made up of Western cowboys and Eastern college athletes. As Colonel, he led this regiment in the storming of San Juan Hill. His energetic and picturesque service in the war brought about his election as Governor of New York in 1898, and both these facts resulted in his election as Vice President in 1900. On the assassination of President McKinley, 1901, he succeeded to the Presidency. In 1904 he was elected President in his own right. After his term was over, he went on two extensive hunting and exploring trips — one in Africa, the other in South America. During the World War he chafed under his enforced inactivity, and soon after the death of his son Quentin, the aviator, he died in 1919. For an estimate of his character see the address by Senator Lodge, p. 155.

His books express his varied interests. Chief among them are *The Naval War of 1812*, 1882; *Hunting Trips of a Ranchman*, 1885; *The Winning of the West*, 1889–1896; *American Ideals*, 1897; *The Rough Riders*, 1899; *The Strenuous Life*, 1900; *African Game Trails*, 1910; *Autobiography*, 1913; *Through the Brazilian Wilderness*, 1914; *Fear God and Take Your Own Part*, 1916.

Note. This selection, a generalized picture of life as it will never be again in America, is successful because the author had knowledge and sympathy in matters of this kind. He lingers over the rifle and the axe, and visualizes the difficulties of frontier life as no mere student would be likely to do. Of *The Winning of the West* Roosevelt might have said, as Parkman (to whom the book is dedicated) said of his own *Montcalm and Wolfe*: " The subject has been studied as much from life and in the open air as at the library table." What method of arrangement makes the selection coherent? Pick out some phrases which show that Roosevelt not only knew about life in the wilderness, but loved it.

BRYCE: THE PLEASANTNESS OF AMERICAN LIFE (PAGE 56)

Biography. James Bryce, Viscount Bryce (1838–1922), English diplomat and writer. Educated at Glasgow University and Trinity College, Oxford, he later became Regius Professor of Civil Law at Oxford. He entered parliament in 1880. Besides being a great diplomat, historian, and student of government and law, Bryce was a botanist and a mountain climber of some note. His talents were recognized in many countries, and his honorary degrees and other distinctions were very numerous. Americans are most likely to remember him as British Ambassador at Washington from 1907 to 1913, and as the author of the best book thus far written on American government, — *The American Commonwealth*, 1888. But Bryce's *Holy Roman Empire*, 1862, and *Modern Democracies*, 1921, are both great books, and his *Studies in Contemporary Biography*, 1903, is a model of what such a volume should be.

Note. This kind of subject tests the intelligence and temper of the writer: stupid, intolerant people are at their worst when generalizing about life in other countries; and such intelligence and sympathy as Lord Bryce's are there shown at their best.

Besides its definite basis of generalized fact, its freedom from a clutter of local details, and its charming urbanity, this selection is a model for its easy lucidity and order: it obeys the rules without seeming to be conscious of their existence.

Are Bryce's statements still true? What can you say about life in some foreign country?

RUSKIN: THE BOW OF A BOAT (PAGE 65)

Biography. John Ruskin (1819–1900), English writer on art and political economy. At seventeen he entered Christ Church College, Oxford. He began his greatest work, *Modern Painters*, at the age of twenty-three. The original purpose was to prove the superiority of modern landscape painting, but as the work (5 vols.) developed during the next twenty years, it became a vast treatise on the principles of art, filled with gorgeous descriptions of nature. Ruskin's studies frequently took him on tours to France, Switzerland, and Italy. From 1869 to 1879 he was Professor of Art at Oxford. Among his other works are *The Seven Lamps of Architecture*, 1849; *The Stones of Venice*, 1851–1853; *Unto this Last*, 1860; *Sesame and Lilies*, 1865; *The Crown of Wild Olive*, 1866; and *Praeterita*, an autobiography, 1887. Ruskin was more than an artist and a critic of art; he was a social reformer and one of the great teachers of modern times.

Note. Ruskin said, "All my work is to help those who *have* eyes and see not." What do you think of his success in carrying out this purpose in the present instance? Here is a kind of exposition different from many of the examples previously studied. Here the writer wishes to explain the meaning of an object, the ideas which flood his mind when he regards it. This sort of exposition — which does not expound a process, or the organization or structure of a thing, but sets forth ideas — is one of the most entertaining to write. Yet here as well as elsewhere you see the value of arrangement. Consider the order of the ideas, and note the transitions. Observe the energy of the sentences and the pictorial force of the words. But above and beyond these technical matters, there is the quality of imagination which kindles the reader as it did Ruskin.

Of the fifth paragraph (p. 66, ll. 34 ff.) Frederic Harrison says: "I would take this paragraph as the high-water mark of Ruskin's prose method." See his article "Ruskin as Master of Prose" in *Tennyson, Ruskin, Mill*, London, 1900.

THE ESSAY[1]

[Since the essay, criticism, and biography are on the whole expository in intention, the methods of employing the principles of composition are much the same as in the case of ordinary Exposition. Instead, therefore, of a detailed account of the principles in relation to these three literary types, the introductions will give brief comment on the nature and qualities of each.]

To write an essay was, originally, to " have a try " at something, and to this day the essay retains, or should retain, the fine old tradition of being tentative and unpretentious. A glimpse at the history of the essay will help us to understand the characteristics of this type. The familiar essay originated with Michel de Montaigne, who in 1580 published a collection of short, informal pieces about himself, his interests and affairs. He called them *Essais* (attempts or trials), and thus frankly indicated the lack of systematic or thorough development. From Montaigne, then, came the three distinguishing traits — personality, informal structure, and an easy, graceful style. Seventeen years later (1597) appeared the first volume of English essays, those of Sir Francis Bacon. The term which he applied to them, " dispersed meditations," shows how they differed from Montaigne's : they were very brief, pithy notes on abstract subjects, the concentrated wisdom of a shrewd observer of human life. During the three centuries from that time to our own both the scope and the technique of the essay have been enriched by many famous writers : Dryden, Addison, Steele, Dr. Johnson, Goldsmith, Lamb, Hazlitt, Leigh Hunt, Macaulay, Carlyle, Arnold, Irving, Thackeray, Emerson, Lowell, and Stevenson. They have found their subjects among the eternal commonplaces of life, — friendship, fame, death, courage, love, honor, patriotism, learning : these are common possessions of every civilization. That is why the great essayists — and the wise general observations in writers who are not essayists — can never die.

An essay can so easily be spoiled ! If it is too learned, too orderly, too serious, too consciously funny, or too anything else, it will be a failure. The flavor that comes from a pleasant personality is the best guarantee of success. If we have all the learning of the ages we may not be able to do a good essay ; if we have a silly little piece of silver paper and the knack of essay-writing, we shall succeed.

[1] For other introductory chapters, see Exposition, p. 451 ; Criticism, p. 464 ; Biography, p. 468 ; Argument, p. 473 ; Description, p. 476 ; Narration, p. 496.

In the old days students wrote essays (when they did not write arguments) more commonly than anything else. Nowadays they attempt the essay too infrequently. Few literary forms offer such pleasant and varied opportunities for showing that one has not only the raw materials of learning, but a little bit also of the finished thought and expression that make Bacon and Lamb and Stevenson, in their different ways, so wise and so delightful.

In recent years there has been a widespread revival of interest in the essay. More people are fond of reading witty, genial, and stimulating essays, and more authors are fond of writing them. Meanwhile the popular " column " of the newspapers has become a vital factor in developing a taste for essays in thousands of readers who take only this daily dip into literature. The list of writers of the present who have won distinction as essayists is so long that it is rather bewildering, but it is a vivid sign of the strength of the revival. Happy the student who makes the acquaintance of G. K. Chesterton, John Galsworthy, A. C. Benson, E. V. Lucas, Hilaire Belloc, Max Beerbohm, Stephen Leacock, S. M. Crothers, Arthur Symons, H. M. Tomlinson, Thomas Burke, A. A. Milne, J. G. Huneker, S. P. Sherman, R. C. Holliday, W. P. Eaton, Heywood Broun, and Christopher Morley.

EMERSON: COURAGE (Page 80)

Biography. Ralph Waldo Emerson (1803–1882), American philosopher, poet, and essayist, studied for the Unitarian ministry and preached for a while, but left the church in 1832; spent most of his life in Concord, Massachusetts; was a friend and correspondent of Carlyle; lectured widely and wrote many volumes of essays. He is eminent beyond almost any other American for his stirring exhortations to self-reliance and for the beauty, fervor, range, and unexpectedness of his thought. The titles of his volumes mean little : virtually all are essays on certain perennial phases of thought and conduct. Some of the separate essays are " Nature," "The American Scholar," " The Over-Soul," " Manners," " Self-Reliance," " Friendship," " Compensation," " Books," " Civilization," and " Success."

Note. Consider the organization of this essay : is it good ? How does it compare with that of other essays by Emerson ? Is the sentence, or the paragraph, the unit which stands out most clearly in this essay ? in most of his essays ?

Study Emerson's condensed, energetic, memorable style, especially his motto-like sentences. Commit a few of them to memory.

Note Emerson's rapidity and scope of allusion. Do his allusions delay progress or enhance the effect ? Is he too profuse in allusion ? What conclusions do you draw about his reading ? Make a modest effort to show your own reading by more frequent allusions.

NOTES AND COMMENTS 463

STEVENSON: ÆS TRIPLEX (PAGE 90)

Biography. Robert Louis Stevenson (1850–1894), Scottish story writer and essayist. Educated at Edinburgh University, he first studied engineering (the family profession) and then law, but abandoned this for literature. The climate of Scotland, too harsh for his weak lungs, drove him to sunnier lands, and his life became a long pilgrimage to France, Switzerland, California, the Adirondacks, and finally the South Seas. Here he settled in Samoa in 1891, and lived picturesquely until his death, in 1894, at the age of forty-four. His heroic struggle against ill-health, his bravery of spirit, and his fascinating personality have made him the best beloved of modern authors.

He distinguished himself in many fields of writing. His books of travel, such as *An Inland Voyage*, 1878, and *Travels with a Donkey*, 1879, are notable for their delightful description and debonair spirit. His short stories rank among the finest in our literature, the most famous being "A Lodging for the Night" and "The Sire de Malétroit's Door" (in *New Arabian Nights*, 1882), and "Markheim" and "Will o' the Mill" (in *The Merry Men, and Other Tales*, 1887). His essays are exquisite in style and astonishingly fresh and original in subject matter: among the most celebrated are "Æs Triplex," "The English Admirals," "Walking Tours," "An Apology for Idlers" (in *Virginibus Puerisque*, 1881), "A College Magazine," "The Manse," "A Gossip on Romance" (in *Memories and Portraits*, 1887), "Pulvis et Umbra" and "A Christmas Sermon" (in *Across The Plains*, 1892). But it is as a writer of prose romances that he has reached his widest fame: *Treasure Island*, 1883; *Prince Otto*, 1885; *The Strange Case of Dr. Jekyll and Mr. Hyde*, 1886; *Kidnapped*, 1886; *The Master of Ballantrae*, 1889; *David Balfour*, 1893; and others. These works revealed Stevenson as a master of thrilling and pictorial narrative, and led to a new Romantic revival. For an appreciation of Stevenson's work see the essay by Professor Copeland, p. 116.

Note. The title of this essay is found in the following lines of Horace (Odes, Book I, Ode 3):

> Illi robur et aes triplex
> Circa pectus erat, qui fragilem truci
> Commisit pelago ratem
> Primus.

"Æs Triplex" is thus the symbol of indomitable courage. This essay deals with abstract and eternal facts, — with man's attitude toward life and death. The definite thesis is "that we do not love life, in the sense that we are greatly preoccupied about its conservation; that we do not, properly speaking, love life at all, but living" (p. 94, l. 7). A subject which thus baldly stated would seem abstract and forbidding can be treated with extraordinary concreteness, humor, and charm. This essay is based on the character of the writer, and it has pathetic and heroic significance when viewed in the light of his fight for health. The consequent "happy valiancy of style" is revealed by the quaint mixture of solemnity and fun, the beauty of single phrases, the trenchant concreteness of the images, and the buoyancy and rhythm of the sentences.

93 35 **Permanent Possibility of Sensation**: a phrase of John Stuart Mill. See *Examination of Sir Wm. Hamilton's Philosophy*, Vol. I, chap. xi.

LUCAS: OF SILVER PAPER (Page 96)

Biography. Edward Verrall Lucas (1868–), English essayist and novelist. He is the author of a series of delightful books of travel: *A Wanderer in Holland*, 1905; *A Wanderer in London*, 1906; *A Wanderer in Paris*, 1909; *A Wanderer in Florence*, 1914; *A Wanderer in Venice*, 1914. He is one of the leaders of the revival of the informal essay: *One Day and Another*, 1909; *Old Lamps for New*, 1911; *Loiterer's Harvest*, 1913; *Cloud and Silver*, 1916; *Roving East and Roving West*, 1921. Among his novels are *Over Bemerton's*, 1908; *Mr. Ingleside*, 1910; *London Lavender*, 1912. He has edited a large number of anthologies, such as *The Open Road*, 1899; *The Gentlest Art: A Choice of Letters*, 1907; *The Second Post*, 1910. His *Life of Charles Lamb*, 1905, is one of the most attractive of modern biographies.

Note. This example of an informal essay offers an interesting contrast with the essays by Emerson and Stevenson. Here is a light subject treated in a light style, and yet it is remarkable that the author gets so much out of so little. The notable fact is that Mr. Lucas *saw* that there was a subject in such a trivial thing as silver paper, — a fact which is most helpful and stimulating to beginners in essay writing. He suggests many other subjects, too, when he goes through his pockets and pulls out the various articles. It would be fun to take this hint and write about the things in your own pockets.

Both the style and the structure of this essay deserve attention. Note the friendly and jaunty tone, the genial humor, the easy flow of the sentences. Study the modeling of the material, the methods by which coherence is obtained. You will notice that as the essay proceeds, "silver paper" becomes a symbol, standing for the many things we do not know about. It comes in as a refrain throughout, and most happily at the end. What is the value of a verbal link like this in producing unity of form? What is the real unity of idea within the essay?

CRITICISM [1]

Criticism, in its broadest sense, is man's conscious relation to art. It has ranged from the magisterial estimate of the value and rank of an author or any work of art to the recital of one's personal impression or

[1] For other introductory chapters see Exposition, p. 451; Essay, p. 461; Biography, p. 468; Argument, p. 473; Description, p. 476; Narration, p. 496.

enjoyment of them. The three critical pieces reprinted in this volume are thought worthy of attention because they show the qualities essential for success.

1. *Judgment.* The indispensable quality in a critic of anything is that he shall be able to distinguish between good and bad. Almost anyone can tell the very good from the very bad, but not so many can tell the fairly good from the slightly bad or recognize the mixture of qualities so admirably indicated by Professor Copeland when he calls Stevenson, for all his skill, a little romantic and Scott, for all his shortcomings, a great one (p. 120, l. 22). A natural sense of fairness, the practice of literary self-control, a constant desire to learn all that one can from the methods of those who criticize in other arts (painting, music, etc.), — these are a few of the ingredients to be sought for in acquiring good judgment of books. A good critic's power to judge books and other works of art should never be thought of as something mysterious, eccentric, and effeminate: it is entirely of a piece with good judgment in other matters.

2. *Wide Reading.* The good critic has read widely, and of course judiciously. Therefore he is not in danger of judging Scott or Stevenson or holiday stories in a vacuum; on the contrary, like a person judging dogs, pictures, hotels, or anything else, the good critic speaks with authority because he is a person of judgment speaking from a wide experience. Knowing that readers must be persuaded instead of being ordered about, he lets it be seen that he has read widely. He does not drag in his knowledge; he does not use it heavily. But he gives a side glance now and then from Stevenson to Scott or from Scott to Weyman. Thus he both beguiles the journey and clarifies his subject. Few tricks are better worth acquiring than the power to talk agreeably, but not overwhelmingly, about one's reading.

3. *Good Temper.* Chesterton does not like certain kinds of pseudo-romance; Copeland's liking of Scott and Meredith is subject to certain reservations; and the dislike of Howells for what he regards as faulty work in the writing of holiday stories is half the theme of his essay. But in each case it is a measured and reasoned disapproval, expressed with the same propriety that governs the expressions of disapproval which pass between one diplomat and another. Or at least it is urbane: the habit of losing one's temper in public is a luxury which the critic cannot afford. There is also a question of good manners when the critic likes his author greatly: unmeasured laudation is as bad as unmeasured censure.

CHESTERTON: SIR WALTER SCOTT (PAGE 111)

Biography. Gilbert Keith Chesterton (1874–   ), English author. He was educated at St. Paul's School, London. After studying art, he took up journalism as a career, and soon achieved fame by the originality of his thinking and the tremendous vigor of his style. He is one of the most inspiring and provocative of present-day writers. When Roosevelt was given a dinner by the authors of London, and was asked whom he would like to have by his side to talk with, he replied "Gilbert Chesterton."

This versatile author has written essays, fiction, poetry, drama, and biography. Among his volumes of essays are *The Defendant*, 1901; *Varied Types*, 1903; *Heretics*, 1905; *Orthodoxy*, 1908; *Tremendous Trifles*, 1909; *What's Wrong with the World*, 1910; *The Uses of Diversity*, 1921. He has invented detective stories of a new and ingenious kind in *The Innocence of Father Brown*, 1911; *The Wisdom of Father Brown*, 1914; and *The Man Who Knew Too Much*, 1923. Among his other books should be mentioned *Robert Browning*, 1903; *The Napoleon of Notting Hill*, 1904; *The Man Who Was Thursday*, 1908; *Magic* (a play), 1913; *The Flying Inn*, 1914; *Irish Impressions*, 1919.

Note. This selection is an example of appreciative criticism. It analyzes the quality of romance which made Scott "the king of the romantics." Note the hearty enjoyment and the thorough manliness of the criticism. The article shows that first-rate criticism is entirely worthy of the highest powers of a robust and original writer. When students' criticisms of books are perfunctory, much profit will result from the study of a critical opinion written with virility and gusto. Note the use of epigram and paradox. To understand this criticism completely, students should read the passages referred to.

113 29 **Sir Arthur Wardour:** see *The Antiquary*, chap. vii.

113 35 **Rob Roy:** see *Rob Roy*, chap. xxiii.

114 6 **Colonel Mannering:** see *Guy Mannering*, chap. xlix.

114 22 **Stanley Weyman:** the author of many historical romances, among them *A Gentleman of France*, *Under the Red Robe*, *The Red Cockade*.

114 31 **Clerk of Copmanhurst:** Friar Tuck in *Ivanhoe*.

114 32 **Mr. Pleydell:** a character in *Guy Mannering*.

COPELAND: ROBERT LOUIS STEVENSON (PAGE 116)

Biography. Charles Townsend Copeland (1860–   ), American writer and teacher. Graduating from Harvard in 1882, he was engaged for some years in writing dramatic criticism. Since 1893, first as Lecturer on Literature and later as Professor of English, he has been teaching at Harvard, where he has exerted upon his students a unique influence by virtue of his personality, his wit, and his power to interpret literature. The essay on Stevenson was written for the *Atlantic Monthly* in 1895. Among his other writings are a *Life of Edwin Booth*, 1901, and an essay on "Carlyle as a Letter-Writer" in *Letters of Thomas Carlyle to His Youngest Sister*, 1899.

Note. This is an example of appreciative criticism which shows the relation between a man's life and his work. Its notable traits are sympathetic knowledge, real feeling, and charm of style. Study the variety and flexibility of sentence structure. Notice the easy command of allusion as contrasted with the heavy references common in many articles. On page 119, line 20, is a particularly good example of a flexible yet perfectly coherent transition from the second to the third point in a series. Cf. Professor Palmer, p. 26, l. 13, where the transition also sums up the first and second points before announcing the third.

116 24 **historian of Wessex:** Thomas Hardy.

116 26 **a strong young Occidental:** Rudyard Kipling.

117 25 *Espérance* **and set on:** the motto of Harry Hotspur at the battle of Shrewsbury in *Henry the Fourth, Part I.*

118 1 **A Christmas Sermon or Pulvis et Umbra:** both in *Across the Plains.*

118 3 **a great novelist:** George Eliot.

118 9 These lines occur in *Andrea del Sarto*, by Robert Browning.

118 25 **The Foreigner at Home:** in *Memories and Portraits.*

118 27 **The Manse:** in *Memories and Portraits.*

118 29 **Probably Arboreal:** suggested by the following sentence in Darwin's definition of the ancestor of man, in *The Descent of Man*, Part II, chap. xxi. "Man is descended from a hairy quadruped, furnished with a tail and pointed ears, probably arboreal in its habits, and an inhabitant of the Old World."

119 3 **memorial:** Skerryvore.

119 19 **Vaea Mountain:** the place of Stevenson's burial in the Samoan Islands.

120 4 **scene in** *Guy Mannering* **which jars on him:** the scene is in *Guy Mannering*, chap. xli. For a discussion of this scene see "A Gossip on Romance" in *Memories and Portraits.*

120 25 **the appearance of Meg Merrilies:** see *Guy Mannering*, chap. viii, toward the end.

120 26 **the abdication of Queen Mary:** see *The Abbot*, chap. xxii.

120 27 **the installation of the abbot:** see *The Abbot*, chaps. xiii, xiv.

120 28 **the appeal of Jeanie Deans:** see *Heart of Midlothian*, chap. xxxvi.

120 28 **a certain scene:** see *Old Mortality*, chap. xlii.

120 33 **Alan and Davie:** see *Kidnapped*, chap. xx.

120 34 **windmills in Holland:** see *David Balfour*, chap. xxx.

120 34 **duel:** see *The Master of Ballantrae*, chap. iv.

121 15 **Providence and the Guitar:** see *New Arabian Nights.*

121 18 **A Story of Francis Villon:** see "A Lodging for the Night" in *New Arabian Nights.*

121 21 **redcoats:** see *Kidnapped*, chap. xx.

121 24 **Hyde:** see *Dr. Jekyll and Mr. Hyde.*

121 29 **forest of Gerolstein:** see *Prince Otto*, Bk. III, chap. i.

121 30 **Bass Rock:** see *David Balfour*, chap. xiv.

122 22 **Wegg:** a character in Dickens's *Our Mutual Friend.*

HOWELLS: ON THE THANKSGIVING AND CHRISTMAS STORY (PAGE 123)

Biography. William Dean Howells (1837–1920), American novelist, critic, and editor. From Ohio, where he spent his early years patiently preparing for his future success by hard, enthusiastic study of the best in many literatures, Howells came to New England in 1860, known chiefly as a promising young writer of verse. Successively Consul at Venice, assistant editor and then editor of the *Atlantic*, and editor of *Harper's Magazine*, Howells wrote steadily for more than sixty years, during which, although he never became conspicuously popular, he gained the deepest respect of those who like novels and essays that are rich in quiet wisdom. Among his very numerous novels some of the best are *A Modern Instance*, 1882; *The Rise of Silas Lapham*, 1885; *A Hazard of New Fortunes*, 1889; *Indian Summer*, 1885; and *The Kentons*, 1902. His essays include delightful chapters about travel, such as *London Films*, 1905, and many essays like those in *Criticism and Fiction*, 1891, from which this selection is chosen.

Note. This selection will repay study on account of its sound sense and its pleasant tone. How does Howells avoid excessive earnestness in this little attack? Would he have been more effective, or less, if he had really gone after these unskillful story-writers with all his might? Why? Can you think of any examples of stories like those of which Howells makes fun? Just what — in the language of rhetoric — is it that he objects to? Read one of Howells's own stories (such as *A Modern Instance* or *The Kentons*) and see how successfully he avoids these faults.

Note the skill and urbanity with which Howells avoids personalities (not mentioning, except in praise, a single individual author or story), while at the same time he completely escapes the danger of vagueness.

BIOGRAPHY

" When all's said, the art of the biographer is the art of the dramatist. He has a story to tell and a portrait to paint. If the story is to grip, it must have its climax in the right place, its drama artistically presented. If the portrait is to live, it must be painted in shadows and high-lights; the many-coloured mantle of life must be shown in true perspective; hidden motives must be revealed, the mainsprings of action brought to light, the soul of man exposed to view."

This passage from Hesketh Pearson's *Modern Men and Mummers* admirably sums up the art of biography. The earlier biographers usually gave the chronicle of a man's life, a record of all the events, external facts, and dates in chronological order. There was no selection of the significant, no subordination of the trivial to the important. Often the man's own personality, that essence of individuality which made him an

ego different from all other men, was lost sight of in a multitude of circumstances. Yet it is this personality which interests us in a man, and which should be the unifying principle in a biography of him. The man himself creates the unity.

It is for the writer to discern this unity, this personality, and make his readers understand it. To this end he employs the artistic methods of selection and emphasis. Out of the great mass of events, facts, deeds, and sayings he chooses, arranges, enforces the vital, the revealing. Thus he makes a work of art. This is the way in which Lytton Strachey produced that brilliant masterpiece *Queen Victoria*, which recently surprised and delighted the world. It was hailed as a new and original type of biography : indeed, some called it the greatest piece of historical biography in the English language. Mr. Strachey himself, however, has remarked that in Dr. Johnson's *Lives of the Poets* there is a foretaste of his own artistry.

The three elements which are woven into the texture of good biography are (1) the descriptive, (2) the narrative, and (3) the analytic.

1. The physical appearance of a person, his features and expression, his build and bearing, gestures, mannerisms, and dress — all these are valuable factors in giving the impression of individuality. Elaborate description is not required : often a few swift, graphic strokes will make a person live before the eye. An example of the descriptive element occurs in *Queen Victoria* (p. 151) — the picture of the young Queen at an impressive moment of her life. For other examples of descriptions of people see pages 284–305, particularly *Tennyson* (p. 284), *Webster* (p. 285), *Two Portraits by Raeburn* (p. 286), and the figure of Napoleon on page 300.

2. The narrative element means something more than the account of a man's career in chronological order. It means, in general, telling the story of his life in such a way as to hold the interest, with attention to the interplay of character and circumstance, and emphasis on significant events. More specifically, it includes incidents and anecdotes which bring out traits of character, and bits of talk which show a man's humor or wisdom or manner of speech. The narrative element is illustrated by *John Gilley* (p. 145) and *Queen Victoria* (p. 150). See also the incidents and adventures on pages 337–347. Being autobiographic, these reveal various characteristics of the writers, notably the selection by Roosevelt (p. 345).

3. The function of the analytic element is to discover the clue to a man's career, to decipher the heart of his mystery. Human character is complex, a mixture of diverse and sometimes warring traits. Yet the

success or failure of a person can often be explained by his strongest or weakest trait. The analysis of his character and life to find out the mainspring of action, the ruling passion, or the dominant quality is thus of the greatest help: it simplifies and explains what might otherwise be confusing and obscure. For examples of the analytic element see *Sir William Temple* (p. 152), *Theodore Roosevelt* (p. 155), and *Abraham Lincoln* (p. 165).

C. W. ELIOT: JOHN GILLEY (Page 145)

Biography. Charles William Eliot (1834–   ) was for forty years (1869–1909) President of Harvard University. During that period he probably exerted a greater influence than anyone else upon American education. Besides many addresses and reports, President Eliot's works include *John Gilley*, 1904; *Five American Contributions to Civilization*, 1898; *Educational Reform*, 1898; and *The Durable Satisfactions of Life*, 1910. His interests and writings have kept pace with the affairs of the whole world, and few other American writers, if any, possess his information, style, and influence.

Note. This selection illustrates the use of the narrative element in biography; incidents are recounted that show character. Make a list of all the traits of John Gilley which you gather from these incidents. What are the characteristics of this narrative style? Note the restrained eloquence of the final paragraph. Contrast the force and pregnancy of the ending with the ordinary perfunctory eulogy. This is the best kind of subject for students who are writing biography: it is well to take men who are not famous, but who ought to be.

STRACHEY: QUEEN VICTORIA (Page 150)

Biography. (Giles) Lytton Strachey (1880–   ), English essayist and biographer. He comes of an intellectual and literary family; St. Loe Strachey, the editor of the London *Spectator*, is his cousin. Since graduating from Trinity College, Cambridge, he has devoted his time to the studies which have led to his books: *Landmarks in French Literature*, 1912; *Eminent Victorians*, 1918; *Queen Victoria*, 1921; *Books and Characters*, 1922. The extraordinary success of *Queen Victoria* was due to the magic touch which revivified the great figures of the Victorian age. Both English and American critics hailed it as a masterpiece of the first rank and agreed that it is one of the surpassingly beautiful prose achievements of our time. An interesting chapter on this author in Hesketh Pearson's *Modern Men and Mummers* ends thus: "One can only compare him with himself. He is the Strachey of biographers."

Note. This selection illustrates that dramatic quality which makes this biography of Victoria as entertaining as a novel. Here is a scene portrayed with all the resources of the narrator's art — pictorial vividness, sense of climax, emotional effect. Note how the marking of the hours produces a feeling of excitement. A momentous day in history is really made to seem momentous. As we reach the great scene at the end, note the means by which it is visualized. Our point of view is that of the assembled lords: we see with them the doors open and the girl queen enter — it is all pure drama. Strachey selects this impressive moment — a moment of action — to describe Victoria's face and bearing, and the portrait in this setting becomes extraordinarily brilliant and eloquent. Note the appropriateness of the words to indicate the qualities of Victoria — " composure," " clarity," " dignity." Observe also the fine rhythm of the last part of the last sentence, and the remarkable emphasis produced by reserving until the very end the word " alone."

MACAULAY : SIR WILLIAM TEMPLE (PAGE 152)

Biography. Thomas Babington Macaulay (1800–1859), English historian and essayist, became famous for his brilliant historical and critical articles in the *Edinburgh Review*, beginning as early as 1825. After having been a member of Parliament, holder of various minor offices in the home government, and a member of the Supreme Council of India, he retired from political life in 1847 and devoted himself to his celebrated *History of England from the Accession of James II* (5 vols., 1849–1861), which immediately gained and still keeps a place among the greatest histories of all time. Not only Macaulay's essays and his *History*, but his *Lays of Ancient Rome*, 1842, and some of his speeches are still valuable. In 1857 he became Baron Macaulay of Rothley.

His essays are of uneven merit. Although written rapidly and often at a distance from libraries, they generally show an almost perfect command of their author's very wide reading, and they can hardly be matched for clearness and vigor of style. Some of the best known are those on Clive, Warren Hastings, Addison, Sir William Temple, Lord Chatham, Madame d'Arblay, Bacon, Milton, and Dr. Johnson.

Note. This selection illustrates the use of the analytical element in biography, resulting in a kind of unity that comes not merely because only one person is being written about, but because in portraying that person one trait of character is explained, illustrated, and amplified. Macaulay was peculiarly fitted to achieve such unified portraiture, for to vast reading he united very strong likes and dislikes about his characters and a perfect willingness to omit details which might interfere with a brilliant single effect.

Among the technical excellences to be watched for are the topic-sentence, the cumulative effect of parallelism, admirable transitions and cadences, and the biting phrase in the final sentence which sums up Macaulay's view of Sir William Temple.

LODGE: THEODORE ROOSEVELT (Page 155)

Biography. Henry Cabot Lodge (1850–   ), American senator and writer. Senator Lodge's long and conspicuous career in politics has not prevented him from writing not only essays and orations, but larger works as well in the field of American history and politics. Such titles as his *Life of Alexander Hamilton*, 1882 ; *Short History of the English Colonies in America*, 1881 ; *Democracy of the Constitution and Other Essays*, 1915, give an idea of Mr. Lodge's varied interests.

Senator Lodge's oration on President Roosevelt is not merely the work of an accomplished historian and writer: Lodge and Roosevelt were intimate friends and in 1895 they wrote together *Hero Tales from American History*.

Note. The address from which this extract is taken consists of two parts, — an account of Roosevelt's life, and an analysis of his chief qualities. This selection is from the analytical part of the address, and that fact explains the absence of dates and external events. The selection is to be judged as a spoken address, by a friend of many years, made to a political assembly which was in an unusually appreciative and unpartisan mood.

The oration is warmed by evident admiration of Roosevelt, and yet free from exaggeration and blind worship. The former quality appears in the very nature of the judgments, of course, and also in the restrained but genuine eloquence of the periods ; the latter, in the frank admission of Roosevelt's mistakes, and still more in the emphasis upon the practical, homely, and natural elements in his career.

ROOSEVELT: ABRAHAM LINCOLN (Page 165)

Biography. See page 458.

Note. This biographical portrait takes its form and expression from the occasion which brought it forth. This occasion was the commemoration of the one hundredth anniversary of Lincoln's birth, held at his birthplace in Hodgenville, Kentucky, February 12, 1909. President Roosevelt did not desire to give a formal analysis of Lincoln's character, but to dwell upon those traits of Lincoln which may be regarded as his legacy to the Americans of our time. Consequently after a rapid survey of many qualities, he selects a few for special and emphatic treatment. Note the skill with which, in that rapid survey, he introduces details of physical appearance so that the lineaments of Lincoln's face and figure come before our eyes. Pick out those touches which contribute to this effect. What are the qualities of style which impress you? What characteristics of his own does Roosevelt reveal while he is discussing Lincoln's? What methods are used to give emphasis to the sentences? Select some of the finest examples of parallel structure.

ARGUMENT [1]

Since the aim of Argument is to make other people accept, and act in accordance with, our own view of the facts, we have to make a greater effort than in the case of Exposition to reach their minds. In our endeavor to convince and persuade, we bring to bear all the power we can extract from the principles of composition.

Unity. Unity is so vital that if we neglect it we run the danger of failure. The most common cry in argument and debate is " Keep to the point! " Now, to keep to the point it is necessary to steer a straight course through the multitude of facts and the complexities of reasoning which beset us. The first thing to do is to limit the field by phrasing the question in a specific and exact way. Next should follow a thorough analysis of the question in order to find out what it means and what are the main issues which lie at the heart of it. The steps of analysis are (1) the origin of the question; (2) the history of the question; (3) the definition of terms; (4) the exclusion of admitted matter; (5) the conflicting contentions of the affirmative and the negative; and (6) the main issues. It is only in very formal arguments that all these steps appear; indeed, it is customary for practical writers and speakers who deal with current problems to set forth the smallest number necessary to a clear understanding, as in *America's Railway Fallacy* (p. 198) and *The Open Shop* (p. 212). Of the steps of an analysis the two which are indispensable in order to secure Unity are the definition of terms and the main issues. Once we have defined the terms, we must limit ourselves to those definitions; once we have determined precisely the main issues, we must concentrate our arguments upon them. The errors which should be guarded against are ambiguity in defining terms, ignoring the question, and arguing beside the point. The best practical device to insure Unity is the Brief (see page 220). Such an outline by means of its definite form will guide us in analyzing the question and will show us what material helps to prove our case and what has nothing to do with it.

Coherence. The order of procedure in Argument is, by the very nature of the task, almost invariable: analysis, proof, conclusion. The process of finding the main issues has been explained above. The main issues themselves become a simple chart by which to arrange the proof. Consequently in constructing the brief, there will be as many main headings in the body of proof (or brief proper) as there are main issues. If there happen to be four main issues (as on page 228), there will be four main headings in the brief proper, and no more. These main headings

[1] For other introductory chapters, see Exposition, p. 451; Essay, p. 461; Criticism, p. 464; Biography, p. 468; Description, p. 476; Narration, p. 496.

should be arranged in the same order as the main issues (see pages 228–246). This order depends on the logical relation of the issues, for they form links in a chain of reasoning. Begin with the one which must be proved before any of the others can be taken up, and treat next the one which is most directly based on the first. Note the order of the issues in *America's Railway Fallacy* (p. 198), *The Open Shop* (p. 212), and *Reclamation or Desecration?* (p. 221). If the order of climax is consistent with the logical order, the steady progression up to the strongest issue will be a double gain in Coherence and Emphasis.

The coherent structure which the brief has thus enabled us to shape will become the framework of the written argument. But this framework should not be allowed to obtrude in a clumsy and mechanical way. To prevent this fault use skillful and varied transitions. Observe the transitions in *America's Railway Fallacy* (p. 198) and *The Open Shop*, (p. 212). Another blemish which often disfigures the written argument is the monotonous repetition of the set order of " statement and proof " which is the method of the brief. Break up this frozen order by continual variety in the manner of introducing evidence.

Emphasis. To seize the attention at the beginning and drive home the chief points at the end is the simplest and the most natural method of securing emphatic structure. The sudden attack and the energetic summary are usually to be found in the practical, businesslike arguments on public questions today. Note the beginnings and endings of *Too Much Soft Coal* (p. 195), *America's Railway Fallacy* (p. 198), and *The Open Shop* (p. 212). As was said above, if the logical order permits placing the strongest reasons or evidence last, this arrangement will be all the more emphatic. The force of an argument depends also on vigor of style, concrete evidence, skillful refutation, and persuasion.

GODKIN: THE EXPENDITURE OF RICH MEN (PAGE 180)

Biography. Edwin Lawrence Godkin (1831–1902), American editor, was born in Ireland, came to the United States in 1856, studied and practised law, wrote for various newspapers, and finally, in 1865, established the New York *Nation*, of which he became editor and part owner. His vigor of thought, fearlessness, and admirable style made his essays highly influential. Many of them were later collected in volumes, of which some of the titles are *Problems of Modern Democracy*, 1896; *Reflections and Comments*, 1895; *Unforeseen Tendencies of Democracy*, 1898.

Note. Americans do not readily listen to those who criticize democracy. And Godkin criticized it often and severely. Yet the essential justice of his criticism, combined with real humor and an uncommonly good style, made Godkin exceedingly influential, even if he was never quite popular.

NOTES AND COMMENTS 475

In the present selection the absence of any ugly feeling toward rich men is conspicuous, and to most readers reassuring, since it disposes us to accept his strictures the more readily. We are also favorably impressed by the perfect honesty and straightforwardness of the style. Not a phrase shows any pride in mere ornament, yet every phrase reaches the mark and advances the discussion to a conclusion which seems peculiarly reasonable because of the careful way in which other possibilities have been examined and rejected.

The article might be made the basis for various compositions, — local studies in which Godkin's thesis is either confirmed or disproved; or Godkin's argument brought down to date; or a consideration of anything that may have happened since 1896 (the date of this article) to remove the reproach that rich Americans do not know how to spend money in a dignified, unselfish way.

KEIR: TOO MUCH SOFT COAL (PAGE 195)

Biography. Malcolm Keir (1887–   ), American economist. After teaching at the University of Pennsylvania, he became Professor of Economics at Dartmouth in 1919. He has written *Manufacturing Industries in America*, 1921, and (with E. W. Goodhue) *The Industrial Order of the United States*, 1922.

Note. This article is of particular value to the student on account of its admirable use of evidence. Written originally as an editorial in a newspaper, this article aims to inform the public about the condition of the soft coal industry and to make readers accept the view here given. It is a representative example of informal argument, the practical use of the principles of argument for a practical, everyday purpose. To seize the attention at once, the points to be proved (the special issues) are stated crisply at the beginning. Why is an elaborate and formal introduction omitted? The proof consists of specific facts each expressed so concretely that it holds the attention. Observe the manner in which figures are used to make facts more easily understood. Draw up a brief to show how the evidence supports the main contentions. The absence of references is due to the fact that this article appeared as an editorial.

DUNN: AMERICA'S RAILWAY FALLACY (PAGE 198)

Biography. Samuel Orace Dunn (1877–   ), American editor. After some years of varied editorial experience, he became, in 1908, editor of *The Railway Age Gazette* and its successor, *The Railway Age*. He has written *The American Transportation Question*, 1912; *Government Ownership of Railways*, 1913; *Railway Regulation or Ownership?* 1918.

Note. This argument is notable for organization of material and logical development. Though built on a larger scale than the preceding article, it follows a simple and coherent plan which is stated compactly in the first paragraph. What are the special issues? Find the place where the treatment of each issue begins and note the transitions and the guide-posts. Observe the logical sequence of these main divisions; that is, the way in which the second depends on the first, and the third on the second. Then analyze the internal structure of the divisions, and note the step which each paragraph makes in the development of the division. In this way you will gain an appreciation of the architecture of argument, and you will enjoy practising the skillful arrangement of material in your own arguments. Study also the use of evidence in this article. As regards the style, note the means by which points are made clear and emphatic.

ABBOTT: THE OPEN SHOP (PAGE 212)

Biography. Lyman Abbott (1835–1922), American editor and writer. First a lawyer, then a Congregational minister (1860–1899), he meanwhile became an editor, and was from 1893 onward editor-in-chief of *The Outlook*. His numerous books cover a variety of subjects and include *The Evolution of Christianity*, 1896; *The Theology of an Evolutionist*, 1897; *Christianity and Social Problems*, 1897; *Industrial Problems*, 1905; and *America in the Making*, 1911.

Note. The convincingness of this argument is due to the combination of reasoning and evidence. It contains an excellent example of refutation. The introduction pays more attention to the steps of analysis than one often finds in practical arguments of today in speeches or magazine articles. It will be noticed that in one of those steps, the clash of opinion, the case for the closed shop is stated with unusual fullness and care. Why is this done? The method of narrowing the question to two main issues deserves attention. The argument on the first main issue is peculiar in that the author refutes a decision which supports his side. Why does he do this, and what effect does he thereby produce? Note the force of the skillful transition from the first to the second issue. The whole article is valuable material for exercises in briefing.

DESCRIPTION [1]

In Description, which is a record of sense impressions, the choice of material is quite as important as the technique. That material which gives opportunity for minute observation can be most effectively depicted. It is not limited, as many students would limit it, to melodramatic subjects, such as turbulent thunderstorms or exaggerated sunsets, but it includes a wide range of familiar subjects of everyday life. In technique, too, Description is not usually limited to the expression of a single element, such as color, sound, motion, but it includes nearly all the elements in combination.

[1] For other introductory chapters see Exposition, p. 451; Essay, p. 461; Criticism, p. 464; Biography, p. 468; Argument, p. 473; Narration, p. 496.

Unity. When we apply the principles of composition to pictorial writing, the fact that this application is more subtle than in the case of Exposition does not mean good-bye to structure. Too often the careless or inexperienced writer thinks that vividness of phrase is the chief virtue of Description, and that order, though it may be the first law of Heaven, is not a statute of pictorial writing. It is true that vividness of phrase does arouse the imagination, but, if the structure is unorganized, the effect is comparable to that of the performance of a Symphony Orchestra, if each member plays an independent melody. Unity of effect is as necessary in Description as in the orchestra.

Inasmuch as Description is a representation of nature as it appeals simultaneously to various senses, the task of recording such representation is very difficult. In order that, amid the possible confusion of sensations, we may understand the principle of Unity in its simplest form, we will deal first with the sensation of seeing. The vision of the eye is limited to what is within range; and the faithful record of what we see in front of us at any one time is the simplest form of Unity in Description. This method of securing Unity by excluding extraneous material is called " the point of view."

There are two varieties of the point of view : the physical, which may be stationary or moving; and the mental. An amusing instance of the violation of the stationary point of view is that of the student, who, describing the pit of an abandoned quarry from a brink high above, gave an idea of the depth of the pit by comparing an overturned gravel-car at the bottom to a child's cart, and then added " beside it lay an old shovel with the initials 'J. W.' carved on the handle." How carefully the skillful writer holds his point of view is shown by Irving in *A Stable-Yard on a Rainy Day* (p. 249). Irving so faithfully follows the maxim " Write with your eye on the object," that he pictures not only the objects which are visible from his window, but the appearance of those objects under a certain condition of weather. A writer has not made an accurate transcript of a scene if he has failed to catch the temporal characteristics of light and shade, sun, or rain.

The moving point of view differs from the stationary only in that it is a connected series of stationary points of view. Instead of a single photograph we have the biograph. In this case the blurred image resulting from the confusion of several points of view may be avoided by a careful indication of the transition from one point of view to another. Note how clearly Conrad informs the reader of the changes in the point of view in *A Tropical River* (p. 270).

In the preceding cases the writer looks at his scene from a physical position in time and in place. The term " point of view " is also figura-

tively applied to a mental attitude. The relation of the two is well illustrated by Stevenson's conscious study (p. 261) of the choice of a point
of view from which he is to describe the Water of Leith. This matter
of the attitude toward the subject, so important in analytic writing, is a
valuable method of securing Unity in pictorial writing. For it means
that the subject-matter is constantly but subtly infused with the writer's
personality. In fact, because of this infusion, pictorial writing is a fine
art. Art is not a photograph, but nature seen through a temperament.

Thus far we have considered only a limited field of vision, as viewed
by one personality. Here are two elements of unity: the exclusion of
irrelevant material and the constant personal attitude. Is there another
element inherent in the subject-matter itself? Whenever we consider a
scene, we are impressed with the presence of some predominant trait or
characteristic which makes itself felt through all the subordinate details
which appeal to all our senses. Treasure Island, by virtue of its sad
coloring, its spires of rock, strangely shaped, its surf " foaming and
thundering on the steep beach," impresses us with an indefinable sense
of gloom (p. 251). Heat radiating "in an oily, quivering shimmer,"
shade " dwindled to the breadth of a mere line," " a pale, scorched sky,"
the prolonged drone of insects, a cat dozing complacently in the sun, hens
wallowing " in the baking hot dust," impress us with the sense of intense
heat (p. 253). A summer day may be prevailingly cheerful ; a street may
be prevailingly squalid. This chief trait, inherent in the material itself,
which suffuses its quality throughout the subject is called "dominant
tone." The selection of details which produce this dominant tone is a
vital means of impressing upon a reader the unity of a scene. Through
this technical element of dominant tone a writer may make his descriptive
writing as firm in structure as ever the analytical writer may make his.

Whether we rely chiefly upon the point of view or upon dominant
tone to give unity of effect, we must so end our description that the
salient details shall be summarized. The summary need not be so formal
as in analytic writing, but it may be light and flexible, analogous to the
all-embracing glance which we take before leaving the hilltop. Examples of this are the concluding sentence in *Autumn on Cape Cod*
(p. 306) and in *The House of Usher* (p. 256).

Coherence. The vividness of Description is due to details, but unless
these details are arranged coherently the vividness will be spoiled. To
help the reader form a mental picture we should give him the details in
an orderly sequence so that one by one he can fit them into place. Of
the many varieties of order, choose that which represents the way in
which the details impress themselves on the senses. (1) The order most

commonly used by great writers proceeds from the most striking elements to the less striking. By this means they swiftly produce the chief impression or dominant tone at the beginning, and after sustaining this tone by significant details, echo it at the end. This method is illustrated in *A Stable-Yard on a Rainy Day* (p. 249), *Treasure Island* (p. 251), *The House of Usher* (p. 256), *In the Luxembourg Gardens* (p. 258), *Autumn on Cape Cod* (p. 306), *El Capitan* (p. 263), *Daniel Webster* (p. 285), *Two Portraits by Raeburn* (p. 286), and many other selections. (2) Then there is the order of direction, which may run from near to remote or the reverse, from right to left or the reverse, from top to bottom or the reverse. For instance, in *A Loamshire Landscape* (p. 264) George Eliot describes the view from Hayslope Green by following the order from the horizon to the foreground. In *The Army of France* is another landscape based on the same order (p. 302). Kipling in *The Grand Cañon of the Yellowstone* (p. 262) glances from top to bottom; and Cable, picturing the Café des Exilés (p. 291), leads the eye from the ground to the roof. (3) If the point of view is a moving one, the order naturally follows the progress of the observer. Some examples of this are *A Tropical River* (p. 270), *London* (p. 274), *The Jungle at Night* (p. 322). (4) The order of time is valuable in cases where we are interested in the successive aspects of a scene. In *The Wheat Pit* (p. 278), Norris begins with silence and emptiness, works up to a maximum of clamorous confusion, and ends diminuendo with silence.

Thus the principle of Coherence adapts itself to the purpose, material, and problems of Description, and plays a vital part in producing a successful result.

Emphasis. The two positions which are most emphatic in any kind of composition — the beginning and the end — are of peculiar value in Description, for they give one the first impression and the final effect. Since the chief factors in producing the first impression are the point of view and the dominant tone, the sooner these are indicated, the greater the force. The " topic-sentence," always useful in securing Unity, serves also the purpose of Emphasis. It strikes the note at once, and seizes the attention. For example, see the beginnings of *A Stable-Yard on a Rainy Day* (p. 249), *Noon in the Plaza* (p. 253), *Running Before the Wind* (p. 254), *The House of Usher* (p. 256), *In the Luxembourg Gardens* (p. 258), *London* (p. 274), *The Voice of the Pacific* (p. 310). The end has even greater carrying power, for an apt phrase, a salient detail, a swift summary, an echo of the dominant tone will make a description linger in the memory long after one has stopped reading. Note the endings of *A Stable-Yard on a Rainy Day* (p. 249), *Treasure Island* (p. 251), *The*

House of Usher (p. 256), *In the Luxembourg Gardens* (p. 258), *The River Dart* (p. 266), *Paris* (p. 277), *Autumn on Cape Cod* (p. 306).

The foregoing methods of securing Emphasis are structural, that is, they have to do with composing. But there is another source of Emphasis, namely expression or style — the vivid and specific language, the figures of speech, the form and rhythm of sentences, which combine to produce a graphic impression. The secret of what Carlyle calls " this so intense pictorial power " is the ability to visualize. It is summed up by Conrad thus : " My task which I am trying to achieve is, by the power of the written word, to make you hear, to make you feel — it is, before all, to make you *see*. That — and no more, and it is everything." (Preface to *The Nigger of the "Narcissus."*)

IRVING: A STABLE-YARD ON A RAINY DAY (PAGE 249)

Biography. Washington Irving (1783–1859), American prose writer, author of *The Sketch-Book*, 1819; *The Alhambra*, 1832 ; *Bracebridge Hall*, 1822; *The Life and Voyages of Christopher Columbus*, 1828 ; *Chronicles of the Conquest of Granada*, 1829 ; a voluminous *Life of Washington*, 1855–1859 ; and other works. Irving's history, now almost obsolete except as good prose, shows his romantic inclination ; his essays also are delightful for their romantic and quietly humorous flavor. *Bracebridge Hall* is not as a whole equal to *The Sketch Book* ; but " The Stout Gentleman," from which this selection is an extract, is nearly as good as anything by Irving, although it is of course less well known than " Rip Van Winkle " or " The Legend of Sleepy Hollow."

Note. This description has been placed first because the material is familiar, the method natural, and the technique so simple that everyone will learn the trick of it at once. Irving uses at one and the same time two devices for obtaining Unity, — point of view and dominant tone. He goes to the window — the simplest way of establishing a physical point of view. The picture is now framed in, and consequently he mentions only those details which are visible from his position. (Note that merely the horse's head, not his whole body, is in the picture.) But the view thus framed in has a quality of its own ; everything is drenched with the rain. To impress upon us this dominant tone of wetness, Irving selects those details which contribute to this effect, and pictures them in language so vivid that we chuckle with amusement. Go over the selection and note the surprising number of words which express the idea of wetness. What serves as the topic-sentence ?

The Coherence and Emphasis are also excellent. The idea of rain introduced in the first sentence prepares us for the dominant tone. Each sentence leads to the next. When we come to the view itself, the general impression is quickly sketched in lines 14 and 15, and then our attention is directed to the details. The ending is particularly emphatic, for it is the climax: the fact that the ducks are having a good time is the strongest proof that everything is soaked with water.

STEVENSON: TREASURE ISLAND (Page 251)

Biography. See page 463.

Note. The dominant tone of this description is gloomy foreboding. This is produced by the choice of significant details of color, form, sound, light, physical sensation. Point out these details. Here again the point of view is skillfully maintained. Jim Hawkins, who tells the story, pictures the island as it appeared when he came on deck in the morning after the *Hispaniola* arrived off the coast. Observe how naturally Jim's condition at the moment (ll. 25 ff.) influences his mental attitude. How does this description differ from a photograph of an island? Note particularly the coherent arrangement. From the first swift impression of the whole scene — "grey-colored woods," "the general coloring was uniform and sad" — we proceed to specific things. In what ways is Emphasis secured? See the third paragraph. Study the admirable choice of words throughout.

NORRIS: NOON IN THE PLAZA (Page 253)

Biography. Frank Norris (1870–1902), American novelist. After studying at the University of California and at Harvard, he served as war correspondent in Cuba and South Africa. Later he was a journalist in San Francisco. *The Octopus*, 1901, and *The Pit*, 1903, are parts of a trilogy, never completed, which was to have been an Epic of the Wheat. The reader of Norris carries away a profound impression of scope, fidelity, and power, somewhat undisciplined and preoccupied with the unpleasant.

Note. Intense heat, of course, and the color effects, sounds, and so forth that go with it are the basis of this description. The brilliancy of the lighting and the consistency of the sounds are well worth study. Contrast the bits of animal life here with those in *A Stable-Yard on a Rainy Day*. What do they contribute to the dominant tone?

MASEFIELD: RUNNING BEFORE THE WIND (Page 254)

Biography. John Masefield (1875–   ), English poet and dramatist. His early life was full of adventure. As a boy he ran away to sea and made many voyages as a sailor. He went around the Horn, an experience which he later described in his narrative poem *Dauber*. In 1902 he found himself in America, almost destitute, and lived by doing odd jobs, working on a farm, and tending a bar in a New York saloon. While employed in a carpet factory, he bought a copy of Chaucer for seventy-five cents and was inspired to become a poet. His early poems were of the sea which he knew so well, *Salt-Water Ballads*, 1902. Then followed sea-yarns and sketches, *A Mainsail Haul*, 1905; and *A Tarpaulin Muster*, 1907. He soon displayed an extraordinary ability in writing long narrative poems, memorable for their vitality, realism, and stirring movement: *The Everlasting Mercy*, 1911; *The Widow in the Bye-Street*, 1912; *Dauber*, 1913; *The Daffodil Fields*, 1913; *Reynard the Fox*, 1919; *Right Royal*, 1920; and

King Cole, 1921. Meanwhile he produced several plays, sombre in tone, but impressive on account of their power. Of these the best are *The Tragedy of Nan*, 1909 (a masterpiece of the modern stage); *The Tragedy of Pompey the Great*, 1910; and *The Faithful*, 1915 (a Japanese play). During the World War he served in the Red Cross at Gallipoli and in France. His book *Gallipoli*, 1916, is one of the most vivid productions of the War.

Note. The dominant tone of this description is one which has not appeared in the preceding selections; hence the study of this passage immediately after those will bring out in the most forcible way the real meaning of unity of tone. What is the dominant tone here, and where is it first announced? Pick out the details which most vividly contribute to the effect. What part does weather play in this description? Does the sentence structure help in producing the impression? This passage is an unusually good example of the relation of subject-matter and sentence form and will show you how valuable technique is in enforcing ideas. Note that the words, though simple and untechnical, are used picturesquely. Point out words of sound, color, and motion.

POE: THE HOUSE OF USHER (PAGE 256)

Biography. Edgar Allan Poe (1809–1849), American poet, critic, and writer of tales. After the early death of his father and his mother, he was adopted by a Mr. Allan of Richmond, Virginia. Having spent several years at school in England, Poe successively tried the University of Virginia, Mr. Allan's counting-room, the regular army, and West Point, in no case with more than partial success. Equally brief and unsatisfactory were his engagements with various periodicals later. His unstable career was the result of a very highly strung nature, poverty, craving for stimulants, a weak will, vanity, his wife's illness, and a variety of other circumstances which together made an unbearable burden. After his wife's death in 1847, Poe was more erratic than ever, and his own death two years later occurred, in Baltimore, under tragic and somewhat mysterious circumstances.

Poe's writings have been the subject of much divergent comment. It is true that he lacks humor, is too much concerned with technique, can conceive only a few varieties of situation and character, and is rather given to being morbid and theatrical. On the other hand, both as a critic and as a creative artist Poe served American literature well by his emphasis on sound, rhythm, the single preconceived effect, and other points of workmanship. At his best he is, within his field, an almost unequaled master of mystery and of beauty.

Some of his principal titles are: (Poems) " The Raven," " To Helen," " Israfel," " Lenore," " Anabel Lee," and " The Bells "; (Essays) " Hawthorne's Twice-Told Tales," " The Philosophy of Composition," " The Poetic Principle"; (Tales) " The Gold Bug," " The Cask of Amontillado," " The Fall of the House of Usher," " Ligeia," and " The Pit and the Pendulum."

Note. The dominant tone of this piece is made clear in the first sentence and is unrelieved throughout. Is it real? Is it intended to be? Notice the methodical way in which the impression is summarized by the final sentence. Notice the skill with which Poe employs unusual words — such as "tarn" — and sombre colors — such as "dark," "black," "grey," "ebon blackness" — to emphasize the effect.

LOCKE: IN THE LUXEMBOURG GARDENS (Page 258)

Biography. William John Locke (1863–   ), English novelist. After graduation from St. John's, Cambridge, in 1884, he became an architect, and was secretary of the Royal Institute of British Architects from 1897 to 1907. Meanwhile he pursued the avocation of novel writing, which led to his first success, *The Morals of Marcus Ordeyne*, 1905, and his best book, *The Belovèd Vagabond*, 1906. In these novels he has given appealing portraits of the whimsical, eccentric Bohemians for whom he shows marked affection in many of his stories. Among his other novels are *Where Love Is*, 1903; *Septimus*, 1909; *Simon the Jester*, 1910; *The Glory of Clementina*, 1911; *The Joyous Adventures of Aristide Pujol*, 1912; *Stella Maris*, 1913; *The Wonderful Year*, 1916; *The Mountebank*, 1921.

Note. The gardens of the Luxembourg Palace are situated in the heart of the Latin Quarter of Paris, and are the chief pleasure ground of the students and artists. The Palace itself is the meeting place of the French Senate.

What is the dominant tone of this sketch? Bear in mind that this is only one aspect of the gardens under a particular condition of weather. In this description what effect does the sunlight produce? What color does the author emphasize? Is this color appropriate? One might do a little gallery of sketches of a place under different conditions of light or atmosphere. There is really a great deal of fun in doing this; for it is continually surprising to observe how sunlight changes colors, how shadows and mists, wind and rain, cold and heat, play upon the earth and produce varying pictorial effects.

HAWTHORNE: THE PRISON DOOR (Page 259)

Biography. Nathaniel Hawthorne (1804–1864), American writer of tales and romances. He graduated from Bowdoin College in 1825. His early life is associated with Salem, Massachusetts, and his later life with Concord, although he lived at several other places, both in New England and in Europe, for short periods. His writings include many short tales and sketches, besides the longer romances of which *The Scarlet Letter* (1850), *The House of the Seven Gables* (1851), and *The Marble Faun* (1860) are the best as well as the best known. Hawthorne's sombre beauty of fancy and style and his peculiar remoteness from reality distinguish him from other writers and prevent him from attaining great popularity. His place among the very greatest of American prose writers is, nevertheless, perfectly secure.

Note. Here, again, is a very distinct dominant tone. What is it and by what descriptive details is it obtained? What is the purpose of the rose-bush? Do you approve of Hawthorne's fancy that the weeds before the prison found the soil congenial? In what way may the prison door and the rose-bush be said to represent two forces which struggle against each other in *The Scarlet Letter*? Glance through the pages of Hawthorne's *American Note Books* and observe his interest in descriptive bits which suggest stories.

STEVENSON: THE WATER OF LEITH (PAGE 261)

Biography. See page 463.

Note. The Water of Leith is a little river which winds through the Pentland Hills, skirts the suburbs of Edinburgh, and flows into the North Sea. On its course through the Pentlands it passes by the manse at Colinton, where Stevenson spent much of his boyhood. The water-door (l. 4) is in the garden wall on the brink of the stream. Colored pictures of this spot, the flour-mill (l. 6), and other places in the Pentlands, such as Swanston Cottage, are to be found in *The Hills of Home*, by L. Maclean Watt, Edinburgh, 1913.

This selection illustrates both the physical and the mental point of view. The first twelve lines deal with the place as seen from the physical point of view; the rest of the article is a sympathetic treatment of the mental point of view. Stevenson realizes that to see the Water of Leith as he saw it when a boy, he must put himself into the boy's frame of mind, when "the trees on the steep opposite side " seemed " to climb to heaven," and "the sand by the water-door " seemed " as low as Styx." Stevenson's experience here suggests a good subject. Revisit a place where you used to play in early years, and write a pair of sketches, — as it used to seem, and as it is now. You will be surprised to find how places shrink in size as you grow older.

KIPLING: THE GRAND CAÑON OF THE YELLOWSTONE (PAGE 262)

Biography. Rudyard Kipling (1865–　　), English poet and story writer. Born in India, where his father was professor in the School of Art at Bombay, he was sent to England to be educated at "Westward Ho," the United Service College, Devon. His school days here he has chronicled in *Stalky & Co.*, 1899, in which " Beetle " is the young Kipling. At seventeen (1882) he returned to India, where he spent seven busy years as a newspaper man. During this period he gained that marvellous first-hand knowledge of all phases of life in India which is reflected in his short stories and poems. In 1889 he was sent to the United States to write descriptive letters of travel for his paper (later published as *From Sea to Sea*, 1899). Proceeding to England with many volumes of stories, he soon became the literary hero of the hour. Except for a four years' residence in America and many voyages to South Africa, Australia, etc., he has lived in England ever since.

As James Whitcomb Riley said of him, " He is a regular literary blotting-pad, soaking up everything on the face of the earth." He has laid the scenes of his stories in India, Africa, the United States, the Newfoundland Banks, London, and the English countryside. He has written soldier stories, children's tales, beast fables, sailor yarns, sporting tales, stories of India, society dialogues, and fairy myths.

Generally speaking, Kipling is the product of an empire rather than of an island kingdom. He has always been the champion of imperialism, discipline, law, and order. His voice became " the war-drum of the white man round the world." The accuracy of his technical knowledge is amazing. Although the reporter in him now and then jostles the man of letters, and his virility sometimes descends into coarseness, the qualities of his style are those that spring from his masculine temperament and attitude to life : force, vitality, vividness, precision, realism.

Kipling's most characteristic poetry occurs in *Ballads and Barrack-Room Ballads*, 1892 ; *The Seven Seas*, 1896 ; *The Five Nations*, 1903. Among the most famous of his short stories are " The Man Who Would Be King " (in *Under the Deodars*, 1888) ; " Without Benefit of Clergy," " The Incarnation of Krishna Mulvaney," " The Man Who Was " (all in *Life's Handicap*, 1891) ; " The Story of Muhammad Din " (in *Plain Tales from the Hills*, 1888) ; " The Brushwood Boy " and " William the Conqueror " (in *The Day's Work*, 1898) ; and the tales in *The Jungle Book*, 1894, and *The Second Jungle Book*, 1895. Although Kipling's longer stories are on the whole not his best work, yet *Kim*, 1901, is a masterpiece in both design and execution.

Note. This is a rapid sketch of a tremendous scene. As often happens in a case like this, a more vivid impression can be given by a short description than by an elaborate one, provided the writer selects salient details and groups them in a striking pattern. Here, almost at a stroke, Kipling flashes into our minds the shape, size, and color of the cañon. Taking a definite point of view is of the greatest help. Compare this description with the photograph taken from the same point of view. Discover as many instances as you can of Kipling's fidelity in delineating the shape of things. Note the figure which paints the river — " a finger-wide strip of jade-green." When it comes to color, Kipling has an advantage over the photograph, for by using specific words he can make us see the gorgeousness of the hues. Coherence is secured by following the natural order in which the eye takes in the details.

BURROUGHS: EL CAPITAN (PAGE 263)

Biography. John Burroughs (1837–1921), American naturalist and author. He is the best known among the considerable number of Thoreau's successors. Like Thoreau, he made literature and life, as well as nature, his subjects. His books, the titles of which are particularly fresh and attractive, include *Wake Robin*, 1871 ; *Locusts and Wild Honey*, 1879; *Fresh Fields*, 1884 ; *Signs and Seasons*, 1886 ; *Camping and Tramping with Roosevelt*, 1907 ; and *Time and Change*, 1912.

Note. This sketch is a companion piece to the foregoing. Observe how Burroughs strikes the note of grandeur at the beginning. Point out the details which reënforce this note throughout. Compare this word picture with the photograph. What do you think of the pictorial value of the similes which Burroughs uses?

GEORGE ELIOT: A LOAMSHIRE LANDSCAPE (PAGE 264)

Biography. George Eliot (1819–1880), the pen name of Mary Ann Evans, English novelist. After a quiet girlhood in the Midland counties, commemorated in *The Mill on the Floss*, she began her literary career of translating and reviewing. *Adam Bede*, 1859, established her importance as a novelist. *The Mill on the Floss* followed in 1860, *Silas Marner* in 1861, *Romola* in 1863. Of the later novels, *Middlemarch*, 1872, is the best. Though these books differ in manner, they all reveal her characteristic interest in mental life rather than in external events, in the thought rather than the actions of her characters.

Note. This selection is an example of the more detailed description of landscape. The point of view is that of a traveler arriving at the village green of Hayslope (which is really Ellastone, in Staffordshire, where George Eliot's father once lived). Two views are given: at first the immediate view of the green and church, and later the distant view to the northwest. The transition between them consists of a general survey of typical Loamshire scenery. The coherence of the distant view, which begins on page 264, line 27, deserves special attention. The order is from the remote to the near, from the masses of hill against the horizon to the foreground. How is this method carried out in detail? This is a very useful order for descriptions of extensive views. What details of color do you find?

PHILLPOTTS: THE RIVER DART (PAGE 266)

Biography. Eden Phillpotts (1862–   ), English novelist. Born in India, the son of an army officer, he was educated in Plymouth, England. He studied acting and art before he chose literature as his profession; but not forgetting these early interests, he still writes plays and enjoys sketching. Selecting as the locality of his novels Devonshire, where he now resides, he has written a vast "Comédie Humaine" of Dartmoor, in which he has portrayed the influence of that wild and primitive region upon human lives. His most powerful novels are *Children of the Mist*, 1898; *The River*, 1902; *The Secret Woman*, 1905; *The Whirlwind*, 1907; *The Mother*, 1908; *The Thief of Virtue*, 1910; *The Beacon*, 1911. More recently he has written a series of novels dealing with various local industries, among them being *Brunel's Tower*, 1915 (Devon potteries); *Old Delabole*, 1915 (Cornish slate quarries); *The Green Alleys*, 1916 (Kentish hop-gardens); *The Nursery*, 1917 (Essex oyster fisheries and nurseries). Other notable books are *The Human Boy*, 1899 (stories of school life), and *My Devon Year*, 1903 (sketches of Devonshire scenery).

Note. This passage is the opening of the novel *The River*, which tells a dramatic story of how the River Dart affects the lives of men and women who dwell along its banks. The Dart gives its name to the vast, rugged tract through which it flows — Dartmoor, and to the port where it empties into the English Channel — Dartmouth.

The landscapes of Phillpotts are famous for their keenness of observation. In a letter accompanying some of his original sketches, he writes thus about his methods:

" The sketches are short-hand notes. Thus I teach myself, and by observing as closely as is necessary to draw, win a few facts sometimes worth using in my own medium of words. My scenery is all painted in the open air and I seldom alter what I have written when I come to the book. If you write from memory alone, you repeat yourself; but by going to nature you cannot, since she never does."

Pick out details in this description which show that Phillpotts went to nature. By going to nature you can acquire the specific touch, that is, the knack of using very specific words to picture the details which you observe closely. Study the choice of words here, the verbs of motion, the color phrases, the figures of speech. What is the effect of the words themselves in creating the dominant tone of the Dart and that of Wistman's Wood? In addition to the pictorial power, note the imaginative beauty of the language, and the rhythm and melody of the sentences.

CONRAD: A TROPICAL RIVER (Page 270)

Biography. Joseph Conrad (1857–   ), English novelist. Born in Poland, his full name is Teodor Jozef Konrad Korzeniowski. Brought up in a country without a coast, where no English was spoken, he had the strange ambition to be an English sailor. At the age of seventeen he first went to sea, shipping from Marseilles. Four years later, in 1878, he landed in England and began to learn the English language. From then until 1894 he made many voyages through the seven seas, as seaman, mate, and finally Master in the Merchant Service. In 1894, on account of a tropical fever, he gave up the sea and settled in England. He then began writing novels and short stories which picture the ocean and the tropics and the tumultuous, passionate deeds of men living under their influence. Although he did not learn English until he was twenty, he is one of the greatest living masters of English prose.

Conrad's chief novels are *Almayer's Folly*, 1895; *The Nigger of the "Narcissus,"* 1897; *Lord Jim*, 1900; *Romance*, 1903; *Nostromo*, 1904; *Chance*, 1914; *Victory*, 1915; *The Arrow of Gold*, 1919. Among his shorter narratives, *Tales of Unrest*, 1898, contains " The Lagoon," the first short story Conrad ever wrote. *Youth*, 1902, contains the story of that name — his most romantic tale. *Typhoon*, 1903, has been called " the most prodigious description of a storm in literature." *The Mirror of the Sea*, 1906, is an eloquent series of memories and impressions.

Note. The vividness of this tropical scene is characteristic of Conrad. Here the point of view is a moving one. Note the way in which the author carefully marks the transitions as the canoe proceeds from the river to the creek, from the creek to the lagoon. The vocabulary will well repay attentive study: it is rich in words of motion, light, and color. What a powerful expression is " darkness oozed," page 271, line 33. A good exercise would be to read the description of darkness on page 271, and then to write a description of darkness, known by personal experience. Compare this extract with another picture of the tropics, *The Jungle at Night*, by Kipling, p. 322.

DAWSON: THE LITTLE HOUSE (Page 273)

Biography. Coningsby Dawson (1883–), English writer. After graduating from Merton College, Oxford, he came to America, where he began literary work by contributing to American magazines, 1905–1910. In the World War he served with the Canadian Expeditionary Forces as a Lieutenant, Field Artillery, and while on active service wrote a number of war books. During convalescence from wounds, he lectured widely in the United States, 1918, and again in 1919. Among his books are *The Garden Without Walls*, 1913; *Khaki Courage*, 1917; *Out to Win*, 1918; *The Glory of the Trenches*, 1918; *Living Bayonets*, 1919; *The Test of Scarlet*, 1919; *The Little House*, 1920; *It Might Have Happened to You*, 1921.

Note. This selection comes from *The Little House*, a charming story which is told by the house itself. What are the advantages of this ingenious point of view? Is it maintained effectively? Descriptions of houses are difficult to do, for it is often hard for the amateur to escape giving a dry catalogue of architectural details. Observe in this case what significant features are chosen, and how they help us to visualize this type of house. Try this method with buildings or streets with which you are familiar.

SYMONS: LONDON (Page 274)

Biography. Arthur Symons (1865–), English poet and critic. An artist in temperament and an admirer of modern French literature, he has written many brilliant essays on the drama, music, literature, and art. Among his books are *London Nights*, 1895; *The Symbolist Movement in Literature*, 1899; *Collected Poems*, 1901; *Plays, Acting, and Music*, 1903; *Cities*, 1903; *Spiritual Adventures*, 1905; *Studies in Seven Arts*, 1906; *The Romantic Movement in English Poetry*, 1909; *Cities and Sea Coasts and Islands*, 1918.

Note. This portrait of a city is an admirable model for several reasons. It presents a characteristic aspect of London, and this gives an immediate impression of the individual flavor which distinguishes this from other cities. It paints the atmosphere of London in language both rich and delicate. It is composed with the greatest skill, and in the process of composing, the author has made effective use of those two fundamental

devices, dominant tone and point of view. Observe that the unity of tone
is kept throughout even though there are several different vistas in the
city. Point out the sentences or phrases which establish and carry on the
tone. Note the ease with which Mr. Symons takes us to the various points
of view, his emphasis on the effect produced by the hour and the weather,
and his management of the details in each of these pictures. Study the
choice of words, particularly the words of color. What do you think of the
way in which these different pictures have been organized into a complete
whole? In connection with this description it is interesting to read the
famous "nocturne" by Whistler:

"And when the evening mist clothes the riverside with poetry, as with
a veil, and the poor buildings lose themselves in the dim sky, and the tall
chimneys become campanili, and the warehouses are palaces in the night,
and the whole city hangs in the heavens, and fairy-land is before us —
then the wayfarer hastens home; the working man and the cultured one,
the wise man and the one of pleasure, cease to understand, as they have
ceased to see; and Nature, who, for once, has sung in tune, sings her
exquisite song to the artist alone, her son and her master — her son in
that he loves her, her master in that he knows her" (*Ten o'Clock*, a lecture
delivered in London in 1885).

GIBBS: PARIS (PAGE 277)

Biography. Sir Philip (Armand Hamilton) Gibbs (1877–   ), the most
famous war correspondent of the World War. He entered journalism in
1902, and acted successively as literary editor of the *London Daily Mail*,
Daily Chronicle, and *Tribune*. His novel *The Street of Adventure*, 1909,
tells of his ten years' experience in Fleet Street (the newspaper centre).
Interested also in history, he published *Founders of the Empire* and *Men
and Women of the French Revolution*, 1906. With this admirable training as
a writer, he was sent out as correspondent with the Bulgarian Army in the
first Balkan War, 1912. On the outbreak of the World War in 1914, he was
given a roving commission to report events on the French and Belgian
fronts. From 1915–1918 he was officially attached to the British Army in the
Field. Few saw as much of the war as he did. Day after day he wrote those
brilliant dispatches which portrayed the struggling men with a vividness,
a tenderness, and a human sympathy unsurpassed by others. For this
service he was knighted, 1920. These dispatches were collected in a series
of books: *The Soul of the War*, 1915; *The Battles of the Somme*, 1917;
From Bapaume to Passchendaele, 1918; and *Open Warfare: The Way to
Victory*, 1919. These were followed by *Now It Can Be Told*, 1920, a tremendous book about the realities of war. He has been editor of the English
Review of Reviews since 1921. In 1923 appeared *The Middle of the Road*,
a novel picturing the present state of Europe.

Note. This description of a city scene is an impression true to the time,
the place, the weather, and, especially important in this case, the emotion

of the moment. It is a glimpse of Paris after the first Battle of the Marne, September 6–9, 1914, when the invading German Army was turned back by Marshal Joffre. The sense of relief at the saving of Paris and civilization, combined with the brilliant light of this September morning, produced in the author an exaltation which expressed itself in this glowing description. Note the pictorial words which create the dominant tone. Study the arrangement, the crescendo of joy, rising to the eloquent climax — a rhapsody which stirs every heart. What technical device in sentence structure is used to keep this last sentence on the wing? Write a description of some city or region of which you are very fond.

NORRIS: THE WHEAT PIT (PAGE 278)

Biography. See page 481.

Note. What peculiarities are to be noted in the structure? Note, for instance, the crescendo to the climax and the diminuendo to the end. This is a very good example of sympathetic observation of details. Very effective is the final sentence on page 280, which sums up and merges into one note all the sounds of the Pit.

CARLYLE: PORTRAITS OF TENNYSON AND WEBSTER (PAGE 284)

Biography. Thomas Carlyle (1795–1881), English essayist and historian. The son of a poor Scottish stone mason (whose memory he has honored in his *Reminiscences*), Carlyle's early life was made stern by poverty, and his entire career is more or less overcast by bitterness and gloom, much of it of his own making. He was dyspeptic and nervous, made friends charily, and was on the whole a pessimist, though with occasional splendid flashes of defiant optimism. His uncouth and powerful style is partly the result of much reading in German literature, in the introduction of which Carlyle was a pioneer. His *Sartor Resartus*, 1835, and *The French Revolution*, 1837, indicated that he was a philosopher and historian of unusual quality, and his *Cromwell*, 1845; *Frederick the Great*, 1858–1865; *Past and Present*, 1843; and *Life of Sterling*, 1851, are only a few of the great events in a long and distinguished career. Carlyle disagreed with nearly all of the causes and leaders of his own day and was more likely to find in the past than in the present his examples of obedience, masterful leadership, hard work, silence, and reverence, which were the principal refrains in his strangely powerful preaching.

Note. These famous portraits, though rapidly struck off by Carlyle in some of his letters, are extraordinarily graphic and true to life, as comparison with the accompanying pictures will show. His method in describing people is often to jot down phrases rather than to make complete sentences. The strokes seem to tell better that way, and for quick, vivid studies the method is to be commended. What is the dominant tone of each portrait, and what details help to enforce it? Note that the most striking details come first. In the case of *Webster*, what particular effect is produced by the large words?

STEVENSON: TWO PORTRAITS BY RAEBURN (PAGE 286)

Biography. See page 463.

Note. In these extracts we are two removes from reality, since we have descriptions of the portraits of the men, yet the effect is that of real life. The secret is partly a matter of method and diction, partly a matter of appreciation of character. The reproductions of Raeburn's portraits make us realize the problem that confronted Stevenson. His method here is to give the chief impression first and then fill in details. Note, in the second sentence, how rapidly he sketches the full-length figure of Admiral Duncan. Next, and most naturally, he pictures the face. What is the order in the second description? The diction throughout is peculiarly fresh and richly flavored. One figure of speech deserves special attention, p. 287, ll. 8–10. What is its pictorial value? What is the force of each word? Pick out the details in both descriptions which suggest character.

286 1 Duncan: Adam Duncan, first Viscount Camperdown (1731–1804). A British admiral who gained the victory of Camperdown over the Dutch fleet, October 11, 1797. For an entertaining account of his character and his battles, see Stevenson's essay "The English Admirals" in *Virginibus Puerisque*.

287 2 Robert M'Queen: a brutal Scottish judge (1722–1799). He is the original of the hanging judge in *Weir of Hermiston*.

THACKERAY: BEATRIX ESMOND (PAGE 288)

Biography. William Makepeace Thackeray (1811–1863), English novelist. Born in India, and educated in England at Charterhouse and Trinity College, Cambridge. He went to Paris with the object of studying art, but later returned to London and began contributing humorous essays and sketches to *Punch* and other periodicals. Of his best-known novels, *Vanity Fair* appeared between 1846–1848; *Pendennis*, 1850; *Henry Esmond*, 1852; *The Newcomes*, 1854; *The Virginians*, 1859. *Henry Esmond* is Thackeray's most ambitious attempt to recall a past age, but it resembles his other novels in its shrewd satire combined with an underlying kindliness of spirit.

Note. Beatrix Esmond coming down the stairs is a famous scene in Thackeray's writings which one always remembers. What makes it memorable is not only the picturesque situation, but also the fine rhythm of certain phrases, — notably on page 288, line 21 ff. Do all the details in this description picture Beatrix as she appeared on this occasion? Should they?

STEVENSON: A PORTRAIT (PAGE 290)

Biography. See page 463.

Note. This is an illustration of Description in the service of **Narration**. The man who appears at the door in answer to Villon's knock is pictured chronologically. When the door is first opened, Villon sees only the man's physical stature. Then, as he looks more closely, the details of the head, face, etc., follow. Notice how effectively the open door frames the picture and the hand-lamp lights it. The total impression is summed up in the last sentence. Meanwhile the story is moving, for it is necessary that the door should open and that Villon should be admitted by this man.

CABLE: CAFÉ DES EXILÉS (PAGE 291)

Biography. George Washington Cable (1844–   ), American novelist. Born in New Orleans, he served in the 4th Mississippi Cavalry in the Civil War. After the war he was for some fifteen years a reporter on a New Orleans paper. *Old Creole Days*, 1879, established him, at a time when local studies in fiction were much in vogue, as the interpreter of the Creoles of Louisiana. He has also written *The Grandissimes*, 1880; *Madame Delphine*, 1881; *Dr. Sevier*, 1885; and *Bonaventure*, 1888. The founding in 1887 of the Northampton People's Institute and the publication of *The Negro Question*, 1890, and *John March, Southerner*, 1894, suggest his later interests.

Note. In this selection Cable pictures a group of characters, and in a very natural manner shows them assembled in their own resort, the Café des Exilés. Thus we are enabled to see them in characteristic attitudes. Find instances that are particularly graphic. Observe that Cable, instead of giving an elaborate description of each man, chooses a few striking details. Pick out some of these that specially please you. Try a description of a group of people, using the same methods.

We should understand that this passage is the opening of a story, and consequently the charming account of the old Café comes first. What is the order of details here? What device is used to link the paragraphs together on pages 291–292?

STEVENSON: VILLON AND HIS CREW (PAGE 294)

Biography. See page 463.

Note. This group of characters is described at a time and place appropriate to the plot of the story "A Lodging for the Night," of which this passage is the beginning. Stevenson's method of portraying Villon and his vagabond companions in their den one winter's night has a dramatic quality. Note their picturesque grouping and their play of gesture. Observe how vividly they are individualized, and yet they all have the flavor of rascality. Do you see how Stevenson accomplishes this result? What are the most telling details here?

The structure of the whole passage is of the finest workmanship. Study the masterly coherence; both the strategy and the tactics of coherence are illustrated in this brilliant series of paragraphs.

François Villon (1431–1484), the French vagabond and poet, so appealed to Stevenson that he also wrote an essay on him in *Familiar Studies of Men and Books*.

HUTCHINSON: THE FARGUS FAMILY (Page 297)

Biography. Arthur Stuart Menteth Hutchinson (1879–   ), English novelist. Born in India, the son of Lieutenant-General H. D. Hutchinson, who has written several books on famous battles, he abandoned the study of medicine to take up writing. He became editor of the *Daily Graphic*, 1912–1916. During the World War he served as captain in the Royal Engineers. His novels are few but distinguished: *Once Aboard the Lugger*, 1908; *The Happy Warrior*, 1912; *The Clean Heart*, 1914; *If Winter Comes*, 1921; *This Freedom*, 1922. The extraordinary success of *If Winter Comes* brings up a number of interesting literary problems. What do you think about the technique of the book, the method of telling the story, the characterization, the management of the climax?

Note. This selection is the portrait of a family, considered not merely as a set of individuals, but as a single group, animated by its own spirit, and displaying its own habits and customs. What an effect of vitality the author produces by showing the family in moments of action! Are these moments well chosen for the purpose? Point out the specific touches which you think most valuable. Do a portrait of a family you know.

CARRYL: THE ARMY OF FRANCE (Page 300)

Biography. Guy Wetmore Carryl (1873–1904), American writer. After graduating from Columbia in 1895, he became an editor of *Munsey's Magazine*, and foreign correspondent for *Harper's Weekly* and *Collier's Weekly*. He published several books of humorous verse, among them *Mother Goose for Grown-Ups*, 1900, and *Grimm Tales Made Gay*, 1902. His stories in prose, particularly *Zut and Other Parisians*, 1903, take high rank for charm of style.

Note. This is a superb description of a great military spectacle. The portrait of the officer in the second paragraph (p. 300) is remarkable in that, though his name is not given, we all recognize him at once. What is the secret of this? In the account of the grand review note the effect produced by details of color, sound, and motion. Here the author paints a great array of different uniforms with a touch so accurate and specific that we share his own delight in the magnificent pageant of military glory. What a contrast with our day when soldiers are obliged to disguise themselves in the colors of the earth! The sentence structure plays a very important part in creating the thrill we feel. Study the sentences (especially on pages 304–305) and try to discover by what means they stir our emotions.

THOREAU: AUTUMN ON CAPE COD (Page 306)

Biography. Henry David Thoreau (1817–1862), American philosopher, naturalist, and writer. Except for a few short journeys (the results of which appear in *The Maine Woods*, 1864; *Cape Cod*, 1865; and *A Yankee in Canada*, 1866), he spent his whole life in Concord, Massachusetts. *Walden*, 1854, is the account of his life at Walden Pond, near Concord, and is probably his best book. Thoreau was much influenced by Emerson, but is no mere satellite and has been steadily gaining in importance since his death. At his best his thought is as valuable as Emerson's and his style is better.

Note. The fundamental metaphor — in this instance a rug — is highly useful. Note that Thoreau not only has a very keen eye for form and for shades of color, but that the naturalist in him insists on naming trees and bushes. What he says about the three shades of green (p. 306, ll. 16 ff.) is minutely true and very effective.

RUSKIN: LIGHT ON THE CAMPAGNA (Page 308)

Biography. See page 460.

Note. This glowing description is an example of Ruskin's wonderful eye for color and his mastery over pictorial language. In what sentence does he express the dominant tone of the scene? Pick out the details of color which are most vivid to you. What figures of speech seem most happy?

STEVENSON: THE VOICE OF THE PACIFIC (Page 310)

Biography. See page 463.

Note. In this description of sound, note the great variety of words which imitate the voice of the ocean. The English language is particularly rich in all sorts of onomatopoetic words. Consider, too, the effect of the movement and rhythm of the sentences, and point out those that specially please your ear.

S. E. WHITE: NIGHT SOUNDS IN THE FOREST (Page 311)

Biography. Stewart Edward White (1873–   ), American author. Born in Michigan, he spent his boyhood in the woods and among the rivermen, and became familiar with the picturesque activity of the lumber camps, and the life of the old ranchers in California. His first articles were about birds. While in college he spent his summer vacations cruising on the Great Lakes. After graduating from the University of Michigan in

1895, he went out to the Black Hills of Dakota in the height of a rush for gold. The knowledge gained in his varied experiences he has woven into many novels and out-door books which portray and interpret the West. Notable among them are *The Claim Jumpers*, 1901; *The Westerners*, 1901; *The Blazed Trail*, 1902; *The Forest*, 1903; *The Silent Places*, 1904; *The Mountains*, 1904; *Arizona Nights*, 1907; *The Riverman*, 1908. He has also written a series of novels depicting successive eras in California history: *The Grey Dawn*, 1915; *The Rose Dawn*, 1920. He has made two exploring expeditions in Africa. In the World War he served as Major in the 144th Field Artillery, 1917–1918.

Note. This extract is part of the essay entitled "On Lying Awake at Night" in *The Forest*. Under the circumstances one's attention is given chiefly to sounds. Pick out those words and phrases which produce the effect of the sounds described. Among things to note are the careful balance in the first sentence of the sixth paragraph (p. 313), the nice distinction between "silence" and "stillness" in the second sentence of the seventh paragraph (p. 313), the italicized words imitating sounds (p. 313), and the description of the white-throated sparrow's song (p. 313, ll. 27 ff.). As regards structure, observe the graceful transitions between paragraphs. Try recording the sounds you hear while lying awake at night.

KIPLING: THE RIDE OF LITTLE TOOMAI (Page 314)

Biography. See page 484.

Note. This selection and the next three show how various kinds of sense impressions may be combined to produce vivid effects of reality. In such cases the author naturally adopts the point of view of the person experiencing the sensations. In this passage the chief element is motion. What other sensations are introduced? When the story was first published, the *Athenaeum* called the account of this ride "simply stupendous." What is the secret of Kipling's success here? Note the specific verbs, and comment on the force of the figures of speech. Observe that Kipling's words are usually short and prevailingly Saxon.

RIDEOUT: SWIMMING THE WHIRLPOOL (Page 316)

Biography. Henry Milner Rideout (1877–   ), American novelist, has written not only *Beached Keels*, 1906, from which this selection is taken, but several other books — such as *Dragon's Blood*, 1909, *Tin Cowrie Dass*, 1918, and *The Foot-Path Way*, 1920 — their scenes ranging from Maine to India, their style always most carefully considered, and their descriptions remarkably vivid.

Note. Note the ingenious (and inevitable) point of view and study the ways in which it is held. No one, the reader feels, could do this description who had not swum much in these waters. Compare Rideout's whirlpool with Poe's in "A Descent into the Maelström."

KIPLING: THE TIME OF NEW TALK (PAGE 320)

Biography. See page 484.

Note. This description of the coming of spring in the Jungle is one of the most famous passages in Kipling. Pick out those details which make a particularly strong appeal to the senses. Read the second paragraph aloud several times to enjoy the melody of the sentences. Note the continual variety in accent by which rhythm is produced. For example, mark the accented or unaccented syllables in the last sentence on page 320.

KIPLING: THE JUNGLE AT NIGHT (PAGE 322)

Biography. See page 484.

Note. After announcing the subject of the first sentence — "a perfect white night" — Kipling fuses together all sorts of sensations — touch, sound, motion, light, odor, color — into a complete unit. Find these details and note in each case how exactly the words fit. What characteristics of Kipling's style do you discover here? By all means read the entire story, "The Spring Running," from which this extract and the preceding come.

NARRATION [1]

Unity. Narration, which deals with events in sequence of time, seems at first to resist the effort to limit the field of material. To know where to begin and where to end a narrative so that the result may leave upon the reader unity of impression, a writer must decide whether his material will yield a simple story of adventure or the more complicated series of events which form a plot. If his material reduces itself to the simple act of catching a fish, he can then very easily limit his field by avoiding a false beginning which might include the arrival in camp, the first night in the woods, the trip to the pond, etc., and by opening with the event itself. And he should end with the natural close of the event. A writer who thus cuts away superfluities in action at the beginning and the end, as Kipling does in *How I Caught Salmon in the Clackamas* (p. 341), will achieve singleness of impression in time no less than the descriptive writer, by limiting his range of vision, achieves it in space. An account of an incident or an adventure which thus has this one main action may be represented by a straight line, which graphically expresses the fact that the event proceeds, logically and without deviation, from beginning to end.

If, on the other hand, the material yields two or more lines of action which intersect, the result is called "plot." Plot in this case does not

[1] For other introductory chapters see Exposition, p. 451; Essay, p. 461; Criticism, p. 464; Biography, p. 468; Argument, p. 473; Description, p. 476.

mean, as many students suppose, conspiracy; but it means the complication or weaving together of events. Our attention is concentrated, not upon any one of these lines of action, but upon their peculiar weaving together to form a new situation. When we achieve a situation which thus produces on the reader a unified effect, we have achieved unity of plot. For examples, see *Tobin's Palm* (p. 384) and *The Red-Headed League* (p. 393). How we may secure "the immense force derivable from totality" Poe explains in his criticism of *Hawthorne's Tales*.

A skillful literary artist has constructed a tale. If wise, he has not fashioned his thoughts to accommodate his incidents; but having conceived, with deliberate care, a certain unique or single *effect* to be wrought out, he then invents such incidents — he then combines such events as may best aid him in establishing this preconceived effect. If his very initial sentence tend not to the out-bringing of this effect, then he has failed in his first step. In the whole composition there should be no word written of which the tendency, direct or indirect, is not to the one pre-established design.

The same principle is reinforced by Stevenson in *A Humble Remonstrance*.

Let him [the writer] choose a motive, whether of character or passion; carefully construct his plot so that every incident is an illustration of the motive, and every property employed shall bear to it a near relation of congruity or contrast; . . . and allow neither himself in the narrative nor any character in the course of the dialogue, to utter one sentence that is not part and parcel of the business of the story or the discussion of the problem involved.

This totality of effect is the form which "dominant tone" takes in Narration. In producing this dominant tone, not only action but characters and background play important parts.

Those characters should be chosen who will help to bring out the particular tone the writer wishes the story to possess. This is true in all narratives. In the novel, however, where there is great opportunity for a character to develop, he not only must contribute his share to the dominant tone of the story, but he must have the many-sidedness of a human being. In short stories, though the character must seem a natural human being and not a mere type, his presence in the tale should exhale a peculiar quality necessary for the preconceived effect.

The purpose of dialogue is to reveal character, to expound the situations, and to propel the narrative. At the same time it must give the illusion of real life by seeming to be the natural talk of human beings.

To make dialogue conduce to the " pre-established design " and at the same time reveal no artificiality of invention is so delicate a method of obtaining Unity, that it demands the keenest observation and the nicest adjustment of the means to the end. Study the dialogue in *The House Opposite* (p. 365) and *Tobin's Palm* (p. 384).

Characters, moreover, should be more than figures which we watch the author manipulate. A character may be the medium through which a writer makes various events significant. An author often lets a character tell his own story, as Defoe let Robinson Crusoe tell his. Or, still limiting the narrative to the point of view of a single character, he may tell the story in the third person, as Mr. White views events through Piggy Pennington's eyes (*The King of Boyville*, p. 375). Whether the phrasing is that of direct or of indirect discourse, the consequent gain in unity of conception and in vividness of treatment is worth the continual care to make the narrative a faithful account of only those facts which this one character knows. This constant factor of one personality through whom all incidents and emotions reach the reader is a subtle means of enforcing dominant tone. Note the use of this factor in *To Windward of the Truth* (p. 355) and *Tobin's Palm* (p. 384).

A writer will not obtain final Unity until his background, or setting, harmonizes with his motive. This harmony may be one of concord or of discord. Stevenson analyzes the harmony of scene and action in a poignant way.

One thing in life calls for another; there is a fitness in events and places. The sight of a pleasant arbor puts it in our mind to sit there. One place suggests work, another idleness, a third early rising and long rambles in the dew. The effect of night, of any flowing water, of lighted cities, of the peep of day, of ships, of the open ocean, call up in the mind an army of anonymous desires and pleasures. Something, we feel, should happen; we know not what, yet we proceed in quest of it. And many of the happiest hours of life fleet by us in this vain attendance on the genius of the place and moment. It is thus that tracts of young fir and low rocks that reach into deep soundings, particularly torture and delight me. Something must have happened in such places, and perhaps ages back, to members of my race; and when I was a child I tried in vain to invent appropriate games for them, as I still try, just as vainly, to fit them with the proper story. Some places speak distinctly. Certain dank gardens cry aloud for a murder; certain old houses demand to be haunted; certain coasts are set apart for ship-wreck (*A Gossip on Romance*).

But it may be the writer's intention to produce the effect of incongruity, and in that case an apparent discord, perhaps of gay action and grim scenery, may be a subtler kind of harmony.

Coherence. Since events occur in order of time, an account of these events will naturally follow the chronological order. If a narrative is a record of actual occurrences, incidents, and adventures, it is a simple matter to tell them in the order in which they actually happened. Often in real life events fall into striking patterns of climax, coincidence, antithesis, etc., and thus the time order is heightened by the presence of some artistic principle. For instance, note the crescendo of excitement in *How I Caught Salmon in the Clackamas* (p. 341) and the crescendo of humor in *Sir Edward at the Carnival* (p. 337).

But when we are inventing a story with plot, the weaving together of the strands and the untying (or dénouement) allow us greater control of arrangement. We may depart from the strict time order and for purposes of mystery or surprise withhold the knowledge of certain events or facts until a later and often final moment. Examples of this method are *To Windward of the Truth* (p. 355), *Tobin's Palm* (p. 384), and *The Red-Headed League* (p. 393). Indeed, this is the customary method in detective stories. Another variation of the actual time order is the so-called "epic order." Here a writer plunges *in medias res*, as in the *Æneid*, and introduces the antecedent action later on by means of a narrative by one of the characters, or dialogue, or other devices. *The Red-Headed League* (p. 393) opens in this manner.

Whatever the arrangement, it is difficult and ineffective to record all the events, and consequently most stories proceed by scenes. The writer selects those episodes which are most important, interesting, dramatic, or picturesque, and develops them by means of detailed action and dialogue. Skillful transitions between the scenes give the feeling of continuity. *The House Opposite* (p. 365) is a scene in itself. *The Story of Muhammad Din* (p. 371) is a good example of a series of short scenes. Consider the effect of the scenes in the other stories.

Emphasis. The spell which Narration has always cast over readers and hearers since the beginning of story-telling will hold an audience even if the opening does not startle or arrest. Human curiosity to know what happened next will lead the reader on. Yet the more strongly an opening arouses curiosity or prepares for the preconceived effect, the more deeply is the reader enthralled. We should try to live up to Poe's standard: " If his very initial sentence tend not to the out-bringing of this effect, then he has failed in his first step." Sometimes a beginning is expository, as in *The King of Boyville* (p. 375); sometimes descriptive, as in *How I Caught Salmon in the Clackamas* (p. 341). But a dramatic beginning with action or dialogue or both is on the whole the most forcible, as in *The Story of Muhammad Din* (p. 371) and *The Red-Headed League* (393).

The end is the place of honor. It should impress the reader with the full force of the effect which the story has been trying to produce. It should not spoil this effect or mar the dominant tone by introducing new and irrelevant interests, or by running on into the slough of anti-climax. It should be rapid, yet not so hurried as to cause confusion. The final sentences and the very last words deserve careful phrasing. For examples of endings which are effective for all these reasons, see *Sir Edward at the Carnival* (p. 340), *To Windward of the Truth* (p. 364), and *The Story of Muhammad Din* (p. 374).

Other structural methods of securing Emphasis are suspense, climax, and surprise. The arrangement of scenes so that there will be a steady rise of interest up to the point of highest tension or greatest complication is always successful. This is illustrated, among others, by *Sir Edward at the Carnival* (p. 337), *To Windward of the Truth* (p. 355), and *The Red-Headed League* (p. 393). The force produced by climax may be doubled if the crisis or dénouement contains a surprise. By keeping the reader in suspense as to the outcome and then revealing the secret by an unexpected turn at the end, the "surprise story" thrills and delights. *Tobin's Palm* (p. 384) is a good example: the author, O. Henry, is well known for his skillful use of this device.

Apart from structure, a story may be emphatic and memorable by virtue of its idea or theme, its vivid style, its power of characterization, its emotional appeal, or its truth to life. These are qualities which spring from the writer's own personality.

HAMILTON: SIR EDWARD AT THE CARNIVAL (PAGE 337)

Biography. Lord Frederic Spencer Hamilton (1856–   ), English diplomat and writer, has made from his travels and his experiences as Secretary in the British Embassies at Berlin and St. Petersburg and in the Legations at Lisbon and Buenos Ayres three delightful volumes, — *The Vanished Pomps of Yesterday*, 1919; *The Days before Yesterday*, 1920; and *Here, There, and Everywhere*, 1921.

Note. This amusing little incident is admirably narrated: Sir Edward's beautiful clothes and austere manner; the respectful secretary, who was so "pained" at the discomfiture of his chief; the contrast between the "ordinary British middle-class householder" and the gay South Americans; the cumulative effect of the earlier episodes leading up to the riotously funny conclusion, — all are amusing in exactly the right way. When undergraduates play pranks upon each other and then try to write about them, this is the way they should try to do it — if they can.

KIPLING: HOW I CAUGHT SALMON IN THE CLACKAMAS (Page 341)

Biography. See page 484.

Note. This selection is an example of simple incident, the kind of narration which most students are best able to write. It handles a single event, and its descriptive introduction is simply to give the setting first, because the scene remains unchanged. When once the movement begins, it is so rapid and so engrossing that there is room for nothing but the business at hand. What details appeal to you most strongly? Note the conclusion.

ROOSEVELT: AN ELK HUNT (Page 345)

Biography. See page 458.

Note. This little narrative exhales the energy of the famous hunter who wrote it. What details of action or of diction help to reveal his personality? The narrative begins *in medias res* and continues with unabated swiftness to the end. Note how admirably the description of the locality keeps pace with the action, — a fact which makes the movement more coherent and at the same time increases our sense of being on the spot. A still greater degree of vividness is produced by the frank and vigorous expression of physical sensations. Pick out examples. Note the many excellent verbs of action. After reading this hunting story by Roosevelt, you will appreciate to the fullest extent what the *New York Tribune* said the day after his death:

" Farewell, mighty hunter! You were the swiftest, cleanest, and most valorous of your tribe. You pressed the hunt fearlessly and to its logical ends, not in fantasy through the clouds, but in fact on this earth, where the consequences are. Innumerable and precious are the trophies. We place them at your feet. Would that there were demons of darkness and unrighteousness in the path you are now on. For you would slay them all and like it more.

" Farewell, O rare American! "

KEMPTON: TO WINDWARD OF THE TRUTH (Page 355)

Biography. Kenneth Payson Kempton (1891–) has long been interested in yachting and maritime pursuits. He graduated from Harvard in 1912. During the World War he served as Lieutenant in the United States Naval Reserve Force, and subsequently acted as Assistant Dock Superintendent for one of the great shipping corporations. All this experience led him to begin writing stories of the sea and other tales of adventure, which have appeared in various American magazines. His first long story was *Phantom Gold*, 1922.

Note. The story *To Windward of the Truth* and the newspaper accounts of the mystery of the *Onato* give us an unusual chance to study the development of a story from its source. In this case we are enabled to know how the story was written, what problems confronted the writer, and what methods he used to solve them. Concerning the inception of the story Mr. Kempton says:

"When I chanced upon the first article, I was naturally attracted by its suggestion of dramatic material; but I saw that, whereas a mutiny is indubitably an exciting event, it can be nothing but the impetus or the finale of a story. I saved the clipping, therefore, and cudgeled my wits for the rest of the tale. Three days later came the second article, and I had it. A mutiny that is not a mutiny — with the monstrous possibility of judgment falling upon innocent heads — afforded opportunity that only a blind man could disregard."

Now there were three chief problems which faced him: (1) the choice of scenes, (2) the point of view, (3) the dénouement, or solution of the mystery.

1. What events should he choose for specific treatment as scenes? Two, — the rescue, and the inquiry. The actual inquiry was held by the British consul in Philadelphia ten days after the rescue. With an eye for dramatic unity and momentum, Mr. Kempton condenses the action into one night, and makes the rescuing Captain, Martin Price, hold the inquiry on shipboard at once. What further advantage results so far as the characterization of the Captain is concerned?

2. Who should tell the story? The author himself, Captain Price, one of the prisoners, or an eye-witness? Consider the advantages or disadvantages of these different points of view. Mr. Kempton decided on an eye-witness, and he found one ready at hand in the newspaper account, — the supercargo. Now it should be explained that a supercargo is a petty officer on a merchant vessel whose duty is the safe delivery of the cargo from consignor to consignee. He has nothing to do with the sailing of the ship. Note the way in which the supercargo's presence at both scenes is managed. Is this a better point of view than that of Captain Price or not? Why? Once the author chose the supercargo, the question of dialect arose. Nautical language would naturally be woven into the speech of any teller of the tale. But Mr. Kempton went further than this: he gave his supercargo an Irish dialect, and thus increased his technical difficulties tenfold. As to his reason for selecting the Irish dialect, he says he felt that only an Irishman would reveal sensitiveness to pathos as contrasted with the bluster of the captain. How remarkably Mr. Kempton triumphed over the difficulties will be realized when you recall that the boy's narrative comes to us through the speech of Red Purvis, and yet we have the impression of a different personality. You should pick out examples, too, throughout the story, of the way Purvis characterizes himself.

3. How could the mystery be cleared up and the mutineers be proved innocent? What facts convinced the consul the second news dispatch does not state. Mr. Kempton says that here he was plunged into the greatest perplexity. It was necessary to contrive some piece of proof that would be quick to produce and certain to convince. But what? What fact would be

accessible on the *Gulfleet* that night and strong enough to convince? Suddenly the idea flashed upon him — make one of the prisoners, the boy, the son of the skipper who had been killed! Such a relationship would have the added advantage of plausibility, since it is customary for members of the same family to sail in various capacities on small trading vessels. Study the management of the suspense whereby the truth is kept till the climax.

In addition to these considerations, regard for a moment the way in which the brief prologue and epilogue frame the story. This is another contribution of Mr. Kempton's over and above the facts in the newspaper. What is the purpose of this frame, and does it produce a valuable effect?

ANTHONY HOPE: THE HOUSE OPPOSITE (PAGE 365)

Biography. Sir Anthony Hope Hawkins (1863–   ), English novelist. At Oxford he was President of the Oxford Union Society. He was admitted to the bar in 1887, but gave up practice in 1894, and devoted himself to writing as the result of the great popular success of his two most famous books, issued that year — *The Prisoner of Zenda* and *The Dolly Dialogues*. Both originated literary fashions which lasted several years: *The Prisoner of Zenda*, a gallant and dashing story of an imaginary principality in Middle Europe, launched the vogue of "Ruritanian romance"; and *The Dolly Dialogues* started a school of epigrammatic drawing-room comedy. The dramatizations of *The Prisoner of Zenda* and its sequel, *Rupert of Hentzau*, 1898, had long runs in England and America. Other stories of Anthony Hope's earlier period are *The Heart of the Princess Osra*, 1896; *Phroso*, 1897; and *The King's Mirror*, 1899. In his later period, his stories have dealt with the social conditions of contemporary life, as in *Tristram of Blent*, 1901; *The Intrusions of Peggy*, 1902; *A Servant of the Public*, 1905; *Mrs. Maxon Protests*, 1911; and *Beaumaroy Home from the Wars*, 1919. He was knighted in 1918.

Note. As an example of dialogue, this selection is remarkable for the naturalness and ease of the talk. The sentences are simple and colloquial, and yet they have the trimness and firmness of structure which is customary among well-bred people. Note the quick give-and-take and the speed. Furthermore, the talk is characteristic of the individuals. Contrast the speeches of Mr. Carter with those of Miss Phyllis. Note the use of stage directions to help visualize the scene.

KIPLING: THE STORY OF MUHAMMAD DIN (PAGE 371)

Biography. See page 484.

Note. "Nowhere in his more elaborate efforts to delineate child-life does he give us so perfect a piece of work as the little child-idyl called 'The Story of Muhammad Din,'" said the *Fortnightly Review*. The structure of this story is beautiful in its simplicity. It proceeds by means of scenes; that is, Kipling chooses certain moments for detailed treatment and omits the intervening ones. This is a very useful method to follow in your own stories. First of all you must decide which events in the whole transaction ought to be revealed to the reader in scenes or episodes. How many scenes are there in the present story? Observe the transitions between them. What is the effect produced by opening with a scene? by closing with one? Does this story exemplify Poe's doctrine of "totality of effect"? This would make a good subject for a critical theme. What details create "local color"?

WHITE: THE KING OF BOYVILLE (Page 375)

Biography. William Allen White (1868–), American editor and writer. Since 1895 editor of the *Emporia Gazette*, Kansas. In his novels he has interpreted the pioneer days of Kansas with great fidelity, and has treated the conflict between "big business" and social conscience. He has also written stories which show his understanding of the pathos and humor of boyhood. His chief books are *The Real Issue and Other Stories*, 1896; *The Court of Boyville*, 1899; *In Our Town*, 1906; *A Certain Rich Man*, 1909; *The Old Order Changeth*, 1910.

Note. What makes this story such a valuable model for amateur writers is that the material is common to everyone. We may not have had adventures at sea or been in India, but all of us have experienced the joys and pains of school days, and remember our first love affairs. Everyone can write a story based on such experiences. In the present instance pick out those events and details which give the story its remarkable vividness and truth to life. Comment on the choice of scenes. What do you think about the expository introduction in this case? usually? Consider the function of the dialogue: (1) Does it reveal character? (2) Does it explain the situation? (3) Does it help the movement of the story? (4) Is it lifelike? What is your opinion of Mr. White's ability to visualize things, to make us see the characters in action? What gives this story its thoroughly American flavor?

O. HENRY: TOBIN'S PALM (Page 384)

Biography. William Sydney Porter ("O. Henry") (1862–1910), American writer of short stories. After trying several occupations in different places, he published *Cabbages and Kings* (1905), *The Four Million* (1906), *The Trimmed Lamp* (1907), *Strictly Business* (1910), and other volumes of short stories. Although at times O. Henry published stories that were thin and cheap, he was at his best almost, if not quite, a genius. He is noteworthy for his prolific invention of plots, for the clever way in which he so often gives his stories an unexpected turn at the very end, for his brilliant (and occasionally tiresome) use of slang and plays upon words, for his rapidity and dramatic sense as a story-teller, and especially for his sympathetic understanding of many kinds of people. In his own words, he "studied cities as women study their reflections in mirrors." New York was his favorite, and he delighted in expressing its characteristic spirit and flavor in one hundred and thirty-eight stories.

Note. *Tobin's Palm* is just a good yarn, an ingenious fulfillment of prophecy. Consider in detail the ways in which it illustrates O. Henry's qualities. Note how the dialogue enriches the various scenes. Pick out some of the speeches which are exuberantly funny and yet absolutely true to life. The coincidence at the end is perhaps too remarkable; but the preposterous diction and general exaggeration throughout — all based on the bed rock of human nature — have made the reader quite ready to accept the pot of coffee from the hand of Katie Mahorner.

DOYLE: THE RED-HEADED LEAGUE (PAGE 393)

Biography. Sir Arthur Conan Doyle (1859–   ), British physician and story writer. While still a physician, he published *A Study in Scarlet*, 1887, the first of the detective studies in which his most famous character, Sherlock Holmes, appears. This vein he followed out in *The Sign of the Four*, 1889; *The Adventures of Sherlock Holmes*, 1891; *The Memoirs of Sherlock Holmes*, 1893; *The Hound of the Baskervilles*, 1902; and *The Return of Sherlock Holmes*, 1904. He also wrote historical novels, among them *The White Company*, 1890, and *The Refugees*, 1891. At the time of the Boer War and the World War, he lent his pen to the public service, and produced *The Great Boer War*, 1900, and *The British Campaign in France and Flanders* (in several volumes). In recent years he has become much interested in psychic research, on which subject he has lectured and has published such books as *The New Revelation* (1918), *The Vital Message* (1919).

Note. A good example of plot: the emphasis is not at all upon character-drawing, and the descriptive element suffices merely to give a plausible setting; but the plot is very skillfully developed. In reading such stories the fun, of course, consists in piecing clues together, as Sherlock Holmes did. The reader must be intensely interested in the outcome, must have some idea whither events are tending, and yet must not guess the complete answer to the puzzle until the right moment. Poe, as early as 1841, established the general method, and in his Monsieur Dupin of "The Murders in the Rue Morgue," "The Purloined Letter," and other stories he invented a detective who is really the literary ancestor of Sherlock Holmes.

But a real man was the direct original of Sherlock Holmes, namely Dr. Joseph Bell (1837–1911), an eminent Scottish surgeon who was one of Conan Doyle's instructors at Edinburgh University. Dr. Bell was gifted with extraordinary powers of observation and inductive reasoning, which he applied both in his professional work and in everyday matters. His hobby was the study of mysterious crimes, and he often aided government officials in unravelling difficult cases.

Conan Doyle himself has successfully employed Holmes's methods in real life, as he tells in "An Intimate Study of Sherlock Holmes," in *Detective Story Magazine*, January 15, 1918. "I can say, though I touch wood as I say it, that I have never entirely failed in any attempt which I have made to reduce Holmes's methods to practical use."

ACKNOWLEDGMENTS

The editors take pleasure in returning thanks to the authors who have kindly permitted the reproduction of selections from their books, and also to the students who, in permitting the use of their themes, have furnished an important part of the book.

They are glad to express their indebtedness to the following publishers who have granted the privilege of printing extracts from copyrighted books: Houghton Mifflin Company; Thomas Y. Crowell Company; D. Appleton and Company; G. P. Putnam's Sons; Charles Scribner's Sons; George H. Doran Company; Dodd, Mead & Company; Harper & Brothers; The Century Company; Harcourt, Brace and Company; P. F. Collier & Son; *The Boston Herald*; *The North American Review*; *The Outlook*; Doubleday, Page & Company; Frederick A. Stokes Company; Robert M. McBride & Co.; Brentano's; Little, Brown & Company; *The Open Road*; Henry Holt and Company; McClure, Phillips & Company.

Thanks are also due to officers of the Yosemite National Park Company and the Southern Pacific Company for their courtesy in arranging for the use of the photograph of El Capitan.

INDEX OF PRACTICAL DEVICES

This index is intended to blaze trails in many directions through the text. It consists of references to a selected number of examples of useful devices in writing, and is not by any means to be regarded as an exhaustive list. The ambitious writer will discover many more examples for himself; in fact, he should not be robbed of the joy of discovery.

The numbers in roman type refer to pages, those in italic type to lines. References to sentences and paragraphs give the lines on which these begin.

507

The Three essentials of description are detailed observation, reproducing, accurate expression, description aims to present a living picture to the reader. A mental picture is the essence of description.

write a description giving one impression in detail.